BORN OF A VIRGIN?

BORN OF A VIRGIN?

*Reconceiving Jesus in the Bible,
Tradition, and Theology*

Andrew T. Lincoln

WILLIAM B. EERDMANS PUBLISHING COMPANY
GRAND RAPIDS, MICHIGAN / CAMBRIDGE, U. K.

© 2013 Andrew T. Lincoln
All rights reserved.

Originally published 2013 in Great Britain by
Society for Promoting Christian Knowledge, London

This edition published 2013 in the United States of America by
Wm. B. Eerdmans Publishing Co.
2140 Oak Industrial Drive N.E., Grand Rapids, Michigan 49505 /
P.O. Box 163, Cambridge CB3 9PU U.K.
www.eerdmans.com

Library of Congress Cataloging-in-Publication Data

Lincoln, Andrew T.
Born of a virgin? : reconceiving Jesus in the Bible, tradition, and theology /
Andrew T. Lincoln.
pages   cm
Includes bibliographical references and index.
ISBN 978-0-8028-6925-8 (pbk. : alk. paper)
1. Virgin birth — History of doctrines. 2. Jesus Christ — Nativity.
3. Infancy narratives (Gospels) 4. Bible. Gospels — Criticism, interpretation, etc.
I. Title.
BT317.L56 2013
232.92 — dc23

2013031432

To Dee
with admiration, gratitude and love

Contents

Contents

Preface

Justification for revisiting a well-worn topic will be provided in the book's first chapter. Some readers may, however, find it helpful to know what led the writer to embark on its further exploration. As a Christian engaged in New Testament teaching and scholarship in both university and theological college settings in my early career, I had given lectures on the historical Jesus, on the resurrection narratives and on Matthew and Luke as a whole, but had not had to teach on the infancy narratives in any detailed fashion and so had had no particular academic reason to come to a clearly worked-out position on the virgin birth. I had, of course, read much of the scholarly literature and commentaries and so was aware of some of the problems and complexities surrounding the historicity and genre of the infancy narratives. I would be reminded of the issues of interpretation when reciting the creed and particularly at the Christmas season, not least when listening to sermons whose preachers seemed to be quite unaware of the thoughts of any critically informed members of their congregations about the status of the nativity stories. While I had clear views about the resurrection and its historical basis, I tended to bracket this issue of the status of the virgin birth. Unless asked directly about what I thought, I kept my reservations pretty much to myself, partly because of the confessional nature of some of the institutions in which I have taught. I did, however, have the experience of being invited to interview for a post at one well-known theological seminary and being requested to submit comments about its statement of faith that could be discussed at the interview. As part of my submission, I wrote,

> The statement uses the language 'being conceived by the Holy Spirit and born of the Virgin Mary.' Whether this language has a historical base is difficult to determine, but it seems clear to me that in Matthew's and Luke's birth narratives theological interests frequently override historicity and, in comparison with the rest of the New Testament, that the virgin birth does not belong to the centre of the gospel, and so I am open to the possibility that the language of conception by the Spirit and virgin birth refers not to a biological or historical fact but is to be seen as the evangelists' depiction in narrative form of their conviction about the divine Sonship of Jesus.

My comments resulted in the immediate withdrawal of the invitation to interview! At another theological institution at which I taught I did find myself objecting publicly and strongly when a rather conservative visiting bishop declared that in his view the virgin birth was the crucial and basic starting point in a robust apologetic for contemporary Christianity. This had to be precisely the wrong place at which to start. Both for the early Christians and for contemporary Christian faith, belief in the resurrection is the far more significant point of departure, and whatever one thinks about the place of the virgin birth in the Christian faith will be consequent upon a belief in the resurrection and not the other way around.

But I did not have to address these matters in any more detailed fashion until I was asked to give some lectures on the use of the Jewish Scriptures in the New Testament birth narratives to a group of those training to become ministers and lay readers in the Church of England and the Methodist Church. Although my topic was not directly that of the virgin birth, it was obvious to me that what I had to say about the pervasive way in which the Jewish Scriptures played a role in the formation of the stories would raise questions about the historicity of all the material, including the annunciation accounts. The students came from a variety of theo-logical traditions and so, if pressed on the historicity of the virgin birth, I wanted to be able to help my audience think through the options theo-logically and pastorally. Yet when I looked for resources for this part of my own preparation, for discussions that not only explored the texts and their historicity but also brought into play the Christian confessional tradition, systematic issues in Christology, and problems arising from contemporary knowledge and sensitivities, I became aware of the rarity of this type of treatment. The reflections begun then eventually became an essay for a symposium on Christology and Scripture.[1] Both the responses at that symposium and a continuing awareness that many thoughtful Christians find the virgin birth a difficulty and are not sure how to handle it confirmed that a fuller treatment might be worthwhile. Anyone familiar with the earlier essay will note that further study, though not changing the overall direction of the argument, has produced a change of mind on some issues, in particular whether it should be assumed that the New Testament has only one perspective on Jesus' birth. I began to discover for myself, therefore, that there was much more to explore about the New Testament itself than I had thought there would be! As it happened, however, major surgery and a longer than expected convalescence, followed

---

[1] Published as 'Born of a Virgin: Credal Affirmation and Critical Reading', in eds A. Lincoln and A. Paddison, *Christology and Scripture: Interdisciplinary Perspectives* (London: T. & T. Clark International, 2007), 84–103.

later by another serious illness, combined with commitments to other projects, meant that beginning work on that fuller exploration had to be delayed for a considerably more extended period than I had anticipated. It is presented now as an attempt to gain greater clarity about the nature and scope of the problems.

I hesitate to mention it but there is one further personal curiosity that has only surfaced consciously recently. I now remember in childhood asking my parents why I was given my middle name and being told that it was the Christian name of a close friend of my father in theological college. Strangely, I never met this close friend and the family seemed to have lost touch with him. It later emerged that at least one of the reasons for this was that the friend had changed his views on theological matters and 'no longer believed in the virgin birth'! What's in a name? Perhaps it was meant to be that I should end up exploring this issue for myself!

More seriously, though none of them bears any responsibility for the conclusions reached here, there are some names that deserve mention for their help, stimulus, critique and support at various stages of my interest in this topic. They include Dr Stephen Barton, Professor David Catchpole and Professor Richard Burridge, and three colleagues at the University of Gloucestershire, biblical scholars Dr Lloyd Pietersen and Professor Gordon McConville, and, most especially, theologian – and my wife – Dr Dee Carter.

Abbreviations

Abbreviations for the titles of ancient sources other than the Bible follow SBL conventions.

JBL	*Journal of Biblical Literature*
JSHJ	*Journal for the Study of the Historical Jesus*
JSNT	*Journal for the Study of the New Testament*
JTS	*Journal of Theological Studies*
NovT	*Novum Testamentum*
NTS	*New Testament Studies*
SJT	*Scottish Journal of Theology*
TS	*Theological Studies*

1

What is there to explore?

Three recent scholarly assertions suggest forcefully, but from quite different perspectives, that the attempt to explore the topic of Jesus' birth in the context of the Church's adherence to scriptural and credal formulations of a virginal conception is likely to be a futile enterprise. The first is the view of a Christian theologian, who, before his recent move to the United States, taught in a British university.

> Although . . . it is possible to set forth a robust two-natures doctrine of the Incarnation that conforms to Chalcedonian Christology in all other particulars apart from its denial of the Virgin Birth, such a doctrine does not reflect the teaching of scripture or the tradition. Consequently, such a NVB [No Virgin Birth] argument is wholly inadequate, indeed, is an unorthodox statement of how the Incarnation took place. (This is so overwhelmingly obvious that it is almost embarrassing to have to state it so baldly.)[1]

For Crisp, Scripture and tradition are so clear and unqualifiedly normative that it is futile to imagine that one could attempt to rethink this topic and still claim to be orthodox in one's Christology. The second is the opinion of a German New Testament scholar who was eventually barred from official teaching in a Protestant theological faculty.

> The statement that Jesus was engendered by the Spirit and born of a virgin is a falsification of the historical facts. At all events he had a human father . . . Any interpretation which fails to take a clear stand here is to be branded a lie.[2]

For Lüdemann the historical facts about Jesus' birth are so obvious that, once this is observed, any attempt to think theologically about the matter is not only futile but is to indulge in a cover-up of the truth. The third is the conclusion of a well-known writer on the historical Jesus who is also

---

[1] O. D. Crisp, *God Incarnate: Explorations in Christology* (London: T. & T. Clark, 2009), 101–2. This section of Crisp's book was originally published as 'On the "Fittingness" of the Virgin Birth', *Heythrop Journal* 49 (2008), 197–221 (217).

[2] G. Lüdemann, *Virgin Birth? The Real Story of Mary and Her Son Jesus* (London: SCM, 1998), 140.

a Catholic layperson. '"Virginal conception" is a theological claim about Jesus and not a biological claim about Mary and the only thing sillier or sadder than taking "virginal conception" literally is opposing it literally.'[3] Unlike Lüdemann, Crossan thinks there is something to talk about theologically but nevertheless dismisses any further historical consideration of the virgin birth[4] tradition as futile, indeed as silly and sad.[5]

What then can be the justification for an exploration of the traditions about Jesus' birth that attempts to be literary, theological and historical in its orientation? And isn't any discussion that involves the virgin birth bound to be not much more than a rehashing of the tired old debates between more conservative and more liberal versions of Christianity? Despite what appears to be so overwhelmingly obvious, but in very different ways, to these three scholars, the situation is rather more complex, and this introductory chapter will try to explain more fully why this is so. To put it briefly at the outset, there are many, and the present writer is among them, who unapologetically find themselves sympathetic both to some of the concerns of Crisp about the status of Scripture and credal tradition, on the one hand, and to some of the concerns of Lüdemann and Crossan about the historical problems of the virgin birth tradition, on the other. Our identity as Christians is shaped by the Church's confession that Jesus Christ is God incarnate and we see no incompatibility in maintaining that identity while attempting to read Scripture and understand tradition critically. In fact, both Christian discipleship and intellectual integrity demand that we do so. Where, as in the case of the tradition about Jesus' birth, there are perceived problems and Christians take different stances, then these need to be investigated seriously. Crisp appears to think that the historical tradition is unambiguous and there are no serious difficulties in holding it. Lüdemann and Crossan appear to think that the historical difficulties are so overwhelming as to no longer require discussion. How is such a chasm between perspectives possible? At the very least, then, part of any exploration will still involve the need

---

[3] J. D. Crossan, 'Response to Robert M. Price', in eds J. K. Beilby and P. R. Eddy, *The Historical Jesus: Five Views* (London: SPCK, 2010), 85.

[4] For the sake of convenience and stylistic variation, 'virgin birth' is employed interchangeably in this book with the more accurate designation for the topic under discussion, namely, 'virginal conception'.

[5] This has not, however, prevented him from having written about it, see e.g. J. D. Crossan, 'Virgin Mother or Bastard Child?', in ed. A.-J. Levine, *A Feminist Companion to Mariology* (London: T. & T. Clark, 2005), 37–55 and M. J. Borg and J. D. Crossan, *The First Christmas: What the Gospels Really Teach about Jesus's Birth* (New York: HarperCollins, 2007), esp. 99–127. It is worth noting that, despite what they claim as so obvious, both Crisp and Lüdemann in their writings also devote considerable efforts to stating the obvious.

to explain what are the historical difficulties in the tradition and to evaluate these rather than simply dismissing this aspect of the debate either as potentially putting one outside the bounds of Christian orthodoxy or as sad or silly. Far too many honest Christians have genuine problems about how to take the tradition for the former form of dismissal to be fair and far too many intelligent Christians believe the virgin birth to be historical for the latter form to be appropriate. Again, if one were to conclude that historical and other difficulties were weighted against the virgin birth tradition, then there would still be at the very least the need to discuss whether and why there might be a theological claim in this tradition that should nevertheless be considered seriously.

It is perhaps not surprising that the present writer, whose primary area of expertise is study of the New Testament, who pursues that study with a theological interest and as a member of a church that recites the creed, and who encounters not only diametrically opposing views among both biblical scholars and theologians but also a great deal of confusion among students and church members on this topic, should optimistically think that further exploration might not prove merely a waste of time over a matter of little consequence. The hope that such an enterprise might not be entirely futile is also fuelled by the belief that the situation in which it now takes place is one that has shifted from the old discussions between conservatives and liberals where one's stance on this topic could simply be reduced to whether or not one believes in the supernatural. Phenomena such as post-liberal theology and post-critical approaches to the Bible have produced a rather different climate in which to discuss such an issue and it is one that affects also those from both evangelical and Roman Catholic traditions. It should also not be surprising that, when it comes to the main part of this book, its exploration will start with a more detailed investigation of the New Testament traditions, the area of the writer's expertise, where it produces some fresh insights, and then look at later developments and the theological issues raised in the process. Here there will be less detailed interaction with secondary literature, and the writer's need to seek indulgence from church historians and systematic theologians for straying into their areas of expertise will be readily apparent. The order in which the exploration is presented should not, however, be thought to reflect a simple two-stage hermeneutic in which constructive theology straightforwardly builds on the foundations supplied by biblical and historical study. The impetus for study of the topic in the first place is theological, and a dialectical relationship between critical reading of Scripture and constructive theology is involved at every stage.

3

An initial justification for the exploration and the way it will be conducted has been offered. But it is worth stepping back and approaching the matter more slowly. Why focus on Jesus' birth at all? What is the significance of anyone's birth in relation to that person's life as a whole? Though some have always turned to astrology to discover the significance of the time of their birth, for most people there is little to explore about the meaning of their births other than to state the obvious – they constitute the beginning of their lives. Any further significance is to be found only within the context of those lives as a whole. If those lives are deemed to have special importance, then their beginnings, in retrospect, are caught up in the impact of lives that have made a difference. In studying such lives due attention will then be paid to the formative influences on them from the very beginning, and the circumstances of their birth to particular parents at a particular time and a particular place can be said to take on meaning. There are, however, other instances in which talk of the significance of a birth would appear to make sense. They have to do with exceptional aspects surrounding a birth. Those who discover they were given up for adoption at birth might have good reason to reflect on the meaning of their arrival in the world in such circumstances. Other unusual factors may contribute to giving special significance to a child's birth, ranging from dramatic rescues from death of women about to give birth to medical choices between the life of the mother and the life of the child. But what about reflection not just on the significance of our birth but also on that of our conception in particular? For many, who know themselves to be the biological product of their present parents' act of procreation, thinking any further about this may be a case of 'too much information, thank you.' But for others it is their conception and not simply their birth that can become crucial in constructing their identity and that raises important questions. Did my parents have difficulty in conceiving and was I wanted and planned or 'an accident'? Was it in fact my present parents who conceived me or was someone else involved? If both nature and nurture have shaped who we are, then accurate knowledge about our conception is not just a matter of curiosity. Advances in medical technology and the complexities of family life can lead to further pressing questions about who supplied the genes that formed my genetic identity at conception and how these have affected my life. Those born with a physical handicap or who develop a major disease often wish to know if there is some genetic explanation and this requires accurate information about the parties who conceived them. Those who are products of IVF treatment or find themselves with adoptive parents or in a one-parent family or with a same-sex couple understandably often think that such information will give them a better sense of who they are. If there is no transparency or disclosure about these matters they can become ticking time bombs within families. It is hardly surprising, for example, that in the UK in 2005 the law was changed in the interest of children so that donors of sperm or eggs no longer had the right to anonymity and had to be prepared to be identified.

Similar reflections impinge on exploring the birth and conception of Jesus. Does the meaning of Jesus' birth derive from what was believed to be the significance of his life as a whole? This question receives further force when we remember that at the time of Jesus it was conventional in telling of the lives of great people, particularly when little was known of their origins, to depict their births in a way that already displayed unique features befitting their future greatness. Or does the meaning of Jesus' birth derive from circumstances surrounding the birth itself, such as his parents living at a time of expectations of a Jewish Messiah in the context of the Roman occupation of Israel? Was it in fact the conception that made this birth significant, because, as some of the traditions appear to claim, there was no male involved or the male involved was someone other than Joseph, the man who reared him? What difference does knowledge about his conception make to Jesus' identity? How might the divergence between ancient views on conception and modern knowledge of genetic identity affect our assessment of such issues? It could well be, of course, that a mixture of the above factors played some part in the meaning that is given to Jesus' birth – the beliefs of his followers about the outcome of his life, something unusual about his conception, and the context of contemporary religious and cultural understanding. A major part of exploring the traditions about Jesus' conception and birth will be to attempt to discover how far this is the case.

The significance of a person's birth is, however, not reducible simply to the results of investigating the original event or the interpretation given it by those closest to it or by those most immediately affected by the impact of the life that followed. Meaning can accrue over a longer period of time. This can be seen to a limited extent within a person's own lifetime and is aided by the practice of marking the day of our birth by a yearly com-memoration. Apart from serving as a reminder of the ageing process, this can be a time not only of celebration but also of reflection, a time of thinking about what we have done with the gift of life, of remembering those who brought us into life, and over time added or different signi-ficance is often given to the way we think about our birth and the role it plays in the stories we tell ourselves about our lives. Something similar applies to the birthdays of those who are close to us. Even after their deaths we remember the birthdays of parents or grandparents and each time attach different memories and meanings to the lives that began on those days. With great figures from the past, particular anniversaries, such as the fiftieth or one hundredth commemoration of their birth, can become the occasion for fresh investigation of their contribution to public life or to a particular discipline and of their continuing impact. In the case of Jesus, where the Christian Church looks back to its origins in his life as well as confessing his living presence, it is again hardly surprising that the meaning attached to his birth, and to the role of his mother, has accrued over the centuries. The Church's creeds highlight his birth in confessing God's purposes of salvation for humanity, theological reflection on the incarnation and the Trinity give further significance to this particular birth, and artistic and musical treatments of the nativity and of the Madonna have made their own contributions to its meaning. Not least, the yearly celebration of Jesus' birth at Christmas, dating from the fourth century, with its accompanying liturgy, carols, sermons, nativity scenes and special customs, often taken over from non-Christian practices and reconfigured, makes a huge impact on how Christians think about the meaning of Jesus' birth. At the same time, more recent critical thinking about Scripture and tradition, about miracles and biology, has played its part in the type of meaning Christians attach to the birth of their Saviour. Any full exploration of that significance, then, will need to take account not only of its historical aspects but also of both its traditional and contemporary dimensions in Christian thought and life.[6]

This account of the growing significance of some births and of Jesus' in particular should not be allowed to disguise the fact that in the latter case the stakes have now been raised considerably. Christians hold that the birth of which we are speaking is not simply that of a figure in history, Jesus of Nazareth, but is also in some sense related to his identity as the second 'person' of the triune God. It is the point in history at which the Son of God or the Word assumed human form. Exploring *this* birth has momentous significance. And it is this claim that accounts to a considerable extent for the strongly held but diverging convictions about Jesus' birth. If this was its import, assert some, then surely the manner in which

---

[6] For reflections on the significance of liturgical recollection of Christmas and its difference from historical reconstruction, see T. O'Loughlin, 'Losing Mystery in History: The Challenge of Recalling the Nativity', in ed. J. Corley, *New Perspectives on the Nativity* (London: T. & T. Clark, 2009), 180–99.

it occurred is unlikely to be through the normal human means of producing children. But, others retort, this view assumes that God only works
significantly in the world through exceptional or miraculous circumstances. And, still others add, if the exceptional circumstances included
no human father being involved in Jesus' birth, then that surely calls into
question whether, whatever else he might have been, Jesus of Nazareth
was a human being like us. Exploration of the tradition of this birth, then,
unavoidably raises not only historical questions but also major theological
ones. What might the claim that God takes incarnate form mean? Does
it involve God intervening in the course of human history in a way that
has biological implications? Or did the means by which this particular
human being became the incarnation of the Word include his birth through
the usual human process of procreation? Does belief that Jesus Christ was
God incarnate necessarily entail belief in his virginal conception? These
questions arising from Christian belief and from its sources in Scripture
and creed are bound to be at the heart of any investigation of the tradition. There has been a long history of reflection on and debate about them
and this itself suggests it would be foolish to imagine there is nothing here
worth further exploration.

Despite such considerations, as we indicated at the beginning, the question 'What is there to explore?' continues to be raised in a rather dismissive
way. On the one hand, there are those who take the rationalistic view that
no educated post-Enlightenment person could seriously entertain the
notion of a virgin birth, the birth narratives are no different from fairy
tales, and so the matter is simply not worth further discussion. On the
other hand, there are those who think that an appeal to the gospel birth
narratives and a belief in miracles makes Jesus' virgin birth a fact and so
only a non-believer would think there is anything further to argue about.[7]
These more popular attitudes on both sides, and the speaking past each
other that they involve, are also found in the writings of biblical scholars
and theologians who think that the issues surrounding Jesus' birth all boil
down to whether one is prepared to believe in the supernatural and in
miracles and, once that has been established, no further exploration is
really necessary. At one end of the spectrum, there are those who hold
that if Scripture and the creed state that Jesus was born without a human
father and all things are possible for the God who is the Creator of the
universe, then only those who disbelieve in the miraculous powers of such

---

[7] Belief in Jesus' virginal conception is, of course, a major feature of Islam, but that is a topic that
cannot be explored here.

a God would be arrogant enough to question the matter.[8] At the other end, there is little to discuss because it is assumed that no intelligent present-day Christian would take the story of the virgin birth literally and it is a simple matter to demonstrate its non-historicity. Anyone who pretends otherwise is really a fundamentalist or an intellectual hypocrite.[9] Biblical scholars who treat the matter more sensitively tend frequently to focus almost exclusively on historical-critical research. The more conservative conclude that the issue cannot be proved either way so that one is free to go with one's church tradition as a matter of faith.[10] Theological treatments of the virgin birth often either summarily state their affirmation of the tradition[11] or assume the legendary status of the topic[12] in pursuing their Christological or Mariological reflections. There are few that take the trouble to explain the range of issues or to do so in a way that indicates that their seriousness has been adequately appreciated.[13] Consequently, traditionalists and revisionists appear to have entrenched positions and to have given up attempting to persuade others about their stance on the core questions.

This situation is strange, both because the earliest traditions are more diverse than is often appreciated and the nature of the Gospels' accounts of Jesus' birth raises large questions about their interpretation which find no simple solution in the appeal to the miraculous, and because the theological task involves continuing to grapple in fresh and coherent ways with questions about Jesus' humanity and divinity and formulating these in relation to both the tradition and our present understanding. But neither the literalism in regard to Scripture and tradition that declines to

---

[8] This type of argument also appears prominently in e.g. Wright's contribution in M. J. Borg and N. T. Wright, *The Meaning of Jesus: Two Visions* (San Francisco: HarperCollins, 1999), 173: 'The God who does not intervene from outside but is always present and active within the world, sometimes shockingly, may well have been thus active on this occasion. It is all very well to get on one's high metaphysical horse and insist that God cannot behave like this, but we do not know that ahead of time.' Despite the language of God always being present and active in the world, Wright's argument depends on the virgin birth being a unique exception to the form of that constant presence and activity, and the result is that, on the matter of Jesus' birth, for the most part, Borg and Wright talk past each other. Both simply present their own views without engaging with the particular reasons that lie behind those of the other.

[9] As we have noted, this is the tone of Lüdemann, *Virgin Birth?*.

[10] Cf. e.g. R. E. Brown, *The Birth of the Messiah* (2nd edn New York: Doubleday, 1993), 517–31; J. P. Meier, *A Marginal Jew* Vol. 1 (New York: Doubleday, 1991), 220–2, though, interestingly, elsewhere in his multivolume work on the life of Jesus he is not reticent about concluding against the historicity of various 'nature' miracles.

[11] Cf. e.g. R. W. Jenson, *Systematic Theology* Vol. 2 (Oxford: OUP, 1999), 200–4.

[12] Cf. e.g. J. Moltmann, *The Way of Jesus Christ* (London: SCM, 1990), 78–87.

[13] Cf. e.g. S. Grenz, *Theology for the Community of God* (Carlisle: Paternoster, 1994), 409–23, who lists some of the objections only to dismiss them as not warranting any disturbance of the tradition.

reflect at all about principles of interpretation nor the cultural arrogance that is content simply to dismiss scriptural accounts of miracle and credal formulations as outdated should be allowed to convince us that there is nothing further to discuss. In fact, as we shall explore more fully later, one of the main problems about the virginal conception is not whether one is disposed to accept the miraculous in general but the nature of this particular miraculous event, which, on contemporary understandings of conception, raises a severe difficulty for the doctrine of the incarnation's assertion of the full humanity of Jesus. On ancient views of procreation and conception, human substance was supplied simply in the contribution of a mother's womb to the process, to which the male seed added the necessary animating principle. We now, of course, consider both parents' contributions to be necessary for human DNA, with, in the case of a male, the mother providing the X chromosome and the father the Y chromosome. Ironically, while on ancient views the virginal conception could be employed to safeguard the humanity of Jesus over against docetic views of his nature, in the light of contemporary biological understanding a virginal conception undermines the notion of Jesus sharing fully in our humanity and introduces a docetic element into the doctrine of the incarnation. Without complete human DNA Jesus would be a semi-divine or wholly divine special creation that appeared to be human.

Institutional and political factors, however, often function as a brake on open exploration of such issues. For some, ecclesiastical pressures are not conducive to any honest airing of the topic. As recently as 1984, David Jenkins' comment in a television interview, shortly after being named Bishop of Durham, that he doubted whether God would have arranged a virgin birth set off a chain of reactions leading to a petition against his consecration signed by 12,000 people and to his opponents attributing to the judgement of God on him the lightning strike and fire at the cathedral just after his consecration. In 1987, Uta Ranke-Heinemann, the world's first woman professor of Catholic theology at the University of Essen, also became the first woman to lose her chair when the Roman Catholic authorities in Germany declared her ineligible to teach, because she had stated that the virgin birth was a theological belief and not a biological fact.[14] And one senses with a number of other Catholic scholars who have treated the virgin birth that their ecclesiastical allegiance and wish to have the Church's *imprimatur* may have prevented them drawing some of the

---

[14] Cf. U. Ranke-Heinemann, *Eunuchs for the Kingdom of Heaven* (Harmondsworth: Penguin, 1991), 346–8 for her own account of the circumstances.

conclusions that their work suggests. But the matter is no different in some other confessional settings. To express doubts about the virgin birth is one of the surest ways for teachers at most institutions in the evangelical tradition to lose their jobs.[15] Two main factors have been at work here among evangelicals – lingering notions that a high view of the authority of Scripture as the Word of God requires belief that all its narrative accounts are strictly historical and, not unrelated, the legacy of the fundamentalist–modernist controversy from the beginning of the twentieth century that elevated belief in a literal virgin birth to one of the five touchstones of evangelical orthodoxy. Barth's warning that theologians and teachers unable to affirm the virgin birth were walking a private road at their own cost and risk and should keep it as a private road by remaining silent about it,[16] however admirable its respect for the Church's teachings, was also hardly calculated to foster any general understanding of the critical issues surrounding the dogma. The pastoral concern on the part of some ministers about disturbing the simple beliefs of the faithful through any serious discussion of the birth accounts has a similar inhibiting effect and is patronizing and ultimately misguided, ensuring at very least that many of the educated in their congregations remain confused about how to understand the Christmas story.

The concerns of ecclesiastical authorities are not, however, totally groundless and are paralleled in the genuine reticence of individual Christians to pursue their questions further. Some appear to be under the impression that the sort of exploration that puts questions to earlier understandings of the virgin birth threatens a high view of Scripture and its authority or a fully orthodox Christology in which Jesus is confessed to be not merely human but divine. Others have a proper respect for the Church's early creeds and the authoritative weight of its tradition and do not wish to be unnecessarily disloyal. Among those who have become used to critical reading of the Bible and have realized there are difficult questions about the virgin birth there can also be the sense that it might somehow be a betrayal of the faith not to affirm the historicity of an event which appears to be required by the Church's creed, is linked closely to other beliefs about the incarnation and about Mary and is so central to the Christmas story. Many end up thinking it may be incumbent on them simply to accept the virgin birth on trust as a miracle, lest further exploration unravels too much. Though prior convictions about Scripture, Christology and church

---

[15] Cf. T. George, 'The Blessed Virgin Mary in Evangelical Perspective', in eds C. E. Braaten and R. W. Jenson, *Mary, Mother of God* (Grand Rapids: Eerdmans, 2004), 108.

[16] Cf. K. Barth, *Church Dogmatics* 1.2 (Edinburgh: T. & T. Clark, 1956), 181.

tradition are important, they also need to be related to informed readings of the relevant texts, to historical investigation, to theological probing and to problems arising from our present state of knowledge. It should not be forgotten that other Christological aspects of the creeds such as the ascension into heaven or the descent into hell are commonly understood as metaphorical rather than literal, since contemporary Christians no longer share the ancient worldview. One of the questions for exploration is whether the virgin birth falls into a similar category or has a different status. This project is undertaken on the assumption that, if one is persuaded that there are indeed issues about a virginal conception that need rethinking, then none of the major prior convictions just mentioned needs to be jettisoned but rather developed and adjusted in the light of any findings. The exploration is then part of the usual hermeneutical circle or spiral in which pre-understandings and developing knowledge and experience are mutually informative. These matters will be addressed more fully as the exploration proceeds but, in my view, it is a mistake to think that these strong prior convictions rule out any reconsideration of a literal interpretation from the start. Instead, the investigation will highlight the question of the nature of Scripture and of the type of writings that God has chosen to employ as the vehicle of authoritative revelation, it will reflect on what it is to have a high Christology that takes account of our best knowledge about the New Testament witness and about how recognition of the earthly Jesus' divinity developed, and it will look at how tradition is a dynamic entity that is itself developing and subject to reinterpretation.

Another obstacle to open exploration can be the sense that, if one were to doubt the miraculous as the chief factor in Jesus' birth, a further step would have been taken in reducing the Christian faith simply to the rational and explicable. One does not need to believe in the inerrancy of Scripture or to have a view of miracle as some kind of magic to be prepared to give the tradition of the virginal conception the benefit of the doubt and to do so because one prefers an openness to mystery and to the possibility of the otherwise unpredictable rather than the prejudice that rules out any idea of miracle as indefensible or that already knows that any discourse that makes use of miracle has to be metaphorical. There is no doubt that a humility and an awe before the presence and action of the Creator within the world is an important part of the Christian faith and that there is a genuine temptation to rationalize and to want everything to make sense from a human point of view. On the other hand, a proper sense of our own limitations and of the richness and incomprehensibility of the divine purposes should not function as legitimation for any and all claims about spectacular divine intervention or as an impediment to open discussion and the exercise of critical judgement. Part of the exercise of critical judgement will be to evaluate various claims, and the reliability of testimony will play a role here, but claims should not be exempted from evaluation simply because they appear in Scripture. And if, for example, one were to conclude that some miracles attributed to Jesus in all probability were accounts developed on the basis of belief in the resurrection, this need not be to reduce the faith to the limits of one's own contemporary knowledge. The same holds for the virgin birth. There is plenty of scope for constant awe and mystery in the face of such realities of the Christian faith as creation, incarnation, atonement, resurrection and consummation.

A situation in which people appear to talk past each other from assumed or entrenched positions on the virgin birth and in which various factors discourage more open attempts at reflection and persuasion is not a healthy one either for the faith and understanding of individual Christians or for the teaching ministry of the Church. This was illustrated relatively recently when for Christmas 2009 a New Zealand church, St Matthew's, Auckland, attempted to encourage people to think more critically about the traditional Christmas story. Its billboard pictured the heads of Joseph and Mary as they lie side by side in bed with Joseph looking slightly sad and rueful and Mary looking away from him with her eyes raised upwards. Underneath was the caption 'Poor Joseph. God was a hard act to follow.' Whatever one thinks of the effectiveness of this particular attempt to raise exegetical, historical and theological questions, it produced a predictably divided response from around the world, with some welcoming its provocation to rethink popular understandings and many others expressing outrage. The billboard proved so offensive to someone that it was in fact defaced in an act of vandalism and had to be removed on grounds of safety. Not only does this indicate the emotions this topic still arouses but the responses from both sides on the church's website also show how easy it is to speak past one another and how much ignorance remains about what the issues for discussion and debate really are.[17] For various reasons, then, those who wish to take Scripture and creed seriously but also to think critically about these sources are often left without much help, and confusion about what is at stake easily distracts from an engagement with the

---

[17] The billboard picture, an explanation and hundreds of comments on it can be found at <http://www.stmatthews.org.nz/nav.php?sid=498&id=999/>. Accessed 23/07/2012.

relevant scriptural texts that is concerned with their theological subject matter. Literary, historical and hermeneutical questions may not always be the most important ones, but in this case they bear directly on what the subject matter is and whether it necessarily includes a particular claim about the miraculous origin of Jesus' human existence and the gynaecological state of his mother. At the very least, some clarity about such matters appears crucial for Christological and Mariological reflection.[18]

Theological interpretation of Scripture frequently faces the issue of how it will relate to historical-critical interpretations and their findings. One dominant way of negotiating the issue has been for the two areas to be kept distinct. Biblical scholars were supposed to do their historical investigations unencumbered by dogmatic or theological convictions, and systematic theologians then accepted what they considered to be the consensus view of biblical scholars on such issues as the basis for their own work of reflection and appropriation. More recently, a variety of perspectives have called such a clear division of tasks into question. When the focus of theological interpretation is Christology, then one of the more obvious areas in which this sort of negotiation needs to take place is the discussion of the relation between what can be discovered with any probability about the life of Jesus of Nazareth from critical study of the ancient sources and Christological assertions about his identity with the God of Israel, the area most frequently spoken of in terms of the relation between the Jesus of history and the Christ of faith.[19] Exploration of the topic of Jesus' birth involves one limited aspect of this area. Yet it also gives rise to a distinctive problem for Christians who engage in serious study of the Gospel texts. Christian students of the Gospels are used to making comparisons between John and the Synoptics in terms of the historicity of their stories of Jesus and then comparisons among and investigations behind the Synoptics' accounts in order to reconstruct probable incidents from the life of the historical Jesus. They carry out such critical studies even though they may hold that they are not decisive for the truth of the

---

[18] In regard to the latter, for anyone who is aware of the critical issues, it seems very strange that some recent writings on Mariology, such as the valuable collection of essays in eds C. E. Braaten and R. W. Jenson, *Mary, Mother of God* (Grand Rapids: Eerdmans, 2004) or the report of the Anglican–Roman Catholic International Commission, *Mary: Grace and Hope in Christ* (London: Morehouse, 2005), can proceed without any acknowledgement of the serious questions that face a contemporary reader of the accounts of the virgin birth.

[19] For recent helpful discussions, cf. e.g. D. C. Allison, 'The Historians' Jesus and the Church', and F. Watson, '*Veritas Christi*: How to Get from the Jesus of History to the Christ of Faith without Losing One's Way', in eds B. R. Gaventa and R. B. Hays, *Seeking the Identity of Jesus* (Grand Rapids: Eerdmans, 2008), 79–95, 96–114.

Gospels and that what matters theologically is the Christ proclaimed by the fourfold Gospel witness. The Apostles' Creed, however, famously says nothing about the earthly career of Jesus. One may seriously doubt, therefore, the authenticity of a variety of sayings of Jesus or of a number of incidents in his life as these are now found in the canonical Gospels and yet find no problems in negotiating the creed. Both maximalists and minimalists in regard to the historical value of the accounts agree that, at least in the bulk of the Synoptic Gospels, there is material about the mission of Jesus that is worth evaluating historically but that the infancy narratives of Matthew and Luke present the most problematic material for such investigation. The irony is, of course, that it is from the midst of precisely this most questionable historical material that the creed selects what is its only historical assertion about the life of Jesus before his passion: 'born of the Virgin Mary'.

By this time some readers may already be asking the question 'What is there to explore?' in yet another way. Surely, there are plenty of treatments of this topic already available for its exploration; why do you think there is any need for yet another? The reply has to be that yes, of course, there are various recent writings, including lives of Jesus, commentaries and theologies, that discuss particular aspects of our topic but, because of their focus, these are not able to bring together the necessary range of issues involved. The same consideration holds even for most monographs that are wholly devoted to the topic of the virgin birth. There are a good number of critical historical or literary treatments of the New Testament material but surprisingly few that relate these to hermeneutical and theological concerns or that approach their investigation with any sympathy for the sort of convictions about Scripture and creed that have already been mentioned in our own discussion. Students of the New Testament might be forgiven for thinking there can be very little yet to add to the magisterial work of Raymond Brown.[20] This project will be indebted to his study in many ways, but Brown's is an in-depth analysis of the birth narratives as a whole and, having completed its work, in relation to the virginal conception itself draws some tentative conclusions about historicity and then unsatisfactorily leaves the major hermeneutical and

---

[20] Brown, *Birth*, 993. H. Wansborough, 'The Infancy Stories of the Gospels since Raymond E. Brown', in ed. Corley, *New Perspectives*, 4–22, provides a survey of some of the literature on the infancy narratives since the second edition of Brown's work. Most recently a wide-ranging collection of scholarly essays has appeared that claims to go beyond Brown's work by enlarging the field of investigation to include the apocryphal infancy gospels, cf. eds C. Clivaz, A. Dettwiler, L. Devillers, E. Norelli with the assistance of B. Bertho, *Infancy Gospels* (Tübingen: Mohr Siebeck, 2011).

theological questions to be determined by its author's church's tradition and its magisterium. A quite different sort of treatment has been given by Bishop Spong.[21] His is a popular and polemical book with an unsympathetic eye much of the time on American fundamentalists and what he sees as their oppressive literalism. Despite some inaccuracies, he makes a number of valid points about the birth stories, but his case is not helped by his generalizations and the sharp polarization between critical scholarship and church tradition, with which he operates. When he proclaims, 'No one in scholarly circles that I know of, however, is willing to defend the historicity or the literalness of the virgin birth story!'[22] not only does he fail to distinguish adequately the historicity of the event and the literalness of the story but also reveals clearly that his knowledge of scholarly circles is a limited one. He can also state,

> Conservative bishops and priests content themselves by asserting that biblical scholarship is an ever-changing, inexact science that cannot be counted on for final answers. They argue that we must, therefore, trust the church's historic teaching authority. It is a weak and almost pathetic argument.[23]

This seriously underplays the substantial role of tradition in theology and shows little respect for the considered position of someone like Brown. Its intemperate formulation is scarcely calculated to persuade those with different but genuine theological concerns. The work of Gerd Lüdemann[24] is a crisp historical treatment but is overconfident about its methods and findings and reductionist in its view that, once a negative conclusion has been drawn on the historical front, the whole matter is no longer worthy of consideration. It does discuss scholars who have theological and ecclesiological concerns and commitments to which they wish to relate their historical investigations but only summarily to dismiss their views. The Jewish scholar Geza Vermes has written a more dispassionate and popular historical account.[25] Unsurprisingly, he is not concerned with the relation of his findings to Christian theology and so only a final half page discusses the theological significance of the birth narratives. More helpful than any of these treatments in many ways is the work of Robert Miller.[26] He gathers together in accessible form a wealth of historical, cultural,

---

[21] J. S. Spong, *Born of a Woman: A Bishop Rethinks the Birth of Jesus* (San Francisco: HarperSanFrancisco, 1992).

[22] Spong, *Born of a Woman*, 139.

[23] Spong, *Born of a Woman*, 140.

[24] Lüdemann, *Virgin Birth?*.

[25] G. Vermes, *The Nativity: History and Legend* (London: Penguin, 2006).

[26] R. J. Miller, *Born Divine: The Births of Jesus and Other Sons of God* (Santa Rosa, CA: Polebridge, 2003).

linguistic and exegetical information necessary for understanding the Gospel accounts and does have a final ten-page chapter that reflects on the hermeneutical and theological consequences.

As readers may already have gathered, although the following exploration will inevitably cover some of the same issues as these books, it does so by acknowledging from the start the commitments that Christians bring to any such study. One of the major purposes of this exploration is, after all, to offer help to those who want to be both confessing Christians and serious, critically informed, students. If there is to be any hope of this happening and of persuading some that there might be appropriate ways of finding some integration that they had not previously considered, it will obviously be necessary to foreground rather than to marginalize confessional commitments and to make clear that the approach taken here to the topic of the virgin birth is one of critical loyalty to the authority of Scripture and creed. But this is not simply a rhetorical tactic. It reflects the basic assumptions that confession of faith and theological conviction do not enter the discussion only after other disciplines have investigated a problem and made their determinations and that, in matters of interpretation of Scripture, the Church's wisdom as found in its creeds and classical formulations is given a default position. While it must be recognized that such formulations are provisional and also subject to error, there can be no automatic assumption that the Church has got much of its teachings wrong and that contemporary readers with their superior critical knowledge are finally in a position to get these matters right. There is also, therefore, no assumption that doubt and suspicion about traditional doctrines are in themselves virtuous. Rather, they are to be treated as dependent on a prior disposition of trust in the gospel about Jesus Christ, as witnessed to in Scripture and mediated by the Church, and therefore as moments in the search of faith for fuller understanding. But it is precisely for this reason that, for many Christians, the virgin birth constitutes a problem. For such people, although historical and literary and biological questions may play a significant role, the really key questions are likely to be somewhat different. Can one remain faithful to the Church's confession while still engaging in a properly critical reading of Scripture? Can there be a continuing conversation between confessional affirmation and critical thinking without this remaining viciously circular? How serious do the problems raised by a critical interpretation of the virgin birth have to be in order to produce a modification of one's confessional presuppositions? There is little point, then, in exploring the virgin birth without being clear that it is questions like these that are crucial for many.

16

The stance of this exploration could be labelled 'post-critical'. It begins by acknowledging a basic trust in the Church's confession as one's framework for interpreting reality and does not imagine that there is some neutral viewpoint from which one can conduct its investigation of the virgin birth. It will not consider historical, literary or biological discourses simply as the master discourses within which the Christian message has to be made to fit. It will, however, bring to bear scholarly tools, critical enquiry and the present state of historical and biological knowledge, again without naivety about their neutral status, in order to pursue a rigorous investigation. A post-critical stance is not one that ignores the hard-won results of criticism but, unlike the criticism that is inclined to think it has the last word, it incorporates those results in order to return to the subject of its enquiry and appropriate it in a fresh way. The perils of allowing prejudice to distort one's critical judgement are obvious, but this is the case for any approach, either one that supposes itself to be totally objective and impartial or one that acknowledges some other standpoint that is not sympathetic to the claims of the Christian tradition and community, and in practice the believing critic will frequently be prepared to accommodate, change or drop aspects of his or her belief in the face of what appears to be compelling evidence. One can only start from where one is, be as aware as possible of the issues, learn critical discernment as one proceeds and be prepared to acknowledge the provisionality and fallibility of one's conclusions along the way.

The hope will be to accomplish something of this in what follows by surveying the most important areas of the discussion, by providing a guide through some of their complexities without getting lost in them, by being scholarly but not cluttered by too many footnotes, and by interacting with some other leading treatments but attempting to remain accessible to those who are not professional biblical scholars or theologians. The focus will be on the problem areas, so readers should not expect a comprehensive and detailed treatment of all the topics on which it touches. As the bibliography indicates, major studies of, for example, the birth narratives or incarnational Christology are already available. It will also have become clear that readers should not expect any systematic treatment of one major area on which this study impinges, namely, the place of Mary, the mother of Jesus, in Christian doctrine, tradition and devotion. The decision had to be taken that, within the constraints of this book, the focus needed to be on the prior Christological issues.[27]

---

[27] One of the most helpful resources for a contemporary Mariology in the light of a critical treatment of Scripture and tradition is E. A. Johnson's *Truly Our Sister: A Theology of Mary in the Communion of Saints* (London: Continuum, 2003), which, however, deals with the virginal conception only in passing.

While the book argues for a particular viewpoint, it also constitutes a call for greater openness and discussion among those concerned about the relationship between reading of Scripture, saying of creed and doing of theology on this topic. The hope is that it will contribute to the sort of discussion that displays a readiness to live with obvious questions without suppressing them, a recognition that too hasty judgements of others in terms of either obscurantism or unorthodoxy are out of place, and a willingness to see that different positions might be compatible with a faithful and critical allegiance to Scripture and creed. At the very least, it is hoped that someone who follows its argument, whether in agreement or not, will not simply be able to say that there was nothing to explore because either one believes in the authority of Scripture and the possibility of miracle or one does not and that is what settles the issue!

One further matter should be made clear at the outset of the exploration. Though, as we shall see, there are implications for some ways of articulating belief in the incarnation, that belief itself is not at stake here. In fact this study has been undertaken by one for whom the belief that Jesus Christ is fully human and fully divine is a non-negotiable element in Christianity's 'scandal of particularity'. So to investigate the notion of the virgin birth is not to question the doctrine of incarnation. First of all, incarnation is not simply a claim about the birth of Christ, however that may have happened. Incarnation refers to the identification of the divine Son with the whole of Jesus' humanity and mission, not just with the beginning of his life. Jesus' conception is one aspect, the necessary initial aspect, of the Son's incarnation. Second, one can raise questions about the adequacy of a particular mode of depicting this initial aspect of the incarnation without denying the reality of that which it depicts. Most defenders of the traditional doctrine of a virgin birth have no problem in conceding this. Indeed, Pope Benedict XVI, in one of his earlier writings as Joseph Ratzinger, while obviously himself holding to the traditional belief in the virginal conception, recognized this remarkably clearly:

> According to the faith of the Church the Sonship of Jesus does not rest on the fact that Jesus had no human father: The doctrine of Jesus' divinity would not be affected if Jesus had been the product of a normal marriage. For the Sonship of which faith speaks is not a biological but an ontological fact, an event not in time but in God's eternity.[28]

---

[28] J. Ratzinger, *Introduction to Christianity* (New York: Herder & Herder/London: Burns & Oates, 1969), 208.

A conservative, though creative, Anglican theologian, Austin Farrer, was also clear on this distinction. In a sermon on 'Incarnation' he declared,

> The virginal birth is not the substance of the Incarnation; it is the peculiar way in which (we have been told) it pleased God to bring it about. Jesus is not the Son of God *because* he had no human father. It would have been conceivable though it did not happen that the Son of God might have become incarnate as the offspring of an ordinary union.[29]

We shall return to the relation between the virgin birth and the beginning of incarnation later, where we shall see that it may well be not so much that doubts about the virgin birth lead to doubts about the incarnation but rather that a robust doctrine of incarnation leads to difficulties with the virgin birth. But for now it should be underlined that this exploration assumes the conviction of Jesus' incarnation, that is, the conviction that God, without ceasing to be God, entered the created world not merely in but as the particular Jew, Jesus of Nazareth, so that Jesus' life, death and resurrection can be identified as that of God in one of the modes of God's being.

The contours of our exploration will become clearer in the chapters that follow but its major stages will be these. First, we shall look at the references to Jesus' conception in parts of the New Testament other than the infancy narratives and indicate, contrary to what is frequently assumed, that the virginal conception is not the only tradition about Jesus' birth in the New Testament. We then turn to the accounts that have been most influential in thinking about our topic, namely the annunciation stories in Matthew and Luke, and attempt to re-examine what they do or do not say about how the life of Jesus began. We next ask how far each of the traditions about Jesus' conception can be traced back and which construction of this past event does better justice to these sources, before investigating how far they can be traced forward in later Christian thinking and when, why and how one of those traditions, the virginal conception, became the dominant view within the Church. Having seen the establishment of this particular tradition and the doctrinal roles it played, we move to explore when and why it began to be considered problematic within Christian theology, looking particularly at Schleiermacher, who was concerned to integrate critical scholarship and Christian theology, as our test case. In the last two chapters we investigate the variety of issues raised by the virgin birth tradition for contemporary Christian thinking in the areas

---

[29] A. Farrer, *The Brink of Mystery* (London: SPCK, 1976), 21.

of Scripture, hermeneutics, Christology and creed. Parts of the terrain to be explored will undoubtedly already be familiar to some readers, but it is hoped that they will find there is enough in this navigation to enable them to look at such parts with fresh eyes. It is also hoped that in the course of the exploration readers will find a few areas that were left blank by previous mapmakers.

2

Beyond the infancy narratives: the so-called 'silent witness' of the New Testament

It is frequently thought that an appeal to the New Testament on the topic of Jesus' conception is a relatively straightforward matter. The New Testament is assumed to contain only one normative perspective on this topic – Jesus was conceived by a virgin without any man involved in the process – and that is found in the infancy narratives of Matthew and Luke. It might indeed appear natural to turn first to the infancy narratives in the Gospels because they contain annunciation accounts, to interpret these as referring to a virginal conception and then to read the rest of the New Testament either as if it were silent about Jesus' conception or in a way that consciously or unconsciously harmonizes its data with the tradition of a virgin birth. However, this approach does not take seriously enough the evidence that appears outside the accounts of the infancy of Jesus but still makes implicit or explicit reference to his parentage, and, in subordinating any further data to the annunciation stories, does not do justice to first hearing the message of each New Testament document on its own terms. Lest our exploration be skewed from the start by immediately focusing on the stories in Matthew and Luke, we would do well to begin by asking whether these two Gospels are our only witnesses to Jesus' conception and whether the New Testament contains more diversity in its witness than is often realized.

Are there other potential witnesses to a virginal conception?

We shall examine first the common view that the rest of the New Testament either provides silent support for the virgin birth or, as is held by a few, offers additional evidence for that tradition. The earliest New Testament writings, as is well known, are those of Paul and in them there is no mention of a virgin birth. Paul does, of course, make some reference to Jesus' birth in three places (Gal. 4.4; Rom. 1.3; Phil. 2.7). But all three passages simply assume Jesus' full humanity in his birth and show no interest in the circumstances of the birth itself. Like any other human being, he was 'born of a woman' and, like any other Jew of the time, he was 'born under the law' (Gal. 4.4). This particular Jew 'was born of the seed of David according to the flesh' (Rom. 1.3)[1] and it was through the Spirit at work in the resurrection that he 'was designated Son of God in power' (Rom. 1.4). In the last reference there is no denial, of course, that Jesus could be seen as Son of God before the resurrection but no indication whatsoever that it was a virgin birth that was decisive for Jesus' status or its recognition. Cranfield, however, claims that the use of the verb *ginesthai* instead of *gennasthai* in these references makes it highly likely that Paul knew of the virgin birth.[2] But this claim has little merit. While the former verb can have the broader meaning of 'to come to exist' or 'to become' and the latter means more specifically 'to be born' or 'to be begotten' with its connotations of male begetting, there are plenty of references, as the lexicons make clear, where the context indicates that 'to be born' is the appropriate translation of *ginesthai* and where this verb is synonymous with *gennasthai*.[3] More significant, as we shall see, is that Paul and the Jewish Christian tradition he takes up in Romans 1.3 show no reservation about employing the term 'seed' in connection with Jesus' birth, indicating that this birth was the result of the continuity of the male seed in the line of David. Elsewhere Paul can speak of Jesus as also the seed (singular) of Abraham (Gal. 3.16, 19), and this is in fact the context for the following reference to Jesus' birth in Galatians 4.4. The one whom God sent as God's Son, born of a woman, is the one who is the fulfilment of the promise to Abraham about his physical seed. Paul has a high Christology, which includes the notion of the pre-existence of Christ, but a virginal conception plays no part in this and it is almost certain that he did not know of such a tradition.

The earliest Gospel, Mark, also shows no sign of knowledge of this tradition. This is not simply an argument from silence, since, in the case of Mark, in the 'sandwich structure' of 3.20–35 and in 6.1–6a the evangelist is quite clear about the attitude of Jesus' mother and brothers towards

---

[1] Where the English wording of the text differs from the NRSV, this is the writer's own translation.

[2] C. E. B. Cranfield, 'Some Reflections on the Subject of the Virgin Birth', *SJT* 41 (1988), 178. T. F. Torrance, 'The Doctrine of the Virgin Birth', *Scottish Bulletin of Evangelical Theology* 12 (1994), 8–25, offers similar arguments to those of Cranfield about the presence of the virgin birth in Paul, Mark and John, but in less restrained fashion. On this question of the use of the particular verb in Paul, for example, he can say, 'This is the strongest disavowal of birth by ordinary human generation in regard to Jesus' (13). In what follows we shall focus on Cranfield's more carefully formulated arguments.

[3] E.g. LXX 1 Esd. 4.15–16; Tobit 8.6. Justin, *Dial.* 48.4; 67.2 actually employs *ginesthai* of normal human birth in contrast to supernatural conception! On this linguistic issue and the whole question of Jesus' birth in Paul's writings, cf. also R. B. Matlock, 'The Birth of Jesus and Why Paul Was in Favour of It', in ed. G. J. Brooke, *The Birth of Jesus* (Edinburgh: T. & T. Clark, 2000), 47–57.

Jesus; it is one of alienation and unbelief.[4] In 6.4 Mark has the saying of Jesus that 'Prophets are not without honour, except in their home town, and among their own kin, and in their own house.' This makes it highly improbable that Mark was aware of a tradition that Jesus' birth was an extraordinary occurrence about which his parents had received some special revelation. What is more, given the tendency in the early Christian movement to honour Jesus' family,[5] it appears highly unlikely that Mark would have presented this negative portrait unless it had been rooted in the tradition. Again Cranfield attempts to read the evidence of Mark as favouring a virgin birth tradition.[6] He takes the reference in 6.3 to the people of Jesus' home town calling him 'the son of Mary' as 'evidence that the charge of illegitimacy, which was certainly levelled against Jesus at a later date, was made very early and quite probably during his lifetime'. But, if this were the correct reading of the disputed appellation (and this will be examined later in the chapter), it would only constitute evidence for their thinking that there was scandal attached to Jesus' birth. For this to constitute evidence for the virgin birth, however, one would have to presuppose the reality of the latter and see their slur as an invalid response to it. But that is, of course, to assume the matter under dispute, and all the evidence from Mark's Gospel itself indicates that a virginal conception was not an assumption held by its writer.

John's Gospel makes very clear that Jesus is more than merely human. Its prologue depicts him as the incarnation of the Word who in the beginning was at God's side and declares that what God was, the Word was (1.1, 14). But for the Fourth Evangelist there is no recourse to a story of virginal conception to make this point. When in the prologue there is a reference to a birth that is not merely human – 'who were born neither of bloods nor of the will of the flesh nor of the will of the male but of God' (1.13) – it is not to that of Jesus.[7] In speaking of generation from God and stating that believers, as children of God, are born not from natural human sexual union but from God, the evangelist is referring to

---

[4] J. G. Machen, *The Virgin Birth of Christ* (2nd edn New York: Harper and Row, 1932), 246–7, disputes this by denying that Mary is included in the reference in 3.21, but see e.g. R. E. Brown, *The Birth of the Messiah* (2nd edn New York: Doubleday, 1993), 520; J. Marcus, *Mark 1—8* (New York: Doubleday, 2000), 277.

[5] Matthew and Luke omit Mark 3.21 and the reference to Jesus' own family in Mark 6.4.

[6] Cranfield, 'Reflections', 178–9.

[7] There is one later variant, an Old Latin manuscript, that has the singular here rather than the plural and is sometimes appealed to by interpreters as support for the virgin birth in John, but the overwhelming manuscript evidence leaves no doubt that the reference is in the plural to the preceding 'those who believed in his name' (1.12).

a spiritual relationship into which those who were born normally from two human parents enter but which is not to be attributed to physical descent from these parents. Cranfield wants to see here an allusion to Jesus' birth, whereby believers' birth is patterned on the birth of Christ which was also solely by the will of God rather than through human procreation.[8] Again this assumes the evidence for which one is looking. Unless the notion of a virginal conception was read into this text from Matthew's or Luke's narrative, it would not occur to any reader to find it here. Significantly, 1 John 5.18 can assert, 'No one born of God sins; instead the one born of God protects them'. If, as in all probability, the one born of God in the second clause refers to Christ, then the Johannine literature as a whole appears to assume that Jesus came into the world in the same way believing humans do and yet both he and they can be said to be 'born of God'. Cranfield appeals also to John 6.41–42 and 8.41.[9] In the former 'the Jews' say, 'Is not this Jesus, the son of Joseph, whose father and mother we know? How can he now say, "I have come down from heaven"?' There is no reason at all to read this as the evangelist's ironic allusion to the virgin birth, knowledge of which would have prevented the audience from thinking that Jesus' origins were incompatible with a descent from heaven. The sense is far more straightforward. The objection has to do with how someone whose earthly origins are known could claim to have a heavenly origin. The Fourth Gospel insists on the paradox of the incarnation in which both perspectives on Jesus' birth are true, because he is the divine Logos who has become flesh. Any irony is derived from the Jewish opposition's limiting itself to the earthly perspective to categorize Jesus and therefore judging simply by earthly appearance rather than with just judgement (cf. 7.24; 8.15). The earthly appearance itself is not being called into question. Indeed, elsewhere Philip's witness to Nathanael also speaks of Jesus as Joseph's son without any hint of this being a questionable designation: 'We have found him about whom Moses in the law and also the prophets wrote, Jesus, son of Joseph from Nazareth' (1.45). Philip's response, 'Can anything good come from Nazareth?' (1.46), in the light of the previous formulation about Moses and the prophets, reflects the fact that Nazareth does not feature in Scripture in connection with the Messiah. It is highly ironic, but not because Jesus is not the son of Joseph or because he does not come from Nazareth but rather because this son of Joseph from Nazareth is not just something good but is in reality also

---

[8] Cranfield, 'Reflections', 179.
[9] Cranfield, 'Reflections', 179–80.

the incarnation of the divine Logos. So, in fact, John introduces Jesus in his narrative as someone in full solidarity with normal human fleshly existence; he has a father (1.45) and a mother (2.1, 3). There can be little doubt that for the Fourth Gospel the Word's becoming flesh did not entail anything other than the normal means of human conception.

As he does with Mark 6.3, Cranfield takes John 8.41 to reflect the charge of illegitimacy in relation to Jesus' birth and therefore also the Fourth Evangelist's belief in the virgin birth. But, even if there is a charge of illegitimacy reflected here, as was pointed out in relation to Mark, the virgin birth does not necessarily follow from it and is an invalid argument from silence. In this case, however, there has to be doubt whether Jesus' illegitimacy is in fact in view. The verse reads: 'They said to him, "We are not illegitimate children [literally, 'not born of fornication']; we have one father, God himself."' While this could be taken as an ironic attack on Jesus by his opponents because of rumours in circulation about the abnormal circumstances of his birth, this is highly unlikely given that John has just had the Jewish opponents say precisely the opposite – that Jesus is the son of Joseph and that they know his father and mother (6.42), and in any case the context of the debate about spiritual paternity and their emphasis on having *one* father makes another interpretation far more plausible. Jesus has just cast doubt on whether his opponents are truly Abraham's children and suggested that their actions indicate that they have a rather different father, who will later be specified as the devil (8.39–41a, cf. 8.44). Since fornication is often employed as a metaphor for idolatry in the Jewish Scriptures, their response that they are not born of fornication is most straightforwardly taken as an emphatic assertion that they are not unfaithful idolaters, who have followed after other gods (cf. LXX Hos. 1.2; 2.4–5) but are loyal to the one God of the Shema (cf. Deut. 6.4). At this stage in the argument they are engaging in a robust defence of their own claims.[10] When they do explicitly attack Jesus later in the dispute, it is not in terms of his scandalous birth but in the same categories that have been used against them. They allege that he is a Samaritan, an idolatrous apostate from Israel, and that he has a demon and is, therefore, the one possessed by the devil (8.48). But even if one were to be persuaded that the force of 8.41 was 'we are not illegitimate – but you are', this would be no more than a trading of insults. It would

---

[10] One can only agree with J. P. Meier, *A Marginal Jew* Vol. 1 (New York: Doubleday, 1991), 228, that 'to see a hidden reference to Jesus' physical illegitimacy in vv. 39–41 is, in my opinion, highly imaginative'.

be a major leap to interpret it as containing a historical reminiscence of rumours about the circumstances of Jesus' birth.[11] The opponents in this dialogue no more think Jesus was likely to have been actually illegitimate than they think he was likely to have been actually a Samaritan rather than a Jew.

The results of this exercise in clearing the ground are these. It has been confirmed that there are no other possible New Testament witnesses to the virgin birth apart from Matthew and Luke.[12] This is not merely a silence elsewhere, but in the case of Paul, Mark and John there are some features that actually tell strongly against their writers holding such a belief and for their taking the view that his conception was like that of other humans. There may be a reflection of some knowledge of scandal or irregularity associated with Jesus' birth (possibly Mark 6.3) but this does not constitute evidence for the virgin birth, unless the latter is presupposed.

Jesus as the seed of David with Joseph as his father

In the discussion of the undisputed letters of Paul above we noted that not only do they reflect no knowledge of a virginal conception but they also make claims about Jesus' patrilineal descent in their use of the terminology of 'seed'. In Galatians 3.16, 19 Jesus is seen as the fulfilment of the promise to Abraham about his physical seed and in Romans 1.3 (cf. also 2 Tim. 2.8) his physical descent is said to be from the seed of David. The latter reference is usually held to be part of a Jewish Christian formulation about Jesus that Paul has taken up. Paul and Jewish Christians before him, then, assumed that the Davidic line of descent continued down to Jesus through his father's seed. The term 'seed' frequently has the extended meaning of 'descendant' but, unless used metaphorically,

---

[11] *Contra* J. Schaberg, *The Illegitimacy of Jesus: A Feminist Theological Interpretation of the Infancy Narratives* (Sheffield: Sheffield Academic Press, 1995; original edn San Francisco: Harper & Row, 1987), 157–8. As eds R. E. Brown, K. P. Donfried, J. A. Fitzmyer, J. Reumann, *Mary in the New Testament* (Philadelphia: Fortress, 1978), 205, concluded, 'if one grants a slight possibility to a hint of a charge of illegitimacy in 8.41, it would be an extraordinary leap from that to a Johannine affirmation of the virginal conception. The more logical conclusion would be that by hinting at illegitimacy Jesus' opponents were rejecting his references to God as Father.'

[12] Cf. also Brown, *Birth*, 521: 'it is perfectly proper to speak of the silence of the rest of the NT about the virginal conception because not a single one of the "implicit references" has compelling force'. He does not see that in the silence about the virginal conception other views about Jesus' conception are found but concedes that 'what the silence of the rest of the NT does call into question is the theory that the memory of the virginal conception was handed down by the family of Jesus to the apostolic preachers and was universally accepted as fundamental Christian belief'.

retains the connotation of being in the line produced by the male role in procreation.[13] In line with the dominant Aristotelian view of procreation in the ancient world, the male seed was seen as giving the matter provided by the female its generation and formation. This point is frequently ignored in discussions of the virgin birth. Brown does not ignore it altogether but fails to appreciate its force. He writes (in a footnote), 'That statement, meant to describe Jesus' human heritage, was most likely shaped without any advertence to the issue of how Jesus was conceived and cannot be used to solve that issue.' He immediately concedes, however, 'At most one may ask whether the evangelists who wrote of the v.c. [virginal conception] would have chosen such phrasing, even though they might have "lived" with it.'[14] Three things need to be said in reply. First, as his follow-up sentence also indicates, Brown is judging all the evidence from the normative perspective of the accounts in Matthew and Luke, which he holds to be in agreement on this matter. Second, as a matter of fact Luke, who wrote of a virgin birth in his Gospel, did also choose to use this phrasing in Acts. We shall explore the significance of this more fully below. But third, once one considers that the virginal conception may not be the only or normative tradition and treats all available witnesses as equally relevant, the picture is different. Then the likelihood that the formulation embedded in Romans 1.3 was 'shaped without any advertence to the issue of how Jesus was conceived' becomes highly significant. It was shaped that way because there was no issue about how Jesus was conceived. Those who formulated it and passed it on had absolutely no reason not to assume that 'of the seed of David according to the flesh' conveyed what it normally conveyed, that the one of whom it was asserted was a physical patrilineal descendant of David. The later deutero-Pauline 2 Timothy 2.8 speaks of Paul's gospel in similar terms but reverses the order of Romans 1 to 'raised from the dead, of the seed of David'. Almost certainly no thought that the latter phrase had to be understood in some other sense because Jesus did not have a biological father and was only Joseph's son legally would have crossed the mind of Pauline Christians who made this confession.

This tradition, as just noted, is also found in Luke's account of the earliest Christian preaching in Acts. Peter's Pentecost speech, with reference

---

[13] The implications of 'the seed of David' terminology in the New Testament more generally and its contradiction to a virginal conception are explored by F. G. Downing, 'Mary: Between Minimal History and Maximal Myth', *Theology* 110 (2007), 163–70, though he does not observe that Luke's writings, as we shall see, contain this contradiction.

[14] Brown, *Birth*, 707n329.

to Jesus, talks of God swearing to David that he would put one of his descendants (lit. one of the fruit of his loins) on his throne (Acts 2.30). Taking up the language of LXX Psalm 131.11, Luke changes *koilia*, 'belly', which he uses elsewhere for the womb, to *osphus*, 'loins'. The loins are, of course, the place of the reproductive organs, the centre of the male's procreative powers, and their fruit, the children produced, are the biological descendants of David. This then appears to be a strong statement of Jesus being in the physical line of descent from David continued through his own father. Paul's first speech in Acts has elements in common with Peter's but they are given their own distinctive twist. So Luke has Paul in his synagogue address in Pisidian Antioch say of Jesus in relation to David, this time employing language from LXX 2 Samuel 7.12: 'Of this man's seed (*sperma*) God has brought to Israel a Saviour, Jesus, as he has promised'. The promise to David that God's holy one would not see corruption is not fulfilled in the case of David but does come to realization in God's resurrection of this one who was David's seed (Acts 13.23, 32–37). Whatever the historical core behind these speeches, Luke evidently thought they reflected earliest post-resurrection beliefs about Jesus. In line with this, even in Luke's Gospel there are, outside the annunciation story, references to the Davidic Joseph as Jesus' parent or father (2.27, 33, 48) and to Jesus as 'Joseph's son' (4.22). Whether this tradition might be compatible with the annunciation story for Luke and, if so, how, will be examined in Chapter 5.

The 'seed of David' terminology for the Messiah is also mentioned in John's Gospel (7.41–42). Here it is more difficult to determine precisely how it is evaluated because it is found in the mouths of those who are questioning whether Jesus is Messiah. In the narrative there is a division within the crowd about this, with some asking, 'Surely the Messiah does not come from Galilee, does he? Has not the Scripture said that the Messiah is of the seed of David and comes from Bethlehem, the village where David lived?' The evangelist provides no explicit perspective on this objection. The narrative as a whole indicates that he simply finds these sorts of disputes about Jesus' earthly origins misplaced, because the important recognition about Jesus' person is his heavenly origin; he is from above, the one sent by God. This is explicit in the preceding chapter, where 'the Jews' cannot understand how someone whose earthly origins are known can claim to have a heavenly origin: 'Is not this Jesus, the son of Joseph, whose father and mother we know? How can he now say, "I have come down from heaven"?' (6.42). The problem is not with the accuracy of their knowledge about Jesus on its own level but with their failure to grasp the paradoxical Johannine perspective on the incarnation where both perspectives on Jesus' origins are true because he is the Logos who has become flesh. In the case of 7.41–42 the phrase 'the seed of David' is subordinate to the geographical emphasis on Bethlehem, as it leads into the main point that a Davidic Messiah should also come from David's birthplace, as the Scriptures (Mic. 5.2) indicate. The issue at stake is simply whether Galilee or Bethlehem is the appropriate place of earthly origin for the Messiah. The evangelist may well be aware of how others (Matthew and Luke) have handled this, but from his perspective such a handling is unnecessary and he is quite prepared to see the Messiah as, on the earthly scene, coming from Nazareth in Galilee (cf. 1.46–47).

In regard to the subordinate designation 'of the seed of David', there is every reason to think that the evangelist would have endorsed this for Jesus' earthly origins, and the uncomplicated testimony found on the lips of Philip to Jesus' identity as 'son of Joseph' (1.45) suggests that he saw Joseph as the means through which the continuity of the Davidic line was maintained. Some have attempted to distance the Fourth Evangelist from his characters, on whose lips the 'son of Joseph' designation is found, but there can be little doubt that the Fourth Evangelist considered Philip's assertion to be a correct one, since it is part of the positive witness to Jesus of one of his disciples, and is unqualified in its context and nowhere undermined in the rest of his narrative. It is very surprising to find that Barrett could comment on this verse, 'It is in accord with his ironical use of traditional material that he [the evangelist] should allow Jesus to be ignorantly described as "son of Joseph" while himself believing that Jesus had no human father.'[15] As we have seen, there is no reason to think that the evangelist believed Jesus had no human father and any irony in this context comes not from Philip's declaration but from Nathanael's response, 'Can anything good come out of Nazareth?' (1.46). That irony arises, as we noted earlier, not because Philip's information is ignorant or incorrect but rather because what has come out of Nazareth is not just something good but in fact also the source of ultimate good, the divine Logos incarnated in Jesus. Indeed, in this passage Philip and Nathanael together represent the view that Jesus is both the son of Joseph (1.45) and the Son of God (1.49) and that there is no incompatibility between the two notions for this Gospel. In the light of the evangelist's positive treatment of Jesus as son of Joseph and of our discussion of the Johannine material at the beginning of this chapter, there should be no difficulty in agreeing with

---

[15] C. K. Barrett, *The Gospel according to St. John* (Philadelphia: Westminster, 1978), 184.

von Campenhausen's assertion: 'This Gospel is . . . a clear witness against the supposedly general acknowledgment of the virgin birth in primitive Christian preaching as a whole.'[16] More positively, John's Gospel is a clear witness to Jesus' place of origin being Nazareth and his physical origin being Joseph's paternity and to the conviction that, whereas others find these an obstacle to his divine or heavenly origin, believers see both origins as precisely the circumstances in which the divine Logos became flesh.[17]

The tradition of Jesus' physical descent from David is also preserved in another New Testament document traditionally associated with John, namely, Revelation: 'I am the root (offshoot) and descendant of David' (22.16, cf. 5.5). There is a further, and often ignored, witness to Jesus' physical descent from David in the Letter to the Hebrews. In mentioning difficulties that could be raised against his proposal for viewing Jesus as the great high priest, its author can say, 'For it is evident that our Lord was descended from Judah, and in connection with that tribe Moses said nothing about priests' (7.14). Just earlier the writer can talk of Melchizedek as 'without father, without mother, without genealogy' (7.3), because none of these is mentioned in Scripture. Yet it does not occur to him to point out that Jesus was without father or genealogy. Quite the reverse: he assumes patrilineal descent through Jesus' father to David and Judah.

So far our focus has been on the 'seed of David' ascription with its more obvious physical connotations, but the more general title for Jesus, 'son of David', that is found more frequently is, of course, also relevant to the discussion. While the emphasis of such a designation may be on its messianic role, normally the expectation to be attached to it would be that it would be employed of someone who could lay claim to be of the tribe of Judah and, more specifically, to a creditable ancestry going back to David.[18] Indeed, whatever Matthew and Luke do with them, as we shall examine later, the different original genealogies of Jesus as Son of David that they employ in Matthew 1.1–17 and Luke 3.23–38 are based on precisely such an assumption. Mark has the tradition of Jesus as Son of David in two accounts: the blind Bartimaeus story in which it occurs twice (10.47–48) and the teaching of Jesus about how it can be said that the Messiah is the

---

[16] H. von Campenhausen, *The Virgin Birth in the Theology of the Ancient Church* (London: SCM, 1964), 17.

[17] For a similar, more detailed assessment of the evidence from John, see J. Frey, 'How Could Mark and John Do without Infancy Stories? Jesus' Humanity and His Divine Origins in Mark and John', in eds C. Clivaz et al., *Infancy Gospels* (Tübingen: Mohr Siebeck, 2011), 189–215.

[18] Cf. e.g. *4 Ezra* 12.32, at the end of the first century CE, which expects a 'Messiah, whom the Most High has kept until the end of days, who will arise from the offspring of David'.

son of David if, according to Psalm 110.1, David calls him Lord (12.35–37). Luke reproduces the former of these accounts (18.38–39) but Matthew takes over both (20.30–31; 22.41–45). Indeed, Matthew has a clear interest in the Son of David title, employing it nine times in comparison with Mark's three (cf. the additional references in 1.1; 9.27; 12.23; 15.22; 21.9, 15). His unique way of combining this Son of David tradition with an annunciation story in which Joseph is not Jesus' father by having him take on the role of father anyway will need to be discussed later in Chapter 4. There is, however, no justification for holding that all the other accounts that refer to Jesus as David's seed or son know of or are assuming either the same annunciation story or the same solution to its contradiction with Jesus' physical ancestry as are found in Matthew.

We have already noted in connection with Romans 1.3 that some scholars, such as Brown, who posit one normative virginal conception tradition in the New Testament, allow it to trump the other evidence in some such way. Occasionally their reasoning is made more explicit and so we should examine it. The most common way of handling the references to the seed of David or to Joseph as Jesus' father is by ascribing some sort of legal paternity to Joseph. Perhaps the fullest presentation of this view is that of Strauss in connection with the references we have presented from Luke.[19] In the course of his overall argument that Jesus' Davidic descent is a key element in Luke's promise and fulfilment motif, he addresses its apparent conflict with the virginal conception tradition. He recognizes the force of 'such physical-sounding language' as that in Acts 2.30 and 13.23 and goes so far as to say, 'If Luke wanted to downplay Jesus' natural descent from David he surely would not have referred to him as coming from David's seed and David's loins!' But he then goes on to claim that Luke can employ

---

[19] M. L. Strauss, *The Davidic Messiah in Luke–Acts* (Sheffield: Sheffield Academic, 1995), 126–9. Machen, *Virgin Birth*, 260–1 cf. 128–30, sees no inconsistency between Rom. 1.3 and the virgin birth because he supposes Paul knew of the latter and interpreted Davidic descent in the way Matthew and Luke do in terms of legal heirship rather than physical paternity, thus ignoring the force of the term 'seed'. Luke, of course, has no explicit reference to any form of legal adoption, but in any case this supposition also ignores the specific reasons why the narratives of Matthew and Luke, written well after Paul's death, see no incompatibility between virginal conception and Davidic descent, reasons of which Paul would not have known. There is a similar problem with the treatment of the presupposition of Davidic descent by A. Le Donne, *The Historiographical Jesus: Memory, Typology and the Son of David* (Waco: Baylor University Press, 2009), 185–9. His proposal that Gentile Christians interpreted Rom. 1.3 in terms of Roman adoption may well be helpful in understanding how later Christians harmonized virginal conception and Davidic descent. It has, however, no bearing on the early stages of the tradition of Davidic descent when there would have been no knowledge of a virginal conception and Rom. 1.3 would have been interpreted in its straightforward sense.

such formulations because he and his readers would not distinguish legal and natural descent and so 'for Luke Jesus' Davidic descent is just as authentic and real whether he is a legal or natural son of Joseph'. Meier makes a similar point, when he asserts, without producing any evidence, that 'in the eyes of the OT, the legal father is the real father, whether or not he physically procreated the child'.[20] These scholars might have adduced, though they do not, later rabbinic evidence, such as Sanhedrin 19b, which asserts that 'whoever brings up an orphan in his home is regarded, according to Scripture, as though the child had been born to him'. This would have some relevance to Matthew's particular and unique depiction of Joseph's relationship to Jesus, but none of these other references to Jesus as David's seed or Joseph's son betrays any awareness of Matthew's story. But the invocation of the Old Testament in general and the notion that any distinction between natural and legal descent is not an issue are highly dubious. Who are these legal fathers that are not the real fathers in the Jewish Scriptures and how is Joseph's case in any way comparable to them? Any references to practices similar to adoption are rare and those that are adduced (e.g. Gen. 48.5–6; Esth. 2.7, 15) involve close relatives in the immediate physical family, not someone from a different family.[21] If it is the practice of Levirate marriage that Strauss, Meier and others have in view, then this only reinforces how important biological paternity was in ancient Israel. In the exceptional case of a death before producing a physical heir, the brother's seed substitutes for that of the deceased and gives the deceased male that heir. But, normally, actual biological paternity was thought to be crucial, not least for socio-economic reasons. Proven paternity of the heir was an essential element in the orderly succession of property and, in the absence of DNA testing, this was ensured through female virginity and marital fidelity and is why such stress is laid on these within biblical patriarchy (cf. e.g. Deut. 22.13–29). Natural paternity was the overriding preoccupation in the Jewish Scriptures and so it seems disingenuous to claim, as does Meier,[22] that the distinction between natural and legal parentage is a present-day concern that is being read back into the interpretation of Davidic descent. It is highly unlikely anyone would have interpreted such texts as Romans 1.3, Acts 2.30 and 13.23 as simply involving

---

[20] Meier, *Marginal Jew* Vol. 1, 217.

[21] Cf. Y. Levin, 'Jesus, "Son of God" and "Son of David": The "Adoption" of Jesus into the Davidic Line', *JSNT* 28 (2006), 415–42, who argues in some detail that legal adoption was not known in either Palestinian or diaspora Judaism. M. Bockmuehl, 'The Son of David and his Mother', *JTS* 62 (2011), 478–9, also rightly questions the notion of legal adoption rather than biological descent.

[22] Meier, *Marginal Jew* Vol. 1, 217.

legal sonship unless they needed to harmonize them with a virginal conception. It is also unlikely that the original compilers of Matthew's or Luke's genealogy thought they were simply supplying a warrant for Jesus' legal inheritance rather than evidence, however idealized and selective, of natural patrilineal succession. If Matthew and his readers had thought there was no issue to be addressed in regard to this matter, it is hard to see why he went to such pains to show that Jesus could be considered to have Davidic descent despite Joseph not being his biological father. And if Luke's earliest extant interpreters had thought there was no issue of incompatibility, some copyists would not have changed the offending texts in Luke 2[23] and a number of second-century writers would not have come up with the notion that Jesus' Davidic descent had to be seen as coming from Mary.[24]

It remains the case, then, that outside the annunciation stories the New Testament writings witness to another tradition about Jesus' conception, namely that he was of the seed of David through Joseph as his biological father. Particularly in documents, in which there is not a hint of the virginal conception tradition, such references would have been understood in their straightforward sense and not as indicating some quasi-legal relationship. Given a readiness to recognize the diversity of the New Testament witness on a range of other issues, it is perhaps surprising that interpreters have not always been willing to be open to differing notions of Jesus' conception and that instead they have too frequently allowed the influence of what became the dominant tradition to marginalize or suppress what in fact is a widespread canonical witness to an alternative tradition. Paul, Hebrews, John and other parts of the canon are not, as is often claimed, simply silent about a virginal conception, either because they do not know of it or have no cause to allude to it; they are instead positive witnesses to the view that Jesus was conceived in the normal human way and that Joseph was his father.

An illegitimate birth?

We have already noted the view of some that there are references, made by those unsympathetic to Jesus' cause, to his being born illegitimately.

---

[23] There are, for example, a few later textual variants that alter 'his father' to 'Joseph' in 2.33 or 'your father and I' to 'we' in 2.48.

[24] This appears to be the thinking behind Ignatius of Antioch's linking 'conceived in the womb by Mary' and 'of the seed of David' (Ign. *Eph.* 18, cf. also *Trall.* 9) and it is made explicit in Justin (*Dial.* 100), Irenaeus (*Haer.* 3.9.2; 3.21.5), the *Protevangelium of James* (10.1) and Tertullian (*Carn. Chr.* 20, 22).

We shall see later that there is also a by no means implausible minority reading of Matthew's birth story that holds it is about an illegitimate rather than a virginal conception. That reading remains to be evaluated, but what is to be made of the evidence adduced for the claim that elsewhere in the New Testament a tradition of Jesus' illegitimacy is reflected? It has already been argued in the discussion at the beginning of this chapter that John 8.41 does not at all constitute a strong piece of evidence. But Mark 6.3, with its apparently offensive designation of Jesus as 'the son of Mary' ('Is not this the carpenter, the son of Mary?'), needs to be considered and its potential significance warrants a more extended discussion. We observed that Cranfield[25] and others have taken it as a charge about Jesus' illegitimacy and then attempted to use this as evidence for the virgin birth by seeing it as polemic directed against an already existing tradition that claimed Jesus was conceived by a virgin.[26] We rejected the latter argument on the grounds that Mark, apparently, was not aware of such a tradition, because not only is he silent about it but his earlier portrayal of Jesus' mother and brothers tells decisively against any knowledge of a miraculous conception.[27] But does the former interpretation of this designation as a charge of illegitimacy hold?

At first sight, the history of tradition appears to support it through the changes to the Markan original. An early variant reading (p[45]) has 'the son of the carpenter, [the son] of Mary', while Matthew 13.55 modifies it to 'Is not this the carpenter's son? Is not his mother called Mary?' and Luke 4.22 to 'Is not this the son of Joseph?' Why make such changes unless the original were understood as being offensive? An offensive remark about Jesus' birth would also fit the context in Mark 6. 'Is not this the son of Mary?' is one of a series of questions whose primary purpose is to discredit Jesus' teaching and deeds by pointing to what people know of his far from exalted status and origins. And, it can be added, it is highly probable that Mark would only have included this apparently shocking phrase in the first place if it were part of his tradition.

Yet such an argument conceals a number of factors that complicate any simple assumption that 'son of Mary' has connotations of illegitimacy.

---

[25] Cranfield, 'Reflections', 178–9.

[26] For a more recent version of the same claim, see L. W. Hurtado, *Lord Jesus Christ* (Grand Rapids: Eerdmans, 2003), 319–21.

[27] *Pace* Hurtado, *Lord*, 322–3 who fails to take account of Mark 3.20–35. In relation to the latter passage, Marcus, *Mark 1—8*, 277, rightly comments, 'if he [Mark] believed Jesus had been miraculously conceived, it is hard to imagine that he would have depicted Mary as sharing in the view that he was insane'.

The first complication is that it is not entirely clear that 'Is not this the carpenter, the son of Mary?' does constitute the earliest text of Mark 6.3. Although this is the best attested reading, it may not be the earliest. It is found in the fourth-century Sinaiticus and Vaticanus, but, as we have noted, the third-century p[45] apparently reads 'the son of the carpenter, [the son] of Mary'. If this earlier and minority witness is accepted, then Mark would have a mention of both parents and any implication of illegitimacy would not be present. But which reading best accounts for the variations? If the minority reading were more original, then the text of Matthew could be explained as simply a minor modification and Luke's redaction would have omitted any mention of Mary and of Joseph's trade. Some have argued that the change from the minority to the majority reading in Mark itself could be explained by a scribe wanting to make clear that the virgin birth was in view, once that doctrine was widely accepted; hence the removal of the reference to the carpenter having a son and making Jesus solely the son of Mary. This is possible, although no scribe thought it necessary to change Matthew's 'son of the carpenter' or Luke's 'son of Joseph' for this reason.

But the majority reading provides a better explanation for the consequent tradition. Matthew would then have changed 'carpenter' to 'son of the carpenter' in line with his stress on Jesus' descent via Joseph in the Davidic line and thereby also avoided any possible offence that might be caused by Jesus being called simply 'the carpenter'. He also avoids any possible misunderstanding or offence from Jesus being designated simply 'the son of Mary' by changing this to the blander 'Is not his mother called Mary?' The text of p[45] can then be explained either as a scribal assimilation in the light of Matthew 13.55 or as a deliberate change because of the offensiveness of the designation 'carpenter'. It may well be the case that, as here in Mark 6 Jesus' status as carpenter is seen by the crowd as incompatible with the claim to impart wisdom and the study that was necessary for such a role, so from early on opponents attempted to use the lowly status of a carpenter or artisan to undermine claims about Jesus being the Messiah or having divine associations. Celsus in the second century is often appealed to as evidence for this perception[28] and as having derided Jesus as nothing but 'a carpenter by trade'. But the context of his comment is rather different. He uses this description as part of his explanation of Christians' constant talk about the tree of life, though it may be significant that Origen

---

[28] Cf. e.g. B. M. Metzger, *A Textual Commentary on the Greek New Testament* (London: United Bible Societies, 1971), 88–9n1.

felt obliged to respond by asserting that Jesus himself was never described as a carpenter in the Gospels (*Cels.* 6.34, 36). Origen had either temporarily forgotten Mark 6.3 or knew it only in the form represented by p[45]. Whether it was possible connotations attached to Jesus' trade or to his birth, to which the scribe of p[45] was responding, his change results in awkward syntax. 'Son of' has simply been removed from before 'Mary' and placed before 'the carpenter' without the sentence being adjusted with an 'and' after 'carpenter' and so reads, literally, 'Is not this the son of the carpenter, of Mary?' The awkward sentence might be appealed to as the more difficult reading, but scribal changes that are not made on grounds of style often inadvertently produce more difficult syntax. On balance, then, the more widely attested reading should probably be preferred.[29]

Yet, even if 'son of Mary' is the more likely Markan text, it is still not altogether clear that it should be understood as an insult about Jesus' birth. The fullest recent attempt to survey the instances of men being identified as sons of their mothers in Jewish usage from around the time of Jesus remains that of Ilan.[30] Where this unusual phenomenon can be explained, it is nearly always in terms of the mother being named because she was considered more important than the father. The superiority was because descent from royalty, priests or sages could be traced to the woman's lineage and attaching such pedigree to one's name clearly contributed to one's status or honour. This cannot, however, provide an explanation for the usage in Mark 6.3 where the context is one of casting aspersions on Jesus' status because of its ordinariness and where Mark also is unlikely to have thought that Mary had superior lineage to Jesus' father. Ilan finds only one case in which a metronymic designation has any odium attached to it. In *Avot of Rabbi Nathan* 7 (B) the emperor Titus is described as 'son of Vespasian's wife' in an attempt to cast doubt on his claims to legitimate royal lineage. This is not the same formulation as simply naming the mother and not the father after 'son', but it is a functional equivalent, and in both cases the different formulations could serve implicitly as an insult about the lack of legal paternity. Could claims about Jesus' royal lineage be being called in question in Mark? Mark does later have the claim to royal descent on the part of Jesus associated with the 'Son of David' title (cf. 10.47–48; 12.35–37), but to hold that readers are meant to see aspersions being cast on it here through the use of 'son of Mary'

---

[29] Cf. also Brown, *Birth*, 537–9; *pace* J. McGrath, 'Was Jesus Illegitimate? The Evidence of His Social Interactions', *JSHJ* 5 (2007), 90.

[30] T. Ilan, '"Man Born of Woman . . ." (Job 14.1): The Phenomenon of Men Bearing Metronymes at the Time of Jesus', *NovT* 34 (1992), 23–45.

by the synagogue worshippers in Nazareth would be too much of a stretch. However it might have arisen historically, the insult, if there is one, here at the narrative level appears to be more general.

A frequently offered alternative explanation for the appearance of 'son of Mary' in this passage is the suggestion that Joseph had died by this time. After all, Joseph makes no appearance at all in Mark's narrative and in the two places where Jesus' family is mentioned and Joseph might have been expected to be included – 3.31–34 and 6.3 – reference is made only to Jesus' mother and siblings. But Ilan uncovers no instances of this type of use of the metronyme in the absence of a dead father and instead offers two counter-examples where orphans continued to be called by the names of their fathers.[31] Her study therefore can offer no explanation for the use of 'son of Mary' in Mark 6.3. In the nature of the case, however, most of the extant usages, to which she points, are from official lists or are formal identifications that do not reflect popular usage, such as that which Mark purports to describe. It might well be the case, therefore, that in more popular usage being called the son of one's mother could still be an indication that one's father had died or an insult about the legitimacy of one's birth. If the former were a popular way of depicting someone whose father was no longer living,[32] then it is still surprising that neither Matthew nor Luke appear to have understood it in this way but have substituted a different formulation. But the latter possibility in popular usage simply raises a further issue. Then, as now, having one's legitimacy queried in a way that was also insulting to one's mother by no means requires that those making the insult actually think or know that there is something suspect about one's paternity. The epithet can simply be a term of abuse with no claims to historical grounding. Yet the context in Mark 6 is one where the people are claiming quite precise knowledge of Jesus' family and so, again at the level of the narrative, if the epithet is pejorative, it is probably intended to reflect actual knowledge.

Is there any other feasible explanation for the unusual 'the son of Mary' in Mark 6.3? Perhaps the most plausible further alternative offered is that which suggests that Mary is named because Joseph had had more than one wife. There are examples in the Jewish Scriptures of sons of the same

---

[31] Ilan, '"Man Born of Woman ..."', 23–4n3.

[32] H. Räisänen, 'Begotten by the Holy Spirit', in eds M. Nissinen and R. Uro, *Sacred Marriages* (Winona Lake, IN: Eisenbrauns, 2008), 325, takes this view: 'The use of the matronymic in informal speech (not to be confused with a genealogical formula) is understandable because the mother of Jesus, as well as his brothers, were known to the early church (Acts 1.14); whereas Joseph was not; he was probably dead by the time of Jesus' public appearance.'

father being distinguished on the basis of their different mothers. So, for instance, David had children by so many women that his sons could be called after their mothers: 'Absalom, son of Maacah . . . Adonijah, son of Haggith' (1 Chron. 3.2). But this would only apply to Mark 6.3 if we speculate about Joseph's marital history on the basis of extra-biblical tradition. The notion that Joseph had children from an earlier marriage is found in the late second-century *Protevangelium of James* and is advocated in the fourth century by Epiphanius, but there is no hint within the New Testament, other than this possible cryptic reference to 'the son of Mary', that Jesus' brothers and sisters were anything other than products of the marriage of Joseph and Mary. In addition, if Jesus were being distinguished from his brothers and sisters in Mark 6 on the basis of different mothers, then one would have expected his siblings' mother also to have been named.

None of the various explanations offered for the unusual occurrence of the metronyme in Mark 6.3 is very convincing. That the variant text of Mark and the other Synoptic accounts avoid the designation may suggest at least that they thought it had potential for being understood as an offensive slur. The passage in which the phrase occurs does not *require* it to be an insult for the overall thrust to be understood. Many in Nazareth are scandalized by Jesus' teaching and deeds because they know Jesus' trade and his family and find these incompatible with his being a teacher who communicates wisdom. Nevertheless, as mentioned briefly earlier, if the phrase were an insult, it would not be out of place. The series of questions raised by the inhabitants of Nazareth in 6.2–3 are meant to undermine Jesus as a teacher and miracle worker by pointing to his less than exalted artisan status and family of origin. A comment about his mother that questioned his legitimacy would simply intensify the perceived contrast.[33] So the interpretation of 'the son of Mary' as a scurrilous remark about the legitimacy of Jesus' birth that may reflect popular rumour remains a possibility but, in the absence of significant supporting evidence from the literature of the time, one on which it would be hazardous to build a firm conclusion about Mark as a canonical witness to the illegitimacy of Jesus' birth. As has been indicated, some claim that Matthew is such a canonical

---

[33] Marcus, *Mark 1—8*, 375, concludes less hesitantly, 'given the hostile nature of the confrontation, it is likely that the use of Jesus' mother's name is a slur against his legitimacy'; G. Lüdemann, *Virgin Birth? The Real Story of Mary and Her Son Jesus* (London: SCM, 1998), 53, 55, characteristically, has no doubt that Jesus 'was without honour because he was of illegitimate descent' or that 'had Jesus been a physical son of Joseph the expression "son of Mary" would never have found its way into an early Christian text'.

witness and it is to the annunciation stories in Matthew and Luke that we shall turn.

In turning to their accounts, it is worth underlining one of the main results of this chapter. We now turn to them not as the main or normative New Testament sources for the conception of Jesus but as part of its diverse witness. In fact, over against the variety of sources that assume Jesus had a normal human conception, the two accounts that appear to witness to a virgin birth function more like a 'minority report'.[34] This is no reason to marginalize them or to treat them with anything less than full seriousness as part of the New Testament's authoritative witness to the person of Christ. It does mean, however, that one's interpretation of them is not as decisive a factor in evaluating what is the scriptural source for how Jesus was conceived or in developing a theology of the incarnation based on Scripture, as is frequently supposed. Nevertheless, since they are in extended narrative form, since they are part of the canon and since they would later become the majority report, there is every reason to give them the close analysis that is provided in the following chapters.

---

[34] Cf. Alan E. Lewis, *Between Cross and Resurrection: A Theology of Holy Saturday* (Grand Rapids: Eerdmans, 2001), 118, who writes of 'the New Testament's "minority report" upon Christ's virginal conception, set in a context where most of its authors show no knowledge of that tradition, and where all of them presuppose and reinforce Jesus' uncompromised humanity'.

3

What are the infancy narratives?

It has now become clear that there is no evidence of the virgin birth tradition elsewhere in the New Testament and that the accounts in Matthew and Luke are the only possible canonical witnesses to such a tradition. In reflecting on the status of assertions about Jesus' conception in their accounts, one clearly needs to take into consideration the nature of the material in which they are embedded and what recent studies have brought to light about these infancy narratives. Just why is it that there is widespread agreement, as was mentioned in Chapter 1, that they present the most problematic material for historical investigation? What sort of literature are they?

This exploration, undertaken in the spirit of faith seeking understanding, proceeds on the basis that such understanding will incorporate our best knowledge of how and when these two Gospels came to be and what sort of documents they are. We shall assume, with the scholarly consensus, that Matthew and Luke were written around 75–85 CE and, therefore, some two generations after Jesus' birth. We shall also assume that, like the other Gospels, they constituted the written stage of a development that had begun with the proclamation about Jesus after the resurrection and had then involved oral and written accounts of the passion and of selected traditions of Jesus' sayings and deeds. The Gospel writers synthesized such material in their own distinctive accounts of Jesus' life, death and resurrection, shaped and elaborated to reflect their own views and to meet the needs of their intended readers. Our thinking about the infancy narratives in Matthew and Luke, in particular, will focus on their relation to three major areas: early Christian belief about Jesus, the Jewish Scriptures, and Graeco-Roman biography.

Christological belief

Dominant in the Gospel writers' presentation of Jesus was their Christological conviction, based on the resurrection, that Jesus was both Messiah and Son of God. As has been discussed, when Paul writes to the Romans in the late 50s CE, he begins by incorporating an earlier Jewish Christian formulation of the gospel: 'the gospel concerning his Son, who was descended from David according to the flesh and was declared to be Son of God with power according to the spirit of holiness by resurrection from the dead, Jesus Christ our Lord' (Rom. 1.3–4). It should be no surprise, then, that something like this core gospel message is determinative in different ways for both Matthew's and Luke's birth narratives, as they interpret the origins of Jesus' life in the light of their post-resurrection beliefs about him. In both Matthew 1.18–25 and Luke 1.26–38 the holy Spirit, who had been operative in creation and in Israel's history and who was at work in the raising of Jesus from the dead, is now seen to have also been at work in Jesus' life from its conception (Matt. 1.18, 20; Luke 1.35a) and indeed to have been at work in power (Luke 1.35b). Both accounts stress Jesus' Davidic lineage (Matt. 1.20, cf. 1.16; Luke 1.27, 32b). Matthew does not use 'Son of God' as a title for Jesus in the annunciation account but underlines that Mary's son is 'God with us' (1.23). He will go on, however, to indicate that Jesus fulfils what was said of Israel – 'Out of Egypt I have called my son' (2.15) – and by the time of Jesus' baptism and temptation the attribution of divine sonship to Jesus has become explicit (3.17; 4.6). Luke, on the other hand, does make explicit in the annunciation itself that Mary's child is to be called Son of God (1.32, 35d). Luke's account of Peter's speech after the resurrection and Pentecost has him state that 'God has made him both Lord and Messiah, this Jesus whom you crucified' (Acts 2.36), and these titles too are found already in the infancy narratives. For Matthew Jesus is the Messiah (1.1, 16, 18) and for Luke he is not only Messiah (2.11, 26) but also Lord (1.43; 2.11).

It may help to set this phenomenon within the broader context of early Christian thinking about Jesus. As we have mentioned, Jesus' earliest followers came to the belief that he was Son of God on the basis of the resurrection and exaltation. A further reflection of this is found in Acts' version of Paul's preaching : 'And we bring you the good news that what God promised to our ancestors he has fulfilled for us, their children, by raising Jesus; as also it is written in the second psalm, "You are my Son; today I have begotten you"' (Acts 13.32–33). The implication, which has become central to Christian theology, was soon seen. If what they had perceived through the resurrection was the case, then this is who Jesus must always have been throughout his life – uniquely God's Son. Indeed, he must have in some sense existed as the Son or the Word prior to his earthly life. In their presentations of Jesus, therefore, the four Gospel writers push back this revealed Christological truth from the resurrection to earlier stages. Mark, who begins his account with the ministry of the Baptist, places it at Jesus' baptism (1.11, cf. also 1.1). John, who also has

no birth narrative, takes a different route and has a prologue that identifies Jesus as the incarnation of the Logos who was with God in the beginning before the creation of the world (1.1–3, 14). Matthew and Luke have
Jesus' divine identity revealed in their birth narratives, so that from the
moment of his conception Jesus is to be seen as Emmanuel (Matt. 1.23)
and Son of God (Luke 1.35).

These birth narratives are composed in a way that not only expresses later
Christological belief but also anticipates what will happen to Jesus himself
and to the message about him. There will be rejection and persecution by
Jewish leaders, adumbrated by Herod's attempt to destroy this child (Matt.
2.1–18) and by Simeon's prophecy to Mary that her child will 'be a sign
that will be opposed' (Luke 2.34–35). At the same time there will be acceptance of the message on the part of Gentiles and so Matthew has the magi
come to pay homage to the child (2.1–12), while Luke has Simeon say of
this child that he has seen God's salvation 'which you have prepared in
the presence of all peoples, a light for revelation to the Gentiles' (2.30–32).

Simeon's words are also an echo of what is said about the servant in
Isaiah – 'I will give you as a light to the nations, that my salvation may
reach to the end of the earth' (49.6) – and alert us to another feature of
the birth narratives and another aspect of the belief about Jesus that
they reflect. Jesus was believed to be the fulfilment of the Jewish Scriptures,
and so Scripture, and by this is meant Scripture as read in Second Temple
Judaism, frequently as interpreted in its Greek translation, and sometimes
as understood in the light of rewritings of its traditions, could be employed
to fill out traditions or construct details about his early life. In the Gospel
narratives as a whole, not least in their passion accounts, a dialectical
process is at work whereby traditions about Jesus' ministry can be seen to
correspond with certain passages of Scripture – this is often what is meant
when they speak about the fulfilment of scriptural prophecy – and at
the same time other aspects of those passages or of different passages can
be employed to provide additional detail for the retelling of the tradition.
When, as in the birth stories, the traditions are particularly sparse, earlier
scriptural stories do even more work in shaping the present narrative.
So the evangelists saw Scripture in the light of Jesus but they also saw
Jesus in the light of Scripture, telling his story by reconfiguring the old
stories. Only a few aspects of this feature of the birth narratives, which
inevitably influences readers' expectations about how to interpret accounts
of Jesus' conception, can be sketched here. In doing so, we shall also indicate a further feature of the birth narratives – the way in which, because
of their introductory role, they anticipate a number of the characteristic

or distinctive overall themes of Matthew and Luke and serve as overtures to the whole of their Gospels.

Use of the Jewish Scriptures[1]

Matthew

One of the characteristics of Matthew's story is his citation of Scripture. The name Emmanuel in 1.23 has already been mentioned and this, of course, was part of a citation of Isaiah 7.14. We need to note that this is one of Matthew's so-called 'formula citations'. He quotes from Scripture much more frequently than any other of the Gospel writers (61 times), but on some occasions he specifically introduces the quotation with a formula about fulfilment of Scripture (ten times). So in 1.22, in introducing the Emmanuel quotation, he has 'All this took place to fulfil what had been spoken by the Lord through the prophet'. The linking of his narrative with the Jewish Scriptures continues in Matthew 2 and one of the main means of signalling this will be through four further quotations, three of which are these formula citations about fulfilment (cf. 2.15, 18, 23). It can be seen, then, that he has frontloaded this type of citation into the birth narrative with four of the ten instances in the Gospel occurring here.

It is worth reflecting a little more on how this notion of fulfilment relates to what has just been said about the dialectic between Jesus and Scripture. The words of Isaiah 7.14 found their fulfilment in Isaiah's time, so their use in 1.23 is not proof from prophecy in the sense of the fulfilment of an unfulfilled prediction. There are, of course, some prophecies in Scripture about the Messiah or predictions about the end times that the New Testament writers see fulfilled in what happened in Jesus. But what fulfilment entails for Matthew is usually rather different. In the case of 1.23 he already had the conviction that Jesus is God with us and then remembered a passage in Scripture about the birth of a child that corresponded with this belief and confirmed it. This method of applying Scripture was common in Judaism. The Qumran writings with their *pesher* interpretative technique ('this is that') offer parallels. This in our situation, they say, is that in the text, and so they see what has happened in the case of the teacher of righteousness and in the events of their community as anticipated in Scripture. What non-Christian Jews would

---

[1] For a fine discussion of a range of issues arising from the use of the Jewish Scriptures in the infancy narratives, see now S. Moyise, *Was the Birth of Jesus According to Scripture?* (Eugene, OR: Cascade, 2013). Unfortunately, its publication appeared too late to allow interaction with Moyise's discussion.

have found controversial about Matthew's use of Scripture was not the method but simply the belief about Jesus it was made to support. The general principle that underlies it is that Scripture indicates patterns of God at work in Israel's history that find their completion in what happens with Jesus and if, in this way, there is a sense that all of Scripture points forward and is prophetic, then what happens in Jesus can be said to be its fulfilment. This is closely related to the phenomenon of typology. Believing that Jesus represents the decisive fulfilment of God's purposes and that those purposes are coherent, one can then look back and find corresponding types in the figures and events of Scripture that anticipate the fulfilment. So Matthew is not so much citing Scripture to prove to other Jews that Jesus is the Messiah as employing Scripture to give expression to the confession that he and his readers share – that Jesus is the Christ, the Son of God. In the light of that confession Scripture as a whole and in its individual parts can now be read as prefiguring Jesus. And if Scripture prefigures Jesus, then it is not surprising that Matthew, as we have suggested above, can go further and in some places use the prefigurement in Scripture to shape his narration of the story of Jesus' birth.

His presentation of Jesus as the Davidic Messiah from the beginning of his life is informed in particular by the Moses stories. The episode of Herod's killing of the baby boys in order to be rid of the child born king of the Jews (2.1–12) is modelled on Pharaoh's attempt to kill all the male Israelite babies (Exod. 1.22). In later Jewish telling of the Moses story this attempt was made specifically in order to deal with the birth of a Jewish deliverer, about whom Pharaoh was warned by magi (cf. *Targum Pseudo-Jonathan* on Exod. 1.15) or informed by a priest-scribe (cf. Josephus, *Ant.* 2.205). In Matthew Herod's informants are both the magi (2.1–3, 7) and the chief priests and scribes (2.4). In Matthew Mary's child will be a saviour of his people (1.21). Moses is depicted as a saviour in Pseudo-Philo, where an angel tells Moses' sister, Miriam, who then relays this to her parents, 'I will work signs through him and save my people' (*L.A.B.* 9.10), and in Josephus where God tells Moses' father, 'He will save the Hebrew people from their bondage in Egypt' (*Ant.* 2.216). What is said about Moses' father, Amram, in these retellings of the Exodus story is particularly interesting for Matthew's depiction of Joseph. Hearing about Pharaoh's plan to kill all the Hebrew boy babies, Amram and others are in a dilemma. In the various rereadings Amram either decides to marry or continues in a marriage with an already pregnant wife or divorces and then remarries his wife, and his or Miriam's dreams that he will have a son who will save his people play a role in the making or confirming of these decisions (cf. Josephus, *Ant.* 2.205–221; Pseudo-Philo, *L.A.B.* 9.1–16; *Targum Pseudo-Jonathan* on Exod. 1). Matthew portrays Joseph as being told in a dream to continue in his relationship with Mary rather than divorce her and to name the child Jesus, 'for he will save his people from their sins' (1.21).

Later parts of the Moses story, particularly LXX Numbers 22—24, feed into Matthew's birth narrative. The king of Moab, Balak, who, like Pharaoh previously, wants to destroy the Israelites, summons from the East (LXX Num. 23.7) a well-known seer, Balaam, to utter a curse against Moses and Israel that would lead to their defeat. Balaam, a non-Israelite practitioner of enchantment, would have been called in Matthew's day a magus, and that is precisely how Philo describes Balaam, as a magus whose magical arts desert him when he is possessed by the spirit of true prophecy (*Mos.* 1.50). In the Numbers story God intervenes and speaks to Balaam, not least through his donkey, and instead of cursing Israel, much to the annoyance of Balak, he ends up blessing them by uttering four oracles. In the fourth oracle he says, 'I see him, but not now; I behold him, but not near – a star shall rise out of Jacob, and a sceptre shall come forth from Israel . . . One out of Jacob shall rule' (Num. 24.15–19). The oracle refers to the emergence of the monarchy, and David was understood to be the star Balaam had foreseen, the one who would be given the sceptre and rule over the united kingdom of Judah and Israel. In Jewish interpretation the passage came to be read messianically and, interestingly, it was to play a role in 135 CE when Rabbi Akibah hailed the revolutionary Simon ben Kosibah as Messiah and Simon was popularly known as bar Kochba, 'son of the star'. In Matthew's story Herod, like Balak, tries to use the magi from the East to help him eradicate God's agent but is thwarted, and just as Balaam saw the star of David rise, so now the magi see the star of the king of the Jews at its rising (Matt. 2.1–2).

The influences of the Moses story continue after the account of the massacre of the innocents. Herod dies and Joseph in Egypt is instructed in a dream to go back to Israel, 'for those who were seeking the child's life are dead' (2.20). Presumably Matthew means Herod is dead, but, in using the plural, the echoes from the Exodus story become more important than consistency in his own. In LXX Exodus 4.19–20 Moses is told by God to return to Egypt, 'for all those who were seeking your life are dead'. Here we also see one of the ironic reversals Matthew builds into his composition. Moses flees from the tyrant in Egypt and then returns to rescue his people, whereas Jesus escapes from the tyrant in Israel to the very land Moses fled, before returning to Israel to rescue his people from their sins. Exodus 4.20 continues, 'So Moses took his wife and his sons, put them on a donkey, and went back to the land of Egypt'. In Matthew Joseph 'took the child and his mother, and went back to the land of Israel' (2.21). Now it also becomes apparent that Matthew has also used this Exodus passage to shape his description of Joseph's original journey to Egypt (2.13–14). The main parallels here are between Joseph and Moses rather than between Jesus and Moses, but because Joseph also takes Jesus with him, this means that the overall parallel between the life of Jesus and the life of Moses continues. What is more, Jesus and Moses are the objects of those seeking the life of the child (2.20). In both stories a child who is to be the agent of salvation has an attempt made on his life; in both this is done by a tyrannical king; in both other innocent children die as a result; in both the king's attempt is thwarted; and in both the child who is to bring salvation is himself saved. In all these ways the details of the birth narrative adumbrate what is to be a major motif for Matthew – Jesus is the new and greater Moses.[2]

In this last part of the birth narrative Matthew depicts Jesus not only as reliving aspects of Moses' story but also as embodying in his experience Israel's story. In the context of his larger narrative the sequence is as follows. Both Israel and Jesus go into Egypt and come out. Israel goes through the waters of the Red Sea; Jesus goes through the waters of baptism. Both Israel and Jesus are then tested in the wilderness. Israel fails in its vocation to be God's son and servant. Jesus in the wilderness and in his ministry faithfully carries out the vocation to be God's Son and servant. Matthew makes this typology explicit in 2.15: 'This was to fulfil what had been spoken by the Lord to the prophet, "Out of Egypt I have called my son."' In the sequence of Matthew's story the citation actually anticipates 2.20–21 and the command to Joseph to leave Egypt and take Jesus back to Israel. The citation is from Hosea 11.1 and this time Matthew uses the Hebrew text that has 'my son' rather than the LXX text that has 'his children'. The reference in Hosea is to Israel at the time of the exodus: 'When Israel was a child, I loved him, and out of Egypt I called my son'. Clearly the singular is more appropriate for Matthew's purposes of seeing Jesus re-enacting the exodus as God's unique son. In relation to our earlier discussion, it is worth underlining that, although Matthew employs his fulfilment formula here, the Hosea text is, of course, not a prediction but an evocation of a past event as part of the prophet's indictment of Israel in his own time. Fulfilment, then, again entails, on the basis of present beliefs about Jesus, finding in Scripture ideas, terminology, events that anticipate that belief. Through the use of this quotation Matthew calls

---

[2] Cf. D. C. Allison, *The New Moses: A Matthean Typology* (Minneapolis: Augsburg Fortress, 1994).

Jesus for the first time God's son, and 'Son of God' will prove to be one of his most important titles for Jesus in the narrative that follows in the rest of the Gospel. And when in the temptation in the wilderness episode, Jesus is shown to use Scripture in resisting the devil, there too it is as God's son that Jesus is equated with Israel. For Matthew, Jesus' role in a new exodus makes him both like Moses and like Israel.

The relation of the Moses theme to the rest of the Gospel is found most immediately through the Sermon on the Mount. The setting – on the mount – is already a reminder of the exodus story where Moses went up Mount Sinai to speak with God and came down with divine instruction – Torah – for the people. Now Jesus speaks from the mountain and delivers instruction that has remarkable echoes of Moses' teaching. He claims, on the one hand, that it is a fulfilment of the law that Moses gave (5.17–20). Yet, on the other, there are also antitheses to the law: 'You have heard that it was said to those of ancient times . . . But I say to you . . .' (5.21–48). Here Jesus deals directly with the words of Moses, qualifying and adding to them. He teaches a righteousness that transcends that of the law, sometimes deepening previous commands, sometimes extending them and sometimes contradicting their letter. In all of this he is to be seen as the new Moses who has the authoritative key to the law's interpretation. And since in the rest of the Gospel Jesus is the great teacher who provides other major blocks of instruction, this portrait of him as the new and greater Moses colours the rest of his teaching for Matthew's community. This is true too of the final great commission in 28.16–20, which builds on, among other scriptural passages, the commission of Moses to Joshua in Deuteronomy 31.14–15, 23 and Joshua 1.1–9. Moses, at the close of his life, commissioned his successor, Joshua, to go into the land peopled by foreign nations and to observe all the commandments Moses had given in the law, and then promised his successor God's abiding presence. Here Jesus, at the close of his earthly ministry, commissions his successors, the disciples, to go into all the world and teach observance of all the commandments that he, the new Moses, had given them, and then promises them his own abiding presence. Matthew had characterized Jesus as Emmanuel, God with us, in the birth narrative, Jesus had then gone on to promise his own authoritative presence to those gathered in his name (18.20), and now the two come together in the great commission as to those who baptize in the name of the triune God is promised the divine presence of the risen Christ (28.20).[3]

---

[3] On this theme in Matthew, see D. D. Kupp, *Matthew's Emmanuel: Divine Presence and God's People in the First Gospel* (Cambridge: CUP, 1996).

More popular writers, and indeed some scholars, often call Matthew's use (and sometimes also Luke's use) of Scripture in this way *midrash* and propose that the whole birth narrative is 'Jewish midrash'. Debate about this designation can be a distraction to a serious exploration of our topic, so it will be dealt with only briefly here. Midrash was a method of 'searching' the sacred text and in the process updating it to make it applicable to later times and settings. Midrash comes in two main types: *halakhic*, commentary on the law, and *haggadic*, commentary on everything else, evincing greater freedom of interpretation, including creative filling in of gaps in scriptural narratives. The writing of both types of *midrashim* commenced in the second century CE, although there were oral forms before that date and this justifies the quest for parallels with such literature in the New Testament. The conviction behind such commentaries was that Scripture was rich in varied meanings that could be drawn out by argument or by rabbinic debate. The basic and characteristic form of midrash in these writings is to begin with the text of Scripture, which can be as large as a whole biblical book or as small as a single sentence, and then to follow this by commentary. So one definition of midrash, to which appeal is widely made, is that it is

> a type of literature, oral or written, which stands in direct relationship to a fixed, canonical text, considered to be the authoritative and revealed word of God by the midrashist and his audience, and in which this canonical text is explicitly cited or clearly alluded to.[4]

Examples from within the New Testament would then include John 6.31–58 or Romans 4 or Hebrews 3.7—4.13. So, strictly speaking, Matthew's birth narrative should not be called midrash, since it clearly does not take this form. Some might still say that such a conclusion is too purist or pedantic and that midrash should be thought of more in terms of the hermeneutical assumptions and techniques found within the midrashim. What Matthew does with Scripture in the birth narratives might then fit. The problem with this view, however, is that the category becomes so broad that it would fit nearly all Jewish exegesis of Scripture in the Second Temple period. We are not discussing historicity directly at this point in our exploration, but the reason this generic term *midrash* can be a distraction is that it tends to be employed as a slogan in that debate. On the one side, there are those who suggest that, since the birth narratives are Jewish midrash, they are obviously employing Scripture for legendary embellishment and

---

[4] Cf. G. Porton, 'Defining Midrash', in ed. J. Neusner, *The Study of Ancient Judaism* (New York: Ktav, 1981), 55–92 (62).

there is no point in discussing their historicity. On the other side, there are those who dispute the literary genre and who think that by showing the infancy narratives are not midrash, they do not have to take very seriously the difficult historical questions that much of the material raises. It seems better, therefore, not least because of the disputed definition, to avoid the indiscriminate use of the term midrash, to look instead at particular ways in which Scripture is employed, and then to reflect on a case-by-case basis on the implications for historicity.[5] Whatever term we employ for Matthew's and Luke's use of Scripture, what remains key to their procedure is what we noted at the beginning of this chapter. They begin not with Scripture but with what is believed about Jesus Christ and then, in a two-way movement, both read Scripture in the light of that belief in order to draw out Christ's significance and employ Scripture to fill out the tradition when they express their belief in narrative form.

Luke

In turning to characteristic features of Luke's opening chapters, we find that here also the scriptural story shapes the story of Jesus' origins. Unlike Matthew, Luke does not sprinkle his account with actual citations. There is only one – in 2.23 – and, as will be noted later, this is problematic. Instead, Luke achieves similar ends primarily by means of pastiches of scriptural language informing the narrative and serving the overall motif of a comparison between John the Baptist and Jesus. John the Baptist's parents are modelled principally on two scriptural couples, Abraham and Sarah and Elkanah and Hannah, who faced the stigma associated with infertility and yet whose situations were resolved by God's miraculous intervention. Zechariah and Elizabeth are described in the same way as Abraham – righteous before God, blameless and keeping God's commandments and regulations (1.6; cf. Gen. 15.6; 17.1; 26.5). Luke also says of them, 'They had no children, because Elizabeth was barren' (1.7) while Genesis 11.30 had stated, 'Now Sarai was barren; she had no child.' What is more, both John the Baptist's parents and Abraham and Sarah share the further complication of 'being advanced in years' – exactly the same phrase in Luke 1.7, 18 and LXX Genesis 18.11. Zechariah's response to the angelic announcement is formulated verbatim from Abraham's response to the

---

[5] Cf. also J. A. Fitzmyer, *The Gospel according to Luke I—IX* (New York: Doubleday, 1981), 308–9, who says of midrash, 'the term is better avoided and is, in any case, quite unsuitable for the Lucan form'; R. E. Brown, *The Birth of the Messiah* (2nd edn New York: Doubleday, 1993), 557–63, 577–9. B. P. Robinson, 'Matthew's Nativity Stories: Historical and Theological Questions for Today's Readers', in ed. J. Corley, *New Perspectives on the Nativity* (London: T. & T. Clark, 2009), 113–15, argues rightly that the label 'creative historiography' is much more apt than 'midrash'.

divine promise about the land. Both ask, 'How am I to know that this is so?' (Luke 1.18 // Gen. 15.8). And Zechariah's objection is the same as that of Abraham in response to the announcement about Isaac, pointing out the old age of himself and his wife (Luke 1.18 // Gen. 17.17).

But there are also echoes of the story of the other scriptural couple, Elkanah and Hannah. Their story begins, 'There was a certain man . . . whose name was Elkanah . . . He had two wives; the name of one was Hannah . . . Hannah had no children' (1 Sam. 1.1–2), while Luke relates, 'There was a priest, whose name was Zechariah . . . He had a wife . . . and her name was Elizabeth . . . they had no child' (1.5, 7). The son who will be born to them will not 'drink wine or strong drink' (1.15). This sort of total abstinence characterized those who had taken a nazirite vow during the whole period of their separation to God (cf. Num. 6.1–4) and is a further reminder of the story of Elkanah and Hannah, in which the mother promises that if God gives her a male child, 'then I will set him before you as a nazirite until the day of his death. He shall drink neither wine nor strong drink . . .' (1 Sam. 1.11). Like Samuel, the nazirite who was also God's prophet and agent in anointing David as king, John is being set apart to bring God's word to Israel and, it will become clear, to be God's agent in preparing for the Davidic king (cf. 1.32, 69, 76).

The angelic announcer to both Zechariah and Mary is Gabriel. He is mentioned in only one place in Scripture: in Daniel 8—12. In both Luke 1.22 and Daniel 9.21 Gabriel's appearance is called a vision. In both Luke 1.10–13 and Daniel 9.20–21 Gabriel comes at the time of liturgical prayer to someone who has been praying. In both Luke 1.12–13, 20, 22 and Daniel 10.8, 12, 15 the recipient of the vision becomes afraid, then is told not to fear, and finally is struck mute. There can be little doubt that Gabriel's appearance to Zechariah is modelled on that to Daniel. This is highly significant for Luke's use of Scripture. Already in the first chapter of his Gospel he has had the law, the prophets and the writings foreshadow what happens at the start of the new era of salvation. Abraham and Sarah are taken from Genesis in the Law, Elkanah and Hannah from the Former Prophets, and Gabriel from the Writings. Later at the end of the Gospel in Luke 24.44 Luke will refer to this threefold division of Scripture when he says that 'everything written about Jesus in the law of Moses, the prophets and the psalms must be fulfilled' and now it becomes apparent that he has embarked on this process himself from the very beginning of his story of Jesus.

The story of Elkanah, Hannah and Samuel influences not only Luke's account of John the Baptist's birth but also his narrative about Jesus' origins. Mary, like Hannah before her, is characterized as a slave of the Lord who has found favour (1.30, 38; cf. 1 Sam. 1.18), and so it is no surprise that her Magnificat echoes Hannah's psalm-like response to her conception of a son (1.46–55; cf. LXX 1 Sam. 1.11; 2.1–10). Its opening words are 'My soul magnifies the Lord, and my spirit rejoices in God my Saviour' (1.46), while Hannah's prayer had begun with 'My heart exults in the LORD, my strength is exalted in my God' (1 Sam. 2.1). Hannah had earlier prayed to the Lord to look on the lowliness of his servant (LXX 1 Sam. 1.11) and here Mary praises God for having looked with favour on the lowliness of his servant (1.48). Both Mary and Hannah call God holy (1.49; 1 Sam. 2.2). Hannah celebrates the reversal brought by God's just judgement: 'The LORD makes poor and makes rich; he brings low, he also exalts. He lifts up the poor from the dust; he lifts the needy from the ash heap, to make them sit with princes and inherit a seat of honour' (1 Sam. 2.7–8). Mary will celebrate the same reversal: 'He has brought down the powerful from their thrones, and lifted up the lowly' (1.52).

The Samuel story continues to influence the details of Luke's account, particularly its final part. His parents' presentation of Jesus in the Temple is patterned after Hannah's presentation of Samuel in the sanctuary at Shiloh in 1 Samuel 1.21—2.21. Hannah brings Samuel to the sanctuary and presents him to the Lord; this is accompanied by an appropriate sacrifice; the elderly Eli blesses Samuel's parents; women who ministered at the sanctuary are mentioned, and the equivalent to the Hebrew name Hannah in Greek is Anna. As he fills out this pattern for his story of Jesus' presentation, however, Luke appears to confuse a number of matters. He thinks the purification according to the law involved both parents – 'their purification' (2.22) – when in fact it was necessary only for the mother. According to Leviticus 12.2–8 a woman who bore a male child was considered unclean for 40 days and had to wait at home until the days of her purification were completed and before she could touch anything sacred or enter the sanctuary. She was then to bring to a priest a one-year-old lamb for a whole burnt offering and a young pigeon or turtledove for a sin-offering. If she could not afford the lamb, then she was to offer two turtledoves or two young pigeons. This is the sacrifice that Luke mentions in connection with the presentation of Jesus according to the law. But there was no law that required the presentation of a firstborn son in the sanctuary. Luke paraphrases Exodus 13.2 in 2.23, but this simply declares that a firstborn male was holy to the Lord. What then had to be done was not to present him physically but to redeem him when he was a month old, to buy him back from the Lord by paying a priest five shekels, as is set out in Numbers 3.47–48 and 18.15–16 and of which there is no mention in Luke's story. Under the influence of the presentation of Samuel in the sanctuary, Luke has made the presentation part of the law and run it together with the law about purification. All of this militates against the view that Luke got the information for his birth story from Mary. Mary would have known the customs, whereas Luke, a Gentile Christian who had probably been a god-fearer, would have had no practical knowledge of these laws. But what he is concerned to assert through his story, even if this is accomplished awkwardly, is that, at a time when official representatives of Judaism had rejected Christian claims for Jesus, thought of Jesus as one who led the people astray and as a false prophet, and considered Paul an apostate, Jesus' life and indeed the circumstances of his birth involved no rejection of Judaism but were to be seen as its continuation and fulfilment.

But let us not lose sight of the Samuel story. Like Samuel's parents after the presentation of their son (1 Sam. 2.20), Jesus' parents now return home (2.39). Then in Samuel there are two statements about Samuel's progress or growth: 'and the boy Samuel grew up in the presence of the Lord' (1 Sam. 2.21b) and 'Now the boy Samuel continued to grow both in stature and in favour with the Lord and with the people' (1 Sam. 2.26). Here in Luke similarly there are two growth notices, which surround or frame the final episode in chapter 2, an episode that provides further evidence of what is being said about the growth. The first is in 2.40: 'the child grew and became strong, filled with wisdom, and the favour of the Lord was upon him' and the second in 2.52: 'And Jesus increased in wisdom and in years, and in favour with God and humans.' Samuel, of course, remains in the sanctuary where he demonstrates his obedience to the Lord, even when this goes against what he believes Eli will want to hear, and so proves himself a trustworthy prophet of the Lord (1 Sam. 3). It is significant that Josephus (*Ant.* 5.348) has this Samuel story, when he begins his vocation as a prophet, taking place in his twelfth year. Luke has Jesus return with his parents to the Temple at Passover at the age of 12, demonstrating his wisdom and exhibiting an allegiance to his heavenly Father that cuts across family ties (2.42–51).

So far we have highlighted the part played by Scripture in shaping Luke's storyline and its characters, but that storyline is interspersed with a number of canticles that are full of scriptural language and allusion. They are commonly known by the Latin version of their opening words: the Magnificat (1.46–55), the Benedictus (1.68–79) and the Nunc Dimittis (2.29–32). It is generally held that Luke has taken these over from his tradition. If this is true, then they serve admirably his purpose of rooting his story of John and Jesus in the hopes generated by the promises made to Israel. Space does not allow treating each of these, and, since part of the background to the Magnificat in Hannah's song has already been mentioned, the Benedictus will be the focus of our brief discussion. This is placed in the mouth of Zechariah as a partial answer to the question raised as a result of the birth of his son: 'What then will this child become?' (1.66). He begins by blessing the Lord God of Israel (1.68a), echoing Psalm 41.13: 'Blessed be the LORD, the God of Israel' (cf. also Pss. 72.18; 106.48). The reason for the blessing is then given: 'for he has looked favourably on [or visited] his people and redeemed them' (1.68b). The language of the Lord's visitation is found in Jeremiah 29.10: 'Only when Babylon's seventy years are completed will I visit you, and I will fulfil to you my promise and bring you back to this place' – a visitation that results in the return from exile. The terminology of God's redemption of God's people is found throughout Scripture. A few examples will suffice – Exodus 15.13: 'In your steadfast love you led the people whom you redeemed'; Leviticus 25.8–55 is full of language of redemption during the year of jubilee – the redemption of property, land and slaves; Deuteronomy 7.8: 'the LORD . . . redeemed you from the house of slavery'; 1 Chronicles 17.21: 'Who is like your people Israel, one nation on the earth whom God went to redeem to be his people?'; Psalm 111.9: 'He sent redemption to his people'; Isaiah 43.1: 'But now thus says the LORD, he who created you, O Jacob, he who formed you, O Israel: Do not fear, for I have redeemed you' (cf. also Isa. 48.20). The Benedictus continues, 'He has raised up a mighty saviour [lit. horn of salvation] for us in the house of his servant David' (1.69), combining Psalm 132.17: 'I will cause a horn to sprout up for David' and Ezekiel 29.21: 'On that day I will cause a horn to sprout up for the house of Israel'. This is in accord with what the prophets had said: 'that we would be saved from our enemies and from the hand of all who hate us' (1.70–71), a formulation that recalls such passages as LXX Psalm 106.10: 'he saved them from the hands of those who hated them and delivered them from the hand of the enemy' and Psalm 18.17: 'He delivered me from my strong enemy, and from those who hated me'.

God has therefore 'shown the mercy promised to our ancestors' (1.72a) which takes up Micah 7.20 – 'You will show unswerving loyalty [LXX mercy] to Abraham, as you have sworn to our ancestors' – and 'has remembered his holy covenant' (1.72b), recalling Psalm 106.45: 'he remembered his covenant' and Exodus 2.24: 'God remembered his covenant with Abraham, Isaac and Jacob.' The covenant is 'the oath that he swore to our ancestor Abraham' (1.73), an incident recounted in Genesis 22.16–18 and mentioned in Deuteronomy 9.5: 'in order to fulfil the promise that the Lord made on oath to your ancestors, to Abraham, to Isaac, and to Jacob' and Jeremiah 11.5: 'that I may perform the oath that I swore to your ancestors, to give them a land flowing with milk and honey'. God's covenantal faithfulness leads to the rescue of God's people: 'that we, being rescued from the hands of our enemies, might serve him without fear' and to living in a way characterized by consecration to their calling and by justice (1.74–75). This not only takes up 1.71 and its allusions but also Judges 8.34: 'the LORD their God, who had rescued them from the hand of all their enemies on every side' and the references to the whole purpose of the exodus in LXX Exodus 7.16: 'Let my people go that they may serve [or worship] me' and LXX Joshua 24.14: 'and serve him in sincerity (uprightness) and faithfulness (righteousness)'.

John the Baptist's specific role as the prophet of the Most High in the coming of this salvation is to 'go before the Lord to prepare his ways' (1.76), recalling Isaiah 40.3: 'In the wilderness prepare the way of the LORD' and Malachi 3.1: 'I am sending my messenger to prepare the way before me'. He will give knowledge or experience of salvation through forgiveness of sins and this is related to God's mercy or steadfast love (1.77–78a), a thought that is paralleled in Psalm 130.7–8 where the Lord's steadfast love brings redemption from iniquities or sins. The salvation of the messianic age is on its way, proclaims the Benedictus: 'the dawn from on high will break upon us' (1.78), and Isaiah 60.1–3 had asserted, 'your light has come; the glory of the LORD has risen upon you . . . kings will come to the brightness of your dawn.' Interestingly, the Greek word for 'dawn', *anatole*, is employed in the LXX to translate the Hebrew term for 'branch' in Zechariah 3.8; 6.12, so that 'dawn' is also the term for the messianic heir to the throne of David. It or he will 'give light to those who sit in darkness and in the shadow of death' (1.79), echoing the language of Isaiah 9.2: 'The people who walked in darkness have seen a great light; those who lived in a land of deep darkness – on them light has shined' and LXX Psalm 107.10, 14: 'those sitting in darkness and the shadow of death'. The dawn from on high will also 'guide our feet into the way of peace' (1.79), wording that recalls Isaiah 59.8: 'the way of peace' and what is said of Wisdom in Proverbs 3.17–26: 'all her paths are peace . . . you will walk on your way securely . . . the LORD . . . will keep your foot from being caught'.

This somewhat lengthy rehearsal of the Benedictus, whether the composition of this canticle is to be attributed to Luke's tradition or to Luke or to a combination of both, demonstrates how thoroughly Luke's infancy narrative is saturated in Scripture. The Benedictus' framework of God's coming deliverance in which John the Baptist has his role as forerunner is expressed in this rich collage of scriptural language that picks up the whole range of divine promises of salvation throughout Israel's history – from the Abrahamic promises about a great nation and the land, through the exodus, the year of jubilee, the future Davidic dynasty, to the return from exile and the coming messianic age beyond this. Images for salvation are heaped up: divine visitation, redemption, horn, rescue from enemies to serve God, forgiveness, enlightenment, peace. All help to display the magnitude of God's purposes for God's people, to give the sense that what God is now doing is in continuity with those purposes but will also exceed previous expectations, and to provide a glimpse of the community of holiness, justice and peace that will be established as a result.

But in Luke's birth story there is a concern not only to demonstrate continuities with the Jewish scriptural tradition but also, in a way distinct from Matthew and characteristic of Luke's work as a whole, to set the action on the broader Graeco-Roman stage. Yet when he does so, this is not a separate emphasis from that on continuity with scriptural tradition, whose significance, as we shall see, remains in play. In 3.1 Luke will set Jesus' actual mission in the broader context, as he spells out the power structures in the midst of which it will be played out. It is in the reign of the emperor Tiberius, when Pontius Pilate was governor of Judea – the Roman political power. It is when Herod was tetrarch of Galilee – the Galilean political power. And it is during the high priesthood of Annas and Caiaphas – the embodiments of the Jerusalem religious and political power structure. There are clear indications of this same concern in the birth story. In chapter 1 the marker for the setting is provided by 'In the days of King Herod of Judea . . .' (1.5), but chapter 2 begins with a much broader marker, that of the whole Roman Empire: 'In those days a decree went out from Emperor Augustus that all the world should be registered' (2.1). The historical problems about this census will be mentioned in a later chapter. Here it is sufficient to note that in Luke's narrative it serves as the means for securing Jesus' birth in Bethlehem, the city of David (2.4). But in terms of the Roman setting it is also important for the angelic announcement that follows in 2.10–11. In that announcement to the shepherds the worlds of scriptural expectation and of Roman political power are brought together: 'I am bringing you good news of great joy for all the people; to you is born this day in the city of David a Saviour, who is the Messiah, the Lord' (2.10–11). To see the force of this, it needs to be recalled that Augustus was revered as the one who had brought the glorious age of pastoral rule over a world made peaceful by virtue. Not long before Jesus' birth a great altar had been erected to celebrate the peace established by Augustus, and this still stands in Rome as a monument to the *pax Augusta*. As emperor he was called 'lord', he was hailed as the 'saviour of the whole world' and his birthday was adopted by the Greek cities of Asia Minor as the first day of the new year. Indeed, the famous Priene inscription says of him, 'the birthday of the god marked the beginning of good news for the world'. With its talk of good news, all people, the day of birth, Saviour and Lord, Luke clearly has the angelic proclamation both echo and contradict the imperial propaganda about Augustus, and this is reinforced in the further angelic praise of 2.14 which talks of peace on earth resulting from the birth of this child to be found in a manger. But all these terms familiar to Luke's Gentile readers as part of imperial propaganda have been given new content from their Christian setting and scriptural background. Here, as elsewhere, what was believed about Jesus in the good news about his death and resurrection is retrojected into the birth narrative. The verb 'to proclaim the good news' used here will be employed by Luke many times to refer to the Christian message, so that, for example, in Acts 5.42 he has the apostles not ceasing to teach and to proclaim the good news of Jesus as the Messiah. And when he provides examples of this proclamation of the good news, the three titles found here are part of it, so that Peter says that God raised Jesus and 'made him both Lord and Messiah' (Acts 2.32, 36) and that God exalted Jesus as Saviour (Acts 5.31).

The significance of such titles and of the other language has already been prepared for through the scriptural language of Luke 1 and through the Scriptures themselves. Proclaiming the good news had been part of Gabriel's language to Zechariah in 1.19 but of course it borrows from Isaiah 40—66. There the herald of good news announces the coming of God (40.9), where that good news is tied to the peace and salvation of God's rule: 'How beautiful upon the mountains are the feet of the messenger who announces peace, who brings good news, who announces salvation, who says to Zion, "Your God reigns"' (52.7) and where it comes to the lowly and the outcasts: 'he has sent me to bring good news to the oppressed' (61.1–2). Similarly the title 'Saviour' is employed in Isaiah 45.15, 21 for Israel's God as helper or deliverer of the people, and the Magnificat has used it in this way – 'my spirit rejoices in God my Saviour' (1.47) – but now that title and the title 'Lord' can be transferred to Jesus. In the LXX *kurios* had become a frequent translation for the divine name. 'I, I am the LORD, and besides me there is no saviour' (Isa. 43.11) is but one prominent example out of many. It is used in respect to God in Luke 1 but already begins to be employed there for Jesus also, as Elizabeth refers to Mary as 'the mother of my Lord' (1.43). The point should be clear. Over against the claims of the empire for its head, Caesar, the God of Israel, who is also the God of the nations, is now acting in the Messiah from the line of David, who so uniquely represents this God that he also can be called Lord and Saviour. It is *his* birth that marks the beginning of good news for the world, the good news of the coming of the rule of God in justice and peace. The *pax Christi* will be quite different from the *pax Augusta* with its enforcing of so-called peace through military might and this is signalled in the circumstances of the birth itself. Contrary to both Jewish and Graeco-Roman expectations, the one around whom this momentous announcement is centred is to be found not in a royal palace surrounded by dignitaries and guards but in a manger, and the first to surround him will be those of low social status, the shepherds.[6] So the reference to Roman imperial power enables Luke to make an ironic theological point. The universal decree of Augustus leads to Jesus being born in Bethlehem and provides the appropriate setting for the announcement of the very different universal messianic rule that Jesus will establish. For Luke, God uses Roman power to carry out the divine purposes unwittingly, just as will be the case with Pontius Pilate in the passion narrative and just as will be the case in the second part of Luke's overall narrative, Acts, when his hero, Paul, takes the gospel to the heart of the empire but does so as a Roman prisoner.

Graeco-Roman biography

The features of the birth narratives that have been sketched here make clear that Matthew and Luke have carefully crafted their accounts. The result is that these reflect their convictions about Christ, show in different ways that their stories of Jesus are rooted in and shaped by the Jewish Scriptures, and express some of their own distinctive emphases. If *midrash* is not a particularly appropriate term for specifying their genre, then what might be? Since they now form an integral part of the two Gospels as a whole, a better approach is to relate them to the genre of these larger narratives. The consensus view about the canonical Gospels as a whole is that, although they are distinctive in the good news they proclaim and

---

[6] On the status of shepherds, see e.g. J. B. Green, *The Gospel of Luke* (Grand Rapids: Eerdmans, 1997), 130–1.

have been influenced by accounts of the history of Israel and of its leaders in the Jewish Scriptures and the writings of the Second Temple period, they find their closest literary analogy in the genre of ancient biography, of which they form a subset.[7] The strongly Jewish setting and content of much of their material is no obstacle to such a conclusion. Later scriptural writings and the works of Josephus and Philo already show the influence of Hellenistic conventions of historiography and biography. The canonical Gospels with their accounts of the mission of Jesus, written in Greek, are most likely to have been thought of by their first readers as sharing the broad characteristics of the *bios* or *Life*. Of course, in addition to their recounting of the deeds and words of Jesus, the Gospel writers pay particular attention to his death, and their purpose is to persuade their readers to believe in Jesus as Messiah and Son of God (cf. Mark 1.1; John 20.31). Ancient biographers, too, were interested in the impact of their subjects and their significance for ethical and philosophical issues, could give the greatest amount of space to what they considered the subject's most important period, wrote their lives for many different purposes, and, in the process, employed a variety of rhetorical techniques to persuade their readers. So the Gospels of Matthew and Luke as a whole follow that of Mark in presenting their message about Jesus in the form of an ancient biography.

It is important to underline that the conventions for an ancient biography should not be confused with those for a modern one. The genre of *bios* was a flexible one and operated within a continuum that stretched from ancient history writing on the one side through to the encomium and the ancient romance or novel on the other. This question of genre is important because it indicates the shared general expectations of author and readers about a particular work. Although we shall be exploring matters of historicity more fully later, it is worth making some general observations about the implications of the literary genre of Matthew and Luke at this point. Seeing the Synoptic Gospels as *bioi* has helped students of Matthew and Luke not to impose modern expectations about biographical or historical writing on them. Modern categories have tended to force polarized answers to the question of their relation to the actual deeds and sayings in Jesus' life. Some have insisted that all the Gospel stories are historical in their detail and have therefore sought complex or speculative harmonizations among them, while others have responded that they are

---

[7] Cf. esp. R. A. Burridge, *What Are the Gospels? A Comparison with Graeco-Roman Biography* (2nd edn Grand Rapids: Eerdmans, 2004).

imaginative, even if theologically profound, creations but that their differences and theological biases mean they are of only minimal worth for gaining historical knowledge of Jesus. But examination of some of the features of ancient biography has reshaped assumptions and indicated the range of expectations about historicity within which Matthew's or Luke's life of Jesus would have been expected to fall.

It has been noted that ancient biography had links with ancient historiography, but the latter was itself a variegated phenomenon, ranging from those writings conforming somewhat more closely to present notions of historical investigation to far more popular accounts dealing in anecdote and aiming to entertain. Even historians, such as Thucydides and Tacitus, who claimed to have investigated their subject matter closely and to have sought out oral or, where available, written sources (cf. also Luke 1.1–4), would compose the discourses that take up a large amount of space in their histories in accord with what they thought would fit the character of the speaker and the occasion. Similarly, in relating events such historians would mix more factual reporting with accounts of incidents that might or could have happened. What was important to them was that this elaborated material be plausible and illustrate the general truths they wanted to draw out about their subject. In ancient biography there was even less of a distinction between what we would call 'factual' and 'fictional' elements. While some biographies stayed closer to the conventions of historiography, some did not, and a sustained correspondence with history was not one of the distinguishing features of ancient biography. Plutarch was a contemporary of Matthew and Luke who wrote slightly later towards the end of the first century. His *Lives* are the work of a biographer who adhered somewhat more closely to the conventions of ancient historiography, but even so the various *Lives* differ considerably in their concern with history. In them, as in ancient history writing, invention or free composition was a central feature. Plutarch frequently rewrote any sources, changing and elaborating emphases and adding anecdotes, as part of a creative exposition of what he perceived to be the significance of his subject's life. What mattered was the plausibility of the portrait, and to achieve this Plutarch was willing 'to help the truth along'. For Plutarch, as a biographer with a historical bent, what counted as historical truth was not, then, what could be authenticated by evidence but what was agreed in prevailing convention to be adequately plausible.[8]

---

[8] Cf. C. B. R. Pelling, 'Truth and Fiction in Plutarch's *Lives*', in ed. D. A. Russell, *Antonine Literature* (Oxford: Clarendon, 1990), 19–52.

Whereas lives of politicians and military leaders, such as those produced by Plutarch, naturally tended to stay closer to history writing, lives of philosophers and religious leaders or holy men were more idealized and often used by adherents of a philosophy or a religious tradition to influence beliefs or to serve as propaganda against competitors. In such biographies the writers' overall convictions are even more in play in their portraits of their subjects. From early on writers such as Xenophon and Aristoxenus used legendary traditions, invented characteristic traits, and fabricated anecdotes, which they employed in a mix with more authentic material, in producing portraits of philosophers that functioned as claim and counter-claim between rival philosophical schools. Accounts of events and discourses became the vehicle for the biographers' ideals taking graphic form within a historically framed narrative, thereby creating verisimilitude. Knowledge of this genre, then, should lead us to expect, as ancient readers would also have done, narratives which contained a substratum of core events from the tradition with some correspondence to what happened in the past but which were now shaped by an interpretative superstructure with varying amounts of embellishment, including some legendary or what we would call 'fictive' elements.[9]

But this survey of the Gospels as *bioi* has been undertaken in order to relate the birth narratives to this overall genre. Do these parts of Matthew and Luke fit what readers would have expected ancient biographies to relate about their subjects' beginnings?[10] Since most subjects only came to public attention as a result of their later careers, there was frequently very little authentic tradition for the early part of their lives and so the composition was particularly legendary as it attempted to show that the future life and career of subjects were already anticipated from the earliest days. A few examples of how ancient biographers treated the beginnings of their subjects' lives and their correspondence with what has been noted in Matthew and Luke will have to suffice.[11] We observed in connection with Matthew's story how accounts of the beginnings of Moses' life had had their influence. Moses' father, Amram, received God's prediction through a dream of his son's future greatness in saving the people from bondage (cf. e.g. Josephus, *Ant.* 2.205–221). This feature in the biographical part

---

[9] Cf. e.g. A. Momigliano, *The Development of Greek Biography* (Cambridge, MA: Harvard University Press, 1971).

[10] Cf. the necessarily very brief discussion in Burridge, *What Are the Gospels?*, 207–8, on the topics of ancestry, birth, boyhood and education in the Synoptics in relation to ancient biography.

[11] Cf. also the treatment in C. H. Talbert, *Reading Luke–Acts in Its Mediterranean Milieu* (Leiden: Brill, 2003), 65–77, in the chapter entitled 'Prophecies of Future Greatness: Contributions of Greco-Roman Biographies to an Understanding of Luke 1.5—4.1'.

of Josephus' work is in fact an integral part of ancient biographies, where predictions, prophecies and omens frequently surround the birth of the subject. In Plutarch's *Lives* there are a number of examples. These include Lampon, the diviner, seeing a horn growing out of a ram's head and explaining this in terms of Pericles' future government (*Per.* 6.2–3) and Philip, the father of Alexander, having a dream about a seal with the figure of a lion on his wife's body, about which a diviner 'assured him the meaning of his dream was, that the queen was with child of a boy, who would one day prove as stout and courageous as a lion' (*Alex.* 3). In regard to Cicero, 'a vision appeared to his nurse, and foretold the child she then suckled should afterwards become a great benefit to the Roman states' (*Cic.* 2) and in regard to Lycurgus, the oracle at Delphi announces that 'he is called beloved of God, and rather God than man; that his prayers were heard, that his laws should be the best, and the commonwealth which observed them the most famous in the world' (*Lyc.* 5). Suetonius in his biography of Alexander (*Aug.* 94) draws explicit attention to this phenomenon in birth stories and to its purpose.

> Having reached this point, it will not be out of place to add an account of the omens which occurred before he was born, on the very day of his birth, and afterwards, from which it was possible to anticipate and perceive his future greatness and uninterrupted good fortune.

He goes on to relate how both Augustus' father and mother have dreams about their son's future greatness before his birth and how

> a few months before Augustus was born a portent was generally observed at Rome, which gave warning that nature was pregnant with a king for the Roman people; thereupon the Senate in consternation decreed that no male child born that year should be reared; but those whose wives were with child saw to it that the decree was not filed in the treasury, since each one appropriated the prediction to his own family.

Further, on the day of Augustus' birth, 'Publius Nigidius, as everyone knows, declared that the ruler of the world had been born'. The same passage tells that Quintus Catulus has a dream about a boy in which Jupiter declares 'that the boy was being reared to be the saviour of his country'. The next day he meets Augustus, having never seen him before, and recognizes him as the boy in the dream. On another occasion Marcus Cicero has a dream in which

> a boy of noble countenance was let down from heaven on a golden chain and, standing at the door of the temple, was given a whip by Jupiter. Just

then suddenly catching sight of Augustus, who was still unknown to the greater number of those present and had been brought to the ceremony by his uncle Caesar, he declared that he was the very one whose form had appeared to him in his dream.

In relation to Tiberius, Suetonius relates how an eagle landed on the roof of his house and underlines that he was confident of his destiny because of the predictions of astrologers (*Tib.* 14). His account of Vespasian lists a number of portents of his future imperial dignity, including a prediction from Josephus and incidents involving a dog, an ox and eagles (*Vesp.* 5). Diogenes Laertius, in his life of Plato, relates that Socrates had a dream about a cygnet that he then identifies with Plato when he meets him the next day (*Vit. Phil.* 3.7). Philostratus recounts that Apollonius' mother had a dream before his birth that was accompanied by the crying of swans and a thunderbolt (*Vit. Apoll.* 1.5).

It should be apparent, then, that in this area Matthew's and Luke's birth stories also provide the features that would be expected of an ancient biography's depiction of the beginnings of the life of a great figure. In Matthew there are Joseph's dreams, the angel's prediction of the child's future role as Saviour, the fulfilment of earlier predictions from the Scriptures, the magi who are the equivalent of the diviners, the portent of the star, and the accompanying attempt to prevent the birth of male children. In Luke there are again angelic predictions of the future greatness of Mary's child, the omen of Elizabeth's baby leaping in her womb at the appearance of the pregnant Mary and the accompanying explanation, the glory of the Lord shining around the shepherds as the angelic announcement is made to them, and both Simeon and Anna immediately recognizing in Mary's child the one who is to bring salvation to Israel, with Simeon also predicting his destiny.

There are further correspondences with Graeco-Roman biographies. Matthew began his story with a genealogy (cf. also Luke 3.23–38). As might be expected, other biographers also provide material on the family lineage of their subjects. Plutarch has an account of Theseus' lineage on his father's and mother's side (*Thes.* 3) and arranges the genealogy of Lycurgus as a family tree (*Lyc.* 1). Suetonius deals with the paternal ancestors of Augustus (*Aug.* 2) and traces the families of origin of Tiberius (*Tib.* 1–4) and Vespasian (*Vesp.* 1–2), while Diogenes Laertius follows Plato's family back through Solon to Neptune (*Vit. Phil.* 3.1). Josephus offers a genealogical depiction of his own family origins (*Vita* 1–6). The naming of Jesus and the meaning of his names are particularly important in Matthew's narrative. A similar concern is found in Plutarch about the names of Romulus and Remus (*Rom.* 6) and of Theseus (*Thes.* 5), in Suetonius about the significance of the naming of Augustus (*Aug.* 7) and in Diogenes Laertius about Plato's name (*Vit. Phil.* 3.5).

Sometimes such biographies recount something miraculous about the birth of the subject. Moses' mother, Jochebed, is enabled to give birth so easily that nobody notices the occurrence (cf. Josephus, *Ant.* 2.205–221) and similarly Cicero's mother delivers her child without any pain or labour (Plutarch, *Cic.* 2). More frequently, and of more significance for our topic, the miracle has to do with conception. Plutarch provides three examples. In relating the origins of Romulus, he says that 'the story which is most believed and has the greatest number of vouchers' is that her uncle, Amulius, made Romulus' mother a vestal virgin. However,

> not long after, she was, contrary to the established laws of the Vestals, discovered to be with child, and should have suffered the most cruel punishment, had not Antho, the king's daughter, mediated with her father for her . . . In time she brought forth two boys, of more than human size and beauty.

The two boys, Romulus and Remus, are taken away and looked after by a wolf and a woodpecker,

> which things, as much as any, gave credit to what the mother of the children said, that their father was the god Mars; though some say that it was a mistake put upon her by Amulius, who himself had come to her dressed up in armour. (*Rom.* 2.5; 4.2)

Like Romulus, Theseus 'got the reputation of descent from gods'; his mother, Aethra, concealed his true parentage and 'a report was spread abroad . . . that he was begotten by Poseidon' (*Thes.* 2, 6; cf. also 36: 'he was said to be a son of Poseidon'). Such accounts are found not only in lives of figures from the distant past but also in those of rulers and philosophers of more recent times. In Plutarch's biography of Alexander, Philip sees Apollo, under the form of a serpent, lying with his wife, Olympias, who later informs Alexander of the secret of his birth 'and bade him behave himself with courage suitable to his divine extraction' (*Alex.* 3). Suetonius has a similar story about Augustus' conception. His mother, Atia, falls asleep in the temple of Apollo. Apollo comes to her in the form of a snake and 'in the tenth month after that Augustus was born and was therefore regarded as the son of Apollo' (*Aug.* 94). Porphyry recounts that Pythagoras was said to be the son of Apollo and the woman, Pythis, the most beautiful of the Samina (*Vit. Pyth.* 2). Diogenes Laertius tells how Aristion, her husband, tried to violate Perictione, Plato's mother, but did not succeed. He then had a vision of Apollo 'in a dream, in consequence of which he abstained from approaching his wife till after her confinement' (*Vit. Phil.* 3). Philostratus relates that Apollonius' mother had an apparition of Proteus, the Egyptian god, in the guise of a demon before the birth of her son and that he told her she would bear Proteus himself. But the people of Tyana called Apollonius the son of Zeus (*Vit. Apoll.* 1.4, 6).[12]

Like Luke's account of Jesus in the Temple at the age of 12, other ancient biographies contain depictions or exploits of their subject as a child or youth that were considered to be omens of his future life. Frequently these were stories of the precocious wisdom of the hero, indicating that the child must already have been what the man was known to be. Josephus does not hesitate to include such material in his autobiography and can relate that at the age of 14, 'I won universal applause for my love of letters; insomuch that the chief priests and the leading men of the city used constantly to come to me for precise information on some particular in our ordinances' (*Vita* 8b–9). Plutarch tells how, in comparison with Remus, Romulus as a youth

> seemed rather to act by counsel, and to show the sagacity of a statesman, and in all his dealings with their neighbours, whether relating to feeding of flocks or to hunting, gave the idea of being born rather to rule than to obey.
>
> (*Rom.* 6)

Of Theseus he says, he displayed 'not only great strength of body, but equal bravery, and a quickness alike and force of understanding' (*Thes.* 6) and of Themistocles that from his youth he showed 'a strong and aspiring bent for action and great affairs' and did not indulge 'in play or idleness, as other children, but would be always inventing or arranging some oration or declamation to himself' (*Them.* 2). In regard to Cicero, Plutarch narrates that

> as soon as he was of an age to begin to have lessons, he became so distinguished for his talent, and got such a name and reputation among the boys, that their fathers would often visit the school that they might see young Cicero, and might be able to say that they themselves had witnessed the quickness and readiness in learning for which he was renowned.   (*Cic.* 2)

---

[12] For a fuller discussion of miraculous conceptions in the ancient world, see C. H. Talbert, 'Miraculous Conceptions and Births in Mediterranean Antiquity', in eds A.-J. Levine, D. C. Allison, J. D. Crossan, *The Historical Jesus in Context* (Princeton: Princeton University Press, 2006), 79–86.

Perhaps closest to Luke's story is his account of how Alexander, when very young and in the absence of his father, entertained ambassadors, asking them profound questions, so that 'they were struck with admiration of him, and looked upon the ability so much famed of Philip, to be nothing in comparison with the forwardness and high purpose that appeared thus early in his son' (*Alex.* 5). Similar stories are told by Philo about Moses (*Mos.* 1.20–24), by Diogenes Laertius about Epicurus (*Vit. Phil.* 10.14), by Iamblichus about Pythagoras (*Vit. Pyth.* 10, 11) and by Philostratus about Apollonius (*Vit. Apoll.* 1.7).

It is worth noting one further feature of Luke's narrative that can also be found in ancient biography. As we shall see, Luke structures his infancy narrative by paralleling material about John the Baptist with that about Jesus, and this step parallelism, in which the second element is greater, is highly significant for his perspective on both figures. The individual accounts of lives from Plutarch that we have referred to above are, of course, part of an overall work entitled *Parallel Lives* where, with a few exceptions the lives are arranged in pairs and compared. There is a concluding section of comparison attached to these pairs, and comparisons are also made at other points in the biographies. Of Theseus and Romulus, for example, Plutarch can say, 'Theseus seemed to me to resemble Romulus in many particulars'. Among these particulars he mentions, 'Both of them, born out of wedlock and of uncertain parentage, had the repute of being sprung from the gods' (*Thes.* 2). Or in comparing Demosthenes and Cicero, he finds their similarities in such areas as character, love of liberty and oratorical skills so striking that he can declare, 'The divine power seems originally to have designed Demosthenes and Cicero upon the same plan' (*Dem.* 3). But the comparison also takes place implicitly within the parallel narrative structure provided for each pair. So Plutarch pairs a Greek statesman with a Roman one, as, for example, with *Alcibiades* and *Marcius Coriolanus*. Just as Luke on a smaller scale parallels, in the case of John the Baptist and Jesus, material about parents, annunciation by Gabriel about conception, the response of the mothers, the birth, the circumcision and naming, prophetic responses to the birth and summaries on the growth of the child, so Plutarch, in the case of Alcibiades and Coriolanus, parallels sections on their origins, their upbringing and training, their physical attributes, their marriages and children, their deeds as statesmen, how they died and what happened after their death.[13] What is more, just as Luke's

---

[13] F. Bovon, *Luke 1* (Hermeneia; Minneapolis: Fortress, 2002), 30, also holds that Luke has combined two independent units in a parallelism in the style of Plutarch.

comparison had a clear apologetic purpose – to show the importance of John but the even greater significance of Jesus, so Plutarch's parallelism had its own apologetic thrust – to show that Plutarch's own homeland of Greece was not in the least inferior to Rome in the statesmen it produced and in its political and military impact on the world.[14]

These examples indicate that major elements in the infancy narratives of Matthew and Luke bear a remarkable resemblance to what is to be found in Graeco-Roman biographies at the places where they treat the early stages of their subjects' lives before their public career. Even these parts of their story confirm strikingly that the two Gospels are to be seen as a subgenre of the *bios*. A subject achieves greatness or renown on the basis of his life, and the form and content of the early part of the written account of this life is selected so as to give readers anticipations of his future significance. In this material ancestry, names and geographical and political setting may well have support from tradition, but much of the content, whether traditional or not, involves notions about the gods, fate, auguries, portents, divination and astrology that are legendary but nevertheless illustrate the significance that became attached to the subject's life. But the point being made at this stage about the Gospels' relation to ancient biography is not so much a 'history of religions' one about the borrowing of ideas and events from other pagan sources. It is primarily a literary point about genre and its implications. Whatever the similarities and the differences in content, the form and the type of material included in Matthew and Luke conform very closely indeed to what ancient hearers or readers would have expected to be told about the births of great figures. Setting the infancy stories in the context of ancient biographies, then, is more appropriate than designating them, with Borg and Crossan, as parables or parabolic.[15] While the latter terms may help to show that the truth of the stories does not depend on their factuality, they too conveniently avoid issues of historicity and are counter-intuitive when applied to the birth narratives. Both Matthew and Luke have distinct features of Jesus' teaching that take the form of parables and these are decidedly not what they employ to discuss Jesus' origins at the beginning of their Gospels. There is no escaping the fact that their infancy accounts are part and parcel of their narrating the life of Jesus in particular historical settings. It is invoking ancient biography with its 'creative historiography' that enables us to discern how far they have meaning that is not dependent on their factuality.

---

[14] Cf. D. A. Russell, *Essays on Plutarch's Lives* (ed. B. Scardigli; Oxford: Clarendon, 1995), 73–98.

[15] M. J. Borg and J. D. Crossan, *The First Christmas: What the Gospels Really Teach about Jesus's Birth* (New York: HarperCollins, 2007), 32–8.

Invoking ancient biography, of course, also puts the evangelists and the recipients of their Gospels in a quite different position from most present-day readers, who, unless they are students of the ancient world, tend to treat the birth stories in isolation and as offering unique information about Jesus rather than as standard biographical fare. Part of the significance of this discussion for our specific topic is that it is often claimed, as we shall see, that a virginal conception is so foreign to the Jewish context of early Christianity that no one would have thought of it unless it was believed it had actually occurred. The reality, however, is rather different. Conceptions without human male involvement belong to the very context in which early Christian traditions were beginning to take shape as written Gospels and to the very genre those written Gospels employed. Educated Jews and early Christians were conversant with such stories, as is indicated by Justin's dialogue with Trypho (*Dial.* 67–70, cf. also *1 Apol.* 21–23). Whatever conclusions are drawn about the status of the virginal conception of Jesus, this literary phenomenon is a datum that cannot be ignored. If Christology in the canonical Gospels comes through this medium of ancient biography and if the earliest parts of such biographies are particularly legendary, then, in determining the theological subject matter of the accounts of the virginal conception, interpretation needs to take seriously the form in which the truth about Jesus' origins is disclosed.[16]

---

[16] This will be discussed further in Chapter 9.

4

Conceiving Jesus in Matthew

When I embarked on my further exploration of the topic of this book, I assumed that the discussion of the annunciation stories in Matthew and Luke would be one of the most straightforward parts of the project, since, whatever one makes of the rest of the New Testament's evidence and whatever one does with Matthew and Luke in appropriating them for today, these two Gospels at least constituted unambiguous witnesses to the virginal conception tradition. I was aware, of course, that some scholars have indeed argued that, when read on their own terms, the passages concerned (Matt. 1.18–25 and Luke 1.26–38) do not demand the traditional interpretation.[1] However, that dominant tradition had already played a part in my assumption and, particularly in regard to Matthew, I had not expected the minority report to have such a strong case. One consequence is that, since Matthew turns out to be arguably the most difficult and complex part of the New Testament evidence, the discussion that follows may, in the eyes of some readers, do the clarity and accessibility of my treatment no favours. But the arguments about the interpretation of this passage are finely balanced and, though I eventually conclude that the traditional view of it may just win the day, I wish readers to gain a sense of why that view cannot simply be taken for granted.[2] This chapter, therefore, constitutes an invitation to examine Matthew's annunciation story afresh without thinking that one already knows in advance what is the best way of interpreting it.

It might, however, be asked why, for one who supposedly takes the canon seriously, the complexity of the discussion could not be sidestepped by

---

[1] Cf. e.g. D. J. Catchpole, *Resurrection People: Studies in the Resurrection Narratives of the Gospels* (London: Darton, Longman & Todd, 2000), 72–80; *Jesus People: The Historical Jesus and the Beginnings of Community* (London: Darton, Longman & Todd, 2006), 84–8; J. Schaberg, *The Illegitimacy of Jesus: A Feminist Theological Interpretation of the Infancy Narratives* (Sheffield: Sheffield Academic Press, 1995; original edn San Francisco: Harper & Row, 1987), though she concedes (82) that her reading of Luke is unlikely to occur to a reader without presupposing 'the illegitimacy tradition'. On Matthew in particular, cf. R. J. Miller, *Born Divine: The Births of Jesus and Other Sons of God* (Santa Rosa, CA: Polebridge, 2003), esp. 7–100, 195–206.

[2] For a more detailed discussion of this matter, see A. Lincoln, 'Contested Paternity and Contested Readings: Jesus' Conception in Matthew 1.18–25', *JSNT* 34 (2012), 211–31.

allowing the clearer account in Luke's annunciation story to be determinative for the interpretation of the more ambiguous Matthew. But while acknowledgement of an authoritative canon commits one to seeking some unity within its diversity, this cannot be done adequately without first knowing clearly the extent of the diversity. We have already seen enough of that diversity in our discussion of the rest of the New Testament outside the annunciation stories to indicate that the very significant differences between the two annunciation stories are also likely to play a role in ascertaining the range of the diversity within which some coherence may be sought. In this light I shall be assuming that best justice is done to Matthew and Luke as New Testament Scripture by treating their two stories in the first instance as distinct interpretations of Jesus in their own right with their own authoritative messages. In doing so, I shall primarily treat interpretation of these two Gospels at the level of their final form. When analysis of the traditions they may have employed is invoked at this stage, it will be in order to cast light on how the evangelists have shaped these for their own purposes. Further exploration of any such traditions behind the stories and how the accounts relate to the attempt at historical reconstruction of the conception traditions as a whole will be reserved for Chapter 6.

One further preliminary point should be underlined. Significant though it is to have some clarity about the most plausible interpretation of Matthew, it should already be clear that the overall argument of this book does not depend on how one resolves this particular contested issue. All the major features of the case being presented would still hold, and, I hope, would still be found compelling, whether or not readers accepted the traditional view of Matthew or were persuaded by the rival approach. A decision one way or the other or indeed a judgement that is content to leave the ambiguities unresolved simply affects the relative weighting one gives to the diverse strands within the canonical witness.

Jesus' Davidic descent and Joseph's dilemma

Matthew's account of Jesus' birth actually begins at the start of his Gospel. Translated literally, 1.1 reads: 'The book of the genesis of Jesus the Christ, the son of David, the son of Abraham.' The term *genesis* can have the broader force of 'origin' or the narrower ones of 'genealogy' or 'birth'. Here the first two meanings are likely to be in play. The broader one fits as the title for the book. Christians believe in Jesus the Christ, the Son of God; now here, says Matthew, is an account of the origin of that belief in his birth, life, death and resurrection. By using this term in its broad sense, Matthew is also beginning his narrative by alluding to the first book of the Scriptures and its title – Genesis. The story Matthew will tell has its links with David and Abraham and Israel's history and he will be at pains to point out the continuities. But it will also be the story of new beginnings, since a new genesis has occurred in the life, death and resurrection of Jesus of Nazareth. But *genesis* in the narrower sense of genealogy recalls another feature in the first book of Scripture. The same phrase, 'the book of the genesis', occurs in LXX Genesis 2.4, where it introduces the account of the creation of man and woman in terms of the genesis of the earth and the heavens, and in LXX Genesis 5.1, where it introduces the listing of Adam's descendants down to the time of the flood. So Matthew's Gospel calls on its readers to make the associations with Genesis but at the same time to note that the one who inaugurates a new genesis is to be identified in terms of Israel's history as son of David, son of Abraham. Its narrative is to be located in and interpreted by that previous narrative, and the one who is its subject can be seen as a summing up of Israel's history in that he is a true Jew (a descendant of Abraham, to whom it was promised that all the nations would bless themselves in him, cf. Gen. 12.3) and he is in the true messianic line (a descendant of David). The identification of Jesus in terms of Davidic descent can be made because of the ancestry of Joseph (1.16).

The annunciation story itself is introduced with another allusion to the notion of genesis. 'Now the genesis [origin or birth] of Jesus the Messiah took place in this way' (1.18). What follows, however, is not so much an account of the birth as of the events surrounding it, and the centre of attention is Joseph. It should not be surprising that Joseph is the important figure because, as the genealogy has already made clear, Matthew wants to establish that, as the Messiah, Jesus is in the Davidic line. For this Jesus needs a father who is a descendant of David, since Jewish ancestry, unlike today when it is reckoned through the mother, was at that time determined through the father. Joseph meets the requirements, as the angelic annunciation to him underlines in its address: 'Joseph, son of David . . .' (1.20). However, Matthew's account relates that, while Mary was the mother of Jesus, Joseph was not actually his biological father. The evangelist has already alluded to this in the somewhat strange way he concluded the genealogy. Instead of what would have been in accord with the patrilineal nature of what has gone before, namely, 'Jacob the father of Joseph, and Joseph the father of Jesus who is called the Messiah', he has 'Jacob the father of Joseph, the husband of Mary, of whom Jesus was born, who is called the Messiah' (1.16). So Matthew, who believes Jesus to be the messianic son of David and yet holds that the Davidic Joseph was not Jesus' father, provides a narrative explaining how this can be. The explanation unfolds through the story of Joseph's dilemma. To understand that dilemma it is necessary to recall Jewish customs and scriptural law. The narrator begins at the time when Mary and Joseph are betrothed (1.18b). Unlike the modern custom of engagement, betrothal was considered part of the marriage not a state prior to it, and here in 1.19 Joseph is called Mary's husband as well as her betrothed. Betrothal was the period in which a young woman, usually aged between 12 and 14,[3] was transferred from the authority of her father to that of her future husband. It had two stages. For the first year or so she would continue to live under her father's roof, but then she would move in with her husband and he would support her financially. It is not certain whether sexual intimacy was allowed during the first stage,[4] but during both stages the couple were considered legally married. Here, according to Matthew's story, during the first stage Joseph discovers Mary is pregnant. Whether she had become pregnant before the betrothal we are not told, but Joseph knows that he is not the father. What is he to do? Being a righteous man (and righteousness according to the law will be a major theme in Matthew's Gospel), Joseph resolves to act in line with the Torah but also compassionately. Legally, there were two alternatives. He could simply present Mary with a bill of divorce, signed by two or three witnesses (Deut. 24.1), or he could ask for an inquiry before the elders that would attempt to determine whether she was pregnant because of consent or because of rape (Deut. 22.23–27). Joseph decides to go for the first option. According to 1.19, he planned to divorce her quietly, being unwilling to expose her to public shaming or humiliation.[5]

But Joseph's plan is interrupted by a dream. At this point it is worth observing that Matthew's is the only Gospel that mentions dreams and it does so six times. Five references are in the birth narrative, and four of

---

[3] Later rabbinic texts indicate that in ancient Judaism betrothal in the case of the female usually took place as early as 12 to 12½ years of age, cf. *b. Yeb.* 62b.

[4] Most scholars think it was probably not permitted, though there is evidence from the second century that it was allowed in Judea (the setting for Matthew's story) but not in Galilee, cf. Miller, *Born Divine*, 88.

[5] M. J. Marohl, *Joseph's Dilemma: 'Honor Killing' in the Birth Narrative of Matthew* (Eugene, OR: Cascade, 2008) offers a different interpretation of Joseph's options. He could either keep her pregnancy hidden, thus disobeying the law, or make it public, thus exposing her to honour killing by male family members seeking to redress the dishonour to them. This reads a great deal into the narrative, and Matthew's concern with interpretation of Torah suggests that he is more likely to have been focusing simply on the legal issues here. There is no indication that Joseph expects Mary to be found guilty and therefore needing to suffer the penalty of being stoned to death or its first-century CE equivalent punishment. What he wishes to spare her is the humiliation of a public investigation into the circumstances of the conception.

these five are to Joseph's dreams. It is probably no coincidence that in Genesis the great receiver and interpreter of dreams was also named Joseph. But the circumstances of this dream in 1.20 are also connected with the story of the birth of Moses from Exodus 1 which was retold in Jewish tradition in a series of *haggadoth* about Moses which fill in the gaps in the biblical narrative. Of particular interest is what is said about Moses' father, Amram, in these traditions. When he and others hear about Pharaoh's plan to kill all the Hebrew baby boys, they are in a dilemma. In one tradition (cf. Pseudo-Philo, *L.A.B.* 9.1–16) they decide not to have sexual intercourse with their wives so that any offspring will not be killed. Amram, however, refuses this option and decides to go ahead and take a wife. Others then follow his precedent. After a lapse of some years his daughter, Miriam, then receives a dream in which God instructs her to tell her parents they will have a son who will be a leader who will save his people. In Josephus (*Ant.* 2.205–221) Amram is already married and his wife is pregnant and so naturally his anxiety about Pharaoh's decree is great. Here God reassures him in a dream that the child will escape destruction and deliver his people from Egyptian bondage. In the much later *Targum Pseudo-Jonathan* on Exodus 2 Amram has divorced his wife because of Pharaoh's decree and then remarries her and she bears Moses. In this tradition Jochebed is 130 years old at the time of the remarriage but her youth is miraculously restored to her so that she can conceive. In yet another tradition (preserved in *Sefer ha-Zikronot* or *The Book of Memory*, a medieval collection of much older traditions) some, including Amram, separate from or divorce their wives rather than staying married and producing sons who would be killed. But then Amram hears Miriam's prophecy that he will have a son who will rescue the Israelites and takes back or remarries his wife, who conceives and gives birth to this son. Matthew's interest in shaping his story in relation to the traditions about Moses' birth appears to be in play, as in his account Joseph is also now told in a dream not to divorce Mary because she will bear a son who will save his people from their sins (1.20–21).

But in Joseph's dream the angel also tells him something that the narrator had already conveyed to readers in 1.18, namely, that the child conceived in Mary is 'from [or of] the holy spirit'.[6] Most commentators simply assume, possibly under the influence of their view of Matthew's later citation of Isaiah 7.14, that this is a reference to a virginal conception.

---

[6] There is no definite article in Matthew's phrase in contrast to the usage in 10.20; 28.19, but, *pace* Miller, *Born Divine*, 40–1, too much should not be made of this, since Matthew appears to be able to use the phrase with or without the article interchangeably, cf. e.g. 12.28 with 12.31–32.

But what would this phrase mean in a Jewish context? It should at the very least give pause for thought that elsewhere in Jewish literature the language of divine begetting does not entail a conception without a human father. Readers would need very clear indications if they were expected to take this phrase in such an unprecedented way. In Psalm 2.6–7 – 'You are my son; today I have begotten you' – God's address to the king meant that the latter had a special status and role in carrying out God's purposes and obeying God's will as a son obeys his father, not that God had been involved in his birth instead of a human father. Indeed, the notion that being God's son meant having a divine or semi-divine nature is foreign to the Jewish Scriptures and more at home in the Graeco-Roman world. Elsewhere, when God is named as the direct cause of certain pregnancies, whether in the case of Eve (Gen. 4.1), Leah (Gen. 29.31–32), Rachel (Gen. 30.22–23), Ruth (Ruth 4.13) or others, this divine causality was never understood as excluding the woman's intercourse with a man. Paul's talk of Ishmael being born according to the flesh and Isaac being born according to the Spirit (Gal. 4.29) confirms how the latter formulation would normally have been taken. His readers would have been clear that Abraham was the biological father of both sons but that Isaac was the son who was the fulfilment of the divine promise. Elsewhere in the New Testament, the phrase 'of or from the Spirit' is used of the birth of believers (John 3.5). In fact, John 1.12–13 explicitly states that believers as children of God are born not from natural human sexual union but from God. This is, of course, not suggesting that their physical births came about through some super-natural means but is speaking of a spiritual relationship that those who have two human parents enter into and that is not to be attributed to physical descent from these parents. There is, then, nothing to this point in Matthew's account that suggests a supernatural or virginal conception.[7] The angel assures Joseph, and the narrator assures readers, that Mary's irregular pregnancy should be seen as part of the divine purposes in which the Spirit was at work in the circumstances of Jesus' birth. There is, how-ever, no interest in spelling out those circumstances as they relate to Mary's pregnancy.

What is of concern is to establish that Joseph was prepared to serve as Jesus' father so that Jesus could be called a son of David, as Joseph himself was, and that Joseph gave this public acknowledgement by naming Mary's child (1.21, 24–25). In Judaism, in order to establish paternity, it was not sufficient to ask the mother, because she might lie about the father so as

---

[7] Cf. also e.g. Schaberg, *Illegitimacy*, 64–8; Catchpole, *Resurrection People*, 76–7.

not to be accused of adultery. Rather a man had to give testimony, since most men would be reluctant to acknowledge a child unless it was their own. The Mishnah, from around 200 years after Jesus' birth, is very clear on this: 'If a man says, "This is my son", he is to be believed' (*Baba Bathra* 8.6).[8] By exercising the father's right to name the child, Joseph indicates his willingness to be considered this child's father. Though adoption as a formal legal procedure was not known in Judaism at this time, the practice of raising another's child as one's own existed and was approved (cf. e.g. Mordecai's adoption of Esther in Esth. 2.7, 15). Indeed later rabbinic texts can assert that 'whoever brings up an orphan in his home is regarded, according to Scripture, as though the child had been born to him' (*Sanh.* 19b) or 'he who brings up a child is to be called its father, not he who gave birth' (*Exod. Rab.* 46.5).[9] The basis for paternity was whether a man accepted a child as his own, and this conferred legitimacy. So, although this account depicts no legal ceremony, Joseph could now expect to be perceived by others, to all intents and purposes, as Jesus' father. Two things are clear in Matthew's story. Joseph is not the actual father of Jesus and yet this child is to have a special role in God's plan as Messiah and Saviour. Joseph enables the latter by co-operating with the divine purposes as a righteous and obedient man so that Jesus can be considered his son and acquire his Davidic ancestry.

The citation of Isaiah 7.14 and a 'virginal' conception

Into this account Matthew inserts his scriptural fulfilment citation in 1.22–23, because he is interested in another name for this child in addition to Jesus, meaning 'saviour' or 'deliverer', and that is Emmanuel, meaning 'God is with us' (1.24). The name was significant for Matthew because it expressed his conviction that through the birth, life, death and resurrection of Jesus the presence of God was manifested among God's people. It is in the citation from Isaiah 7.14, in which this name is found, that there occurs

---

[8] Cf. R. E. Brown, *The Birth of the Messiah* (2nd edn New York: Doubleday, 1993), 139.

[9] Y. Levin, 'Jesus, "Son of God" and "Son of David": The "Adoption" of Jesus into the Davidic Line', *JSNT* 28 (2006), 415–42, as we have noted previously, provides a thorough review of the evidence from which he argues that legal adoption was not known in either Palestinian or diaspora Judaism. He shows that analogous practices that can be cited from Scripture were within the extended family and cannot be shown to have had legal consequences (423). His own solution to the problem of how Matthew and Luke could have considered Jesus to be a descendant of David, though he was not actually Joseph's son, is that they were far removed from Jewish tradition and must have been assuming Roman adoption practices when they composed their accounts (433). However, this scarcely seems likely in the case of Matthew and, as we shall see, there is a more plausible explanation of Luke's combination of virginal conception and Davidic descent.

the one possible explicit indicator in this account that not only was Joseph not Jesus' biological father but also no human male was involved in Jesus' conception. Here the term that can be translated 'virgin' appears (1.23), but, as is well known, Matthew's use of the Isaiah text, where his main interest is in the name Emmanuel, is highly debated. Commentators on Isaiah discuss whether the young woman, whose giving birth is to be a sign to Ahaz, is a wife of the king or Isaiah's wife or just some other young woman, who, because Syria and Israel have received judgement, will be grateful for God's faithfulness to Judah and call her son Immanuel. But what is clear is that in the Isaiah passage itself there is no question of the young woman being a virgin when she conceives Immanuel.[10] In Hebrew the term employed is *almah* and that simply means a young woman, who would have been understood to conceive by the usual means. The sign to Ahaz derives its force not from the manner in which the young woman will conceive but from its timing (Isa. 7.15–16). However, when Matthew takes up the Isaiah text, as in nearly all his scriptural quotations, he is more dependent on the LXX, which here translates 'young woman' with the Greek term *parthenos*. Although another term, *neanis*, might have been used (and was employed in the Greek versions of Aquila and Theodotion), the former is a perfectly good translation, since its primary reference in Greek is also to a young woman of child-bearing age who had not yet had a child. The interesting complication, however, is that 'virgin' could also be one of its more precise connotations. The LXX translators do not, then, change the force of the Hebrew, and even if, somewhat improbably, they intended the term to be taken in the more technical sense of 'virgin', the Greek version of Isaiah would still involve no notion of miraculous conception but mean only that a woman who is at present a virgin will become pregnant.

The key issue is, of course, how the quotation now functions in Matthew's story. Is the potential of the Greek term for referring to a virgin being exploited? This is what most interpreters have assumed – that Mary conceived as a virgin in a totally extraordinary pregnancy. This is possibly what the evangelist intends. Yet it is by no means obvious. Since nothing in the account so far has indicated that the conception of Mary's child took place supernaturally, it is perfectly plausible to continue to read the story in that light. On such a reading *parthenos*, in line with the Hebrew and the LXX,

---

[10] *Contra* J. G. Machen, *The Virgin Birth of Christ* (2nd edn New York: Harper and Row, 1932), 288–93, who holds that the term 'sign' must refer to a birth that is miraculous. The reception-history comment of U. Luz, *Matthew 1—7* (London: T. & T. Clark, 1990), 123–4, is worth repeating: 'Luther declared his willingness to pay "the stubborn, condemned Jews" one hundred guilders if Isa. 7.14 really means "young woman" and not "virgin." He owes them.'

is understood in its more general meaning as 'young woman'.[11] For Matthew this conception and birth of a child to a young woman of child-bearing age is a fulfilment of the Isaiah text because the child involved is to be seen as uniquely Emmanuel, 'God is with us'. For those who assume Matthew is relating a virginal conception, the statement that Joseph 'had no marital relations with her until she had borne a son' (1.25) serves to underline that Mary remained a virgin until after she had given birth. Again, however, this is by no means the only way to understand its function. It can be read as simply continuing to make clear that Joseph was not the father and to underline that he remains righteous throughout this whole affair. He behaves precisely how someone concerned to uphold the law strictly should do. So, for example, when Josephus discusses the Essenes, he sees their conduct as exemplary for all Jews and goes on to claim that the law permits intercourse only for the procreation of children and therefore any man who has sex with a pregnant woman is impure (*C. Ap.* 2.199, 202).[12]

Other than telling its readers that Joseph was not the father of Jesus and that Jesus' conception was dependent on the working of the Spirit, which, as we have seen, does not usually entail the absence of a man's part in procreation, Matthew's account appears to reveal nothing more about how Mary conceived. Unless we assume that this matter was of no interest to Matthew and his first readers, there are only two viable explanations of this gap in the account. One is that they are so familiar with a tradition that Jesus was conceived miraculously without any male involved in the process that this can simply be presupposed. Readers can then be

---

[11] As has been noted, a standard meaning for *parthenos* is that of a young woman of child-bearing age who has not yet given birth, a maiden, a young unmarried woman. Biological virginity is not in view in this usage, although frequently it is likely to be the case, discernible from contextual factors, that such a young woman is also virginal. For the general use, see e.g. Pausanias 8.20.4; Diodorus Siculus, *Bibliotheca historica* 20.84.3; Lycophron, *Alexandra* 1141, 1175; Sophocles, *Oedipus Rex* 1462. A clear instance in which *parthenos* cannot refer to a virgin is provided by Sophocles, *Women of Trachis* 1216–1229, where the dying Heracles implores his son to marry a *parthenos* who has already been his own lover, and for a non-virginal use in the LXX, see Gen. 34.3. For some of the ambiguities and complexities surrounding the meaning of *parthenos* in distinction from the abstract noun *parthenia* (virginity) in Greek literature, cf. M. F. Foskett, *A Virgin Conceived* (Bloomington, IN: University of Indiana Press, 2002), 25–9. Cf. also Miller, *Born Divine*, 189–93.

[12] Cf. also Pseudo-Phocylides, *Sent.* 186: 'Do not lay your hand upon your wife when she is pregnant', a Hellenistic Jewish text from between 100 BCE and 100 CE. Cf. Catchpole, *Jesus People*, 87. Philo also has this view, speaking of those who behave unchastely with their own wives, seeking pleasure rather than procreation (*Spec.* 3.9, 113), because 'the end we seek in wedlock is not pleasure but the begetting of lawful children' (*Ios.* 43). D. C. Allison, 'Divorce, Celibacy and Joseph', in *Studies in Matthew* (Grand Rapids: Baker Academic, 2005), 163–72, suggests that righteous Joseph providing 'an illustration of proper sexual conduct within marriage' can be seen as supplementing the traditional interpretation of 1.25a and cites further Hellenistic and patristic texts that indicate that intercourse during pregnancy was considered to be 'against nature'.

expected to pick up on the one possible allusion to this tradition the account offers and realize that the term *parthenos* in the Isaiah citation should now be interpreted not, as expected from its LXX source, as a young woman but as a virgin. This is certainly possible and, despite the account's lack of interest in depicting the conception as a miracle, is how most of its later readers have interpreted it, presumably under the influence of Luke's story and later credal tradition. But there is, of course, another fairly obvious explanation. Matthew was aware of another tradition, one that Jewish opponents would use against Christian claims about Jesus, namely, that some other unidentified male was the father.

It needs to be said at this stage of our exploration that this explanation should not be ruled out immediately simply because it may be shocking to later Christian sensibilities. For early Christians who believed that the Messiah died in the most scandalous of all circumstances, as a common criminal crucified by Romans, it would not necessarily have been unthinkable that he had also been born in scandalous circumstances. But this digression into possible explanations of the gaps in Matthew's account is already in danger of taking us too far ahead of ourselves.

So far our reading of Matthew's actual narrative has indicated the plausibility of the view that it may not, contrary to what most assume, require a virginal conception for its coherence. Before attempting to assess this view further, we need to note three other factors that could tell in its favour and that require serious consideration.

Matthew's redaction

Since there is general agreement that Matthew has employed traditional material in his annunciation narrative, his use has potential to shed light on his assumptions, including those about the knowledge with which he expected his readers to be familiar. Tradition-historical approaches are beset by uncertainties and so our own analysis will be relatively conservative, restricted to looking for signs of highly probable editorial activity on preceding traditional material.[13] The opening sentence, 'Now the birth of Jesus the Messiah took place in this way' (1.18a), has been supplied by Matthew. So has his advance notice to readers that Mary's pregnancy is 'from the holy Spirit' (1.18d), anticipating a major element in the resolution of Joseph's dilemma. The qualifying description of Joseph in

---

[13] On this, see Catchpole, *Resurrection People*, 73–4; cf. also the reconstruction and analysis of pre-Matthean material in Brown, *Birth*, 104–19, 154–63.

the address at the beginning of the announcement – 'son of David' (1.20c) – is also redactional with its stress on the Davidic lineage that Matthew had already made through his use of the genealogy.[14] Most extensive is the evangelist's addition, 'Now all this took place to fulfil the word of the Lord . . .', followed by the citation of LXX Isaiah 7.14 and the explanation of the name Emmanuel (1.22–23). These verses are an insertion into the traditional material, which would have run more smoothly from the angel's command to Joseph to name Mary's son Jesus (1.21) to his obedience to the command once his dream was over (1.24–25). Finally, the mention of Joseph having no marital relations until Mary had borne the child (1.25a) interrupts the straightforward account of his obedience to the angelic command. Removing these editorial additions suggests that Matthew inherited a story that begins with Mary being found pregnant during her betrothal to Joseph and of Joseph, believing the child not to be his, planning to divorce her. This course of action is prevented by the appearance of an angel to him in a dream and by an announcement, telling him to marry Mary, because the child is 'from the holy Spirit'. In addition, he is to name the child Jesus, because he will save his people from their sins. This he does. In this traditional material there is no mention of Mary's virginity and no reason to take 'from the holy Spirit' as having, from the standpoint of Jewish Scripture, an unprecedented meaning of miraculous activity that bypasses normal human procreation. In addition, nothing here suggests Joseph was incorrect in his original analysis. The angel does not tell him he was wrong in thinking that Mary was pregnant by another man but does tell him that he was wrong in the conclusion he has drawn from this, namely, that he should divorce her. The alternative or revised reading of Matthew proposes, then, that this source material does not have in it a virginal conception and that the final form of the narrative with Matthew's additions is more likely to be in continuity with its source than to take it in the quite different direction of a virginal conception without much more explicit indicators from its narrator that this is in fact taking place.

The women in the genealogy

Preceding the annunciation story is the genealogy, which prepares readers for interpreting the birth that follows and whose pattern Matthew strikingly

---

[14] A phrase qualifying the addressee does not occur enough to be thought a standard feature of scriptural annunciations, *pace* Brown, *Birth*, 156–8.

disrupts through the addition of five women to the conventional list of males. At its end Joseph is described as 'the husband of Mary, from whom Jesus was born' (1.16). But before that, four other women, Tamar, Rahab, Ruth and the wife of Uriah, otherwise known to us as Bathsheba, have been included (1.3, 5, 6). This is a very rare phenomenon in ancient genealogies. Why are these women there and why are these four singled out, while well-known matriarchs such as Sarah, Rebekah and Rachel, who needed divine intervention in order to conceive, are not included?

Among the variety of answers, two predominate. It could be that both are right and they are therefore complementary, but the second in fact turns out to be more compelling. The first suggests that these women were all non-Israelites. Tamar was the Canaanite wife of Judah's eldest son, Er. Later tradition (*Jub.* 41.1; *T. Jud.* 10.1) specifies that she was an Aramean. Rahab was a Canaanite from the time of the conquest of the land. Ruth was a Moabite, and Moabites were specifically excluded from the Israelite community, even after ten generations (cf. Deut. 23.3; Neh. 13.1). So she was a foreigner who could not, according to the law, be part of Israel. Bathsheba is described as the wife of Uriah the Hittite. This does not necessarily mean that she was herself a Hittite, though Matthew might have inferred that, but it does mean that she had been in a marriage with a foreigner, and according to later rabbinic law that would have caused her to be considered a foreigner herself. So in all four cases the point would be that foreigners were included in the story of Israel and were indeed part of the ancestry of the great king David. Matthew, then, is seen as already indicating that the story of Israel is open to the inclusion of Gentiles, anticipating the coming of the magi (2.1–12), Jesus' response to the faith of the Gentile centurion (8.5–13) and of the Canaanite woman (15.21–28) during his ministry, and the mission to all the nations that will follow that ministry (24.14; 28.19). Two points tell against this construal being the only or the most satisfactory explanation. It is not clear that at the time of Matthew Jews would have seen these women simply as Gentiles or would rather have considered them Jewish proselytes, which would clearly not have fitted the Gentile mission theme so well. But, more importantly, this proposal does not directly connect the mention of the women to their immediate context in Matthew or to the other woman in the genealogy, Mary, whom they surely anticipate. Mary was, of course, not a foreigner.[15] What one needs to ask is not whether they have some

---

[15] Though, as we shall see later, in providing a historical reconstruction of the illegitimacy tradition, some argue that the father of her child may well have been.

connection to the Gospel narrative as a whole but, more specifically, what it is that the five women in the genealogy have in common.[16]

This is where the second answer to the question about the presence of the women makes better sense. It points to what is known about their sexual activity and underlines its irregularity or scandal. Tamar's husband, Er, died, and his brother, Onan, then refused to consummate a union with her as part of his duties as brother-in-law, because he knew that though he would be the biological father, he would not be the legal father – that would be his dead brother. So Tamar was promised by her father-in-law, Judah, that, on coming of age, his youngest son, Shelah, would be her husband (cf. Gen. 38). But Judah failed to keep his word and so, by dressing up as a prostitute, Tamar tricked Judah himself into having intercourse with her and making her pregnant. On learning that she had become pregnant, Judah wanted his daughter-in-law to be put to death by burning, but she was able to prove him to be the father and he ended up by having to acknowledge, 'she is more in the right [righteous] than I, since I did not give her to my son Shelah' (38.26). Rahab did not just pose as a prostitute on one occasion but was a professional prostitute, yet one whose hospitality towards and protection of the Israelite spies made the conquest of Jericho possible (Josh. 2; 6.25). In looking for a husband, Ruth, the widow, attracts the attention of Boaz who turns out to be a relative who can act as next of kin. To get Boaz, who would not be expected to marry a Moabite enemy of Israel, to act in this way, Ruth takes the initiative, going to him at night, putting him in a compromised position on the threshing floor and uncovering his feet, which can be a euphemism for uncovering the genitals, in a story with much sexual innuendo (Ruth 3). The story of Ruth has the royal line of Judah as a major concern and it is significant that it concludes with an explicit reference back to Tamar's story (4.12) and with a genealogy that includes four of the men who are linked with the four women in Matthew's genealogy (4.18–22): Perez (with Tamar), Salmon (with Rahab), Boaz (with Ruth) and David (with the wife of Uriah). The last of these, David, produces Solomon by another man's wife, Bathsheba. This was an adulterous relationship in which she was the

---

[16] P.-B. Smit, 'Something about Mary? Remarks about the Five Women in the Matthean Genealogy', *NTS* 56 (2010), 191–207, allows for the Gentile interpretation as secondary but argues that gender issues are more significant than ethnic ones, that the five women are to be viewed as one group and that the function of the first four is to prepare for and vindicate the awkward circumstances of Jesus' irregular birth. He points out that the use of the verb and preposition (*gennaō ek*) 'to describe the birth of Jesus from Mary is consistent with the expression used (only!) in 1.3, 5–6 of the genealogy' (198) and therefore provides continuity rather than discontinuity between Mary and what is said of the women in the earlier formulaic pattern.

victim of David's lust and of what we would be inclined to call an act of
rape, since she was powerless to resist the demands of the monarch (2
Sam. 11). Seen in this light, the four women prepare for the account
involving Mary as the mother of Jesus and what would be considered the
scandal surrounding her pregnancy.[17] If it were thought that her child was
not Joseph's, then Jesus would have been treated as a *mamzer*, a child born
of a prohibited sexual union, an Israelite of suspect paternity,[18] and according to Deuteronomy 23.2, no *mamzer*, no one born of an illicit union,
should be admitted to the assembly of the Lord, nor his descendants down
to the tenth generation. In this story Joseph initially thinks that Mary's as
yet unborn child will have this status, and his later naming and taking
him as his own child is meant to deal with that. But Matthew's point is
that, if the Abrahamic and Davidic line of descent to the Messiah was
carried forward through the anomalous sexual activity involving these
four women, and if indeed the very first 'son of David' who was Israel's
king was the result of an adulterous relationship, then there should be no
surprise if Jesus' conception and birth involved a sexual scandal in the
case of Mary. It is no accident that the four women are unevenly distrib-
uted in the genealogy. They are included immediately before and immediately after David – and nowhere else. David's own ancestry and that of
his first successor are shown to have anomalies. What connects Mary with
the four women, then, is the similar scandal or irregularity surrounding
her relationship with Joseph and her conceiving. Such a stigma should be
no obstacle to viewing Jesus as the Messiah in the line of David.

In itself this interpretation of the presence of the four women in the
genealogy might be regarded as compatible with a reading of Matthew as
involving either a virginal or a non-virginal conception, because it simply
stresses the irregularity of the birth. But the point of introducing these
four as in some way the precursors of the fifth woman, Mary, is that each
could be included in the messianic lineage despite their participation in
scandalous sexual activity within ordinary human relationships. Whether
the scandal surrounding the fifth woman is best explained by a miraculous

---

[17] For similar interpretations of the significance of the four women, cf. also e.g. Schaberg, *Illegitimacy*, 20–34; Miller, *Born Divine*, 82–5. Brown, *Birth*, 73–4, appears to agree with this interpretation: 'It is the combination of the scandalous or irregular union and of divine intervention through the woman that explains best Matthew's choice in the genealogy.' In the Supplement (594–5) he explains that what he really meant by 'divine intervention' was that the women became vehicles of God's messianic plan. He misrepresents Schaberg's view, however, by characterizing it, and then criticiz-ing it, in terms of the five women having in common the giving of birth illegitimately (593–4).
[18] On this, see B. Chilton, *Rabbi Jesus: An Intimate Biography* (New York: Doubleday, 2000), 12–13.

conception remains to be explored. But at the level of Matthew's account and its coherence there would appear to be greater continuity between the situation of the preceding four women and that of the fifth, if the scandal surrounding Mary's conceiving involved sexual irregularity within human relationships rather than their complete disruption.

It should be noted here that this reading of Matthew's account as involving Joseph initially thinking Jesus would be a *mamzer* should be distinguished from any view that Matthew depicted Jesus as continuing to have this status. Just as in Matthew's Gospel as a whole there is no sign that belief in a virginal conception has affected the plot or characterization at any other point in the narrative, so also there is no indication that a belief that Jesus was illegitimate has affected the rest of the narrative. If Jesus had had the status of a *mamzer*, then, as we noted earlier, according to Deuteronomy 23.2, he should not have been admitted to the assembly of the Lord, yet Matthew does not hesitate to depict Jesus as teaching in the synagogues throughout Galilee (4.23; 9.35), teaching in the synagogue of his home town, Nazareth (13.54), healing in a synagogue (12.9–14) and giving extended parabolic teaching and disputing with Pharisees and Sadducees in the Temple (21.23—24.1). If Jesus were known to be of suspect paternity, he would simply have been disbarred from entering such places. What is more, while someone considered illegitimate was marginalized and had no social status, this is not at all how Jesus is portrayed elsewhere in the Gospel.[19] Texts such as Ecclesiasticus 23.22–26; Wisdom of Solomon 3.16–19; 4.3–6 make very clear that the children of illicit unions share the punishment and dishonour of their adulterous parent for their entire lives. Rabbinic literature indicates that they were socially ostracized, segregated from the rest of Jewish society and regarded as outcasts.[20] When, then, in 9.10–13 (cf. also 11.19) Matthew records that the Pharisees took offence at Jesus eating with tax collectors and sinners, this would make little sense if they already considered Jesus himself to be an outcast. Such behaviour would be only to be expected; other outcasts would be Jesus' natural companions. The offence is that Jesus is doing something that is not in accord with his social status as a religious teacher and is ignoring purity regulations in doing so. Again, if he were a *mamzer*, he would have been regarded as impure anyway. The trading of accusations is part of Matthew's extensive portrayal of

---

[19] See the convincing case made by J. McGrath, 'Was Jesus Illegitimate? The Evidence of His Social Interactions', *JSHJ* 5 (2007), 81–100, in regard to the traditions about the historical Jesus.
[20] Cf. McGrath, 'Was Jesus Illegitimate?', 85.

the encounters between Jesus and the Pharisees. Within a Mediterranean society dominated by the values of honour and shame the controversies and their challenges that are part of these encounters only make sense if Jesus is regarded as of similar social standing to his interlocutors. According to the social code, only equals can take part in such disputes. Those of superior status simply did not take part in public controversy with those of lesser status because their honour was not engaged by the affront of an inferior and had nothing to suffer. Likewise, someone who was a social outcast, such as a *mamzer*, would have been perceived as having no honour to defend and an entirely unsuitable participant in such controversies. For this key part of Jesus' ministry, as Matthew presents it, to have any plausibility, both the Pharisees and any onlookers would have had to perceive Jesus as having sufficient social standing in order to be a worthy participant.[21] These considerations effectively rule out the view that Matthew actually thought that Jesus was illegitimate in the sense of being a *mamzer*. What remains plausible, however, is that Matthew held that Jesus was illegitimate simply in the sense that he was illegitimately conceived by someone other than Joseph and that he depicts this issue as immediately resolved through Joseph's public acknowledgement of Jesus as his own son. Although Jesus had been conceived irregularly, Joseph's acceptance of him meant that he would not have been seen as a *mamzer*; there would have been no public questioning of his paternity or treatment of him as having any other status than Joseph's son. Matthew's account effectively further excludes any good reason for Jesus' compatriots to question his paternity because, by the time his parents set up home in Nazareth, they already constitute a bona fide family (2.23).

The role of the male assumed but omitted in scriptural accounts of conception

One further factor can be brought into play in a reading that takes Matthew's account to be about a conception involving a human male, even though that male was not Joseph. There are scriptural accounts of conception, especially about those who are to have a significant role in Israel's history, in which only the divine agent and the mother are mentioned, although the accounts assume the role of a human male. Against the backdrop of the ancient view that what was needed for conception

---

[21] Cf. also McGrath, 'Was Jesus Illegitimate?', 95.

was the generative male seed and the female womb, whose blood or fluids provided the material substance to which the seed gave life and form, the Jewish Scriptures emphasized the role of Israel's Creator God in this process. God is seen not only as opening or closing the womb to bring about the birth of a child but also as the one who creates the embryo in the womb. So Job can say of God, 'Did not he who made me in the womb make them? And did not one fashion us in the womb?' (Job 31.15, cf. also 10.8–12). The well-known psalm, attributed to David, proclaims, 'For it was you who formed my inward parts; you knit me together in my mother's womb. I praise you, for I am fearfully and wonderfully made . . . Your eyes beheld my unformed substance' (Ps. 139.13–16). What is significant is that in such depictions it is simply God and the mother's womb with its unformed substance that are involved in conception. Present-day readers tend to assume too quickly that this language was understood metaphorically. These writers, we think, knew that in fact both male seed and the substance provided by the female produced an embryo and they are simply attributing the whole process to God generally as the creative source of life in the first place. In other words, we understand such language by reading it in the light of the theological distinction, inherited particularly from Aquinas, between primary and secondary causation and suppose the ancient writers would have thought similarly. But the matter is not so simple. The writers of such scriptural texts shared the dominant Aristotelian view of how conception occurred but adapted it distinctively so that there were three parties involved in conception – God, the male with his seed, and the female with the blood or fluids of her womb – and all three parties were understood to be actively involved in the production of a human foetus. In the birth of Cain, all three parties are involved; 'the man knew his wife, Eve, and she conceived and bore Cain, saying, "I have acquired a man with the Lord"' (literal translation of Eve's words – Gen. 4.1–2).[22] Cain's conception is a three-party affair but Eve's pronouncement gives the credit to the divine rather than the human male party. When Rachel says to Jacob, 'Give me children, or I shall die!', Jacob angrily responds, 'Am I in the place of God, who has withheld from you the fruit of the womb?' (Gen. 30.1–2). Later it is, of course, God who heeds Rachel and opens her womb, so that she conceives (cf. Gen. 30.22–23). When in Judges 13 the angel of the Lord appears to Manoah's previously barren wife and announces, 'You shall conceive and bear a son' (13.3), what

---

[22] Most translations make the Hebrew easier for readers by interpreting Eve's words with a phrase such as 'with the help of the Lord' (NRSV).

follows stresses her preparation for this conception and birth of one who will be a nazirite to God from birth by refraining from drinking alcohol or eating anything unclean but does not mention Manoah's 'going in to her' or 'knowing her'. Readers rightly fill in the gap and assume that the third party, Manoah, did his part, but the narrator feels no compunction to state this.

So ancient biology and Jewish theology are not kept in separate spheres but are intermingled and when God's activity is emphasized, the male's role can frequently be elided. 'In the Hebrew Bible, the woman is God's primary partner in bringing forth Israel.'[23] While in the biblical literature this view of reproduction is mostly implicit, it is made explicit in the rabbinic writings that employ biblical texts. Again there is the tradition of three partners. The emphasis is on the role of the divine partner, the male seed is present, though without God it is unable to create the embryo, and there is the contribution of the female through her blood to the substance of the embryo.[24] God's active involvement is seen in a particularly striking fashion in *Leviticus Rabbah* 14.5, which takes Psalm 51.7 (5) and its statement about David's conception – 'Behold I was brought forth in iniquity, and in sin did my mother conceive me' – and explains it as follows.

> David said before the Holy Blessed One, 'Master of all the worlds, my father Jesse had no intention of having me, he only intended [to satisfy] his own needs. Know that this is such because when they were taking care of their needs, one turned his face this way and the other turned her face the other way. And You inserted each and every drop [into my mother's womb].' Like that which David said, Though my father and my mother have forsaken me, the Lord will gather me in (Ps. 27.10).

Here David is said to have been conceived in iniquity because his parents had no intention of procreating and engaged in some form of *coitus interruptus*, but though in this sense David was forsaken by father and mother, God gathered David in, literally, by inserting the semen in his mother's womb. This example conveys graphically the extent to which God's creative activity was envisaged as ongoing and as necessary for conception.[25] 'Rabbinic traditions about procreation bring together the macrocosm (cosmos) and the microcosm (embryo), and attribute the creation of both to God.'[26] Yet because of this concern to show God as active in procreation,

---

[23] G. Kessler, *Conceiving Israel: The Fetus in Rabbinic Narratives* (Philadelphia: University of Pennsylvania Press, 2009), 113.

[24] See Kessler, *Conceiving*, 89–126 for this analysis of rabbinic 'bio-theology'.

[25] Cf. Kessler, *Conceiving*, 97–9, 121–3.

[26] Kessler, *Conceiving*, 126.

what is also noticeable is 'the extent to which men's contributions through seed are de-emphasized relative to God's'.[27]

To return to the Jewish Scriptures, it becomes especially significant that the male partner in the reproductive threesome is omitted from the picture in the conception of key figures. In Isaiah 7.14 itself no male partner is mentioned for the young woman who will conceive Emmanuel but he is presupposed. This also occurs with David, if the language of Psalm 139, noted above, was, as is highly probable, read in the light of its traditional ascription to David. Similarly in the case of the prophet Jeremiah, God says, 'Before I formed you in the womb I knew you, and before you were born I consecrated you; I appointed you a prophet to the nations' (Jer. 1.5) and the servant figure is told in Isaiah 44.2, 'Thus says the Lord who made you, who formed you in the womb and will help you' (cf. also 44.24; 49.1–6). In each case the life force that generates and develops the foetus in the mother's womb is divine, and in emphasizing the divine initiative any mention of male seed, to which in any case God is required to give life, disappears.

In the light of this discussion, then, it could be claimed that the absence of the mention of male involvement in Matthew's account of Jesus' conception simply means that readers are supposed to assume this. After all, the evangelist would simply be following what Scripture had done with other key figures in Israel's history in eliding any mention of the male contribution to the conception of this child who had been elected from the womb for an extraordinary role in the salvation of God's people. By talking only of God's Spirit and Mary's womb and by announcing the child's future role, the narrative indicates that Joseph is to play his part, whoever the actual father, by obeying the angelic instruction instead of divorcing Mary, because God has a special purpose for this child.

The traditional reading

Given the strengths of this alternative reading, how does the traditional reading, which sees the account as entailing a virginal conception, fare and how might its advocates respond? The dominant interpretation has usually thought its view was so self-evident that it needed little discussion.[28]

---

[27] Kessler, *Conceiving*, 115.

[28] So e.g. W. D. Davies and D. C. Allison, *The Gospel according to Saint Matthew* Vol. 1 (Edinburgh: T. & T. Clark, 1988), 221, state, 'Matthew, we can be sure, believed in the virginal conception of Jesus', having previously asserted without further ado, 'Joseph now knows what the reader knows from 1.18. Mary has conceived miraculously by the Holy Spirit' (208). Brown, *Birth*, 124–5, 138, simply

In case at this stage we need reminding, it has held that the narrator tells readers in advance that Mary 'was found to be with child from the holy Spirit' (1.18d), anticipating the angel's announcement that is a crucial part of the resolution of Joseph's dilemma – 'the child conceived in her is from the holy Spirit' (1.20d). Joseph has to know that he was wrong about the suspicion that led him to decide on divorce. Though he is not the father, this child has been conceived through the agency of the divine Spirit and this is seen as a direct, non-sexual act of creative power. If there were any doubt about this conception not involving any human male, this is decisively removed by the narrator's own interpretation of what has been recounted through his citation of the Isaiah 7.14 scriptural text that the one who shall conceive is a virgin. The original passage may not have had a miraculous birth to a virgin in view, but the LXX translation of 'young woman' by *parthenos* has opened up a possibility of meaning that is exploited in Matthew in the light of what was believed to have happened in the case of Jesus. In any case, the narrator's view that Mary is a virgin is confirmed in the last part of the passage. Why else would he underline that Joseph 'had no marital relations with her until she had borne a son' (1.25a)? He wants to leave no doubt that Joseph was not the father, that the male role had been replaced by the agency of the Spirit and that Mary would give birth as a virgin.[29] To this basic outline some would add that such an interpretation is already anticipated in the wording of 1.16 – 'Mary, of whom Jesus was born' – in which the aorist passive form of the verb *gennaō* should be taken as a *passivum divinum* with God as the implied agent of the action of begetting. Others would underline its further continuity with the genealogy, as we have seen, by noting that what matters about the other four women is the suggestion of scandal surrounding their sexual activity or procreation and this would certainly characterize public reaction to the claim of a virginal conception in Mary's case. Again this appears to be a plausible and coherent reading and certainly generations of readers have found it to be so. Yet we have seen that the main planks in its case have come under strong attack from the alternative

---

assumes that the language of 'through the Holy Spirit' rules out any human agent in the conception and asserts that the manner of begetting is creative rather than sexual, though, interestingly, later when discussing the four other women in the genealogy, he can say, 'they played an important role in God's plan and were instruments of His Providence (or of the Holy Spirit)' (143)! His later response in the Supplement to Schaberg's detailed discussion of 1.18, 20 is essentially a non-response, content to assert that her argument is 'most extraordinary' and that a claim that Jesus' father could have been a rapist 'destroys the theological identity of Jesus' intended by Matthew (601).

[29] Cf. Davies and Allison, *Matthew*, 218; Brown, *Birth*, 138.

reading which also argues that its plausibility and coherence only hold if one first assumes that the evangelist and his readers already know of a tradition of a virginal conception and yet what is at issue is whether Matthew's account itself witnesses to a virginal conception. Before prematurely deciding that the debate may be at an impasse, it is worth further evaluating the comparative merits of the two readings and exploring whether there are other factors that might strengthen the exegetical case for the traditional interpretation.

Reassessing readings

Women in the genealogy and 1.16

We begin with the last two points listed in the case for the traditional reading, since they are not particularly strong and can be dealt with briefly. In fact we have already indicated that, if the primary reason for the inclusion of the previous four women in the genealogy is, as has been proposed, irregularity in their sexual activity that evokes an element of scandal, then the alternative reading may have the better of the argument since it provides greater continuity with Mary if the sexual irregularity occurred between humans rather than as a result of the divine suspension of the normal means of procreation. It is possible, of course, that Matthew and his readers were not as concerned with this logical coherence and were content to find in the mention of the women an anticipation of the scandal that would surround Mary, whatever its cause. It is also possible to read the aorist passive in 1.16 as a divine passive. On the traditional view this is accompanied by the assertion that of course the divine role was creative and bypassed the sexual and procreative. It is frequently not realized, however, that this view of 1.16 requires a significant shift in the force of the verb *gennaō*. Throughout the genealogy 'to beget' has been used of the normal human action of procreating through sexual activity, but now without warning readers would be expected to know simply from the passive form, which would anyway be appropriate if the reference were to some male other than the one whose genealogy was being claimed, that the meaning of the verb had changed and no longer had the previous connotations of begetting in view. The earlier discussion of Jewish 'bio-theology' also casts some doubt on whether a notion that separates God's creative activity so neatly from the actual processes of reproduction would have been easily entertained. The traditional reading might well have to accept Räisänen's version of it, when he concludes, particularly in relation to 1.18, 20, 'it could hardly be stated more clearly that the Spirit fulfils the role of the father in Jesus' birth. Mary has indeed been impregnated by the Holy Spirit.'[30]

Use of LXX Isaiah 7.14

We saw earlier that one of the lynchpins in the traditional reading – the mention of a virgin conceiving in the citation of LXX Isaiah 7.14 – is not necessarily secure. The traditional view, as articulated by its recent upholders, claims that Matthew, ignoring the force of *parthenos* in his source, has exploited another more technical sense of the term in order to underline that Mary's conception was not through the normal means assumed by the LXX text of Isaiah but occurred while she was still virginal. On this version the evangelist knows of this virginal conception tradition and is able to find a text from Scripture that in the light of the new event can be seen to point towards it. The alternative reading, as we have seen, holds that Matthew has given readers no reason to think, that although Joseph was not the father, no male was, and therefore no reason to think that the term *parthenos* has a meaning other than that in the LXX source, namely, a young woman of child-bearing age.

Supporters of the traditional reading might well claim in response that the alternative approach has not paid sufficient attention to the phenomenon that we mentioned in Chapter 3, namely Matthew's formula quotations, the ten times he specifically introduces a quotation with a formula about fulfilment of Scripture. Here, in 1.22, in introducing the Emmanuel quotation, he has 'all this took place to fulfil what had been spoken by the Lord through the prophet'. While in the quotations of Scripture common to Matthew and Mark the LXX is the primary source and while, in those peculiar to Matthew, the non-formula ones are generally LXX in form or show only minor variations, this is not the case with the formula quotations. In these, and in some of the adaptations of quotations he has in common with Mark, the evangelist shows his knowledge of Hebrew text forms. In fact, most of the formula quotations are either his Greek rendering of the Masoretic Text (MT) or are mixed citations that combine the LXX and MT text forms.[31] His virtually complete agreement in wording with the LXX in the formula citation of 1.22–23 therefore stands out as

---

[30] H. Räisänen, 'Begotten by the Holy Spirit', in eds M. Nissinen and R. Uro, *Sacred Marriages* (Winona Lake, IN: Eisenbrauns, 2008), 330.

[31] M. J. J. Menken, *Matthew's Bible: The Old Testament Text of the Evangelist* (Leuven: Leuven University Press, 2004), however, proposes that in the fulfilment quotations Matthew employs an already existing revised text of the LXX.

exceptional. In this light, then, it looks as though Matthew has deliber-
ately chosen the LXX wording here, when he could have done what he
has done elsewhere in his formula quotations and worked with forms of
the Hebrew text. The reason he has followed the LXX so closely here, it
can be argued, should be obvious; its use of *parthenos* allows him to express
what he and his readers would be assuming all along, namely, a virginal
conception.[32] This appears to be a fairly strong point on the side of the
traditional reading.

It is not completely decisive, however, for the following reasons. First,
it can be questioned how far the text forms of the formula quotations
should be seen as in a quite separate category from the text forms of
Matthew's other distinctive citations of Scripture.[33] Second, with the possible minor exception of 2.23, the formula quotations do not require
giving the words of the scriptural passages as they are now rendered by
Matthew a meaning that they did not originally have. To be sure, what
has happened in the life of Jesus now gives those words a whole new
dimension, not by requiring them to mean something different from what
was meant originally but by that original meaning being illuminated and
filled out in the new context of Jesus' mission.[34] Third, there is in any case
another and perhaps clearer reason for Matthew's choice of the LXX text
that is frequently ignored. His interest in the text is primarily in the name
Emmanuel, indicated by his making at this point his one minor change
in the LXX wording in order to adjust the text to its new context – the
shift from the LXX's 'you shall call' to 'they shall call' – and it is the LXX
and not the MT that will go on to give him precisely the wording he needs
for the explanation following the citation: 'God with us' (LXX Isa. 8.8; cf.
also 8.10).[35] The appeal to the character of Matthew's formula quotations
does not, therefore, rule out thinking that Matthew understood Isaiah 7.14
in the way the LXX does, as referring to one who was at the time a virgin
but who would conceive naturally. But the traditional reading makes a
good point and can be strengthened by asking, even though Matthew's
main reason for employing the LXX text may be his interest in the

---

[32] Cf. Brown, *Birth*, 150.

[33] Cf. also e.g. Luz, *Matthew 1—7*, 156–62.

[34] On the relationship between the quotation wording and its new context in the formula quotations,
cf. e.g. G. M. Soares Prabhu, *The Formula Quotations in the Infancy Narrative of Matthew* (Rome:
Biblical Institute Press, 1976), 159–61.

[35] The assertion of Menken, *Matthew's Bible*, 120–1 that 'it is impossible to decide from where the
very literal translation . . . derives' inexplicably overlooks LXX Isa. 8.8, 10 as the source. Brown,
Birth, 152–3, does, however, see this as a factor in Matthew's use of Isa. 7.14.

Emmanuel title and its meaning, how likely it is that, aware of the range of meanings of *parthenos*, he would have chosen a version that had this term in order to gloss his annunciation story if he also knew or suspected that the child was in fact conceived normally but illegitimately.

'Begotten by the holy Spirit', Graeco-Roman biography and Philo

The crucial issue for the traditional interpretation is whether the alternative reading is right in its claim that 'begotten by the holy Spirit' would not, without clear further indications, have been understood in a Jewish context as excluding any male involvement in the conception. If that terminology could already be seen to signal a virginal conception, then the other aspects of the traditional reading would fall into place more coherently. Important here is how one defines 'Jewish context'. The alternative reading may well be in danger of forgetting the extent to which Jewish culture was part of the Hellenistic world and the extent to which the interpenetration of Judaism and Hellenism would have been part of the setting of Matthew's Gospel. While the language of 'begotten by God/the Spirit' to refer to a conception without a human father may not have been characteristic of Second Temple Jewish literature, similar formulations are, of course, used in Graeco-Roman stories of both legendary and historical heroes who were said to be the sons of a god. In Herodotus Hercules is one of the 12 gods begotten (*egenonto*) from the previous eight (*Hist.* 2.43, 145), Plato distinguishes present merely human legislators from both the ancient lawgivers and the heroes and sons of gods for whom they legislated, all of whom were offspring of the gods (*Leg.* 9.853; cf. also 12.948), Aristotle says that Hesiod and the mythologists asserted 'the first principles to be gods and born (*gegonenai*) of gods' (*Metaph.* 1000a) and Plutarch can talk of the report that Theseus 'was begotten by Poseidon' (*Thes.* 6) and speak of Alexander carrying himself 'very haughtily before the barbarians, as if fully persuaded of his divine birth (*geneseōs*) . . .' (*Alex.* 28). Plutarch in his book of table talk also has a section headed '. . . and about the reported birth (*geneseōs*) from gods' (*Quaest. conv.* 8.1), in which there is discussion about begetting and being begotten as repugnant to the immortality of the deity. None of these references are, of course, about being begotten by the Spirit specifically, but Plutarch again can comment that wise Egyptians find it possible that 'a woman can be approached by a divine spirit (*pneuma*) and made pregnant' (*Num.* 4.2–4; cf. also *Quaest. conv.* 8.1).

Such examples would suggest that, if Matthew and his tradition were assuming familiarity with Graeco-Roman or Egyptian stories about the gods begetting children, the language of being conceived or begotten by God's Spirit could well have signalled a virginal conception. Such stories circulated widely across the Mediterranean world and it would be surprising if they had passed Matthew and his readers by.[36] Trypho in the dialogue with Justin provides clear evidence that educated Jews would no doubt have been aware of them (cf. *Dial.* 67–70). Perhaps more telling is the first-century evidence from the writings of Philo, a Greek-speaking Jew who appears to be familiar with such stories while engaging extensively in retellings of Jewish Scripture. What is striking is that, while he does so on the allegorical level, in a number of his scriptural interpretations he can talk about God generating life in female characters, specifically described as virgins, without any male agency. In particular, in *De cherubim* 40–50 he can draw on the notion of a divine begetting through mortal women, when, in order to expound divine generation of the virtues, he depicts Sarah, Leah, Rebecca and Zipporah being made virgins and then becoming pregnant by God's seed without the aid of their husbands. Philo does this through developing hints and gaps in the text where the male contribution is overlooked. So he makes much of LXX Genesis 21.1, which does not mention Abraham but talks of the Lord looking on Sarah (who was by herself, Philo adds) and doing for her as the Lord had said, as a result of which she conceives (*Cher.* 45). In the case of Leah, he points out that God is said to do what the husband normally does – 'God opened her womb' (LXX Gen. 29.31) – and so 'virtue received the divine seed from the Cause', i. e. God (*Cher.* 46, cf. also *Leg.* 2.47). On the basis of LXX Genesis 25.21, Philo talks of Isaac making supplication on behalf of Rebecca, who represents perseverance, and of her conceiving by the One who received the supplication, while Moses is said, without having to make supplication, to have found that Zipporah had conceived by no mortal and thus, by implication, by God (cf. LXX Exod. 2.22). In the same passage Philo holds Jeremiah, like himself, to be one who has been initiated into the mysteries, since LXX Jeremiah 3.4 speaks of God as the husband of Israel's virginity,

> clearly showing that God is . . . the husband of wisdom sowing the seed of blessedness for the mortal race into good and virgin soil. For it is fitting for God to hold converse with a nature undefiled and untouched and pure, the nature truly virgin, in a manner different from our manner; for in the case

---

[36] Cf. also A. Runesson, 'Giving Birth to Jesus in the Late First Century: Matthew as Midwife in the Context of Colonisation', in eds C. Clivaz et al., *Infancy Gospels* (Tübingen: Mohr Siebeck, 2011), 317–18.

of men the union for the begetting of children makes virgins to become women, but whenever God begins to converse with a soul, even if the soul was a woman before, he makes it again a virgin ... (*Cher.* 49–50)

Elsewhere, when employing this type of discourse, Philo can speak of God making Sarah, or virtue, pregnant by seeds from heaven, so that Isaac should be seen not as offspring of creation but as the work of the uncreated God, who can therefore 'most properly be said to be the father of Isaac' (*Det.* 59–60, 124). Similarly, Philo interprets Sarah's words about the lord who is older than her and who can cause Isaac's conception to refer to the divine Lord and 'the Lord has caused me laughter' to mean 'the Lord has begotten (*egennēsen*) Isaac' (*Leg.* 3.218–19; cf. also *Migr.* 142). For him, Hannah too is one of those women who can be said to have 'become pregnant, having received the divine seed' (*Deus* 5). Philo's discussions are usually dismissed as irrelevant on the grounds that he is allegorizing and does not think in terms of an actual virginal conception. But this is to miss the point. His discussions indicate clearly that the notion of God impregnating a virgin was readily available to him,[37] presumably from his acquaintance with Egyptian and Graeco-Roman legends, that he can employ this notion in the interpretation of the Jewish Scriptures, and that in the cases he mentions formulations using 'to beget' (*gennaō*) for the activity of God or 'of' (*ek*) in relation to the divine agency communicate this notion. Although Philo's work appears to have had little influence on later rabbinic literature, earlier his work was known to Josephus, for example, and finds some echoes both in the New Testament and in early rabbinic exegesis.[38] Philo's witness, therefore, constitutes strong evidence against a major claim of the alternative reading and in support of the traditional interpretation.

Matthew's setting and 1.25a

Some upholders of the traditional reading of a virginal conception are, however, loath to accept this sort of support, since they also work with too neat a distinction between Jewish and Hellenistic culture and wish to find the backdrop for Matthew's annunciation story simply in the Jewish Scriptures and their retellings.[39] In response, it has to be said that there is nothing in such sources that provides any anticipation of a virginal

---

[37] Cf. also Runesson, 'Giving Birth', 317n55.

[38] Cf. e.g. D. T. Runia, *Philo in Early Christian Literature: A Survey* (Assen: van Gorcum, 1993), 13, 63–86.

[39] Cf. Davies and Allison, *Matthew*, 21–2; Brown, *Birth*, 523, 579.

conception or accounts for Matthew's motif of the suspicion of adultery.[40] The closest one comes to a parallel in Jewish writings remains the strange birth of Melchizedek in *2 Enoch* 71, of much disputed date and provenance, where it is made clear that Nir had not slept with Sopanim, who is on the point of death, recently enough for her pregnancy to be explained and the child appears out of her corpse as a developed three-year-old with the badge of priesthood on his chest. But Philo's allegorical retellings of Jewish Scripture stories under the influence of Hellenistic notions of the gods begetting offspring with virgins demonstrates that the two need not be seen as separate categories and we have already seen in Chapter 3 that, while Matthew's infancy narrative has been shaped by Jewish haggadic traditions about the birth of Moses, it also has major features that correspond remarkably to the treatment of the early stages of their subjects' lives in Graeco-Roman biographies.[41] This is precisely what might be expected of Matthew's Gospel, produced in a Hellenistic Jewish setting, where before its composition Matthean Christians have also already embarked on a Gentile mission.

Recognition of this factor also helps the traditional reading of 1.25. Although the alternative approach offers a different plausible interpretation, which

---

[40] I am assuming, though there is not the space to demonstrate this here, that the recent attempts by R. D. Aus, *Matthew 1—2 and the Virginal Conception* (Lanham, MD: University Press of America, 2004) and Allison, *Studies in Matthew*, to find a Jewish precedent for virginal conception in this material or by A. J. Welburn, *From a Virgin Womb: The Apocalypse of Adam and the Virgin Birth* (Leiden: Brill, 2008) to find it via the *Apocalypse of Adam* have proved unsuccessful. In any case there is no evidence of the language of 'begotten by God / the Spirit' in their alleged parallels. I am also assuming that the disputed wording of the Qumran Rule of the Congregation, 1QSa, does not provide evidence. If the wording were 'When God begets the Messiah', then, like God's begetting the Davidic king, it would not imply absence of male involvement. But in any case the damaged fragment more likely reads: 'When God leads the Messiah'. M. J. Borg and J. D. Crossan, *The First Christmas: What the Gospels Really Teach about Jesus's Birth* (New York: HarperCollins, 2007), 105–10, propose that the suspicion of adultery arises from Matthew's use of the traditions about Amram to present Jesus' conception as that of the new Moses. There, as we have seen, discussion of the need to divorce or actual divorce is followed by a revelation that instructs Amram either to stay in his marriage or to remarry. According to this proposal Matthew needs a different reason for Joseph to consider divorce than the one Amram had – Pharaoh's decree – and so, in order to maintain the overall Joseph–Amram pattern, invents one: suspicion of adultery. This is possible, though Matthew does, of course, have the missing parallel to Amram's situation with Herod's decision later in 2.16 and it would not have been beyond his creativity to have moved this back into the setting for the announcement to Joseph. But in any case a more adequate analysis of Matthew's redaction indicates that suspicion of adultery would have been in Matthew's tradition and the proposal ignores the other elements in that tradition that have suggested a natural rather than a miraculous conception.

[41] Luz, *Matthew 1—7*, 117–18, is one advocate of the traditional reading who also holds that Matthew's tradition in a Hellenistic Jewish Christian context is linked with reports of the divine begetting of kings, philosophers and heroes.

could possibly be supplementary, the motif of abstention from intercourse during pregnancy does in fact correspond to what can be found in Graeco-Roman biographical accounts of conception from the gods. The various tellings of the birth of Plato all mention that Apollo, who had intercourse with Plato's mother, Perictione, appeared in a vision to his father, Ariston, and ordered him to have no intimacy with Perictione for ten months until after she had given birth (cf. e.g. Olympiodorus, *Vit. Plat.* 1; Diogenes Laertius, *Vit. Phil.* 3.1).[42] In this light it can also be noted that the interpretation of 1.25a as not only underlining that the child was not Joseph's but also indicating that he was doing what any righteous Jew would do, abstaining from intercourse during pregnancy, does not fit very well at this point in the account. It would be strange to emphasize again at this stage that the child was not Joseph's but someone else's when, on this reading, that had already been dealt with by the angelic announcement and equally strange to insert a comment about this aspect of Joseph's law-observant righteousness just here. It makes better sense to see it as an expansion on Joseph's obedience to the angelic instructions that underlines the absence of his own involvement in the extraordinary conception of this child by the Spirit.

Conclusion

Reassessing the rival readings has allowed us to see that a good and possibly more compelling case can be made for Matthew's account being about a virginal conception. Once one accepts, on the basis of Philo's writings and on the assumption that the evangelist and his readers had some familiarity with accounts of the birth of major figures in the Graeco-Roman world, that a begetting by the divine Spirit could entail a virginal conception, then the other issues more or less fall into place for some version of the traditional reading. It can now be seen, in the light of this terminology in 1.18, 20, that Matthew may well have had added reason to opt for the LXX of Isaiah 7.14, given the possibilities its use of *parthenos* opens up for an actual virginal conception. While the discussion of Jewish 'bio-theology' and its assumption that three parties were involved in procreation even when the human male was omitted in the depiction of the conception of key figures may have appeared to favour the alternative reading, it can also now be seen that it was precisely such elisions in scriptural texts that provided the basis for Philo then interpreting these

---

[42] Cf. also Luz, *Matthew 1—7*, 122.

in the sense of God begetting offspring through the woman without male involvement. If in Philo absence of the mention of the male need not necessarily mean that this is to be presupposed but can in fact signify actual absence of the male, then this certainly should not be ruled out for Matthew. And while the appearance of the women in the preceding gene-alogy appears to have a better explanation on the alternative reading, namely there was sexual irregularity in the case of all five women, the evangelist's point can now be given a different force. If there was actual sexual irregularity and scandal surrounding the first four women and yet God could still incorporate them within the line of Davidic descent, how much more is God able to include in the Davidic lineage this child whose conception only later gave rise to rumours and suspicions about illegitimate human sexual activity.

Since I have in the end preferred a version of the traditional reading, it might be asked why I did not simply treat the passage from this perspective in the first place. I hope that the preceding discussion has shown that the objections to this interpretation are simply too strong to be ignored in a critical reading and also that deciding for the traditional reading has required discussion of factors not usually found in the expositions of those who advocate it. Indeed some have felt the arguments for the alternative to be strong enough that they cannot decide between the two explanations of the passage and conclude that the text has enough gaps and ambiguities to support either reading, depending on the interests that are brought to that reading.[43] It is true that the text remains ambiguous at key points and that on neither reading does it make explicit the means of Jesus' conception. Since, however, the two rival readings are mutually exclusive on a matter of major significance for each, we have attempted to come to a probable evaluation of which has the better case. On the question of ambiguity and lack of explicitness, the alternative reading has a ready explanation of this phenomenon. If one is dealing with a tradition of an illegitimate conception, one might well not want to be explicit about its details but to refer to it only indirectly.[44] But there is a similar issue of

---

[43] This appears to be the conclusion of E. Wainwright, *Towards a Feminist Critical Reading of the Gospel of Matthew* (New York: de Gruyter, 1991), 74 and n55, 171–5, who thinks Schaberg 'makes clear the enigmatic nature of the Matthean text and the extreme difficulty of establishing the historicity of either an illegitimate pregnancy or a virgin birth from the text and its silences' and so incorporates Schaberg's reading as an option in what she calls 'an inclusive re-reading'.

[44] Cf. J. Schaberg, 'Feminist Interpretations of the Infancy Narrative of Matthew', in ed. A.-J. Levine, *A Feminist Companion to Mariology* (London: T. & T. Clark, 2005), 35: 'the illegitimacy tradition by its very nature would not lead us to expect anything but murkiness, silences, hints, convoluted admissions, misunderstandings and rebuttals'.

delicacy on the traditional reading. In a Greek-speaking Jewish environment one might well want to avoid any too crude anthropomorphism in speaking of God's involvement in directly generating human life within Mary. In this connection, it is telling that in the case of Philo, where this notion of virginal conception does occur, it is reserved for allegory and frequently further restricted to the instruction of those whom Philo calls the initiated. If Matthew wants the language of 'begotten by God' to be understood on a more literal level than Philo and to refer to an actual conception, then this is more dangerous linguistic territory and he negotiates it by avoiding some of the more graphic turns of phrase that one finds in Philo, such as 'being impregnated by the divine seed', and instead speaks more obliquely of being 'begotten by the holy Spirit'.[45] What is more, it is not so unusual for writers, for a variety of reasons, to produce accounts that speak obliquely of events that would already be known to their readers. So, for example, we would not be able to tell from John 1.19–34 whether Jesus was actually baptized by John. The Fourth Evangelist assumes his readers know of this event and chooses, probably for apologetic reasons, not to spell this out. In comparison with the accounts that follow in Matthew's infancy narrative, 1.18–25 stands out for its sparseness of detail. A plausible explanation is that, in contrast to the stories he will go on to tell in chapter 2, Matthew can assume some previous knowledge of the conception and chooses not to elaborate because the means of conception is less important to him than the significance of the one who is conceived, conveyed through the names Jesus and Emmanuel.

We have concluded, then, that the alternative reading needs to be taken seriously as a minority report that raises significant questions about the traditional reading that have often been avoided and should cause the latter's adherents to rethink its justification, but that on balance the alternative is not quite compelling enough to cause the abandonment of the view that Matthew, though not as clearly as has often been thought, remains a witness to the virginal conception.[46]

Questions about the historicity of the virginal conception tradition or, on the view of the minority report, of the illegitimacy tradition will be

---

[45] I owe this last observation to Professor John Barclay of the University of Durham in email correspondence.

[46] B. P. Robinson, 'Matthew's Nativity Stories: Historical and Theological Questions for Today's Readers', in ed. J. Corley, *New Perspectives on the Nativity* (London: T. & T. Clark, 2009), 119–21, after setting out the case for the alternative reading, comes to a similar conclusion: 'Whether Matthew wishes to teach a virginal conception must, in my view, remain less than certain. As I have indicated, I am inclined to think that he does but that he may be using a source that does not.'

addressed in Chapter 6. But the issue of whether or not Matthew is a witness to the virgin birth tradition should not cause us to lose sight of this witness being part of the broader witness of his annunciation story to the significance of the child who is conceived. As suggested above, the very lack of explicitness in Matthew's account should alert us to the fact that his main interest lies elsewhere. Drawing on the Jewish Scriptures and their retellings and within the conventions of ancient biography, Matthew's Gospel's birth announcement is most concerned with the identity of the one who is to be conceived. The preceding genealogy has already located that identity within Israel's story. Jesus is to be seen as a true Jew, son of Abraham, and as truly in the messianic line, son of David, but his story will also signal a new beginning in God's purposes, a new genesis that is inaugurated in the life to be recounted. Now in the announcement that resolves righteous Joseph's dilemma, the conception of the child is said to be 'from the holy Spirit' (1.18). The very beginnings of this life are the work of the creative divine Spirit who will ensure that it will be separated to God in the fulfilment of the divine purposes. Whatever suspicions Joseph may have entertained about Mary's pregnancy and whatever scandal may have attached itself to it, this conception is to be seen as in line with the divine purposes, as had been the irregular sexual activity of the first four women in the genealogy, and Joseph taking the child as his own shows how Jesus can be said to be descended from David. Recalling the Moses story, in which Moses is depicted as the one who will save his people from Egyptian bondage, the instruction to name the child Jesus indicates that he is to 'save his people from their sins' (1.21). By refocusing this salvation on the sins that are at the root of all bondage, the narrative is later able to make clear that the one conceived will be a Saviour not only of Israel but also of the nations (cf. 28.19). Indeed this son of a young virginal woman fulfils what was meant in Scripture by giving another such son the name Emmanuel. Just as the birth of the young woman's son in Isaiah was a sign that God would stand by the divine promise to the house of David and be with God's people, so, Matthew tells his readers, the birth of Mary's son is the decisive sign that God has fulfilled that promise. The future greatness of the one conceived lies not only in his being the messianic son of David or Israel's Saviour but also in his uniquely embodying God's reassuring presence with God's people.

5

Conceiving Jesus in Luke

It would be an unlikely anomaly if, from very early, the Church had completely misunderstood its own Scriptures on this matter and they contained no clear account of a virginal conception. Readers may be relieved to know that, though there have been a few dissenters[1] and the exegetical case still needs to be made, there is far greater agreement that Luke's annunciation story is about a virginal conception. Yet what is said about Jesus' origins in the rest of Luke's writings complicates matters interestingly. But this is to jump the gun and these cryptic introductory comments remain to be elaborated in what follows.[2] We begin with Luke's annunciation story and again the attempt will be made initially to treat the narrative on its own terms.

The structure of Luke's infancy narrative

Though there are a few overlaps, Luke's story is very different and the focus is on Mary rather than Joseph. Two observations about Luke's structuring of his narrative will help to set his account of Jesus' conception in context. In his preface he talks not simply of the events that happened

---

[1] Cf. J. A. Fitzmyer, 'The Virginal Conception of Jesus in the New Testament', *TS* 34 (1973), 566–72, where he asserts that Luke's account is far more ambiguous about a virginal conception than Matthew's, and *The Gospel according to Luke I—IX* (New York: Doubleday, 1981), 338, although in this later work he had become persuaded by R. E. Brown ('Luke's Description of the Virginal Conception', *TS* 35 (1974), 360–2) that the step parallelism in Luke's story suggested a more extraordinary conception for Jesus than for John the Baptist, namely, a virginal one. Cf. also G. Parrinder, *Son of Joseph: The Parentage of Jesus* (Edinburgh: T. & T. Clark, 1992), 31, 35; D. J. Catchpole, *Jesus People: The Historical Jesus and the Beginnings of Community* (London: Darton, Longman & Todd, 2006), 86; J. Schaberg, *The Illegitimacy of Jesus: A Feminist Theological Interpretation of the Infancy Narratives* (Sheffield: Sheffield Academic Press, 1995), 78–144; E. D. Freed, *The Stories of Jesus' Birth* (Sheffield: Sheffield Academic, 2001), 11, 65, who holds that Luke believed Joseph was Jesus' father and that 'Fitzmyer's original view is still the correct one'. G. Vermes, *Jesus the Jew* (London: Collins, 1973), 218–22 and *The Nativity: History and Legend* (London: Penguin, 2006), 78–81, takes a non-virginal interpretation on the basis of a technical rabbinic definition of a virgin as a girl who has not reached puberty and not one who simply has not had sex. This is a definition unlikely to have been known to Luke or his readers, and 'I have not yet menstruated' is scarcely a plausible interpretation of 'I do not know a man' (1.34).

[2] For a more detailed treatment of the issues, see A. Lincoln, 'Luke and Jesus' Conception: A Case of Double Paternity?' *JBL* 132 (2013), 639–58.

among us but of 'the events that have been fulfilled among us' (1.1). He sees what he will relate as the culmination of something earlier, and it becomes clear that that something was the divine purpose that had unfolded in the history of God's people and been disclosed in Scripture. So in the overall structuring of his two-part work, Luke–Acts, he wishes to show that the history of salvation has a chain of continuity that runs through it from God's promises to Israel to their fulfilment in the mission of Jesus and on into the mission of Jesus' followers leading to the Gentile Church of his own day. Within this continuous chain of God's purposes in history, there are three main periods, which are distinct but also overlap, so that in this way they are soldered together. The first is the period of Scripture, the time of the law and the prophets, which runs up to John the Baptist. The second is the period of fulfilment in Jesus' ministry, which begins with John the Baptist. The third is the next instalment of fulfilment in the time of the ministry of the Church, which is clamped together with what has preceded it through the ascension and the giving of the Spirit. The reason for mentioning this is that Luke 1—2 with its depiction of the faithful remnant among the Jewish people and the births of the Baptist and of Jesus serve as the bridge between the first two periods – that of scriptural prophecy and the fulfilment in Jesus' mission.

The second observation is about the structuring of these two chapters. All the Gospels start their accounts of Jesus' ministry proper with John the Baptist acting as a forerunner, herald or witness preceding Jesus. Only Luke, however, has the idea of starting his story by reading back the later view of Jesus' followers about his relation to John the Baptist into an account of both their births. Now the relationship between John and Jesus from the early stages of Jesus' mission is depicted as also holding for the stories of their birth. In fact, the whole of Luke 1—2, after the preface, is structured so as to set out this relationship. There is a parallelism between the episodes about John the Baptist and Jesus throughout, though as will become clear, it will not be parallelism between two figures of equal status. Indeed, Jesus' story receives nearly twice as much space in the two chapters as does John's. In this sense it is a step parallelism in which the second element is greater. It starts with the introduction of their parents (1.5–7 // 1.26–27) and then an annunciation by Gabriel (1.8–23 // 1.28–38). This is followed by the response of the mother (1.24–25 // 1.39–56). Then in each case the birth is recounted (1.57–58 // 2.1–20). But the parallelism does not stop there. It continues with circumcision and naming in both cases (1.59–66 // 2.21–24), a prophetic response to the birth (1.67–79 // 2.25–39), and a summary on the growth of the child (1.80 // 2.40–52).

The two stories are not simply parallel and totally distinct. Luke has them converge in 1.39–56 by depicting Elizabeth and Mary as relatives and having Mary visit Elizabeth, and in this section Mary and her unborn child are the focus of attention. So the two stories are part of one overall story of promise and fulfilment of God's actions in history to bring deliverance, redemption and peace. Both births have a role in this but that of Jesus has the clearly primary one.

The annunciation and a virginal conception

While Matthew has an angelic announcement to Joseph some time after it is clear that Mary is pregnant, Luke has an announcement to Mary before she becomes pregnant and, unlike Matthew's account, in Luke 1.26–38 there is no hint of scandal or sexual irregularity. The angel Gabriel is sent to Nazareth and the recipient of his announcement is in the same situation as Matthew had described – betrothed to Joseph who belonged to the house of David. She is described as a *parthenos* (1.27), the term found in Matthew's scriptural citation. At this stage there is no particular reason to suppose that this term has a meaning beyond the standard one of a young woman of child-bearing age who has not yet given birth to a child.[3] Since in this account there is no prior knowledge of a conception or pregnancy, information about this will come as news to Mary as part of the angelic annunciation (1.31).

To appreciate the issues that surround the interpretation of the manner of that conception, we should note the form the annunciation takes. It follows the form of the earlier annunciation to Zechariah in 1.8–23, and both follow the pattern of annunciations in the Jewish Scriptures. There are four scriptural scenes in which either God or an angel announces the birth of a boy who will play a significant role in Israel's history and two scenes in which God or an angel appears to an adult male to announce he has been chosen for such a role. An angel announces Ishmael's birth to his mother, Hagar (Gen. 16.7–13). The Lord twice announces Isaac's birth to his father, Abraham (Gen. 17.1–21; 18.1–15) and an angel announces Samson's birth to his parents (Judg. 13.2–23). In addition, God announces to Moses from the burning bush his future leadership role (Exod. 3.1–12) and an angel announces to Gideon his future leadership role (Judg. 6.11–24). There are five basic aspects to such scenes, and most, though

---

[3] As noted in regard to Matthew, the term can refer to either a woman's age or her sexual condition or both, depending on the context.

not all, have all five: (a) a divine appearance (God or an angel); (b) a human reaction of fear or amazement; (c) an announcement of the message; (d) a human objection or request for a sign; (e) a giving of a sign in confirmation of the message. All five appear in both annunciation scenes here in Luke. (a) An angel of the Lord (revealed later to be Gabriel) appears to Zechariah (1.11, 19) and to Mary (1.26–28). (b) Zechariah is terrified and fear overwhelms him (1.12) and Mary is much perplexed or deeply disturbed (1.29). (c) Gabriel announces the message to Zechariah (1.13–17) and to Mary (1.30–33), beginning each time with the typical 'Do not be afraid'. (d) Zechariah asks for a sign: 'How will I know that this is so?' (1.18), while Mary objects: 'How can this be, since I do not know a man?' (1.34). And finally (e) a sign is given in confirmation, as Zechariah is told he will become mute until the promise is fulfilled (1.20) and Mary is told that her relative Elizabeth has conceived a son in her old age (1.36). Luke has followed the scriptural form of annunciation precisely in constructing his accounts.

The first two formal elements of the annunciation to Mary have already been mentioned. What is the content of the third element, the message about conception in 1.31–33? The angel announces that she will conceive, her child will be a son and she is to name him Jesus. What is more, this son is to be the Davidic king. Here the formulations are taken from the promise about the future Davidic king in 2 Samuel 7. 'He will be great' (1.32a) recalls 2 Samuel 7.9: 'I will make for you a great name', while 'The Lord God will give to him the throne of his father David. He will reign over the house of Jacob for ever, and of his kingdom there will be no end' (1.32b–33) recalls the promise of 2 Samuel 7.13: 'I will establish the throne of his kingdom for ever.' Even further, 2 Samuel 7.14 had talked of this Davidic king in terms of being God's son: 'I will be a father to him and he will be a son to me', and now Mary's son will also be called 'the Son of the Most High' (1.32) or the title by which he will be most well known, the 'Son of God' (1.35). So Luke's story is claiming that the promises to David are about to be fulfilled, and so far nothing suggests that this will be other than through the normal means of conception. Even when the sonship of the Davidic king was expressed in terms of being begotten by God (cf. Ps. 2.6–7), this was, of course, as noted previously, always understood in a way that did not exclude a human father.

It is with the fourth and fifth of the formal elements of the annunciation that the matter of a virginal conception, together with dispute about its interpretation, arises. Mary's response to the angel's announcement is the typical human response of such announcement scenes, with her question expressing puzzlement, astonishment and initial disbelief at what she has been told: 'How can this be, since I do not know a man?' (1.34). It corresponds to the questions of Abraham: 'Can a child be born to a man who is a hundred years old?' (Gen. 17.17), of Sarah: 'After I have grown old, and my husband is old, shall I have pleasure?' (Gen. 18.12), and of Zechariah earlier: 'How will I know that this is so? For I am an old man, and my wife is getting on in years' (1.18). But old age cannot be the problem in Mary's case, so Luke makes the impediment that Mary raises one from the other end of the age spectrum – she is still a young woman who is not yet having sex with a man. Those who find here no clear account of a virginal conception argue that Mary's objection is no more than a conventional literary device that is meant to prompt the next stage of a dialogue.[4] In terms of any verisimilitude in the narrative, her question makes little sense. She has not, of course, been told that there will be anything extraordinary about the manner of her conception. She is betrothed to Joseph, as the narrator has made clear (1.27), and therefore should be expected to think that, although they have not been intimate yet, intercourse will take place and the child who is to be Davidic king will be the fruit of their future union. Those for whom Mary's question is no more than a literary device reject attempts to give the question some straightforward sense in the context, holding that the need to supply the supposition that Mary had taken the announcement to imply an immediate or imminent conception, although her betrothal had not yet reached the second stage of cohabitation with Joseph, to be, at best, an awkward and forced solution. On this view, Mary's astonishment at being chosen as the mother of the messianic king prompts what follows in the next stage of the dialogue that consists of the angel's further explanation of what will occur, further identification of Mary's son and the promise of a sign: 'The holy Spirit will come upon you, and the power of the Most High will overshadow you; therefore the child to be born will be holy; he will be called Son of God'.[5] This is simply taken to mean that God by the divine Spirit will superintend the conception and birth of this child, so that the child to be born will be holy, that is, separated to God for a special role from his mother's womb. 'To come upon' (*eperchomai epi*) is found frequently in the LXX, and the one reference to the Spirit as subject

---

[4] This is emphasized by Fitzmyer, 'Virginal Conception', 568–9: 'Mary's query is merely a Lucan stage-prop for the dramatization of the identity of the child.'

[5] There is no definite article before 'holy Spirit' in the Greek text but, like Matthew, Luke can use this terminology with the article or without the article interchangeably.

in LXX Isaiah 32.15 depicts the Spirit as making the wilderness fruitful. Elsewhere in Luke–Acts the holy Spirit can be said to come upon the disciples (Acts 1.8) and on the believers in Ephesus who are baptized in the name of Jesus by Paul (Acts 19.6, though here without the intensifying verbal prefix). These are references to empowerment by the Spirit, but in none of them is there any suggestion that the Spirit replaces any agency or activity that humans would normally be expected to exercise. As the parallel clause here, 'the power of the Most High will overshadow you', suggests, the thought in this account is also of divine empowerment. 'To overshadow' is used literally in 9.34 of the cloud, representing the divine presence that is depicted in the transfiguration scene, and in Acts 5.15 of Peter casting a shadow. LXX Exodus 40.35, where it is also employed of the cloud representing the divine glory that covers the tabernacle, may well have influenced the depiction in 9.34 and, via that text, the reference here, though the verb can also be used metaphorically in LXX Psalms 90.4; 139.7 to mean 'to cover' or 'to protect'. At work in the circumstances of the conception and birth of Mary's special child, then, will be the powerful and protective divine Spirit.[6]

The reading that sees 1.34 as a mere literary device continues as follows. It might seem unthinkable to Mary that she should be the mother of the son of David and Son of God and so, as evidence that 'nothing will be impossible with God', the angel points to Mary's relative, Elizabeth, who, despite her advanced age and previous inability to have children, is six months pregnant (1.36–37). This echoes the assurance given to Abraham (despite Sarah's laughter about being able to have a child): 'Is anything impossible for the Lord?' (LXX Gen. 18.14). So, if her barren relative can bear a child, Mary will be able to conceive and give birth to the messianic Son of God. Finally, Mary declares herself a slave of the Lord and therefore ready to play her part in the fulfilment of the message she has heard (1.38); 'Let it be with me according to your word' is in line with Luke's later depiction of Mary in 8.20–21, where he softens the Markan account (Mark 3.21, 31–35) in order to allow the inclusion of Jesus' physical mother and brothers among 'those who hear the word of God and do it'. On this reading of the last part of Luke's account, then, there is still nothing that requires one to think that Mary's conceiving will be virginal in the technical sense, that is, without Joseph being involved in the process.

---

[6] G. B. Caird, *The Gospel of Luke* (Oxford: Clarendon, 1963), 31, makes a similar point to the one that we have seen plays a major role in the interpretation of Matthew: 'It would never have occurred to a Jew to consider the overshadowing of Mary by the Holy Spirit as a substitute for normal parenthood.'

But this is, of course, not the only way of reading the fourth and fifth formal elements in the annunciation. In fact, the more traditional reading can make a better case. On it there are two plausible ways of handling Mary's question, 'How can this be, since I do not know a man?' (1.34). The first agrees that it is a literary device that makes no sense at the level of the narrative. Mary is betrothed to Joseph and so should be expecting to 'know' him! Nevertheless it thinks it would be strange if no force at all were to be given to the content of the question. Luke must, therefore, at this point have some purpose other than any realism in the depiction of Mary. So Brown, for example, takes the lack of verisimilitude as signalling that Luke is more concerned about making a point to his readers.[7] It is his way of making clear that Mary is not just a *parthenos* in the general sense (1.27) but that, when she conceives, she is the sort of *parthenos* who is also a virgin technically, one who has not had intercourse with a man. In the LXX it is precisely the qualifying clause, 'who has not known a man', or its equivalent (cf. Gen. 19.8; 24.16; Num. 31.18, 35; Judg. 21.12), that makes clear that the young women in view (*parthenos* in Gen. 24.16; Judg. 21.12) are also technically virgins. Furnished with this explanation of Mary's question, readers are now expected to take the language of the angel's reply about the holy Spirit coming upon Mary and the power of the Most High overshadowing her (1.35a) as having a significance here that it would not normally have and so to think that in this unique case the Spirit or the divine power excludes the role of any male in the procreation of Mary's child. At the same time, for readers familiar with stories of gods engaging in intercourse with women in order to produce exceptional offspring, this language will not necessarily lead them to infer sexual contact in this instance.

The second approach to Mary's question contends that its lack of verisimilitude at the narrative level has been assumed too easily. After all, Luke's characterization elsewhere does not contain this sort of implausibility. Should we really think that here he has allowed a rigid conformity to an annunciation pattern to impede making sense of Mary's question as a plausible one from that of a character within his narrative? Landry has offered a persuasive version of this second approach.[8] Making clear that he is not discussing the psychology of the historical Mary but the plausibility of Luke's presentation of the character, Mary, he claims that 'an

---

[7] R. E. Brown, *The Birth of the Messiah* (2nd edn New York: Doubleday, 1993), 307: 'It is meant . . . to tell *the reader* how the child was conceived.'

[8] D. T. Landry, 'Narrative Logic in the Annunciation to Mary (Luke 1:26–38)', *JBL* 114 (1995), 65–79.

ancient reader would conclude that as a betrothed virgin, Mary objects because she assumes that the angel is telling her she will become pregnant *almost immediately*, before she could possibly have sexual relations legally with her husband'.[9] This is in line with the future tenses of the angelic announcement, which only rule out a conception taking place during the announcement, not one that occurs shortly after and before the second period of betrothal when Joseph would take her to his home. The scriptural annunciations, which provide the pattern Luke is following, are about conceptions that have already taken place or will take place immediately, not after several months' delay. The lack of any significant delay in the case of Mary is also indicated by the chronological clues in the immediately following passage. Elizabeth is already six months pregnant at the time of the annunciation (cf. 1.36), Mary's visit to Elizabeth lasts for three months and is still before the birth of John, and, although it is not explicitly stated, Mary appears to be pregnant at the time of the visit.[10] Though Elizabeth's greeting of Mary with 'blessed is the fruit of your womb' and calling her 'the mother of my Lord' (1.42–43) might just be taken to have a still future reference, Mary's own assertion that 'the Mighty One has done great things for me' (1.49) is more plausibly interpreted as referring to the angelic promise already having begun to be fulfilled than as simply a reference to the promise itself. This second approach that grants some coherence to Luke's account of the annunciation at a narrative level appears preferable to one, like Brown's, that holds that Mary's question is a mere literary device that makes no sense at this level. On this reading the angel's response is also, of course, no longer a non-response to Mary's question. The talk of the divine agency of the Spirit and of nothing being impossible with God is to be read as an explanation to Mary of how she will conceive shortly while she is still a virgin in her relationship with Joseph.

On either version of the reading that a virginal conception is in view, the last part of the angel's reply now has a different force from the reading that sees only a natural conception entailed. Elizabeth's pregnancy, despite her old age and lack of ability to conceive previously, now produced as evidence that with God nothing is impossible, has relevance not only to Mary's ability to have a child who is Son of God but also to the *manner* in which she will have this child. If a barren woman can bear a child, a virgin can conceive. After all, nothing is impossible with God! Mary's response, expressing her obedience to the divine word, is to be seen as

---

[9] Landry, 'Narrative Logic', 73.
[10] Cf. Landry, 'Narrative Logic', 75–6.

including her acceptance of a miraculous conception for her future son. This reading of the latter part of Luke's account is, of course, in essence the traditional interpretation. On a sequential reading it entails that with Mary's question the account moves from one wholly comprehensible within Jewish cultural expectations to one that narrates an event totally unprecedented in Jewish Scripture, namely God bringing about the birth of a human without the presence of a male seed.

Here one must surely agree with Brown that this reading does much better justice to the structure of Luke 1—2 with its step parallelism that we set out earlier.[11] The first reading does satisfy the demand of this structuring that the second element, that concerning Jesus, should involve something greater. While in the annunciation to Zechariah John the Baptist is to be filled with the holy Spirit and to have the spirit and power of Elijah as the forerunner who will prepare the people of Israel for the Lord (1.15–17), in the annunciation to Mary Jesus' future role and status is superior as the one who is both Davidic King and Son of God. But the earlier annunciation also makes clear that the conception of John the Baptist will be a miraculous one. The event involves a childless couple well past the age that the wife could be expected to conceive (cf. 1.7, 18). Since the sign for Mary that with God nothing is impossible is that Elizabeth has indeed conceived in old age (1.36), it is not unreasonable to think that the step parallelism would include the manner of conception and entail a greater miracle in the case of Jesus. Indeed, the step parallelism would be significantly undermined if John's conception involved the miraculous but that of Jesus did not. The traditional reading, of course, supplies just such a miracle, greater in that, unlike John's conception, it was unprecedented in the Jewish Scriptures. If an infertile woman can bear a child, then the greater miracle is for a virgin to conceive without any male seed being involved. In this light one function of the immediately following pericope, 1.39–56, with its mention of Mary's speedy departure from Nazareth, her three-month stay with Elizabeth in the Judean hill country, and then her return to her *own* house seems to be to underline her absence and independence from Joseph during much of the period before she gives birth and thus the virginal nature of the conception.[12]

The only qualification that might need to be made in regard to the claim about the manner of Jesus' conception being superior is that at the level of the narrative and its Jewish context it would not necessarily be so

---

[11] Brown, *Birth*, 300–1.

[12] Cf. also M. Coleridge, *The Birth of the Lukan Narrative* (Sheffield: Sheffield Academic, 1993), 96.

obvious. If a miracle was held to be a public sign that God had been at work in an extraordinary fashion, the birth of a child to parents past the age of producing and to a wife who had previously been barren would have been clearly miraculous. But seeing a betrothed teenager produce a child would not have been extraordinary and her claim to have conceived virginally would not have been impressive. Since her virginity was not a matter of public verification, the only person for whom this could have been clearly miraculous would have been Mary herself.[13] If Luke, in all probability a Gentile Christian who had been a god-fearer, did intend the conception of Jesus to be understood as a superior miracle, then it needs to be added that he is not thinking of it on the level of public knowledge or attestation and that its effectiveness for readers is dependent on their prior conviction of Jesus' superiority as Son of God and on their familiarity either with an already existing tradition about a virginal conception or with analogous stories about the birth of heroes.

Luke's virginal conception and Graeco-Roman stories

It seems clear that familiarity with analogous stories is indeed operative for Luke. We have already shown in Chapter 3 how the birth narratives conform very closely indeed to what ancient hearers or readers would have expected to be told about the births of great figures. In particular, we observed how these resemblances include stories that are handed down about miraculous conceptions so that the origins of subjects' future greatness can be traced to the gods.[14] Plutarch related such conceptions for Romulus, whose mother was a vestal virgin and whose father was Mars (cf. also Cicero, *Resp.* 1.41; 2.2), Theseus and Alexander; Suetonius did the same for Augustus, Porphyry for Pythagoras, Diogenes Laertius for Plato and Philostratus for Apollonius of Tyana. As we have also seen, it is Luke, not Matthew, who has the title 'Son of God' in his annunciation story. Gabriel tells Mary, 'he will be called the Son of the Most High' (1.32) and 'he will be called Son of God' (1.35). One of the main conventions, then, for a son of a deity, whether of Zeus or Apollo or Mars, in ancient biography and more broadly in the Graeco-Roman world was that he would have a supernatural conception that involved no human father. Luke's

---

[13] Cf. R. J. Miller, *Born Divine: The Births of Jesus and Other Sons of God* (Santa Rosa, CA: Polebridge, 2003), 236–7.

[14] Cf. esp. C. H. Talbert, 'Prophecies of Future Greatness: Contributions of Greco-Roman Biographies to an Understanding of Luke 1:5—4:1', in *Reading Luke–Acts in Its Mediterranean Milieu* (Leiden: Brill, 2003), 65–77.

story is in line with this convention.[15] If Jesus is Son of God, then that is shown by depicting him as having no human father, whose role in conception is replaced (though not physically) by a divine agent, the Spirit and power of the Most High. That Luke himself is familiar with such claims for great figures is plain. He gives his birth narrative a Roman setting in 2.1–14, where he specifically mentions Augustus (2.1) and where the angels' announcement to the shepherds evokes the Priene inscription about Augustus (2.10–11, 14). That inscription spoke of the birthday of 'the god'. After the deification of his adopted father, Julius Caesar, by the Roman senate in 42 BCE, Octavius became *divi filius*, son of God. Then, as Augustus Caesar, he was deified by the senate shortly after his death in 14 CE. The inscription retrojects this status to his birth and, as noted above, he is later reported by Suetonius (*Aug.* 94) to have had a divine birth from his mother, Atia, and the god Apollo.

We also noted earlier that Luke's paralleling of the early part of the lives of John the Baptist and Jesus for the sake of comparison has its counterpart in ancient biography in Plutarch's *Parallel Lives*. But any doubts that Luke's Gospel follows ancient biographical conventions should be dispelled when it is observed how Luke ends his life of Jesus. Not only does his Gospel begin with a virginal conception, but it is also the only one of the Synoptics to end with an explicit ascension. Mark ends with the empty tomb and the promise of an appearance in Galilee, Matthew finishes with the resurrected Jesus commissioning his disciples, but Luke concludes with an ascension in which Jesus is carried up into heaven from Bethany and with the worship of the disciples (Luke 24.51–52; cf. also Acts 1.9–11). The ascension brings Luke's ending into line with that of a number of ancient accounts of those who were considered to be among the immortals.[16] A prime example is Plutarch's life of Romulus. This not only attributes a virginal conception to its subject but also at the end of his life has him taken up to heaven as a god. Plutarch relates that Romulus disappeared, so that only the time and not the manner of his death is known, and records the tradition that Romulus vanished while he was holding an assembly of the people and when 'the light of the sun failed, and night came down upon them, not with peace and quiet, but with awful peals of thunder and furious blasts driving rain from every quarter'. The nobles then 'exhorted them all to honour and revere Romulus, since he had been

---

[15] Surprisingly, Schaberg, *Illegitimacy*, 126–7, acknowledges the similarity of Luke's account to Graeco-Roman biographies but is unwilling to see in it anything miraculous about Jesus' conception.

[16] Cf. C. H. Talbert, 'The Concept of Immortals in Mediterranean Antiquity', *JBL* 94 (1975), 419–36.

caught up into heaven, and was to be a benevolent god for them instead of a good king' (*Rom.* 27). Later one of the patricians went on oath that he had seen Romulus coming to meet him and asked why he had left 'the whole city sorrowing without end at the loss of its father'. Romulus had replied,

> It was the pleasure of the gods, O Proculus, from whom I came, that I should be with mankind only a short time, and that, after founding a city destined to be the greatest on earth for empire and glory, I should dwell again in heaven. So farewell, and tell the Romans that if they practise self-restraint, and add to it valour, they will reach the utmost heights of human power. And I will be your propitious deity, Quirinus.
>
> (*Rom.* 28; cf. also *Numa* 2.2–4)

Because of the oath of this witness and his character, the Romans consequently found these things credible and 'they prayed to [Romulus]Quirinus, and honoured him as a god'. Plutarch's own comment on this tradition is to interpret Romulus' ascension as that of the soul and to claim of good men that we must

> believe that their virtues and their souls, in accordance with nature and divine justice, ascend from men to heroes, from heroes to demi-gods, and from demi-gods, after they have been made pure and holy, as in the final rites of initiation, and have freed themselves from mortality and sense, to gods . . . thus achieving the fairest and most blessed consummation.
>
> (*Rom.* 28)

Luke, then, has a number of correspondences with the end of the tradition about Romulus found in Plutarch: an appearance by Jesus to travelling disciples who express disappointed hopes (24.15–21a),[17] an ascension of Jesus into heaven in the midst of witnesses of the event (24.51) and then worship of him (24.52). In other biographies Suetonius has a miraculous conception of Augustus as son of Apollo, as we have seen, and also has an ascension at the end, where a witness goes on oath that he has seen the form of the emperor on its way up to heaven (*Aug.* 94, 100) and Philostratus not only begins his story of Apollonius with a miraculous conception but also ends it with Apollonius' ascension from the Dictynna temple on Crete (*Vit. Apoll.* 8.30).

The discussion of the beginning of a subject's life through miraculous conception and its ending through ascent to heaven is not, however, confined to ancient biography, of which Luke's Gospel is a subgenre. Evidence

---

[17] Cf. also A. Ehrhardt, 'The Disciples of Emmaus', *NTS* 10 (1963–4), 187–201.

for this sort of thinking about great lives is more widespread in the ancient world. According to Homer, Perseus was the son of Zeus and the woman Danae (*Il.* 14.315–28). Diodorus of Sicily has Heracles as the son of Zeus and a human mother, Alcmene (cf. also Homer, *Il.* 14.315–28), and also tells of his ascent (*Bibliotheca historica* 4.9, 38). In addition, he has an ascent for Aristaeus, depicted as the son of Apollo and a woman, Cyrene (*Bibliotheca historica* 4.81–82). Diodorus also talks of Dionysus who was the son of Zeus and Semele, daughter of Cadmus, the founder of Thebes, and who at the end of his life became one of the demigods (*Bibliotheca historica* 4.2) and of Asclepios, the son of Apollo and a woman who was either Coronis or Arsinoe, who at the close of his life was taken up among the stars (*Bibliotheca historica* 4.71; cf. also Cicero, *Nat. d.* 3.22). The historian Dionysius of Halicarnassus also relates how Romulus was the son of Mars and the vestal virgin Ilia or Rhea (*Ant. rom.* 1.76–77) and has an ascent for Aeneas (*Ant. rom.* 1.64), while Ovid talks of the latter being the son of a goddess and a human father (*Metam.* 14.588). As in ancient biography, this pattern for a life was first attached to these legendary figures from the past but then became the convention for depicting the lives of more recent rulers and philosophers. Diogenes Laertius relates how the philosopher Empedocles disappeared after a meal with friends, one of whom claimed to have heard a voice from heaven calling Empedocles, and how it was then believed that the philosopher had been taken up to heaven (*Vit. Phil.* 8.67–68). Dio Chrysostom in the late first century CE has an account in which Alexander the Great is depicted as discussing with Diogenes. The latter impudently calls Alexander a bastard. When asked for a reason, he says that this is what Olympias, Alexander's mother, claims by attributing his conception to a god. When asked if he thinks such a claim is true, Diogenes replies that it is true of those who are self-controlled, noble and able to impart the knowledge of kingship (*Or.* 4.18–31). Pseudo-Callisthenes' third-century CE romance tells of Alexander's mother, Olympias, being made pregnant by the god Ammon, and then has an ascension for Alexander (*Alexander Romance* 3.24, 30).

It should go without saying, after the discussion in Chapter 3, that underlining major similarities of Luke's narrative with such biographies is not meant to be at the expense of also noting the significant differences that come from the rooting of his own biography in the Jewish Scriptures and its shaping in terms of the character of Israel's God and this God's promises of salvation. Just as Luke applies distinctive Jewish and Christian sensibilities to his depiction of the beginnings of his subject's life, so he does with the conventional Graeco-Roman ending of ascension by combining it with Jewish associations (the Elijah tradition with its notion of Elijah's return in the end times) and Christian convictions (Jesus' resurrection and in Acts 1.11 his eschatological return). Three of the features of this distinctiveness in regard to Jesus' conception are worth comment. First, Luke's account makes no mention of the mating, mediated or otherwise, between the divine and the human that was common in the Graeco-Roman biographies and in other stories. Luke is telling a story that stresses the Gentile mission's continuity with God's dealings with Israel and remains alert to Jewish sensibilities. Avoiding any explicit sexual reference in his account, he focuses instead on the power of the holy Spirit, which was believed to have been at work both in the creation of the world and in the resurrection of Jesus, and on the purity of the female recipient of this power. It should be noted, however, that a non-sexual encounter between the divine and a woman is also discussed by Plutarch, who can say 'that an immortal god should take carnal pleasure in a mortal body and its beauty, this, surely, is hard to believe' but at the same time comments that wise Egyptians find it possible that 'a divine spirit [*pneuma*] so apply itself to the nature of a woman as to imbreed in her the first beginnings of generation' (*Numa* 4.2–4; cf. also *Quaest. conv.* 8.1).[18]

Second, the main similarity between Luke's account and ancient biographies is the subject's conception from the gods without a human father. In only a few of the Graeco-Roman stories of the conception of heroes or sons of god is the human mother a virgin. Yet in Luke's account, as we have seen, Mary's virginity is accented. This has a number of resonances in the Jewish Scriptures and their interpretation. In those Scriptures God's people can be called 'virgin daughter Zion' (cf. 2 Kgs 19.21; Isa. 37.22; Lam. 2.13), 'virgin daughter Judah' (Lam. 1.15) or 'virgin Israel' (Jer. 31.4, 21–22; Amos 5.2). Here God's relationship with God's people is viewed as one in which God has laid claim to and acts as guardian for the people and in which, in return, they owe God loyalty. As the virgin who gives birth to the Messiah, Mary can be seen as representative of the people of Israel and this is made clear in her Magnificat, which links what God has done for her with what God has done for Israel.[19] Her virginity would also have been important because it signified that she was in an appropriate state for an encounter with the divine. In the Jewish Scriptures purity

---

[18] Cf. also G. Lüdemann, *Virgin Birth? The Real Story of Mary and Her Son Jesus* (London: SCM, 1998), 73–6.

[19] Cf. also M. F. Foskett, *A Virgin Conceived* (Bloomington, IN: University of Indiana Press, 2002), 56, 129.

in the sense of abstinence from sex was seen as necessary for being in the divine presence (cf. e.g. Exod. 19.15; Lev. 15.18; 1 Sam. 21.5) and a priest who served in the sanctuary before the Lord had to have married a virgin (cf. Lev. 21.13–15). In regard to virginity *Joseph and Aseneth* should also be mentioned. Most scholars have treated it as a Jewish work, though there have also been one or two recent proposals that it may be Christian in origin. Unfortunately there is no consensus on its date, which has been placed anywhere between the first century BCE and the fourth century CE. It retells the biblical story in Genesis 41 and 46 of how Aseneth, the daughter of an Egyptian priest, who becomes the bride of Joseph, is converted from paganism to Israel's God. Joseph himself is presented as the son of God (6.2, 6; 13.9) and as a virgin (4.9; 8.1), and it is important to him that Aseneth also is a virgin (7.9; 8.10). The narrative has stressed from the start (cf. 1.4–5) that she is indeed a virgin who has been surrounded and waited upon by other virgins and that she has had no contact with men, whom she disdains (2.1). Later, having met Joseph, she repents of her worship of other gods and of her pride. The chief of the angels appears to her and commands her to 'put on a new robe that you have never worn before, and tie your bright girdle round your waist – the double girdle of your virginity' (14.13, 16). When she has done this, the angel tells her that she is now 'a pure virgin' and what is more,

> Penitence is the Most High's daughter and she entreats the Most High on your behalf every hour . . . And Penitence is herself a virgin, very beautiful and pure and chaste and gentle; and God Most High loves her, and all his angels do her reverence. (15.7–8; cf. 15.1, 6)

If this work does have its origins in early Judaism, it is certainly significant not only for the prominence it gives to female virginity but also for its view that virginity and penitence have their counterparts in the heavenly realms. But, in any case, both Jews and pagans 'believed that abstinence from sexual activity, and especially virginity, made the human body a more appropriate vehicle to receive divine inspiration'.[20] Philo presents Moses as disdaining sex 'from the time when, possessed by the Spirit, he entered on his work as a prophet, since he held it fitting to hold himself always in readiness to receive oracular messages' (*Mos.* 2.68–69). Luke himself talks of the outpouring of the Spirit in fulfilment of Joel's prophecy that

---

[20] P. Brown, *The Body and Society* (London: Faber and Faber, 1990), 67. For Graeco-Roman discussions of female seers and priestesses needing to be virgins in order to receive oracles from or to carry out their duties before the gods, see Foskett, *Virgin*, 37–44.

envisages both males and females prophesying (Acts 2.17–18) but it is significant that the only explicit reference to actual female prophets, the four daughters of Philip, specifies that they are virgins (Acts 21.9). In the annunciation scene the Spirit that comes upon Mary is not explicitly said to be the Spirit of prophecy and in uttering the Magnificat Mary is not explicitly depicted as a prophet, but the implication may well be that her hymn of praise is speech inspired by the Spirit.[21]

Within Hellenistic Judaism Philo could also entertain this notion of the interaction between divine power and female virginity. While, as we have seen, he does not, of course, assert that such a thing actually happened, in expounding the divine generation of the virtues he can speak, as an integral part of his allegorizing of the Pentateuch, of Sarah, Leah, Rebecca and Zipporah being made pregnant by God's seed without the aid of their husbands, since it is appropriate for God to communicate with a virgin, and to make ordinary women virgins in order to do so (*Cher.* 40–50). It is worth quoting again some of the language from this passage that we cited in the previous chapter. Philo holds Jeremiah, like himself, to be one who has been initiated into the mysteries, since LXX Jeremiah 3.4 speaks of God as the husband of Israel's virginity,

> clearly showing that God is . . . the husband of wisdom sowing the seed of blessedness for the mortal race into good and virgin soil. For it is fitting for God to hold converse with a nature undefiled and untouched and pure, the nature truly virgin, in a manner different from our manner; for . . . whenever God begins to converse with a soul, even if the soul was a woman before, he makes it again a virgin . . . With Sarah, therefore, he will not hold converse until she has ceased from all the ways of women and has returned to the rank of pure virgin. (*Cher.* 49–50)

The point of citing this material here is not that this passage had some direct influence on or is a precise parallel to the virgin birth tradition[22] but that it indicates rather clearly that the general notion of God impregnating a virgin and of virginity being necessary for this sort of relationship with the divine was readily available to Philo, and, though he frequently reserves his discussion of it for the initiated, not at all abhorrent to him for his allegorizing exposition. What is significant is that Philo also adopts

---

[21] On the rhetorical function of Mary's virginity and its relation to ascetic women in Luke–Acts, see T. E. Klutz, 'The Value of Being Virginal: Mary and Anna in the Lukan Infancy Prologue', in ed. G. J. Brooke, *The Birth of Jesus* (Edinburgh: T. & T. Clark, 2000), 71–87.

[22] The main grounds on which, e.g. J. G. Machen, *The Virgin Birth of Christ* (2nd edn New York: Harper and Row, 1932), 297–312, dismisses its significance.

into Judaism a version of the divine begetting through a mortal woman that he has purged of any explicit sexual depictions and made distinctive by insisting on the virginal state of the woman who is favoured in this way. In taking up birth stories similar to those in other ancient biographies, then, Luke too makes adaptations along these lines, just as the Gospels as a whole apply their own Jewish and Christian distinctives to ancient biography as a genre.

A third distinctive feature that may well have contributed to Luke's use of the notion of a divine conception of a great figure that was widespread in his and his audience's world comes from his Jewish Scriptures and has already been discussed in setting out our reading of Matthew. This is the phenomenon of only God and the woman being mentioned in the conception of significant figures, among whom are the prophet Jeremiah (cf. Jer. 1.5), and the servant in Isaiah (cf. Isa. 44.2). Prophet and servant are, of course, two of the ways Luke will characterize Jesus as the fulfilment of God's promises to Israel. Jesus is not only called a prophet (cf. e.g. Luke 4.24; 7.16; 13.33; 24.19; Acts 3.22–23) but his predictions are also shown to be fulfilled in the course of the narrative (cf. e.g. Luke 24.6–8, 44; Acts 1.4–5, 8; 2.4). Luke depicts Jesus as taking as his own the words of Isaiah's prophet/servant (Luke 4.17–21), portrays him as the servant (cf. e.g. Luke 22.27; Acts 3.13, 26; 4.27, 30; 8.32–36), and indicates that, like the servant in Isaiah 49.6, he is to be 'a light to the nations' (cf. Luke 2.32). When, therefore, Luke has Gabriel announce the conception of the one who fulfils Israel's role as servant, who is greater than the prophets, and who is superior to John the Baptist, whose aged barren mother attributes his conception to the Lord (1.25), it should not be surprising that this pattern of eliding the male's role and simply talking of God and the female womb in order to emphasize the divine initiative should suggest itself. Luke now gives it actual narrative form and, in the step parallelism with the Baptist material, takes it one stage further by making the female womb a virgin one. The narrative form that lies at hand to be adapted for this further step is, as we have seen, that of the birth of heroes or great figures in ancient biography.

Non-virginal conception in Luke's writings

We have concluded that Luke's annunciation story is best interpreted as intending to present Jesus' conception as miraculous and as bypassing any involvement on the part of Joseph. But alert readers will have remembered that in Chapter 2 Luke's writings were appealed to as one of the New

Testament witnesses to the tradition that Jesus was of the seed of David and had Joseph as his biological father. There we discussed in particular the mention of Jesus' conception in the speeches in Acts where, in formulations that Luke would have believed reflected earliest post-resurrection beliefs about Jesus, he is described as the fruit of David's loins and David's seed and concluded that it was highly unlikely that such references would have been understood in some legal or adoptive fashion rather than in terms of actual biological patrilineage. But there are also references to Joseph as Jesus' father within Luke's Gospel but outside the annunciation story that need to be looked at more closely.

It is commonly observed that if the annunciation to Mary is about a virginal conception, then knowledge of such a conception has no impact on the understanding of any of the characters later in the narrative and that the narrator's own depictions, even within the second half of the infancy narrative itself, appear to show no awareness of this earlier announcement.[23] Joseph makes his first appearance in the narrative at 1.27, where it is mentioned in passing that Mary is betrothed to him but where also, in preparation for Mary's son being given the throne of his ancestor David (1.32), it is underlined that Joseph is of the house of David. The story of the actual birth of Jesus, via Luke's notorious census, further underlines Jesus' Davidic descent by having Joseph, who is introduced again as betrothed to a now pregnant Mary, travel with her to Bethlehem, so that her firstborn would be delivered there (2.7). Luke tells us why this was necessary. It was because Bethlehem was David's city and because Joseph was from the house and family of David (2.4, cf. 2.11). If Joseph had no part in his betrothed's pregnancy, then all this stress on Jesus' Davidic ancestry would make little sense. And, indeed, in the incident where Simeon responds to the birth of the child, the narrator talks straightforwardly of the parents (2.27) and then of Joseph as the child's father (2.33) and has both parents amazed at Simeon's words as if there had been no annunciation by Gabriel to Mary, no salutation from Elizabeth and no Magnificat on Mary's own lips. Later in the Temple incident, when Jesus is 12 (2.41–51), both Joseph and Mary are consistently referred to as 'his parents'. Mary even speaks to Jesus about Joseph as his 'father' (2.48) when Jesus will go on to talk of the Temple as his 'Father's house' (2.49). The play on the term 'father' indicates that Jesus has an allegiance that cuts across family ties but there is no hint that his special relationship to the heavenly Father excludes his having a physical father. Luke goes on to

---

[23] Cf. e.g. Fitzmyer, 'Virginal Conception', 552 and *Luke I—IX*, 435.

provide his own distinctive genealogy of Jesus, tracing it back through Joseph and later David (3.23–38). But also, according to Luke, those most familiar with Jesus' family, outside his immediate relatives, the people of Jesus' home town, Nazareth, hold Joseph to be his physical father, as they respond to his synagogue sermon with 'Is not this Joseph's son?' (4.22). If the earliest text of Mark 6.3 was 'Is not this the carpenter, the son of Mary?', then, whatever the force of this unusual use of the metronymic, it is significant that Luke had no qualms about his alteration to 'Is not this Joseph's son?' raising queries about Jesus' real origins. Instead, in his account there is nothing at all negative about this designation; it is part of an initially positive and welcoming attitude towards him on the part of his fellow Nazarenes.[24]

There is one possible exception to the ignoring of the annunciation story's virginal conception in the rest of the Gospel narrative. When Luke places a genealogy of Jesus in 3.23–38 after his accounts of John the Baptist's ministry and Jesus' baptism, he begins it: Jesus 'was the son, as was supposed, of Joseph son of Heli' (3.23b). The verb *nomizō* can mean 'to think, to hold, to assume, to believe, to suppose'. It is part of the linguistic subdomain of regarding something as presumably true, but without particular certainty,[25] and often the context will indicate what level of certainty might be attached to the belief or supposition in question or whether such a belief or supposition was warranted or not. Although it does not alter the bigger question of the difference between the annunciation story and the other references to Joseph as apparently Jesus' natural father, here is the one place where Luke would be concerned to bring other material into relation with Gabriel's announcement. The clause, 'as was believed/held/supposed', then becomes telling. On the one hand, it suggests that the genealogy Luke has taken over was based on the early belief that Jesus was indeed Joseph's son and in this sense of the seed of David. On the other hand, its presence here supports the reading of Luke 1.26–38 in terms of a virginal conception. Especially if, as many hold,[26] an earlier version of the Gospel started at 3.1, then, when Luke added the infancy narratives for the final edition, his gloss on the genealogy that he had placed towards the beginning of his original composition acknowledges that it contains a different perspective on Jesus' conception from

---

[24] Cf. also R. Nadella, *Dialogue not Dogma: Many Voices in the Gospel of Luke* (London: T. & T. Clark, 2011), 37–8.

[25] Cf. J. P. Louw and E. A. Nida, *Greek–English Lexicon of the New Testament: Based on Semantic Domains* Vol. 1 (New York: United Bible Societies, 1998), 31.29.

[26] They include Fitzmyer, *Luke I—IX*, 310–11; Brown, *Birth*, 240–1.

the one he had depicted earlier.[27] But it should be recognized that it is a further, and not necessarily justified, move to conclude that the gloss must mean 'as was falsely believed or supposed'. Of the eight other uses of *nomizō* in Luke–Acts, one is irrelevant to this discussion, since it involves Paul telling the Athenians what not to think (Acts 17.29) and one is disputed (Acts 16.13).[28] In the other six places Luke employs the verb of a belief or supposition that is false, but in five of these this is made clear in the immediately following wording (Luke 2.44; Acts 7.25; 8.20; 14.19; 16.27), and in the sixth (Acts 21.29) the immediately preceding passage (21.21–26) makes clear that Paul would not have done what the Jews of Asia think he has done. Here, in Luke 3.23, there is no marker in the immediate context to indicate that the supposition is false. If that were meant, it would, of course, undermine the rest of the genealogy,[29] and indeed, as we have seen, Luke has already used this supposition and will repeat it in the ensuing narrative without any correction or qualification. There is nothing about Luke's redactive gloss, 'Jesus was the son, as was held, of Joseph', then, that requires passing a negative judgement on the tradition of Joseph as Jesus' father or that would rule out what has been suggested to this point, namely that his writings reflect two traditions about Jesus' conception.

Co-existence of two perspectives

Unless one denies that there are two different traditions within Luke through explaining away the Davidic seed material and reading Matthew's

---

[27] F. Bovon, *Luke 1* (Minneapolis: Fortress, 2002), 136, rightly dismisses the meaning '"he was considered to be Joseph's biological son" (but I, Luke, know this is not true)' because this would rob the genealogy of its significance. However, his preferred alternative '"he was rightfully declared to be Joseph's son" (and I, Luke, agree with this)' appears to give the verb too strong a sense and entails Bovon's view that Luke is stating his own conviction that, through adoption by Joseph, Jesus was a legal descendant of David. This is to read Matthew's account into Luke. Schaberg, *Illegitimacy*, 83, claims that Luke corrects the supposition because he holds that a human other than Joseph was the biological father of Jesus, but this has to presuppose that Luke is telling a story similar to her reading of Matthew's and involving illegitimacy, a presupposition that we have not found to be reflected anywhere else in Luke's account. Indeed all the supporting details Schaberg adduces for her reading of Luke's account (78–144) are dependent for any force on bringing the notion of Jesus' illegitimacy to the text rather than finding it in the text.

[28] For the view that the supposition in Acts 16.13 is correct, see e.g. C. K. Barrett, *A Critical and Exegetical Commentary on the Acts of the Apostles* Vol. 2 (Edinburgh: T. & T. Clark, 1998), 781; J. A. Fitzmyer, *The Acts of the Apostles* (New York: Doubleday, 1998), 585. For the view that the supposition was erroneous, see e.g. T. E. Klutz, *The Exorcism Stories in Luke–Acts* (Cambridge: CUP, 2004), 212–14.

[29] As Vermes, *Jesus the Jew*, 215, put it, if the supposition was erroneous, 'why did Luke, and the tradition responsible for the genealogical table before him, waste their time compiling a sequence of irrelevant ancestors?'

story of some sort of adoption by Joseph into Luke – an approach we have earlier rejected – one faces the question of how these apparently contradictory perspectives can exist within writings by the same author. A few have attempted to solve the problem by excising the virginal conception verses, whether 1.34 alone or 1.34–35 or 1.34–37, from the original text of the Gospel.[30] While early corruption of the text is possible, this suggestion involves speculation on the basis of no evidence in the manuscript tradition. In addition, this later interpolation solution plays havoc with the annunciation pattern that Luke appears to have followed in the case of both Zechariah and Mary. Most frequently, however, those who take seriously the juxtaposition of two perspectives on Jesus' conception find a solution through a tradition-historical analysis, which claims that Luke took over traditions that knew nothing of a virginal conception and somewhat carelessly failed to bring them consistently into line with his own earlier account.[31] More generously, the awkward redaction can be attributed to that earlier account in fact having been written as the last part of the Gospel and probably of the two-volume work. If an earlier draft of the writing began, in similar fashion to Mark, at 3.1 with an introduction to John's proclamation and baptizing activity, then it would have involved too much difficulty to have gone through the earlier draft to ensure that it all conformed to the newer material in the birth narratives or that its characterization of Jesus, his mother and his disciples was now informed by the knowledge of Jesus' origins and identity conveyed in that material.

Yet, as has become clear, even within the infancy narrative itself in Luke 2, Joseph is referred to conventionally as Jesus' father or parent. This led Vincent Taylor to the complex theory that Luke 1.34–35 constitute a later interpolation but one that, because of the Lukanisms of these verses, must have been made by Luke himself when he learned about the virginal conception story after he had completed the Gospel as a whole. He inserted these verses into an account that was originally about a natural birth to Mary and Joseph, possibly after Theophilus had received his copy but before the Gospel gained a wider circulation.[32] Others have produced more speculative explanations. So, for example, A. R. C. Leaney reconstructed

---

[30] So, e.g. R. Bultmann, *History of the Synoptic Tradition* (tr. J. Marsh; San Francisco: Harper, 1976), 295 stated bluntly, 'Mary's question in v. 34 is absurd for a bride' and on this basis relegated it to a later textual addition, which in Bultmann's view extended to v. 37.

[31] Brown, *Birth*, 480, 689–90 n285, who is generally cautious about distinguishing tradition from Lukan composition, apparently accepts this as the best explanation for the usage in 2.41–52; so also Fitzmyer, *Luke I—IX*, 311, 436.

[32] See V. Taylor, *The Historical Evidence for the Virgin Birth* (Oxford: Clarendon, 1920), 22–87.

two different sources for the infancy narrative, in the earlier of which there is no mention of John the Baptist or a miraculous conception and Joseph is the guarantee of Jesus' Davidic descent, while in the later second source Mary is central and the conception is virginal.[33] Since Leaney holds that the reference to the betrothal in 1.27 and Mary's objection that she does not know a man are incompatible, he also thinks that this source did not contain 1.27b, which is Luke's editorial accommodation to the earlier source. While the view that Luke placed a later virginal conception tradition within other traditional material that did not know of it is entirely plausible, Leaney's reconstruction of the two separate sources can be no more than guesswork and illustrates that the separation of tradition and redaction in Luke's infancy narrative is a hazardous enterprise and one that has failed to produce consensus. Whatever tradition-historical analysis one finds plausible, at best it might only illuminate how the two different perspectives on Jesus' conception originated. There remains the question of whether Luke and his readers would have found the conjunction of the two in the final product as jarring as those scholars who have attempted to ease it by such tradition-historical means.

A better solution, and one that explains why Luke and his readers might not have found the juxtaposition uncomfortable or contradictory, can be found by returning to Luke's use of the conventions of ancient biography. The writers of such biographies were also sometimes content to juxtapose two different sorts of tradition, one natural and one miraculous, about their subjects' origins and in some cases to leave readers to sort out the connection or to decide for themselves which to accept. In telling of Theseus' conception, Plutarch can talk of his lineage on his father's side and tell of Aegeus, his father, sleeping with Aethra, Pittheus' daughter, and only much later acknowledging Theseus as his son, who in the meanwhile had been brought up by Pittheus, his grandfather. At the same time he can convey the report, said to have been initiated by Pittheus, that Theseus was conceived by Poseidon or Neptune (*Thes.* 2, 3, 36). Plutarch also offers a number of accounts of the conception of Romulus. Some, he tells us, hold that he was son of Aeneas and Dexithea, others that he was born to Latinus and Roma. Both of these would have been natural conceptions. But then Plutarch reports 'the story which is most believed' about Romulus' origins. It concerns Amulius, whose niece, Ilia, is a vestal virgin. After she is discovered to be pregnant and has given birth to the twins Romulus and Remus, she claims their father is the god Mars (*Rom.* 2–4). Similarly,

---

[33] A. R. C. Leaney, *The Gospel according to St. Luke* (London: A. & C. Black, 1958), 20–7.

in his biography of Alexander, after first telling how Alexander was believed to be the son of Apollo, who, in the form of a serpent, lay with Olympias, Plutarch then offers two apparently contradictory reports. In one Olympias tells Alexander this secret of his conception at the time of his first army expedition and instructs him to behave with the courage suitable to his divine extraction. In the other report she denies ever having said anything of the kind and instead insists she was in the habit of saying, 'When will Alexander leave off slandering me to Juno [or Hera, the goddess and protector of marriage]?' Finally, when Philip hears the news of the birth of Alexander, Plutarch relates this in terms of Philip receiving it with great delight as the birth of his own son, which coincided with three other victories for Philip on the same day (*Alex.* 2, 3). Suetonius, at the beginning of his life of Augustus, simply talks of him as the son of Octavius by Atia and deals with his paternal ancestors but then towards the end can include the quite different story of Apollo coming to Atia in the form of a snake and of her giving birth to Augustus ten months after this so that it was held that he was the son of Apollo (*Aug.* 2, 4, 94). Just over a hundred years later, Dio Cassius gives his version of Augustus' beginnings, also juxtaposing the two perspectives. First he relates that Atia emphatically asserted that her child had been fathered by Apollo, but then, when the child is born, he has the senator Nigidius Figulus exclaim to Octavian, 'You have fathered a master over us' (*Hist. Rom.* 45.1).

The same phenomenon is found in lives of Plato. So Diogenes Laertius begins by stating that Plato was the son of Ariston and Perictione and by giving his parents' genealogies but follows this with reports of the story of Apollo appearing to Ariston in a dream after which the latter is convinced that the god has made Perictione pregnant. The account closes with two poems about Plato, the first of which begins,

> If Phoebus [Apollo] did not father Plato in Greece
> How did Plato heal the souls of mortals with words?
> (*Vit. Phil.* 3)

Later, in the sixth century CE, Olympiodorus still juxtaposes right at the start of his biography of Plato the two different traditions about his father, one that said Ariston was his father and one that said he was the product of Apollo having intercourse with his mother, Perictione (*Vit. Plat.* 1). Philostratus relates that 'the people of Tyana say that Apollonius is a son of Zeus; the sage himself says that he is the son of Apollonius [his father of the same name]' (*Vit. Apoll.* 1.6). It is worth concluding this brief rehearsal with reference to a *Life* where the two traditions are not only juxtaposed but where the biographer, interestingly, also makes his own view explicit and does so in a way that indicates how he can still include both traditions in his account. Iamblichus, writing around 300 CE about the early life of Pythagoras, first talks of his natural parents, Mnemarchos and Pythia. He then names those who claimed Pythagoras had been fathered by Apollo and gives their report of this event but says their assertions 'are by no means to be admitted'. Nevertheless, he goes on,

> No one will deny that the soul of Pythagoras was sent to mankind from Apollo's domain, . . . which may be inferred both from his birth, and his versatile wisdom . . . though he was still but a youth, his aspect was so venerable, and his habits so temperate that he was honored and even reverenced by elderly men, attracting the attention of all who saw and heard him speak, creating the most profound impression. That is the reason that many plausibly asserted that he was a son of god.[34]   (*Vit. Pyth.* 2)

So Iamblichus, while himself holding that the popular miraculous belief about the conception that he records was not true in any literal sense, can see why it was made and uphold its intent.

Evidently it was thought not to be inconsistent or inappropriate simultaneously to entertain different stories about the origins of a great figure, one involving ordinary physical lineage and the other, suitable in the light of the later heroic achievements of such a figure, involving a miraculous conception and an origin with the gods. The juxtaposition of different perspectives on a subject's conception is, therefore, by no means foreign to ancient biographies. Nor is it foreign elsewhere in the ancient world. Over 40 years ago, Cyrus Gordon had already observed this. In a brief one-page critical note,[35] he suggested that Jesus as God's Son also being legitimated as having Davidic descent through Joseph reflects a concept widely known in the East Mediterranean world. Having observed the paradoxical formulation of Homer's *Iliad* 10.144 in which Odysseus is called 'the Zeus-sired son of Laertes', he then discusses the phenomenon in Egyptian history where each pharaoh was regarded as the son of the god Re but inherited the throne through a human father. So, Odysseus and the pharaohs were regarded as having, on the one hand, a divine father and human mother and, on the other, a human father and human mother, but their right to kingship was transmitted through the mother's human husband, the child's biological father.

---

[34] Cf. also Miller, *Born Divine*, 149–52, on this account.
[35] C. H. Gordon, 'Paternity at Two Levels', *JBL* 96 (1977), 101.

It looks, then, as if Luke–Acts contains both a virginal conception of Jesus and the tradition that he was of the seed of David through Joseph not because the evangelist is a hopeless editor or unable to see what to present-day readers appears to be a blatant inconsistency but because ancient conventions about dual paternity allow him and his readers to be quite comfortable holding both notions. For readers familiar with such conventions double paternity can be seen even within the annunciation story. The two parts of Gabriel's announcement in 1.32 – 'he will be called the Son of the Most High' and 'the Lord God will give to him the throne of his father David' – would by no means be in tension or incompatible. The following material in the annunciation about a virginal conception of the Son of God through the power of the Most High (1.34–35) would explain the first part by representing the origin of this divine sonship as involving no human male, a claim familiar to readers, while the material in the rest of Luke–Acts would substantiate the second part by indicating the physical descent of Jesus from David through Joseph.

If this proposal is right and it was possible for Luke and his first readers to entertain simultaneously the notions that Jesus was Joseph's son and that he was the Son of God whose conception was miraculous, then it also has to be said that in the reception of Luke's writings, for a variety of reasons that will be explored further in Chapter 7, any dialogue between the two notions soon became a monologue, in which the virginal conception tradition was privileged to such an extent that the other tradition was marginalized and reinterpreted in the light of the former. From a present-day perspective, however, the juxtaposition can prove illuminating. Luke holds with the earliest Christian formulations that Jesus was of the seed of David and Joseph's son, but he also holds that in the light of his resurrection Joseph's son was vindicated as God's Son. To stress that conviction he includes an annunciation story in which the conception of this Son of God is narrated in a fashion similar to that of other figures in the ancient world who were thought to be sons of gods, omitting any participation on the part of a human male. Once the literary conventions of ancient biography are recognized in this phenomenon, this offers strong support for interpreting the miraculous tradition in Luke's story of Jesus' conception in relation to the human conception through Joseph no differently than we would in the case of this element in the stories of Romulus, Theseus, Plato, Philip, Alexander, Pythagoras or Augustus.

We should not overlook, however, the force of Luke's claim for this Son of God. Expressing the claim through the literary conventions about the conception of sons of gods does not, of course, mean that he merely places Jesus alongside these other figures in the ancient world. As we saw previously, Luke gives his birth narrative a Roman setting in 2.1–14, where he specifically mentions Augustus (2.1) and where the angels' announcement to the shepherds evokes the Priene inscription about Augustus (2.10–11, 14), which spoke of the birthday of 'the god'. Augustus, born as Gaius Octavius, had become *divi filius*, son of God, after Julius Caesar's deification and was later himself deified by the senate shortly after his death in 14 CE. The inscription retrojects this status to his birth and, again as we have seen, he is later reported by Suetonius to have had a divine birth from his mother, Atia, and the god Apollo. In this light Luke's insistence on Jesus being Son of God from his conception can be seen both as a retrojection of later Christological belief about the Spirit being at work in the person and mission of Jesus and as an integral part of his presentation of Jesus as the alternative to imperial ideology. For Luke Jesus is both the Davidic king who brings salvation to God's people, Israel, and the Son of God whose status and sovereignty transcends and undermines that of Caesar as he brings light to the nations.

6

Behind the New Testament:
historical exploration

The place of historical exploration

For the purposes of the overall argument of this book, historical issues are in an important sense secondary. That overall argument is not dependent on a historical reconstruction of traditions behind the New Testament that attempts to determine what actually happened in the circumstances of Jesus' birth and on the basis of its conclusions about historicity adjudicates whether or not a virginal conception is to be believed and how it is to be appropriated in contemporary theological reflection. The stance taken here is that the more significant primary factor for Christian theology is the canonical witness and that in this case that witness is diverse. If the previous findings about this diversity are persuasive, then the theological arguments that will be made in the book's last two chapters follow. So far the claim has been made that there are definitely two and possibly three different traditions within the New Testament itself about Jesus' conception. The annunciation stories in Luke and most probably in Matthew witness to a virginal conception, Paul, John and Hebrews bear witness to Jesus being a physical descendant of David through Joseph, and Luke combines this perspective with that of a virginal conception, while the minority reading of Matthew and possibly Mark 6.3 suggest illegitimacy. So the primary hermeneutical question is how such canonical diversity is to be handled.

That having been said, even at the canonical level historicity immediately rears its head, because in this particular case of canonical diversity, whatever the theological value of each tradition, it is obvious that they cannot be reconciled as historical affirmations. In regard to Jesus' conception, it cannot be the case historically that Joseph and someone else was the biological father of Jesus or that Jesus had a human biological father and was miraculously conceived without a father! So, however the diversity is handled, it will inevitably have consequences for the historicity of one or other of the traditions. Historical exploration, like the literary discussion of genre that has already been in play, can help to explain how the diversity of traditions came about. It has a further role that depends on the approach one takes to relating the three possible traditions. Do the sparse data support the view that dominated until the modern era, namely, that it is the virginal conception tradition that is historical, that the 'Joseph as father' tradition is about some form of adoptive fatherhood and that any hint of illegitimacy is as a result of opponents' reactions to claims of a virginal conception? Or do they provide backing for the hypothesis, already being developed here on literary grounds, that Joseph was Jesus' father, that the virginal conception was a conventional way of elaborating Jesus' status as Son of God and that a possible illegitimacy tradition is therefore to be explained in some other way? Or how likely is it that the illegitimacy tradition reflects what actually happened and that both the virginal conception and the assertion of Joseph as father are ways of dealing with this awkward datum? In this chapter we shall explore each of the three possible alternative witnesses in turn in the light of such questions, but some preliminary observations are necessary before proceeding.

In principle, the issue about Jesus' conception is no different from that of other historical clashes among New Testament witnesses. Did the Temple incident occur at the beginning of Jesus' mission (John) or towards the end (the Synoptics)? Did Jesus die on 14 Nisan (John) or 15 Nisan (the Synoptics)? What is important at the level of canonical coherence is the portrayal of Jesus' authority in relation to the Temple and its practices in the first instance and of his death in the second. Investigation of the probability of one or other or neither of the depictions being historically more accurate then becomes one part of illuminating what each of the witnesses has done in elaborating the significance of the basic event for its own purposes. Similarly here the basic event is Jesus' human conception, whether with or without a human male. In terms of ancient biology a virginal conception secures this because the mother supplies all that is necessary for the human substance of the foetus. The means of this conception of Jesus in his humanity is secondary and the various alternative depictions of the means can be explored historically as one part of the investigation of the significance of the conception for those who have elaborated on it in these different ways.

So far we have been using the term 'historical' and the phrase 'what actually happened' in a relatively straightforward and common-sense way but those acquainted with contemporary historiography and with historical Jesus studies will realize that they cover a multitude of more complex issues. As late modern readers, we bring a distinctive set of concerns about history to our engagement with the Gospels. On the one hand, we are heirs of the Enlightenment preoccupation with what actually happened in the past and its accompanying series of quests for the historical Jesus. On the other, we share the more recent recognition that all historical 'facts' already involve interpretation and the accompanying perception that the writing of history is also the writing of narrative containing inevitable elements of fictionalization. Some take this further and argue that the historian's task is not so much to reconstruct what happened in the past, since 'the past' only exists as already interpreted by memory, as to account for how and why the past was remembered. Memory here is also not simply an individual's recall of what was said or done but a social memory, a process, involving the interaction between individual and communal perception and interpretation, that is ongoing as each generation attempts to make sense of the past for its own new situation.[1] Despite this, the question 'Did that happen?' is hardly an uncommon response to a Gospel story and it remains a legitimate one. It may be asked in a naive fashion, presupposing a clear distinction between fact and fiction, between recall and the shaping of social memory over time, that is vulnerable to obvious criticisms. But the rejection of a purely positivistic notion of historiography should not debar both ordinary readers and scholars from pursuing historical investigation in a chastened fashion and attempting to make probable judgements not only about how and why particular records remember the past in a distinctive way but also about the most plausible explanation, on the basis of such records, of the events, deeds and words that they have interpreted. Of course, such historical investigation produces yet another story rather than 'objective facts', as the various phases of historical Jesus research amply demonstrate. Yet each generation inevitably has to satisfy its own concerns about the past and about how far significant figures and events are rooted in history. For Christian faith what remains normative are the stories of the New Testament witnesses in their diversity and not the various historians' stories about them, but the latter will play an important role in understanding and illuminating the former. Part of the latter's role will be the attempt to distinguish, among core historical traditions, material of dubious historical quality and legendary elements in the ancient texts being studied. Such distinctions are not imposed by unbelieving or

---

[1] On the consequences of some of these issues for historical Jesus studies, see e.g. D. C. Allison, *Constructing Jesus: Memory, Imagination and History* (London: SPCK, 2010), esp. 1–30; A. Le Donne, *Historical Jesus: What Can We Know and How Can We Know It?* (Grand Rapids: Eerdmans, 2011).

sceptical prejudice but arise inevitably from taking the Gospel texts seriously in an investigation of their relationship to each other, to earlier texts and traditions, and to the worlds in which they were written and which they depict.

One further preliminary point should be made. There are major disputes and debates about historical methods and their results in dealing with Jesus' words and deeds in the bulk of his public mission nearly 30 years after his birth. The historical task is likely to be even more difficult when it comes to this non-public aspect of his conception at a time when there would have been little interest in the circumstances surrounding the birth of this unknown child from Nazareth. As a consequence it is hardly surprising that in the New Testament the details around his conception, known only to his parents and possibly their immediate families at the time, are filled out in quite different and contradictory ways that fit the later purposes of those who had cause to write about him because of their estimate of the significance of his mission, death and resurrection. This fits with what we have already noted about the form in which we have some of the key New Testament witnesses, that of ancient biography with its depiction of the beginnings of a subject's life. As we have seen, we should expect that in its mix of core traditional events and interpretative embellishments, the latter, with its elements of legendary and fictive material, would feature particularly prominently in accounts of the early part of lives. While most ancient hearers or readers of the Gospels' versions of Jesus' life would not have been especially concerned to sift critically this mixture of material but would have been satisfied if the resultant portraits were plausible in the light of what they knew from elsewhere, most present-day readers will have rather different criteria of plausibility and therefore want to pursue further the legitimate questions of which parts of the infancy narratives are likely to be closer to what they would consider to be reliable tradition and which material is likely to have been part of the less historical embellishment one would expect in an ancient biography. Of course, in evaluating the most plausible construction of what lies behind the literary witnesses to Jesus' conception, conclusions will nearly always be in terms of greater or lesser probability. And if most ancient recipients of the texts were both disinclined and frequently not in a position to disentangle the historical and the legendary, the paucity of evidence and sources and the lapse of so much time will make it a lot more difficult than is sometimes assumed for present-day readers to distinguish these elements, and so sometimes the conclusion that the evidence is inconclusive will be a warranted one.

The virginal conception tradition

Are Matthew and Luke independent witnesses to this tradition?

So far it has been shown that there are no other possible New Testament witnesses to the virgin birth apart from Matthew and Luke.[2] But if the reading of Matthew as containing a virgin birth is accepted, then does this constitute one of two independent witnesses or is Luke in fact dependent on Matthew for his account so that we have only one original witness to this tradition? The consensus view of the relation among the Synoptic Gospels is some form of the Two Source theory or Two Document hypothesis, on which Matthew and Luke should be treated independently. Both have employed Mark as a common source and where they have further agreement this is due to their use of a common tradition, usually referred to as the 'Q' source. The birth narratives clearly do not fall into either of these sources and so are places where the two evangelists have gone their own way and creatively used whatever other traditions might have been available to them. The substantial differences and the paucity of any agreements in the two birth stories appear to confirm their lack of dependence on each other. There are, however, two main challengers to the Two Source theory. The first is the Griesbach hypothesis, named after the eighteenth-century scholar who advocated it. On this hypothesis Matthew was written first, was then used by Luke and then both were used by Mark. The second is commonly known as the Farrer-Goulder hypothesis, named after its two influential advocates in the twentieth century. On this hypothesis Mark's Gospel came first, then Matthew employed Mark, and finally Luke used both Mark and Matthew. Since both alternative hypotheses propose that Luke employed Matthew, it would be unwise simply to dismiss this possibility without a brief look at its implications for our exploration. It is from these hypotheses that the issue arises of whether Luke knew of and used Matthew's birth narrative and whether, if Matthew's narrative were thought to contain a virginal conception, this means that there is only one independent witness to this tradition within the New Testament, because Luke would have taken the

---

[2] Cf. also R. E. Brown, *The Birth of the Messiah* (2nd edn New York: Doubleday, 1993), 521: 'it is perfectly proper to speak of the silence of the rest of the NT about the virginal conception because not a single one of the "implicit references" has compelling force'. He does not see that in the silence about the virginal conception other views about Jesus' conception are found but concedes that 'what the silence of the rest of the NT does call into question is the theory that the memory of the virginal conception was handed down by the family of Jesus to the apostolic preachers and was universally accepted as fundamental Christian belief'.

notion from Matthew and developed it in his own way. On these hypotheses also, if Matthew's account does not contain a virginal conception, as held by the minority report, then again we would have only one witness, this time Luke, who would have added it to his version of Matthew either from a tradition with which he was familiar or as a result of his creative embellishment of Matthew.

But did Luke know and use Matthew's birth narrative? Despite its initial implausibility, there are points that can be made in favour of this view.[3] It is not a matter of inevitability that one would begin a life of Jesus with a birth narrative. After all, neither Mark nor John does so. It is his knowledge of Matthew that has given Luke the idea of beginning in this fashion. But he finds Matthew's attempt unsatisfactory and so engages in a major revision at this point. The ambiguities of Matthew are clarified and he makes clear that Jesus was conceived virginally, corresponding to the lives of Graeco-Roman rulers and heroes in the context of which he sets his story, and in the process he removes any hint of scandal from the account. He wants to give Mary the primary human role in the story and thinks he can do a better job of relating the two items of Jesus' birthplace as Bethlehem and Jesus' home town as Nazareth. He is not impressed by Matthew's placing of a genealogy first or by his proof-texting method, preferring to treat the theme of fulfilment differently and to situate a genealogy later in his account. He omits a visit from magi because they have negative connotations for him (cf. Acts 8.9–24) and replaces it with a visit from shepherds because they better represent his emphasis on Jesus' concern for those of lowly status and on status reversal. These and other arguments that could be adduced offer good explanations for why Luke has crafted his narrative in the way he has. But do they contain sufficient points of contact with Matthew to suggest that Luke has done this specifically as a means of improving upon Matthew? In response, advocates of Luke's use of Matthew point to a number of features that the birth narratives have in common. Unique to their two accounts within the New Testament, it is claimed, are Bethlehem as Jesus' birthplace, Joseph as the name of Jesus' father, the inclusion of a genealogy for Jesus and, if Matthew has a virginal conception, this supernatural explanation of Jesus' origin.

---

[3] Cf. A. J. McNicol, D. L. Dungan, D. B. Peabody, *Beyond the Q Impasse: Luke's Use of Matthew* (Valley Forge, PA: Trinity Press International, 1996), 47–70, from representatives of the Griesbach hypothesis and M. D. Goulder, *Luke: A New Paradigm* Vol. 1 (Sheffield: JSOT Press, 1989), 221–37; M. Goodacre, *The Synoptic Problem* (London: Sheffield Academic Press, 2001), 131–3; *The Case Against Q* (Harrisburg, PA: Trinity Press International, 2002), 54–9, from representatives of the Farrer-Goulder hypothesis.

In addition, both begin their story of Jesus' birth from the time of Joseph and Mary's betrothal, both stress Jesus' Davidic descent, both have an angelic annunciation and in the annunciation both have the angel declare the birth of a son who is to be called Jesus, using the formulation 'you will give birth to a son and you shall call him Jesus' (cf. Matt. 1.21; Luke 1.31). Such claims, however, are not very convincing. Jesus' Davidic descent is part of early Christian tradition (cf. Rom. 1.3) and it is likely that Bethlehem as his birthplace became associated with this also at an early date (cf. also John 7.42). It is not the case that Joseph as the name for Jesus' father is found only in these two Gospels; it is found also in John, as we have noted. In any case, the names of Jesus' parents are likely to have been common knowledge for early Christians. Luke is likely to have known about the convention of employing a genealogy in writing a *bios* without needing Matthew to remind him of this. Angelic annunciations of births would have been a convention known to both from the Jewish Scriptures and, while the coincidence of wording is at first sight interesting, it loses persuasive force when one realizes that it reflects the standard wording for giving birth and providing a name in such scriptural announcements (cf. LXX Gen. 16.11; 17.19) and other narratives (cf. LXX 1 Sam. 1.20; Isa. 7.14).

The mention of Isaiah 7.14 raises one further claim that can be made by those who hold that Luke used Matthew, namely, that both reflect knowledge of this text. Since Matthew's citation of the text is part of his editorial activity, if it could be shown that Luke also had this text in view, it might then constitute evidence that Luke knew Matthew and not just some tradition common to both. It can be argued that Luke's formulation of the angelic announcement in 1.27–33 contains seven possible parallels to LXX Isaiah 7.10–17.[4] Three of these – 'will conceive', 'will bear a son', 'you will name him' – as has been noted, are common to other birth announcements in Scripture. 'The Lord' (1.28, cf. LXX Isa. 7.10) is too common a title for God to be a convincing parallel. This leaves 'virgin' (1.27, cf. LXX Isa. 7.14), 'house of David' (1.27, cf. LXX Isa. 7.13), and 'over the house' (1.33, cf. LXX Isa. 7.17). The last of these is not at all persuasive. In Isaiah the context is judgement 'on the house of your father', while in Luke it is Jesus' reign 'over the house of Jacob for ever'. The mentions of 'virgin' and 'house of David' remain as the strongest links to Isaiah 7.13–14, but commentators dispute whether they constitute a definite

---

[4] Cf. e.g. J. B. Green, *The Gospel of Luke* (Grand Rapids: Eerdmans (1997), 85; J. D. Crossan, *Jesus: A Revolutionary Biography* (San Francisco: HarperCollins, 1994), 17–18.

reference to that text.[5] The depiction of Mary as a 'virgin' is in any case essential to the different story Luke wishes to tell and 'house of David' is a common enough way of speaking about Davidic lineage. If these two terms were to be echoes of the Isaiah passage, then it is still not clear that Luke would have needed Matthew to remind him of them. As we have seen, his birth narrative is full of allusions to scriptural texts and it would not be surprising if this were simply one of the many that he takes up quite independently of Matthew. It cannot then be shown with any great degree of probability that Luke is dependent on Matthew's use of Isaiah 7.14.

This is not the place to attempt to resolve the Synoptic Problem. Perhaps the best that can be said for the alternative hypotheses is that, if in connection with the rest of the two Gospels one is convinced there are good grounds for holding that Luke knew and used Matthew, then the difference in the birth accounts might not necessarily be an insuperable stumbling block for such a view. The similarities in the birth narratives, however, are simply not remarkable or numerous enough to persuade anyone to abandon the dominant Two Source theory on which they are readily explained by independent use of common traditions. If, as we have argued, we allow that Matthew probably contains a virginal conception, we are left, then, with two witnesses to this tradition.

Tracing a common tradition

Earlier in our exploration we examined the accounts of Jesus' conception in Matthew and Luke primarily at the level of the narratives in which they are now found, asking whether these stories as we now have them contain accounts of a miraculous divine conception. In the case of Matthew we also discussed briefly the tradition Matthew probably used because it was appealed to particularly by the minority report in support of its reading of Matthew's narrative. Here this question of tradition needs to be followed up, as we ask how far, if at all, any tradition that their authors might have employed for these divergent stories, where Matthew has the announcement of Jesus' birth given to Joseph in a dream in Bethlehem well after it is clear that Mary is pregnant and Luke has a similar announcement made to Mary in Nazareth before she has even conceived, already contains the notion of a virginal conception.

In the case of Matthew we will pick up the threads of our earlier analysis in Chapter 4. After taking away the clearest signs of Matthew's redaction

---

[5] J. A. Fitzmyer, *The Gospel according to Luke I—IX* (New York: Doubleday, 1981), 336 and Brown, *Birth*, 299–300 do not think that any influence from Isaiah 7 on Luke's account can be demonstrated.

in his annunciation story, we were left with two pieces of underlying tradition: a dream appearance and its setting, and an announcement of birth. In the former Joseph is told to take Mary as his wife because she will bear a son who is to save his people and he is obedient to the dream (1.19–21, 24–25b). In the latter, which is also based on scriptural precedents, the recipient of the announcement is addressed as 'Joseph', told not to fear, given the message that the woman involved will conceive a child 'of/from the holy Spirit' and give birth, and instructed about the name by which her child is to be called (1.20c–d, 21a). Whether Matthew is responsible for the combination of the two earlier traditions or whether they had already been combined before they reached him is disputed. Since it makes little difference to the argument, we will work with the hypothesis that Matthew employs traditions that had already been brought together. The combined traditions simply have a story of Mary being found pregnant during her betrothal to Joseph and of Joseph, believing the child not to be his, planning to divorce her. This course of action is prevented by the appearance of an angel to him in a dream and by an announcement, telling him to marry Mary, because the child is 'from the holy Spirit'. In addition, he is to name the child Jesus, because he will save his people from their sins. This he does. There is no mention of Mary's virginity or of abstinence from intercourse during the pregnancy – the two more explicit clues in the final narrative that 'from the holy Spirit' might have a meaning, unprecedented in Scripture itself, of miraculous activity that bypasses normal human procreation. This certainly makes the tradition much more ambiguous. If one interprets it as involving a virginal conception then one would need to presuppose that it originated in a Hellenistic Jewish setting where knowledge of Philo's sort of retelling of Scripture or of stories of birth of heroes in the Graeco-Roman world was already embedded. Otherwise it looks as though the tradition was simply about a natural conception or at best ambiguous and Matthew has drawn on and developed the potential of 'from the holy Spirit' in his elaboration of the tradition for his own narrative.

But what can be said about any tradition behind Luke 1.26–38? In Chapter 5 we noted that, in the attempt to explain the two different traditions of Jesus' conception within Luke, scholars such as Taylor and Leaney held that Luke had employed traditional material which did not know of a virgin birth and that 1.27b or 1.34–35 are instances of Luke's redaction of such earlier material. However, Taylor's view involves Luke's final redaction of his own material and Leaney's depends on a highly speculative reconstruction of two different sources behind Luke's infancy narrative.

It is generally agreed that in his birth narrative Luke's Septuagintal style is thoroughly pervasive and so, with the probable exception of the canticles attributed to Mary, Zechariah and Simeon, detection of pre-Lukan sources is a hazardous enterprise. In his account of the annunciation to Mary, there are editorial seams visible as Luke links his John the Baptist story to that of Jesus at the beginning and towards the end. He situates the story in 'the sixth month' (1.26a), thereby connecting it to Elizabeth's five months of seclusion (cf. 1.24) and has the angel mention Elizabeth's miraculous conception as a sign to Mary that nothing is impossible with God (1.36–37). But this does not mean that the rest of the story is traditional. It has no obvious signs of later editorial work on it and is in the same style as the rest of Luke's birth narrative. It too is Luke's composition. That does not rule out his employing pieces of traditional information available to him but does mean that it is unlikely that he had an extended source that he incorporated and adapted. If he knew a tradition of a birth announcement, similar to the one in Matthew's tradition, it is he who has filled it out and given it its typical scriptural elements, just as he did in the case of the announcement about the birth of John the Baptist.[6] For the bulk of 1.26–38, then, there is no obvious way of finding a written tradition behind Luke's narrative and therefore determining whether a virginal conception was in such a tradition as well as in the narrative.

Instead, the best that can be done in the attempt to get behind Luke is to see whether in his composition there are sufficient commonalities with the tradition behind Matthew to suggest that he has used independently information from that tradition. The points in common between the very different traditional material in Matthew 1.18b, 19–21, 24–25b and the account in Luke 1.26b–35, 38 are these: (i) the setting during the period of betrothal between Joseph and Mary (Matt. 1.18b; Luke 1.27); (ii) the angelic announcement that Mary will give birth to a son, preceded by a command not to be afraid (Matt. 1.20–21; Luke 1.28–31); (iii) the notion that the holy Spirit is involved in the conception of this son (Matt. 1.20d; Luke 1.35); (iv) the instruction to name the child as Jesus (Matt. 1.21a; Luke 1.31); (v) a statement about the future role of the child in God's purposes for Israel (Matt. 1.21b; Luke 1.32b–33); (vi) an indication of the compliance of the recipient of the announcement with its terms (Matt. 1.24–25; Luke 1.38). To these points might be added (vii) the notion, though reflected quite differently and depending on one's reading of

---

[6] For similar views of Luke's use of traditional sources in the infancy narratives, cf. Fitzmyer, *Luke I—IX*, 309–12; Brown, *Birth*, 244–50.

Matthew's tradition, that Joseph is not the father of the child (Matt. 1.19–20; Luke 1.34).

How are these common points to be assessed? At the heart of both the pre-Matthean tradition and the Lukan material (points ii–v) is the angelic announcement of the birth of a son, who is to be named Jesus, who will play a special part in the divine purposes for Israel, and in whose conception the holy Spirit is involved. The formulation of the first parts of the announcement is already based on scriptural models of such announcements of the births of special figures. The actual formulations about the future role of Mary's son are very different in Matthew's tradition and in Luke. The agreement about the last part, the involvement of the holy Spirit, is striking and probably reflects the belief that the Spirit at work in the resurrection in designating Jesus Son of God in power (Rom. 1.4) is to be seen as operative from the very beginning of his life. Since in the pre-Matthean tradition it is not altogether clear whether the Spirit's role already has the function of replacing the role of a human in conception, we cannot be sure that the agreement is about a virginal conception. This is found explicitly only in the Lukan material. This observation affects point (vii). Because of the ambiguity of Matthew's tradition a plausible reading of it is that Joseph is not the father of the child because someone else is, while in the Lukan account Joseph is not the father because no human father is involved. The agreement about point (i) is probably less significant. The natural time period for an announcement about a special firstborn son is likely to be before a marriage and therefore in the time of betrothal, but, in any case, in the pre-Matthean tradition Mary is already pregnant at this point, whereas in the Lukan material she is not. Similarly, point (vi) only provides a formal agreement. The details of the compliance vary according to the two different recipients of the annunciation, in the one case Joseph and in the other Mary.

It is worth clarifying where we have come to at this point of the historical exploration. If we accept the rough division of three stages in the process leading to the written Gospels, where the first is the life of Jesus, the second is the growth of oral and written traditions about his life and the third is the incorporation of such traditions into the evangelists' written compositions, then, in the cases of Matthew and Luke, we have worked back from the third stage to the second. In regard to Jesus' conception we have found at this second stage a pre-Matthean tradition that may or may not contain a virgin birth and Lukan material, where any tradition and Luke's own composition are virtually indistinguishable, that does contain a virgin birth. Working further back in this second stage of

Gospel formation, we have found it most likely that behind these disparate traditions there does lie a briefer common tradition of an angelic appearance during the period of betrothal between Joseph and Mary in which Jesus' birth was announced, the Spirit's part in his conception stated, his name given and a divinely chosen role within Israel predicted. This proposal then cautions against a too easy acceptance of the view of the tradition history that is frequently held in which both Matthew and Luke are thought to have drawn independently on a common tradition of a virginal conception. The brief common tradition that has been outlined and where it is not clear that a virginal conception would have been understood may be as far back as we can go by working from the annunciation stories in Matthew and Luke. The further back the common tradition is pushed, the less likely it is that in a primarily Palestinian Jewish context the phrase 'from the holy Spirit' simply by itself would trigger the thought of a virginal conception. What the rest of the New Testament evidence will not support is any claim that the virginal conception tradition was so well known among Jesus' early followers that the simple reference to 'from the holy Spirit' would be enough to bring that prior knowledge into play. It should be clear, however, that even if this proposal about the tradition history of the virginal conception is thought to be persuasive, it is still not decisive for historicity. It could still be the case that, in employing the earlier and at best ambiguous form of the tradition, Matthew and Luke or his tradition were in possession of more accurate information about the conception as virginal and incorporated this more reliable source into the adaptation of the earlier material. The question, then, is whether this or some other explanation is the more plausible or probable interpretation of the development of the traditions. In responding to that question we shall attempt to move from the brief common tradition forward to the accounts in Matthew and Luke.

Development of tradition in Matthew and Luke

We shall look at possible explanations for the development from the common tradition to the minority view of the annunciation story when we examine the illegitimacy tradition. Here we take the traditional interpretation of Matthew's narrative to be the more probable, which would then mean that the brief common announcement of birth has been taken up in the pre-Matthean tradition which combines it with a dream appearance to Joseph and thus gives it a setting in a story about Joseph. If this part of the tradition originated in a Hellenistic Jewish setting, then it is possible that the 'from the holy Spirit' reference in the earlier announcement now already becomes an oblique reference to a virginal conception, though the alternative reading of the pre-Matthean tradition as involving a natural conception but one in which some male other than Joseph was involved may be more compelling. In any case, it is the evangelist who by his elaboration on the tradition either moves its Joseph story in a different direction or clarifies its ambiguity. The insertion of the citation from LXX Isaiah 7.14 and the reference to abstention from intercourse during the pregnancy now indicate more clearly that 'from the holy Spirit' is to be understood in relation to a virginal conception. This suggests that Matthew's explicit knowledge of a virgin birth emerges relatively late in the process leading up to the writing of the Gospel. This is also supported by the common observation that the account of a virginal conception plays no role in the rest of the Gospel narrative either in the characterization of Jesus or the response of his family or followers to him. There is no hint of its knowledge on the part of any of these characters. It appears that it is not sufficiently embedded in Matthew's views to have been integrated into his overall narrative construction of the life of Jesus.

There are three main possibilities for explaining the lateness of an explicit notion of a virginal conception in the development of the Matthean tradition. One is that Matthew came across what he considered to be a plausible or reliable tradition late and used it to inform the traditional material he inherited. But the only other evidence we have for such a tradition from elsewhere is in Luke's Gospel, where it is treated so differently from Matthew, and we have not been able to find a common tradition at the level of the virginal conception but only at the more basic level of the brief birth announcement, where there is no compelling reason for thinking that 'of the holy Spirit' concealed the implication that no human male would be involved. Another is that Matthew himself is responsible for creatively interpreting his tradition in terms of a virginal conception and he did so under the influence of the cross-fertilization of the stories of the birth of heroes from the gods in the broader culture and Jewish retellings of Scripture. On this view his tradition was originally telling a story, set in the context of Joseph's dilemma, about the illegitimacy of Jesus' conception, which the Spirit nevertheless overrules. Matthew then sees the potential for 'of the holy Spirit' to be taken as a reference to a virginal conception and attempts to make this clear in his narrative by his redactional additions. This is certainly plausible but may need to be qualified, given that the Lukan material also expands on their brief common tradition of a birth announcement in the same direction of a virginal conception. It could well be, then, that the virginal conception interpretation of the birth announcement was beginning to be developed in Hellenistic Jewish circles before Matthew writes, that the pre-Matthean tradition, despite its original meaning, had already begun to be interpreted in this way, and that Matthew in continuity with this interpretation takes the development further in his version of Joseph's story. A third possibility is that Matthew and the tradition before him have told the story of the virginal conception in the context of Joseph's dilemma and his suspicion of adultery as a response to scurrilous suggestions already being made by Jewish opponents reacting to the claim of a virginal conception. But, as we shall see, any extant evidence for the charge of illegitimacy in response to the virginal conception is much later in the second century and if the claim itself has only begun to emerge shortly before Matthew develops it, this gives very little time for there to have already been counterclaims that were serious or widespread enough to need to be refuted.

But what might be said in explanation of the development of the Lukan form of the tradition? If the earliest form of the story of Jesus' conception was a brief birth announcement indicating that the Spirit was involved, then Luke or his tradition has elaborated on this by having the announcement made to Mary, providing the full framework of scriptural birth announcements with their five basic elements, depicting Jesus' future role as that of Davidic king, and most importantly for our purposes, having no human male involved in the conception. In principle, as discussed in relation to Matthew, this last point could have been derived from access to reliable information. The historical element here would be the bare datum that Mary found herself pregnant without ever having had intercourse with a man. By its very nature this was not a public event but an occurrence for which one only had Mary's word. So, in terms of historical investigation, one is essentially reduced to asking whether there is enough evidence that Mary and/or Jesus' family members passed down such a claim or whether there is some other explanation that better accounts for the Lukan material. The attestation for a virginal conception tradition is minimal. As we have seen, at best it only emerges elsewhere relatively late in the development of the Matthean tradition. The lack of mention of a virginal conception in the earliest birth announcement tradition and the absence of it in Paul or in Mark also indicate that its circulation was not widespread and that the Lukan material's familiarity with it is unlikely to have originated very much earlier than the time of the final version of the Gospel. This is in line with the commonly held view that, though the infancy narrative is now integral to Luke's Gospel, it is likely to have been written last. Given the probability that Luke was written in the late 70s or the 80s, it is unlikely that any tradition about the virginal conception would have reached him very much earlier, otherwise it would surely have made some impact on his narrative as a whole. Yet, as we also noted in regard to Matthew, the announcement of a virginal conception does not affect the narrative that follows in terms of its depictions of the responses to Jesus of those close to him or of his own awareness of his mission and identity. In fact, as we have seen in Chapter 5, Luke is content to allow material that talks of Joseph as Jesus' father to sit side by side with a virginal conception, even in the infancy narrative. These factors make it very difficult to give any weight to the explanation that Mary decided to pass on the virginal conception part of her family history after the disciples had been convinced that Jesus had been raised. And if there was a family tradition that had been passed down, why then does Luke make so little use of it in the rest of the birth narrative?[7] Access to a tradition of Mary's eyewitness testimony would have rescued him from inaccuracies about, for example, the Roman census and the Jewish law.

It is worth digressing briefly to underline this point. Luke 2.1–7 has a pregnant Mary accompanying Joseph, during the time Quirinius was governor of Syria, on a journey from Nazareth to Bethlehem as a result of Joseph's requirement to register there in compliance with the decree of the emperor Augustus. As is well known, there are significant problems with what Luke says about this census. Here are some of them. (i) There is no evidence from anywhere else about a Roman census at this time. (ii) There is external corroboration for a census during the governorship of Quirinius in 6 CE but this was several years after Jesus' birth and ten years after the death of Herod the Great, in whose reign Luke has situated the births of Jesus and John (1.5). This census is mentioned in Josephus, *B.J.* 2. 117–118; *Ant.* 18.1–11 and it had sparked a popular revolt. It was not a worldwide census but did include Syria and Judea but not Galilee. (iii) Neither this census nor any other Roman census required people to travel various distances to the places of their ancestors. Such an arrangement would have produced chaos across the empire and would defeat the whole purpose of a Roman census, which was to assess current property for taxation. In the midst of this chaos of movement would be thousands of descendants of David, who had lived a millennium earlier, and it would be quite impractical to require them all to return to his

---

[7] There is no good reason for questioning the consensus view that the birth narratives show no sign of having been influenced by family traditions, cf. e.g. Brown, *Birth*, 521, 525–6; Fitzmyer, *Luke I—IX*, 307–8, 341–2; J. P. Meier, *A Marginal Jew* Vol. 1 (New York: Doubleday, 1991), 221.

birthplace.[8] (iv) Only the head of a household was required to report to a local administrative centre. It would make no sense to take one's betrothed on a journey of some 85 miles, especially if she were heavily pregnant.

Luke's inaccuracies in regard to the law in 2.22–24 have been observed earlier in Chapter 3. He thinks the purification according to the law involved both parents: 'their purification' (2.22), when in fact it was necessary only for the mother.[9] According to Leviticus 12.2–8 a woman who bore a male child was considered unclean for 40 days and had to wait at home until the days of her purification were completed and before she could touch anything sacred or enter the sanctuary. She was then to bring to a priest a one-year-old lamb for a whole burnt offering and a young pigeon or turtledove for a sin-offering. If she could not afford the lamb, then she was to offer two turtledoves or two young pigeons. This is the sacrifice that Luke mentions in connection with the presentation of Jesus according to the law. But there was no law that required the presentation of a firstborn son in the sanctuary. Luke paraphrases Exodus 13.2 in 2.23, but this simply declares that a firstborn male was holy to the Lord. What had to be done was not physically to present him but to redeem him when he was a month old, to buy him back from the Lord by paying a priest five shekels, as is set out in Numbers 3.47–48 and 18.15–16 – something of which there is no mention in Luke's story. Under the influence of the presentation of Samuel in the sanctuary, Luke has made the presentation part of the law and run it together with the law about purification. All of this militates against the view that Luke got the information for his birth story from Mary or a tradition stemming from her. Mary would have known the circumstances of the birth of her child and the customs surrounding purification and presentation. Luke, however, a Gentile Christian who had probably been a god-fearer, would have had no practical knowledge of Jewish laws, and his largely Gentile audience around 70–80 CE would have been unlikely to quibble about this or about the chronology and nature of the census. They would have granted both

---

[8] J. G. Machen, *The Virgin Birth of Christ* (2nd edn New York: Harper and Row, 1932), 243, attempts to solve this issue by suggesting that not many families would have preserved their genealogy as far back as Joseph's had done and so would not have needed to make this sort of journey. On the census as a whole he is forced to admit, 'although the problem of the enrolment has not as yet been fully solved, there is no reason to think that it might not be solved if our knowledge should become more complete than it is at present' (242). This is no doubt true in principle, but in assessing historical probabilities one has to work with what one knows at present and on this basis Luke's account has to be judged highly improbable.

[9] See also e.g. Brown, *Birth*, 447–9, *contra* the implausible attempt by Machen, *Virgin Birth*, 72–4 to avoid this conclusion.

depictions some degree of plausibility, which, after all, is what counted in ancient biography.

So the likelihood of a piece of reliable information derived from Mary reaching Luke, but not others, in the 60s at the earliest is not at all strong. When the clash of such a piece of information about Jesus' origins with the probably reliable tradition about Jesus' family underlying Mark's narrative is also taken into consideration, this only underlines how problematic the Lukan material is at this point in regard to historicity. The more probable explanation of the independent development of an earlier birth announcement by the Lukan tradition and/or Luke is the conforming of the life of Jesus to other ancient biographies about significant figures, and the striking similarities to their conventions about conception, ascension and double paternity were set out in Chapter 5. The ambiguity between 'Lukan material' and 'Luke' in the previous sentence has been deliberate. This is because of the difficulty, mentioned earlier, of distinguishing between tradition and redaction in Luke's infancy narrative. In regard to the account of the annunciation to Mary, apart from the likelihood of an original brief birth announcement that his tradition has in common with the Matthean tradition, it is impossible to tell whether Luke's carefully crafted composition draws on a further development of that original announcement. It could be that a move towards a clear virginal conception of Jesus and towards one of the conventions of the *bios* had already been made in some form in the material that Luke was able to employ but, to all intents and purposes, because of his pervasive creative work in the birth narrative, we owe the clear tradition of a virginal conception to Luke, just as we owe to him the tradition of a distinct ascension of Jesus to heaven.

The conclusion that the most plausible reason for the Lukan material containing a virginal conception is not that it had more reliable information than the earliest form of the tradition of a birth announcement but that it adapts the tradition to conform more closely to standard elements in the accounts of the lives of great figures in ancient biography fits with another feature of Luke's storytelling. Elsewhere in the New Testament 'Son of God' remains a metaphor for Jesus' unique relationship to Israel's God. But by adapting the annunciation story to Graeco-Roman biographical conventions, Luke historicizes the metaphor so that Jesus' divine sonship is shown by his having no human father, whose role in conception is replaced by a divine agent, the Spirit. Something similar occurs with resurrection and exaltation. While some other early Christians saw Jesus' resurrection and exaltation as one complex, Luke separates them out and portrays both as realistically as possible, insisting that the resurrected Jesus was not a ghost but could eat fish (24.39, 43) and presenting the exaltation as a physical ascension on a cloud (24.51; cf. Acts 1.9). Again, while Matthew's infancy narrative has angels appearing in dreams, Luke much more graphically has angels interrupting the activities of everyday life. While in Mark 1.10 and Matthew 3.16 the descent of the Spirit at Jesus' baptism is depicted metaphorically, 'like a dove', Luke 3.22 changes the metaphor into part of the historical narrative so that the Spirit actually takes the form of a dove and is portrayed as literally descending 'in bodily form as a dove'. Luke is also certainly not averse to using popular legendary material, as can be seen when elsewhere, in Acts, he is rather undiscriminating in his selection of miracles and has people being healed by Peter's shadow falling on them (5.15) and matches this with the account of Paul's handkerchiefs having healing properties (19.11–12).

What has been provided at this stage is an outline of the history of the tradition about Jesus' conception reflected in the annunciation stories on the assumption that Matthew's Gospel is indeed a witness to the virginal conception. It has been suggested that the earliest source the two Gospels may have had in common was a brief birth announcement in which the mention of the holy Spirit was in itself highly unlikely to have evoked the notion of a virginal conception. In the development of this announcement in the pre-Matthean tradition about Joseph that Matthew employs it is still uncertain that this would have been understood as indicating that Mary was a virgin. Matthew in a Hellenistic Jewish setting does, however, provide indications that in his narrative no human male is involved in the conception and in doing so it is possible that he is in continuity with an emerging understanding of the tradition in the light of stories of the birth of heroes in the broader culture. Independently Luke employed the early common tradition of a birth announcement, possibly mediated through further development, and adapted it even more explicitly to the conventions of Graeco-Roman biographies about the beginnings of a subject's life. If both Matthew and Luke were written in the late 70s or early 80s CE, then the virginal conception interpretation of the birth announcement is unlikely to have emerged any earlier than the 60s and there is no compelling evidence to suggest that its emergence resulted from access to knowledge passed on by Joseph in the case of Matthew or Mary in the case of Luke.

Historical arguments for the virgin birth?

In the suggested outline above, a number of the arguments commonly put forward for the historicity of the virginal conception have been treated.

It might, however, be suggested that since our exploration has wound its own way through the tracing of traditions behind the annunciation stories, it has not done justice to the main arguments of those who defend the historicity of the virgin birth. It is worth, then, briefly interacting with those arguments in a more focused way before continuing our exploration. Theological arguments about the authority and therefore historical reliability of the Gospels or about alleged anti-supernaturalist bias will be dealt with in a later chapter. Here our interest is in the historical arguments employed. It needs to be clear from the start, however, that almost all defenders of the tradition carry out their defence on the supposition that the virginal conception is the only tradition in the New Testament. Once it is acknowledged that there is at least one other tradition about Jesus' conception represented in the New Testament writings as our earliest witnesses, then not only would this starting point be undermined but the defence would also need to take a different form. It would be insufficient to point out difficulties for opposing hypotheses about how the virgin birth tradition came about and then claim that because other views are not totally satisfactory and because there are some indications that the virginal conception could be seen as historical, there is enough warrant to take it as such. Instead, the argument would need to show why the witness to the virginal conception has better claim to historicity than the at least equally well-attested witness to Jesus' normal birth from both parents.[10] That is a very different and far more difficult task.

Despite this highly significant qualification, for the sake of completeness we shall survey major elements of common defences of the tradition with their mix of positive and negative historical arguments.[11] (i) It is claimed that a virgin birth is a complete anomaly in Jewish thought and so no Jewish Christian would have come up with such an idea unless compelled to do so because of the conviction that it had really happened. While it is true that there is no precedent for virgin birth in the Jewish Scriptures, this claim assumes an outmoded notion of Second Temple Judaism as cut off from all contact with Graeco-Roman society and culture. We should think, rather, of the interpenetration of Judaism and Hellenism

---

[10] Attempts to dismiss the evidence for this tradition, see e.g. J. Redford, *Born of a Virgin: Proving the Miracle from the Gospels* (London: St Paul, 2007), 70–92, are another matter. What is in view here is a recognition of different perspectives within the New Testament.

[11] This is the shape taken by the classic defence of Machen, *Virgin Birth*: positive testimony (2–268), negative examination of alternative explanations (269–379).

in Palestine.[12] As we have noted, the Gospels themselves are a subgenre of ancient biography and there is no reason to think that their writers and readers would be unfamiliar with the way the births of those considered sons of deities were imagined and portrayed. Justin's *Dialogue* 67–70 makes explicit that in the second century an educated Jew, Trypho, knew these stories, and earlier Philo too, we saw, was familiar with and employs the notion of virgin births in his own way in the retelling of Scripture. (ii) It is observed that, despite the differences between their accounts, Matthew and Luke have a significant agreement on a virginal conception. There must then have been a common earlier tradition to which they both had access independently. The existence of an earlier tradition to this effect would, of course, still not be equivalent to its historicity. But if it is granted that Matthew is indeed a witness to the virginal conception, our examination of the tradition behind Matthew still casts some doubt on whether it would have been understood as entailing a virginal conception and we have indicated that in all probability the agreement between Luke's tradition and Matthew's tradition would have amounted to a brief birth announcement in which the Spirit's part in Jesus' conception was stated and Jesus' divinely chosen role within Israel predicted. But, as we have seen, it is much more difficult to demonstrate that in such an early tradition the mere mention of the conception as the work of the Spirit would have been understood as involving no human male rather than the activity of the Spirit in relation to a normal human birth. (iii) Some defenders, of course, have suggested that an agreement between Matthew and Luke stems not so much from a common early Christian tradition but from knowledge derived originally from Jesus' family, Matthew's sources ultimately going back to Joseph and Luke's to Mary. We have given reasons earlier why it is highly unlikely that such family knowledge would only emerge at such a late stage in Christian tradition. Here it need only be underlined that this proposal entails a harmonizing of the conception stories that fails to recognize the nature of these stories and ends up presenting us with anomalies. If the two stories go back to the parents, how is it that one annunciation takes place in Judea and one in Galilee? And if Joseph had known that before her pregnancy Mary had been visited by an angel telling her in some detail

---

[12] D. Boyarin, *Border Lines: The Partition of Judaeo-Christianity* (Philadelphia: University of Pennsylvania Press, 2004), 18, can say, 'many if not most scholars of Judaism currently do not operate with an opposition between Judaism and Hellenism, seeing all of Jewish culture in the Hellenistic period (including the anti-Hellenists) as a Hellenistic culture'.

of its significance and had then travelled away from home to have this confirmed by Elizabeth, then his dilemma would already have virtually disappeared. Otherwise we would have to suppose that they never talked to each other about the extraordinary revelation Mary had received and that Joseph had expressed no curiosity about Mary's three months' absence from Nazareth.[13]

(iv) A variation on the previous argument attempts to account for the Gospels' lack of mention of any influence of the virginal conception during Jesus' ministry and the late appearance of this tradition by seeing it as Mary's secret. Mary kept secret the miraculous origin of Jesus during his lifetime because it would have given rise to suspicion and slander. She only began to speak of it to sympathetic friends after Pentecost when she would finally be believed and then the tradition began to circulate gradually.[14] In itself, this argument has some plausibility. However, it assumes what is at issue – the historicity of the tradition – and ignores the fact that, unlike Mary, the evangelists in their narratives no longer had any reason for keeping such significant information under wraps. In addition, as discussed earlier, if Mary later set the record straight on this matter, how is it that her memory failed to influence the accounts on other matters to do with the birth? (v) Appeal is made to the virgin birth tradition clashing so obviously with the Davidic descent tradition and the conclusion drawn that therefore no one would have invented the former. Again, this argument appears initially to have some force. But it really only applies to Matthew's account. While it is true that Matthew's story goes to some lengths to reconcile the tradition that Joseph was not the father with the claim of Davidic descent, the majority of the New Testament witnesses reflect no such clash because they know only of the tradition of Davidic descent. More importantly, as has been indicated in our treatment of Luke, many ancient writers and their readers would have seen no clash at all between an account of the origin of a major figure supernaturally from the gods and an account of his normal human descent complete with genealogy. The dual paternity of such figures was a common convention in the Ancient Near East and in ancient biography.

---

[13] Treating the narratives as straightforward history, Machen, *Virgin Birth*, 194–6, attempts to supply possible psychologizing reasons why indeed Mary would not have spoken to Joseph about her experience but would have told Elizabeth.

[14] Cf. e.g. Machen, *Virgin Birth*, 244–5, 263–5; Redford, *Born of a Virgin*, 72–3, 76, 151–76, who certainly overplays this explanation by having it also account for the New Testament evidence that Joseph was Jesus' father on the grounds that those who knew the secret would by no means have wished to discourage the latter idea.

The other major strand in defence of the traditional view is to attempt to take other possible explanations individually and show each to have problems in providing a sufficient basis for the emergence of the virginal conception tradition, so that again the conclusion can be reached that what is affirmed in that tradition offers the most satisfactory explanation of its origin. (i) If it is argued that the tradition developed as an embellishment of the early pre-Pauline Jewish Christian formulation that Jesus 'was descended from David according to the flesh and was declared to be Son of God with power according to the spirit of holiness by resurrection from the dead' (Rom. 1.3), then defenders of the virginal conception as historical can counter with the objection that it might be plausible to have developed the tradition that Jesus was born in Bethlehem rather than Nazareth on the basis of his descent, but there is no clear reason, when the holy Spirit's involvement in his Sonship is retrojected to Jesus' birth, for it taking the particular form of a virginal conception. It is true that this factor alone is insufficient to explain why the tradition of a virginal conception took the form it did. But our argument has not taken it alone and has supplied plausible reasons why the birth of one considered the Son of God would have been shaped in this way and why his mother would have been depicted as a virgin. (ii) If it is claimed that the tradition developed on the basis of early Christians searching the Scriptures for prophecies and anticipations of Jesus and then finding LXX Isaiah 7.14 as appropriate for telling of Jesus' birth, it can be countered that it is highly unlikely that any Jew would have interpreted this text as involving Jesus' virginal conception unless a tradition already existed of such a birth and was in need of scriptural support. This is an objection to which wholehearted agreement can be given.[15] But it is one that does not apply to our proposal in which Isaiah 7.14 does not have such a role. If Matthew's redaction is indeed using the Isaiah text to highlight the virginity of the conception, then it is because Matthew or the pre-Matthean tradition is already presupposing that 'from the holy Spirit' can indicate a conception in which no human male is involved.

(iii) If it is proposed that the tradition developed on the basis of the stories about Greek and Roman heroes who were considered to have been conceived by gods, then defenders of the tradition's historicity question whether it is in fact clear that any of the women in such stories were

---

[15] *Contra* e.g. G. Parrinder, *Son of Joseph: The Parentage of Jesus* (Edinburgh: T. & T. Clark, 1992), 24, who asserts that 'critical study suggests that Matthew, or his circle, composed the narrative to fit in with interpretation of prophecy'.

virgins and claim that this, together with the more physical, sexual depictions of such unions between gods and women, means the Graeco-Roman stories do not provide any exact parallels to the canonical ones. However, a more careful use of this Graeco-Roman material, such as has been offered in our exploration, does not claim that it offers precise parallels. The point of the comparison with such stories about the miraculous or divine origins of major teachers or heroes is that they provide the sort of pattern to which the tradition could apply its distinctive Jewish and Christian modifications, just as ancient biography provides the genre within which the canonical Gospels have their own such distinctives. As we have seen, Luke's Gospel in particular is familiar with other elements in this pattern, which it employs in its own fashion – especially the ending of a subject's life with an account of his ascension to the divine realm. It is also mistaken to claim that there are no examples of any of the mothers in the other stories being virgins. The mother of Romulus and Remus was said to be a vestal virgin, Perseus' mother, Danae, was claimed to be a virgin, and Plato's mother, Perictione, conceives by Apollo before any intercourse with her husband.[16] Again, plausible reasons have been provided why in the Christian version of such stories Mary's virginity would have been thought to be significant. But in many ways this line of objection misses the point. The key factor for Christology in invoking these comparisons is not the sexual experience, or lack of it, on the part of the mother but the absence of any human father.[17] There can be no avoidance of the fact that the convention for telling of the origins of a great figure, who was held to be the son of a god, was a story in which he had no human father. The canonical story of Jesus' birth omits any sexual aspects in the relation of the deity to a human mother. But then not all reports of the belief that a particular figure was born from a deity give an account of how that conception was believed to have taken place and in the canonical story God through the holy Spirit still replaces a human male in somehow supplying what is biologically necessary for Jesus' conception. (iv) Against those who have suggested that the tradition grew from an attempt to put a favourable light on popular knowledge that Jesus was born illegitimately, the response is made that it is more likely that such a view of Jesus' origins was a later

---

[16] F. Prescendi, 'Divine Fathers, Virgin Mothers and Founding Children: Italic Myths about Conception and Birth', in eds C. Chivaz et al., *Infancy Gospels* (Tübingen: Mohr Siebeck, 2011), 3–14, examines various myths surrounding the conceptions of Servius Tullius, Romulus and Remus, and Caeculus, where virgins are said to be impregnated by divine fire.

[17] Cf. also R. J. Miller, *Born Divine: The Births of Jesus and Other Sons of God* (Santa Rosa, CA: Polebridge, 2003), 242–3.

attempt by opponents to counter Christian claims about a virginal conception than that such an extraordinary miraculous claim should have been invented by Jewish followers of Jesus when it would have been sufficient to defend his honour by insisting that Joseph was his actual father. Yet, if Mark 6.3 is taken as evidence for popular knowledge of illegitimacy, then because this knowledge came from those who were familiar with Jesus' family, it would not have been sufficient to insist on the very point that they contested and in Mark there is no indication of knowledge of any claim that Jesus had a virginal conception. In any case, this is an issue that arises mainly in relation to Matthew's account, where, as has been seen, the connection between knowledge of illegitimacy and a virginal conception that has been suggested is rather different from the notion of a sole and immediate link that defenders of the virgin birth criticize.

Some of these negative arguments by defenders of the historical value of the tradition are not without worth, when advanced against those who maintain in an unqualified fashion that any one alternative explanation is the obvious one. When, however, some of these alternative explanations become part of a more complex and nuanced historical proposal such as has been offered above, then criticizing each one as insufficient in itself no longer has the same force.

Finally, one other feature of the defence of the tradition on historical grounds should be mentioned. This suggests that since proof for or against the historicity of the virgin birth is not attainable, one is left free to accept its historicity on other grounds, either the witness of Scripture or the tradition or both. Again this assumes there is only one witness in Scripture, and there are Roman Catholic and evangelical versions of the argument. But the argument involves confusion about the notion of 'proof'. Historical reconstructions rarely involve proof but are in terms of probabilities. One of the more sophisticated versions of this aspect of the defence is that of Brown, who, after his major analysis of the birth narratives, came to the conclusion that 'the scientifically controllable biblical evidence leaves the question of the historicity of the virginal conception unresolved'.[18] Two points should be noted about Brown's conclusion. First, he qualifies what he means by this biblical evidence by speaking of a 'tradition that is traceably preserved and not in conflict with other traditions'.[19] But we have argued that the virginal conception is in conflict with another tradition and that his focus on the birth narratives has skewed his interpretation

---

[18] Brown, *Birth*, 527; cf. also Meier, *Marginal Jew* Vol. 1, 222.
[19] Brown, *Birth*, 527n26a.

so that he is unable to give due attention to that other tradition of Jesus' Davidic descent through Joseph. Second, even on its own terms, Brown's argument about historical investigation leaving the issue unresolved still appears to see the goal of such investigation as attaining certainty or proof. But if the question is about the most probable explanation for the various pieces of evidence we have about the conception and birth of Jesus, then our exploration has evaluated that evidence rather differently, seeing the difficulties for the traditional explanation as being more severe than he allows[20] and suggesting that an alternative explanation is not as difficult as he claims. Enough has been said, however, to indicate that it is insufficient simply to conclude that the non-historicity of the virgin birth cannot be proven. The issue is not one of proof but of probabilities.[21] Here the balance of probabilities is against the virgin birth belonging to the earliest stratum of Christian memories about Jesus' life and for it being a particular elaboration of affirmations about Jesus based on belief in the resurrection.

The illegitimacy tradition

Mark, Matthew and pre-Matthean tradition

We have already seen that whether the New Testament itself contains witness to a tradition that Jesus was conceived illegitimately is disputed and have concluded that there are only two possible sources. One is Mark 6.3, which we examined in some detail in Chapter 2. The other is Matthew's annunciation story as read by the minority report on it. While these sources may not appear to constitute strong evidence, there are, of course, further sources for the charge of illegitimacy outside the New Testament. Furthermore, in an historical exploration the illegitimacy tradition needs to be taken into account as the possible source for what is found in the New Testament. Indeed illegitimacy as the historical explanation for the

---

[20] W. D. Davies and D. C. Allison, *The Gospel according to Saint Matthew* Vol. 1 (Edinburgh: T. & T. Clark, 1988), 216, take a similar view of where the probabilities lie. After talking of 'the doubtful character and meagre number of the extant sources and the limitations of historical research in general', they then list a number of factors that 'all point strongly in one direction: affirmation of the virgin birth entangles one in difficult dilemmas. Hence if the traditional belief be maintained, it will have to be on the basis of strictly theological considerations; historical reasoning offers little support.'

[21] Responding to improbabilities in the accounts pointed out by others, Machen, *Virgin Birth*, frequently resorts to highly conjectural explanations or is content to assert that the matters in question 'cannot be shown to be impossible' (cf. e.g. 237).

data about Jesus' conception is a view increasingly advanced in some recent discussions and more popular presentations.[22]

In our earlier discussion the Markan reference to Jesus as 'son of Mary' being a scurrilous comment about the legitimacy of Jesus' birth that reflected popular views was judged to be one possibility for its interpretation. Given Mark's lack of knowledge of a virginal conception, including the evidence of the attitude of Jesus' family towards him in this Gospel, the remark would not reflect any reaction to a claim about an extraordinary divine conception. The insulting remark comes from those in Jesus' home town who are depicted as knowing the family and its history. In regard to Matthew there are both the minority reading of the annunciation story in the actual Gospel and, perhaps even more plausibly, the pre-Matthean tradition where any editorial indicators that 'of the holy Spirit' is to be taken as a reference to a virginal conception are absent. In both accounts the announcement in the dream is given to Joseph in order to resolve his dilemma about an already pregnant, though still only betrothed, Mary. He obviously believed that he was not the father and that another male had fathered Mary's child. Wishing to be righteous but also merciful, however, Joseph had opted to divorce Mary quietly rather than 'to expose her to public disgrace' (1.19). He could have chosen the sort of divorce proceedings that would have determined whether the intercourse had taken place in the town or in the country and therefore whether she was deemed to have given consent or whether rape had taken place (Deut. 22.23–27). Presumably he thought that forcible violation was involved but did not want to put Mary through the ordeal and humiliation of having to bring the circumstances into public scrutiny. In commenting on these laws, Philo too urges careful judgement and compassion for the woman who has been forced (*Spec. Leg.* 3.76). Again, unless one holds that 'of the holy Spirit' here clearly has the unusual connotation of divine agency replacing human agency, nothing in the pre-Matthean tradition suggests Joseph was incorrect in his original analysis. The angel does not tell him he was wrong in thinking that Mary was pregnant by another man but that he was wrong in the conclusion that he has drawn from this, namely, that he should divorce her. The usual command not to fear because of the appearance of an angel has been adapted, so that, instead, Joseph is now

---

[22] Cf. e.g. J. Schaberg, *The Illegitimacy of Jesus: A Feminist Theological Interpretation of the Infancy Narratives* (Sheffield: Sheffield Academic Press, 1995); G. Lüdemann, *Virgin Birth? The Real Story of Mary and Her Son Jesus* (London: SCM, 1998), 137–9; J. D. Tabor, *The Jesus Dynasty* (London: HarperElement, 2006), 64–80. T. Dennis, *The Christmas Stories* (London: SPCK, 2007), esp. 143–5, accepts the view that both Matthew and Luke presumably held Jesus to be illegitimate.

told not to fear going ahead with the marriage, since the Spirit has anyway been at work in overruling and authorizing this conception.

But why did the story take this form? If Joseph was to be the main figure in an annunciation story, that story could have had the angel appear to him in a dream well before it became obvious that Mary was pregnant and forewarn him about what was going to happen, much as Luke's story about the angelic announcement does for Mary. But no, the announcement is left until after Joseph suspects adultery. It looks as though more is involved than a particular elaboration of the characterization of Joseph as a law-observant Jew and that it was thought necessary to show that, whatever irregularity may have been involved in Jesus' conception, it could be seen as part of the divine purposes and attributed to the work of the Spirit, and Jesus could still be held to be of Davidic descent through Joseph. There are two possible reasons for this presentation, both of which also fit the inclusion of the women in the genealogy in Matthew's final narrative: either the composer(s) of the tradition thought that Joseph was not the father of Jesus and someone else was or the latter was the content of an accusation about Jesus' origins to which a response was needed.

The first explanation, then, holds that the Matthean tradition assumed it was actually the case that some form of sexual scandal was associated with Jesus' conception and that this conception was through irregular but nevertheless human sexual relations.[23] Again, as shown in Chapter 4 in regard to Matthew's narrative, but this time at the level of the historical Jesus, this view is to be distinguished from that which claims that throughout his mission Jesus had the social status of a *mamzer*, an Israelite of suspect paternity. Matthew's depictions of Jesus' activities and interactions rule this out and, if, as is extremely likely, Matthew's overall portrayal of Jesus' mission has a historical core, this also rules out that, during his lifetime, his compatriots seriously held Jesus to be illegitimate and treated him accordingly.[24] The Matthean tradition assumes that Joseph's acknowledgement of the child conceived out of wedlock as his own secures that child's future social status and, if this child's illegitimate conception has a historical basis, then his belonging to Joseph's family was also sufficient to give him the legal status to have operated as he did. For any who

---

[23] Cf. Schaberg, *Illegitimacy*, 20–77; D. J. Catchpole, *Resurrection People: Studies in the Resurrection Narratives of the Gospels* (London: Darton, Longman & Todd, 2000), 73–9; Miller, *Born Divine*, 99: 'My reading of the evidence leads me to the conclusion that Matthew probably thought that Jesus had a human father other than Joseph' – see also his fuller discussion, 195–206.

[24] Cf. J. McGrath, 'Was Jesus Illegitimate? The Evidence of His Social Interactions', *JSHJ* 5 (2007), 81–100.

suspected his origins to recall those when it suited them would be a different matter. This consideration also makes unlikely the suggestion that Joseph and Mary had intercourse before they actually lived together and that it was the resulting early pregnancy that gave rise to rumours that Joseph was not the father.[25] Again, under the normal conventions of the time, Joseph's public acceptance of the child as his own should have been sufficient not only to give Jesus legal status but also to stop any rumours about paternity. In any case, if it was this sort of scandal – that intercourse had taken place at too early a stage in the betrothal – that lay behind the Matthean tradition, it would have been much more straightforward to have an angelic announcement to Joseph that this was nonetheless under the providence of God and 'from the holy Spirit' than to tell a story in which Joseph is not the father at all.

The second possible explanation of the Matthean tradition, which is not necessarily incompatible with the first, continues to take seriously the feature of illegitimacy in the story and sees it as integral to a charge to which the tradition is responding. After all, Matthew's Gospel reflects a sharp intra-Jewish polemic between Christ-believing Jews and those who rejected their claims, whether it was written before or after any actual break between the two groups. If the pre-Matthean tradition already reflects the same sort of conflict, then it could of course be claimed that the accusation of scandal or illegitimacy itself arose as a misunderstanding of and slur on the claim of a virginal conception for Jesus. Yet there is no other clear evidence for this Christian claim of a virginal conception so early and the story in the tradition does not attempt to set the record straight and to make clear that Jesus' conception was virginal. Instead it assumes the scandal and seeks to put a quite different perspective on it. Its apologetic might, however, be seen as a response to charges by unbelieving Jewish opponents not at this stage in relation to a virginal conception but in relation to Jesus' Davidic messiahship. As we have seen, the earliest assertion about Jesus' origins, as reflected by Paul in Romans 1.3, was that he was 'born of the seed of David' and the Son of David title is highly significant for Matthew, who employs it nine times in comparison with Mark's three. In addition to the dispute about the 'Messiah' and 'King of the Jews' in the trial (26.63–66; 27.11) and passion (27.28–29, 37, 42) narratives, two of the occurrences of the 'Son of David' title earlier in the

---

[25] Cf. B. Chilton, *Rabbi Jesus: An Intimate Biography* (New York: Doubleday, 2000), 5–13. It is Chilton who also suggests that, since there was no way to prove the rumours wrong, Jesus was considered a *mamzer* from his earliest days.

narrative involve controversy. The chief priests and scribes become angry when children in the Temple cry out, 'Hosanna to the Son of David' (21.15) and Jesus disputes with the Pharisees about how it is that, if the Messiah is Son of David, David can call him Lord (22.41–45). It is not surprising that any claim that Jesus was the Son of David who was greater than David met resistance, and one obvious way for opponents to attempt to undermine it was to throw doubt on Jesus' descent from David by disputing his paternity and alleging that Jesus was not in fact the son of Joseph. The Matthean tradition, which may not have had any precise information about Jesus' conception with which to counter this allegation or which may have had information that lent the charge some credibility, deals with it by telling a story in which Joseph believes the child is not his but is instructed by an angel to marry Mary and accept the child anyway, thereby also imparting to this child his family lineage.

So far, then, we have argued that one very plausible reading of the pre-Matthean tradition – and, on the minority view of Matthew's continuity with this tradition, this would include Matthew's account itself – can be seen as a response to a charge of illegitimacy levelled by others that may or may not reflect actual knowledge of a tradition of illegitimacy and that Mark 6.3 *may* be interpreted as hinting at a charge of illegitimacy levelled by inhabitants of Nazareth where Jesus had grown up. For any further evidence of such a tradition it is necessary to look beyond the New Testament. *Gospel of Thomas* 105 – 'He who knows the father and the mother will be called the son of a harlot' – is obscure. It probably reflects knowledge of the charge of illegitimacy but, as will be argued in the following chapter, is itself most plausibly interpreted as evidence for the view that Jesus had two human parents. It is in Jewish responses to Christian claims that charges of illegitimacy are found. Despite being later, can they be of help in the historical quest?

Non-Christian Jewish sources

From relatively early on there is evidence that Jews disputed Christian accounts of Jesus' birth in terms of a virginal conception. Justin's dialogue with Trypho reflects both Jewish objections that were made to Christian use of Isaiah 7.14 and Jewish comparison of Christian claims to legends like that of Perseus being born of a virgin (*Dial.* 43, 67–69). Here the objector simply holds that Jesus was born like other humans and did not have a miraculous divine conception. But other objectors in the second century went beyond a straight rejection of Christian claims and a comparison of them to mythological fables and included the charge that Jesus was born illegitimately.[26] Origen (*Cels.* 1.28–39, 67) engaged the earlier work of Celsus who reports this charge. There are strong indications that, like Celsus himself, his Jewish informant already knew the Matthean account and so was responding to Christian reading of it in terms of a virginal conception. But there are also assertions that exceed any mere response to the Christian claim, namely, that Joseph cast out Mary for her adultery with a Roman soldier named Panthera. This is the first extant reference to the name and occupation of a person said to have fathered Jesus out of wedlock. What is to be made of it? Is it simply an embellishment of a counterclaim to the virgin birth? Where does the name come from and how is it related to other mentions of such a figure in Jewish writers?

The name is found in connection with other Jewish charges against Jesus recorded in the Babylonian Talmud, namely, that he was a practitioner of magic and a heretic who led the people astray. One passage reports a saying of Rabbi Eliezer that Ben Stada brought spells from Egypt in a cut on his flesh and then identifies Ben Stada as Ben Pandira (*b. Sabb.* 104b). That this is meant to be a reference to Jesus is made highly probable by the fact that Celsus's Jewish informant, in talking about Jesus as the son of Panthera, also charges that Jesus learned magical practices while in Egypt (*Cels.* 1.28, 38). There is general agreement that Ben Stada was a heretic accused of sorcery and that at some point he was associated with Jesus, his name becoming a code term for the name of Jesus. The same pattern is found in a passage that hints at Jesus' illegitimate origins: 'And thus they did to Ben Stada in Lod and they hung him on the eve of Passover. Ben Stada was Ben Pandera. R. Hisdah said: "The husband was Stada, the paramour Pandira . . ."' (*b. Sanh.* 67a). Again, Pandera/Pandira is the figure who is expected to be known to readers. The identification of Jesus with Jesus ben Pantera in the Talmud is put beyond doubt when mention of Jesus ben Pantiri is followed and replaced with mention of Jesus the Nazarene (*b. Abod. Zar.* 16b–17a). Two stories in the Tosefta, codified somewhat earlier than the Talmud, speak of a Jesus who is the son of Pantera. One is the case of Eliezer ben Dama who was bitten by a serpent. 'Then came in Jacob, a man of Cephar Sama, to cure him in the name of Jesus ben Pantera, but R. Ishmael would not allow it' (*t. Hull.* 2.22–23). The other is the story of R. Eliezer who was arrested for *minuth* or heresy. He is released but cannot understand why he should have been

---

[26] Jewish charges that Jesus was illegitimate, 'born of fornication', are mentioned somewhat later in *Acts of Pilate* 2.2–4, where a sufficient response is thought to be the provision of witnesses to the betrothal of Joseph and Mary. Again, see the discussion in the following chapter.

arrested until R. Akiba tells him a heretic must have spoken to him in a way that pleased him. He responds,

> By heaven, you have reminded me! I was once walking along a street of Sepphoris, and I met Jacob of Cephar Sichnin, and he spoke to me a word of *minuth* in the name of Jesus ben Pantiri, and it pleased me.
>
> (*t. Hull.* 2.24b)

Jacob, mentioned in both stories, appears to have been a prominent Jewish Christian who healed and spoke in the name of Jesus. It looks, then, as if Jesus ben Pantera as a name for Jesus in the Babylonian Talmud has roots that go back through the Tosefta to a much earlier stage of Jewish polemic in the second century, reflected in Celsus's Jewish informant, and that it was later in the development of the tradition that Ben Stada is assimilated to this figure in the way that is evidenced in the Talmud. The much later medieval *Toledot Yeshu*, containing polemical Jewish counterclaims to the Christian gospel, also has the name Pandera in its counter-narrative to the infancy story. There are various recensions of the written material. In the Wagenseil and Huldreich recensions, for example, Mary's seducer is a neighbour named Joseph Pandera, while in the Strassburg manuscript he is a soldier with the name of Ben Pandera. All appear to offer a counter-narrative to that found in Matthew, and the Strassburg version has elements in common with the earlier material reported from Celsus. Behind the written versions of the *Toledot Yeshu* there are, of course, oral traditions but it is difficult to tell how far these are likely to go back, though the comparison with Celsus suggests this may be quite early.[27]

This still leaves the questions of where the name Pantera came from and whether there is any likelihood that it has anything to do with Jesus of Nazareth. It is just possible, as some have suggested, that the name derived from a word play on *parthenos* (virgin).[28] But even if this were a factor, all the evidence points to it being a real name. Both Origen and the rabbinic sources presume this, and patristic writers take the name seriously enough to attempt to explain it by including it within Jesus' own family tree. In the fourth-century writer Epiphanius we find the claim that

---

[27] For a discussion of various recensions and the suggestion that the oral traditions might go all the way back to the formation of the canonical narratives themselves, see P. Alexander, 'Jesus and his Mother in the Jewish Anti-Gospel (the *Toledot Yeshu*)', in eds C. Clivaz et al., *Infancy Gospels* (Tübingen: Mohr Siebeck, 2011), 588–616.

[28] The word play has been described in terms of Panthera being an anagram of *parthenos* in Greek, where, leaving aside the word endings, the same main consonants and vowels are switched around. But it should be remembered that Jesus was not called 'son of the virgin' in early Christian circles of the first two centuries and so it is unlikely that any designation referring to Jesus himself generated the supposed word play or the name ben Panthera.

Joseph's father was Jacob Panthera and this was why Jesus could be called ben Panthera (Epiphanius, *Pan.* 78), while much later, in the eighth century, John of Damascus can claim that Panther was the name of Mary's great-grandfather and Barpanther was her grandfather (*An Exposition of the Orthodox Faith* 4.14). More significantly, at the beginning of the twentieth century the German scholar Adolf Deissmann made a study of the various inscriptions from around the first century CE that used the name Panthera or Pantera and showed that the name was employed at that time and in particular was a surname of Roman soldiers.[29] One of the inscriptions, to which he draws attention, was discovered on a tombstone in Germany in 1859. It reads, 'Tiberius Julius Abdes Pantera of Sidon, aged 62, a soldier of forty years service, of the 1st cohort of archers, lies here' (*Corpus Inscriptionum Latinarum* XIII. 7514). As Deissmann observes, this refers to a Panthera who had come to Germany from Palestine with the Roman army and had died there around the middle of the first century. In a recent somewhat sensationalistic and speculative book, Tabor suggests this could well be the Panthera who was the father of Jesus.[30] Under a section headed boldly but misleadingly 'The Mystery of Pantera Solved' he tells of a visit to the cemetery in Germany where the tombstone still exists and then reconstructs the career of this Panthera.[31] According to Tabor, he was a Roman soldier, possibly a Jew, a native of Syria-Palestine, just north of Galilee, and a contemporary of Jesus' mother. 'So we have the right name, the right occupation, the right place, and the right time.'[32] But this is somewhat too hasty. Tabor is likely to be right that the names Tiberius Julius suggest that the man was a slave who became a freedman and received Roman citizenship from Tiberius for his army service some time after Tiberius came to power in 14 CE. But if Deissmann is correct that the indications are that he died in the middle of the first century, let us say 50–60 CE for the sake of argument, and that he died while still a soldier, then he would have become a soldier 40 years earlier at the age of 22, between 10 and 20 CE. So, he could not have been a soldier at the time of Jesus' conception, usually placed between 2 and 6 BCE. Instead he would have been born between 2 and 12 BCE and so at the relevant time was

---

[29] A. Deissmann, 'Der Name Panthera', in ed. C. Bezold, *Orientalische Studien: Theodor Nöldeke zum siebzigsten Geburtstag gewidmet* (Giessen: Töpelmann, 1906), 871–5.

[30] Tabor, *Jesus Dynasty*. The book fails to mention that this possibility had been raised previously by Morton Smith, *Jesus the Magician* (New York: Harper & Row, 1978), 47, who claimed, 'It is possible, though not likely, that his tombstone from Bingerbrück is our only genuine relic of the Holy Family.'

[31] Tabor, *Jesus Dynasty*, 70–80.

[32] Tabor, *Jesus Dynasty*, 77.

either himself newborn or no more than ten years of age. The problem with timing alone means that other difficulties in Tabor's thesis are not worth detailing. Significantly, despite his section heading, Tabor himself appears loath to give his original suggestion full backing. Instead he concludes that 'Jesus' father remains unknown but possibly was named Pantera, and if so, was quite possibly a Roman soldier.'[33] We can conclude that the Pantera buried in Germany was almost certainly not a Pantera connected with Jesus' birth and that we are left with no more than the possibility that the Pantera of Celsus's Jewish informant might not simply have been the product of strong polemic.

It looks highly likely that this latter Pantera has a real name and, as we have seen from Deissmann's study, one that could plausibly be attached to a Roman soldier. The earliest tradition in Jewish polemic was simply that Jesus was illegitimate and this matches one reading of Mark 6 and of the Matthean tradition, where the charge may have been directed originally against claims that Jesus was of Davidic descent. Somewhat later it was used as a response to the story of his virgin birth. As the polemic developed, further details were added to the charge, namely that the illegitimacy was through Mary's adultery with a Roman soldier. In further tellings the father is also given a suitable name, Pantera. Later still Jesus can simply be called Jesus ben Pantera. What is virtually certain, however, is that this name was not at the beginning of the tradition and was not a historical reminiscence about Jesus' illegitimate biological father. It would have been unprecedented for a child born illegitimately to be known officially or referred to as the son of the suspected father. The only exception would be if the father later married the mother and gave recognition to the son as his own son.[34] If there were ever an actual person named Jesus ben Pantera, he would not have been illegitimate.

This detour into the later traditions has been necessary, but in the end it adds little to the New Testament evidence except to show that the charge of illegitimacy remained as part of Jewish polemic. If there were to be any historical basis for the illegitimacy tradition reflected on a probable reading of the pre-Matthean tradition and a possible reading of Mark 6.3, what is it likely to be? There is obviously no way of knowing any precise circumstances. But the only real possibility is that Mary was raped. The patriarchal structure of the family, the cultural values of honour and shame, and Mary's youth (betrothal of a young woman between the ages

---

[33] Tabor, *Jesus Dynasty*, 80.
[34] Cf. also McGrath, 'Was Jesus Illegitimate?', 91–2.

of 12 and 14 was the norm) make any other relationship highly unlikely.[35] Talk of a love affair or a seduction to which Mary responded is the product of a modern romantic imagination.[36] In reality young girls would have been closely protected and watched in most law-observant Jewish households. There was only one set of circumstances where these restrictions would have been of no avail. Here, instead of pursuing the ben Pantera references, Tabor might have done better to reflect on the implications of his own sketch of the history of Sepphoris.[37] Despite his reliance on a late sixth-century tradition that Mary was born in Sepphoris, he does remind his readers of the fact that in 4 BCE this major city, four miles from the village of Nazareth, was the centre of a revolt that was brutally crushed by Roman armies.[38] Sepphoris was burnt to the ground and its inhabitants sold into slavery. The pillaging and raping invaders rounded up rebels from the surrounding countryside and its villages and over 2,000 men were crucified. Children born nine months after these events might well have been suspected of being the product of humiliating encounters with the invaders and of having a Roman soldier as their father. The most that can be said for the scenario that Jesus was one such child is that it is plausible and that the timing fits the dates usually assigned to Jesus' birth (between 2 and 6 BCE).[39] It might also be supported by the way the pre-Matthean tradition depicts Joseph as not wishing to put Mary through further humiliation by being exposed to interrogation about what had taken place and by the later Jewish accusations mentioning a Roman soldier, though it must always be remembered that these are from opponents out to discredit Jesus and that the earliest extant evidence for them is probably at least 150 years after the alleged event.

---

[35] *Contra* Tabor, *Jesus Dynasty*, 78, who claims that we should not imagine anything sinister or ugly about a relationship Mary had chosen.

[36] William Blake held that Mary had an adulterous relationship that was sanctified by Joseph's forgiveness, cf. *Jerusalem*, plate 61: <http://www.blakearchive.org/exist/blake/archive/object.xq?objectid=jerusalem.e.illbk.61&java=no>. Accessed 10/10/2012; *The Everlasting Gospel*, section i: <http://www.bartleby.com/235/129.html>. Accessed 10/10/2012. Thomas Hardy, 'Panthera', in *Time's Laughingstocks and Other Verses* (London: Macmillan, 1909), was familiar with the Pantera tradition and has as the narrator of his own version an old soldier, who muses on his army superior, Panthera, and on Panthera's talk of his encounter and lovemaking with Mary at a well on a march north from Judea to Tyre and then of his later recognition of her in Jerusalem at the execution of their son. Cf. also the posthumously published poems of James Whitehead, *The Panther* (Springfield, MO: Moon City Press, 2008).

[37] Tabor, *Jesus Dynasty*, 39–43.

[38] If the Roman bath house excavated in Nazareth in the 1990s is confirmed as dating from Roman times, then this, of course, no longer puts significant contact with Romans four miles away but right in Nazareth itself.

[39] Cf. also Lüdemann, *Virgin Birth?*, 77–9; Miller, *Born Divine*, 220–1.

Two further points should be made here. First, if the tradition of suspect paternity were to be historical and it were the case that Jesus was illegitimate, this would not be a sufficient cause for the emergence of the virginal conception tradition – as an attempt to provide a different, miraculous explanation of the circumstances. That may have played a role in Matthew's handling of the tradition, if he knew this reading of it, but other factors such as knowledge of Graeco-Roman stories of heroes' conceptions were operative in his taking conceived 'of the holy Spirit' in the tradition in an explicit virginal conception direction. It plays no role in Luke's account for which we have shown ample alternative explanation for such a virginal conception and where, in any case, as we have seen, Luke appears to have developed the latter while being aware of another tradition, not of illegitimacy but of Joseph as Jesus' father. The second point is not so much a historical one but might well affect how the historical possibility is viewed. If the tradition of suspect paternity were judged to have most in its favour in terms of likely historicity, such a historical reconstruction need not, as some have thought, be offensive or undermine the Christian faith.[40] It would provide no obstacle to Christian claims about Jesus but would in fact be entirely theologically coherent. If God could be seen to have reversed the greater scandal of the end of Jesus' mission in his shameful and ignominious death on a Roman cross, then the beginning of his life being associated with violence and sexual humiliation would simply be part of the same pattern.[41]

In the end, however, early attestation of the illegitimacy tradition rests on a possible interpretation of 'the son of Mary' in Mark and a plausible, but by no means the only necessary, reading of the pre-Matthean tradition. As such, it remains a historical possibility that cannot simply be dismissed but one which it would be hazardous to treat as preferable to other explanations of Jesus' conception.[42]

---

[40] Machen, *Virgin Birth*, 273–5, considers illegitimacy to be the only plausible alternative to the historicity of the virgin birth tradition but describes it, even if it simply involved Jesus being born to Joseph and Mary out of wedlock, as 'repulsive'.

[41] Cf. also e.g. J. A. T. Robinson, *The Human Face of God* (London: SCM, 1973), 62, who sees God's disclosure taking place through 'one who is born, as well as dies, under the curse of the law'; Miller, *Born Divine*, 222: 'If Christianity can believe that God could reverse the humiliation of Jesus' degrading death as a criminal by raising him from the dead, it can learn to believe that God could overcome the shame of Mary's degrading violation by making her the mother of the Messiah.'

[42] Cf. also J. D. G. Dunn, *Jesus Remembered* (Grand Rapids: Eerdmans, 2003), 346, 'Given the limited data available, a historical judgment cannot exclude the possibility of Jesus' illegitimacy. But the basis for the inference is exceedingly thin.'

The seed of David and Joseph as father tradition

Evidence for the claim that Jesus was of Davidic descent and the accompanying assumption that this was through his being Joseph's physical son is, as we saw in Chapter 2, early and widespread, being found in such disparate sources as the Pauline Corpus, John and Hebrews. Particularly striking is, as we argued in Chapter 5, that it is found in Luke–Acts, where it sits side by side with the virginal conception of the annunciation story with no attempt to reconcile the two traditions by explaining that Davidic descent was through some form of adoption by Joseph. It is still, of course, possible to doubt that the claim had any historical warrant and to suspect it of having been a way of legitimating early Christian belief that Jesus was Messiah, just, as seems probable, Bethlehem as Jesus' birthplace was a further legitimating elaboration.[43] Once Jesus' followers believed that he had fulfilled Israel's hope for a Messiah, it is argued, then, since most Jews at the time would have thought of the Messiah as being in the line of David, Jesus had to be given the title of 'Son of David' and a Davidic lineage. The premises in this argument are not as clear-cut as they might appear, however. While the notion of a Davidic Messiah was the dominant one in Second Temple Judaism, it was not the only one. In the Qumran writings there is also the expectation of a priestly Messiah, and later R. Akiba had no problem acclaiming bar Kochba as Messiah, despite the latter's apparent lack of Davidic credentials. It is not, therefore, obvious that Davidic credentials would have had to be found for Jesus if they did not exist.

But how likely is it that claims to Davidic descent would have been given credibility when there had been no royal successor to David for over five centuries since Zedekiah? Perhaps surprisingly, claims to a variety of tribal descents continued to be made well into the rabbinic periods and were by no means treated as fanciful. For those in significant lines of descent, such as from Levi or from David, oral preservation of family history would have been important, and Josephus and then later rabbinic literature refer to public genealogical records.[44] Indeed the Mishnah and the Tosefta continue to refer to the descendants of David as a distinct and identifiable

---

[43] For a cautious but in the end primarily negative assessment of the historical worth of the latter tradition, see Brown, *Birth*, 513–16. J. P. Meier, *A Marginal Jew* Vol. 3 (New York: Doubleday, 2001), 615–16, has moved from the more cautious approach on this issue in his first volume to being able to summarize his conclusions with the assertions that Jesus was born in Nazareth and the Bethlehem traditions 'are probably later Christian theological dramatizations of the belief that Jesus was the royal Davidic Messiah'.

[44] Cf. e.g. Josephus, *C. Ap.* 1.31; *Vita* 6; *m. Qidd.* 4.4; *Gen. Rab.* 98.8.

grouping, the former in connection with responsibilities for sacrificial duties and the latter in connection with the defeat of Israel's enemies in the end times.[45] From the time of Zerubbabel down into the period of medieval Judaism claims to Davidic descent were made, apparently unproblematically, for various individuals.[46]

There is no reason, then, to dismiss a claim to Davidic descent for Joseph and therefore for Jesus as implausible. The earliness of the pre-Pauline Jewish Christian formulation of 'seed of David' as the means of designating Jesus' origins (cf. Rom. 1.3) makes it likely that this tradition was known, not only among Jewish Christians in Rome but also in the Jerusalem church. While opponents of Christian claims may have wanted to dispute this one because of the theological significance being placed on it, it is difficult to think that James, the brother of Jesus, or other relatives of Jesus associated with the Jerusalem church would have gone along with the formulation in the first place if they had known it to have no basis at all in their family traditions. Indeed a case can be made that the first part of the pre-Lukan genealogy, tracing Jesus back through Zerubbabel and Nathan to David, derives from authentic oral genealogical tradition that has been manipulated to fit the scheme, found in *1 Enoch*, of dividing world history into generations of seven and that this tradition was current in the Palestinian Jewish Christian circles with which Jesus' relatives were associated.[47] And there is some later evidence that this family tradition was preserved, since Domitian is reported to have interrogated the grandsons of Jesus' brother, Jude, about whether they belonged to the Davidic line. They confessed their Davidic descent under potential threat of persecution but were let go once it became clear that they were not expecting that the Messiah's kingdom would be an earthly one that challenged Domitian's rule.[48] Early in the third century, in his *Letter to Aristides* Julius Africanus claims that the *desposynoi*, 'those who belong to the Master', the designation used for Jesus' relatives, preserved their family genealogy and used it in their interpretation of the gospel on their travels in Palestine.[49]

---

[45] Cf. *m. Ta'an* 4.5; *t. Sanh.* 4.11.

[46] For a fuller discussion of these, see M. Bockmuehl, 'The Son of David and his Mother', *JTS* 62 (2011), 486–90.

[47] That case is made in detail in R. Bauckham, *Jude and the Relatives of Jesus in the Early Church* (Edinburgh: T. & T. Clark, 1990), 315–73.

[48] Eusebius, *Hist. eccl.* 3.19–20.

[49] Eusebius, *Hist. eccl.* 1.7. For a discussion of this passage, defending the plausibility of the tradition behind it, which may go back to the middle of the first century, see Bauckham, *Jude*, 355–63. See also now C. Guignard, 'Jesus' Family and their Genealogy according to the Testimony of Julius Africanus', in eds Clivaz et al., *Infancy Gospels*, 67–93.

If, as we have seen plausible, the Matthean tradition's annunciation story was shaped to deal with polemic, it is interesting that the polemic is not directed against Joseph's likely Davidic heritage but more specifically against Jesus having shared it by being a legitimate link in the chain.

A good argument can be made that knowledge of Jesus' Davidic descent must have been current in his lifetime. For Meier, it is more likely that Davidic descent was a catalyst for a particular interpretation of the resurrection than that belief in the resurrection led to the claim of Davidic descent:

> seeing the resurrection of the crucified Jesus as the enthronement of the royal Davidic Messiah seems totally unmotivated *unless* some of Jesus' disciples during his earthly life thought he was of Davidic stock and fixed their hopes on him partly because of his lineage – hopes that they then considered fulfilled by his resurrection.[50]

Bauckham, in fact, is prepared to go further:

> The fantasy, entertained by some scholars, that Jesus was first considered the messianic 'Son of David' without reference to his ancestry must now be laid to rest. We must now see the family of Jesus as Davidides, conscious, through family tradition, of the hopes of Davidic restoration which had been cherished in their line since Zerubbabel. Their insignificant social status would have made the family tradition of this potent ancestry no less tenacious or significant. The tradition may not have been important to Jesus himself, but it was there to be activated and developed when Jesus' relatives became some of his most convinced and dedicated followers.[51]

On the whole, then, it seems more likely than not that the early claim that Jesus was of Davidic descent through Joseph has historical grounding.[52] But whatever one's conclusion about its relationship to Jesus' actual origins, the conviction that Jesus was of Davidic descent remains an early one. This conviction would also have been one of the major factors in the title 'son of God' originally being used of him, since this was the way in which Jewish Scriptures spoke of the Davidic king (e.g. 2 Sam. 7.14; Ps. 2.7) and in which expectations of a royal Messiah were expressed (e.g. 4Q246; 4Q174 (4QFlor) 1.10–12). Of course, a fuller and unique sense of divine sonship was very soon part of early Christian belief about Jesus, but there

---

[50] Meier, *Marginal Jew* Vol. 1, 219.

[51] Bauckham, *Jude*, 376. In summarizing his own views in a later volume, Meier, *Marginal Jew* Vol. 3, 617, can state that he believes it to be the case that Joseph's family claimed to be of Davidic descent.

[52] Cf. also Brown, *Birth*, 505–12, who concludes, 'the NT evidence that Jesus was really a Davidid outweighs, in my opinion, doubts to the contrary ... there is no insuperable difficulty in positing that Joseph belonged to one of the non-aristocratic, lateral branches of the House of David'.

would be little dispute that the application of that fuller meaning to Jesus' conception came later. Our main point here, however, is that the early conviction would have assumed normal patrilineal descent from David. If the Qumran documents spoke of God begetting the Messiah (1QSa (1Q28b) 2.11–12),[53] this royal Messiah would still have been expected to be in David's physical line. It is significant that this assumption remains even when, as we shall see in the next chapter, a number of later Christians hold to a virginal conception. Since their belief excludes Joseph being able to provide the required physical Davidic descent, they see this as supplied instead through Mary, whose status as a Davidide is never suggested in the canonical texts.[54]

The dominant tradition, then, was that Jesus was of Davidic descent and this was through Joseph as his father. This view would also have relatively early support from the evidence to be examined more fully in the next chapter that, among others, the Ebionites, a group of Jewish Christians, denied the virgin birth by asserting Jesus was the son of both Joseph and Mary (cf. e.g. Irenaeus, *Haer.* 5.1.3; Epiphanius, *Pan.* 30.14.4; Justin, *Dial.* 48.4—49.1 may also be a reference to Ebionite beliefs about Jesus' human origins).

Conclusions

How should these various probes behind the different New Testament witnesses be assessed? It bears repeating that, given the relatively sparse

---

[53] As mentioned in the discussion in Chapter 4, the fragment is damaged and a number of scholars hold that the text is better translated in terms of God leading forth the Messiah.

[54] Though Bockmuehl, 'Son of David', 491–3, surprisingly views the later attempt to associate this belief with the exegesis of Luke 1.27 as 'not altogether implausible' and not to 'be regarded as a particularly strained reading of Luke's admittedly complex account'. It requires reading 'engaged to a man whose name was Joseph' as a parenthesis, so that 'of the house of David' can then refer to 'a virgin' instead of to the immediately preceding Joseph. Such a reading is possible if this verse is taken in isolation but is excessively awkward syntactically and ignores that Joseph has been introduced at this point precisely because of his link to the house of David, which prepares for his next mention in the narrative in 2.4, where he travels to Bethlehem for the census 'because he was descended from the house and family of David'. In the logic of the narrative Mary is with him for the registration (2.5) not because she too is a Davidide and therefore would be required to be registered (only heads of households would have been involved) but because she is about to have their child and, for Luke, its birth needs to be in Bethlehem. There can be little doubt that the later attempt to find Davidic lineage for Mary is primarily derived from the need to hold together a virginal conception and the strong tradition of Jesus being of the seed of David. Tabor, *Jesus Dynasty*, 55–61, despite holding that Jesus was conceived illegitimately, believes Jesus was of Davidic descent through Mary, basing this on speculation that Luke's genealogy is not, as it claims, that of Joseph but of Mary.

sources and given our distance in time from them and our different take on what might constitute historical reality, any historical judgement will have to be a fairly cautious one. It is, of course, possible that the three traditions – the virginal conception, suspect paternity and the seed of David with Joseph as the father supplying the Davidic seed – arose quite independently of each other, so any proposal that attempts to trace development among them will need to be made tentatively. Those qualifications having been made, what follows is this writer's summary of what has seemed to him at present to make best sense of the preceding exploration of the evidence.

Jesus as 'the seed of David' is the earliest tradition. It was part of Jewish Christian thinking before Paul, who, as the earliest New Testament writer, repeats it in Romans 1.3. He does so as an expression of the gospel that he believes he has in common with other Jewish Christians and expects it to be totally uncontroversial. There is good reason to think, therefore, that it goes back to the Jerusalem church. Indeed, Luke in the speeches in Acts also assumes this notion was part of the earliest Christian proclamation. This notion and its corollary – that Jesus received his Davidic lineage through Joseph as his biological father – are, as we have seen, multiply attested in a variety of sources. When Joseph is mentioned in various passages in Matthew, Luke and John as Jesus' father, it is only Matthew who has made this an adoptive arrangement. The claim that Jesus was Messiah and more particularly the messianic title 'Son of David', found throughout the Synoptics, again among the earliest Christian convictions, are unlikely to have had much viability if there were any major doubts among his followers about his physical descent from David through his father. In addition, whatever their redaction by Matthew and Luke, the genealogies that they employed assumed that that Davidic descent was to be traced through Joseph. Further, if we are right in tracing as a common tradition behind the annunciation stories in Matthew and Luke a brief birth announcement, that common tradition, in which the Spirit's part in Jesus' conception is stated, his name is given and a divinely chosen role within Israel is predicted for him, appears to corroborate this understanding of Jesus' conception, since there is nothing in it that suggests that the conception will not be through the normal means.

Just as clearly the virginal conception tradition emerges at a relatively late stage. As we have discussed, some dispute that it is there in Matthew at all. But, if we are right that, on balance, Matthew's story does have a virgin birth, then it is only clear because of Matthew's redactional additions to his tradition. That pre-Matthean tradition might also contain it but it can equally well be understood to be telling of an illegitimate conception. So even in Matthew's circles the development of this tradition awaits the final composition of the Gospel before it attains a degree of clarity. The tradition is clear in Luke's annunciation story but, as we have argued, there it sits together with other material in the Gospel and Acts that assumes the earliest tradition and where at only one point (Luke 3.23) is a minor editorial adjustment made that recognizes the presence of the later tradition. This fits with the widely held view that the infancy narrative was the last part of the Gospel to be composed. Of course, earliest tradition does not equate straightforwardly with reliable historical reminiscence and, in theory, it could be the case that, although the virgin birth tradition is latest, it comes on the scene because it contained a genuine historical memory that was not widely known at an earlier stage. But we have already given substantial reasons why, in this case, it is highly unlikely that there were reliable traditions stemming from Joseph in the case of Matthew and from Mary in the case of Luke that only became accessible at a late date. It could even be that Matthew and Luke themselves thought that their additions to their traditions provided historical information or at least reconfigured historical memories but we have provided equally plausible reasons why they developed the traditions in this direction, especially the shaping of their accounts in ways that reflected the conventions of ancient biography.[55]

The tradition of a suspect paternity is in some ways anomalous and is the most difficult to assess in relation to the other traditions. It is well attested after the New Testament period but then primarily in sources that express hostility to Christian claims. In theory again it could reflect the reality that Jesus was conceived illegitimately, a reality that for obvious reasons other traditions attempted to conceal. However, with the possible exception of Mark 6.3, a plausible reading of the pre-Matthean tradition, and, on the minority reading, Matthew's development of this, would be the only and the clearest early attestation of this tradition. If it is accepted that the pre-Matthean tradition is best interpreted as involving the resolution of how Jesus could be recognized as Joseph's son and therefore inheriting his Davidic lineage despite his illegitimate conception, then it is earlier than Matthew's own reshaping of this tradition in terms of a virginal conception and possibly also earlier than the virginal conception

---

[55] Allison, *Constructing Jesus*, 435–59, provides a cautionary discussion of how far it is possible to know whether the evangelists believed their own stories were historical and of the dangers of assuming our sense of historical reality was the same as theirs.

tradition that Luke incorporates. It is unlikely therefore that this possible early source for an illegitimacy tradition arose as a response to claims about a virgin birth. There are two possible explanations for its existence. One is that the pre-Matthean tradition gave it credibility because it was thought to be a reliable memory of what had happened. The other is that it was incorporated for apologetic reasons as a response to the attempt of opponents to discredit Jesus' Davidic descent by claiming that there was something irregular about Jesus' birth and that Joseph was not his father. Not being in possession of any precise knowledge of the circumstances of Jesus' conception, the tradition dealt with the objection by showing that, even if the charge were true, it would not invalidate the claim to Davidic descent and the fulfilment of God's purposes through this child. On this latter view the tradition would fit with the other evidence by occupying a mediating role in the development of the tradition in Matthew's setting, which moved from an understanding of the brief birth announcement as involving normal human means of conception to the need to incorporate the illegitimacy tradition to seeing the possibilities for reinterpreting this tradition in terms of a virginal conception. But the illegitimacy tradition plays scarcely any role in the Lukan tradition. At most, if the evangelist understood Mark 6.3 as a reference to it, he dismisses it in favour of the earlier tradition that Jesus was Joseph's son (Luke 4.22). But explaining the origins of the illegitimacy tradition has been the most speculative part of our exploration. In any case, given the doubts about the interpretation of its two earliest sources, proposing that it best explains the origins of the other traditions would be to go way beyond the evidence. For these reasons, in regard to Jesus' conception, the earliest tradition with its varied attestation does appear most likely to constitute the most reliable memory of what his first followers thought about Jesus' origins, and Joseph can with some probability, but by no means certainty, be regarded as Jesus' natural father.

A reminder of where the significance of this chapter for the book's overall argument lies may be needed. It is *not* simply that its probable historical conclusions trump the Church's traditional teaching about the virgin birth, which on this basis can be dismissed. It is rather that the diversity of the witness in the Church's canon prompts this sort of historical exploration in the first place. Only on the supposition that the canon contains one clear and substantial perspective on Jesus' conception, namely, that it was virginal, will it be thought that the task of a contemporary Christology will involve affirming, discarding, revising or reinterpreting this perspective and that the results of historical investigation have a major role in that process. What is being argued here is rather different. It is that a responsible reading of the New Testament itself has to reckon with a number of different perspectives on Jesus' conception: the tradition of the seed of David, involving paternity through Joseph; the tradition of a virginal conception in the annunciation stories; the tradition of dual paternity, both virginal and through Joseph, in Luke–Acts as a whole; and a possible tradition of suspect paternity. If the canonical level is the authoritative level for Christian theology, then the attempt to peel away the surface theological and sociological functions of these traditions to arrive at a core factual memory, even if it could be satisfactorily achieved, would be beside the point. What the historical exploration does, alongside literary and theological explorations, is help us as contemporary readers interpret the nature of the diverse canonical witnesses, including discerning those whose value includes more reliable historical memory and those whose value lies primarily elsewhere.

7

After the New Testament: the rise to dominance of the virginal conception tradition

Contrary to what one is sometimes led to believe, doctrinal tradition is not something that is monolithic nor does it function as a dead weight. Instead it frequently entails re-appropriations of earlier sources and traditions for later times and circumstances under the guidance of the Spirit. It can develop by dispute and conflict over what is essential and what is peripheral and such development can involve continuities and discontinuities, confirmations and corrections. This chapter can only survey some key stages in the tradition of reflection on Jesus' conception and some of the factors that were involved. Although inevitably this reflection is intertwined with issues surrounding Mary and her status, Marian tradition is, of course, a much broader topic. Given the constraints of our exploration and its focus on Christological implications, Mary will feature in what follows only in relation to her role in the conception as mother and virgin.

We have proposed that the origins of theological reflection on Jesus' conception within the New Testament itself do not form one monolithic perspective but have a number of distinct strands – paternity through Joseph in the line of David, virginal conception, possible suspect paternity, and dual paternity involving both a virginal conception and descent through Joseph. This immediately raises two further related questions. Is there evidence that any of the strands other than one involving a virginal conception continued to be held into the second century? How is it that, despite the alleged diversity within the New Testament, by the fourth century Christian interpretation and tradition had made only one tradition, the virginal conception, normative and any divergent New Testament material was being read in the light of this particular model?

From the early second century to Irenaeus

The use of 'After' in our chapter title, of course, needs some qualification. It may well be that the latest compositions within the New Testament overlap chronologically with the earliest second-century writings we shall examine. However, it is worth beginning our sketch of developments by observing that in the earliest writings, with two important exceptions, those of Ignatius of Antioch and the *Ascension of Isaiah*, to which we shall return, there is no discussion of the circumstances of Jesus' birth. Writings such as *1* and *2 Clement*, the *Didache*, the *Epistle of Barnabas*, the *Shepherd of Hermas*, the *Epistle of Polycarp* and the *Epistle to Diognetus* appear not to have been aware of the tradition of a virginal conception. In a number of cases this is clearly not because they did not have the occasion to say anything about Jesus' origins. The *Epistle of Barnabas* 5 has an extended discussion about the incarnation and the sufferings of Christ but simply talks of Christ's coming or appearing in the flesh, and elsewhere this letter speaks of Christ as the son of David (12). Similarly, the *Epistle to Diognetus* 9 reflects on the manifestation of Christ but is content to talk about the sending of the Word to humanity. Elsewhere the incarnation is seen in terms of a Spirit Christology. The *Shepherd of Hermas* speaks of God making the holy Spirit dwell in the chosen flesh of the Son and of this flesh then being subject to the Spirit in holy living (*Herm. Sim.* 5.6), while *2 Clement* holds that Christ the Lord was 'first spirit, and then became flesh' (9.5; cf. also 14.2).

When later in the second century attention is paid to aspects of Jesus' birth and parentage, does the diversity reflected in the New Testament writings continue? We have already supplied some of the answer to this question in the course of our earlier discussion. The strand reflecting possible suspect paternity continued not in Christian circles but in lingering suspicions among those Jews antagonistic to Christian claims about Jesus. As we have seen, however, these objections changed shape somewhat in response to developing Christian views. Whereas originally the suspicion of illegitimacy may well have been used to attempt to discredit claims about Jesus' Davidic messiahship by casting doubt on his Davidic pedigree, it later became elaborated in response to the dominant Christian claim about Jesus' virginal conception. That claim was easily interpreted as a Christian cover-up for what had actually happened and seen as a way in which Christians had had to come to terms with the fact that Joseph was not Jesus' father – they had invented a story of a miraculous conception. The response to the claim then intensified. New details were added to the illegitimacy tradition in an attempt now to discredit any notion of a virginal conception. Origen's (*Cels.* 1.28–39, 67) response to the earlier work of Celsus and his Jewish informant is a response to information that in all probability goes back to before the middle of the second century and that has the assertion that Jesus' mother was driven out by her carpenter husband because of her adultery with a soldier named Panthera who fathered her son.

A different and simpler charge of illegitimacy also appears to have remained current during this period. *Gospel of Thomas* 105 – 'he shall be called the son of a harlot' – in all probability reflects this charge and Tertullian knows of those who call Jesus 'the son of a carpenter or of a prostitute' (*Spect.* 30.6). *The Acts of Pilate*, probably to be dated in the late fourth century, continues to be aware of a charge of illegitimacy, as it has the Jewish elders accuse Jesus of being 'born of fornication' at his trial before Pilate (2.2–4). Interestingly, the counter to the charge offered by those sympathetic to Jesus, certain Jewish disciples, is not that he was miraculously born of a virgin but simply that his birth was without sin because his father and mother were betrothed and they, his later followers, were present at the betrothal. For this to be a plausible response, the charge must have been understood as one that involved illegitimacy in the sense that Jesus was born out of wedlock because Joseph had fathered the child prematurely before he was betrothed to Mary.

This same passage is therefore, both in its charge and the counter to it, also a witness to the continuation of the tradition that Jesus' birth was a natural one with both Joseph and Mary as his parents. It is not recognized enough that this view continued for some time after the first century. This strand of the tradition involving paternity through Joseph, separate from a virginal conception, is attested, not surprisingly, in various Jewish Christian circles.[1] The information we have from various sources about the Ebionites[2] indicates that they held that Jesus was the son of both Joseph and Mary. When Justin in his response to Trypho says,

> 'For there are some, my friends,' I said, 'of our race,[3] who admit that He is Christ, while holding Him to be man of men; with whom I do not agree, nor would I, even though most of those who have the same opinions as myself should say so . . .'

---

[1] On the ambiguities and complexities surrounding the term 'Jewish Christian', see eds O. Skarsaune and R. Hvalvik, *Jewish Believers in Jesus* (Peabody, MA: Hendrickson, 2007), esp. 3–52.

[2] There is much debate about this designation and its scope. The term 'Ebionites' is first found in Irenaeus (*Haer.* 1.26.2). The relationship between such a group and those named 'the Nazarenes' is not clear, and the continuities and discontinuities between both groups and pre-70 Jewish Christians, including the Jerusalem church, are disputed. This scholarly discussion does not significantly affect our presentation here, which is concerned simply with the existence of such groups and the views about Jesus' conception that are ascribed to them. For a review of the issues, see Skarsaune and Halvik, *Jewish Believers*, 419–87.

[3] This is the translation in the *Ante-Nicene Fathers* collection. A footnote refers to the alternative reading 'of your race'. The latter is in fact more likely to be original and is found in the 1364 Paris manuscript of the *Dialogue*.

this is frequently and plausibly seen as referring to Jewish Christians and, more specifically, the Ebionites, whom he does not view as heretics but rather as mistaken in their interpretation of prophecy and the apostolic witness to Christ (*Dial.* 48.4—49.1, cf. also 47.4–5). Irenaeus, believing that, as with Adam, a new form of generation was necessary for the incarnation of the Son of God, is much harsher on the Ebionites, whose views about Christ's natural origins are characterized as remaining 'in the old leaven of birth' and a consequence of not wishing 'to understand that the Holy Spirit came into Mary' (*Haer.* 5.1.3). He holds that 'they assert he was begotten by Joseph', because they follow the reading of Isaiah 7.14 that has 'young woman' instead of 'virgin' and thereby 'are setting aside the testimony of the prophets' (*Haer.* 3.21.1). Presumably, they would have seen themselves as simply holding on to an older tradition that they then defend against claims of a virgin birth by questioning the viability of its dependence on proof from this particular prophecy. The extent of Irenaeus' attempted refutation in 3.21 of the view that Jesus was the son of Joseph suggests that this tradition was still a live option among Christians in his time. Hippolytus says of the Ebionites that 'they assert that our Lord himself was a man in a like sense with all' (*Haer.* 7.22). Later Eusebius clarifies that this means he 'was the fruit of the intercourse of a man with Mary' (*Hist. eccl.* 3.27.2) and elsewhere says that 'the heresy of the Ebionites, as it is called, asserts that Christ was the son of Joseph and Mary, considering him a mere man' (*Hist. eccl.* 6.17).

Tertullian also reports that Ebion viewed Jesus as 'mere man and only of the seed of David' (*Carn. Chr.* 14) and himself held that a divine seed rather than a human seed was needed for Jesus' conception, 'lest, if He were wholly the Son of a man, He should fail to be also the Son of God, and have nothing more than "a Solomon" or "a Jonas", as Ebion thought we ought to believe concerning Him' (*Carn. Chr.* 18).[4] It appears that those whose views Tertullian combats continued to believe that it was Jesus' descent through Joseph that enabled the claim that he was the Davidic Messiah. Epiphanius also comments on the Ebionites,

> Since they wish Jesus in reality to be man ... Christ came in him having descended in the form of a dove and was joined to him, and became the Christ from God above, but Jesus was born from the seed of man and woman. (*Pan.* 30.14.4–5)

---

[4] There is no evidence for an individual named Ebion as a leader of those whom others called 'the Ebionites'. This appears to be part of a tendency within patristic writings to categorize Jewish believers in Jesus as a sect with a founder.

There are also accounts that later there was a division among Ebionites and some were willing to accept the virgin birth tradition, while others held 'that he was not born in this way but like other men' (Origen, *Cels.* 5.61; cf. also *Comm. Matt.* 16.12 and Eusebius, *Hist. eccl.* 3.27.3). Adding to information found in Irenaeus and Eusebius, Epiphanius claims that the Ebionites 'receive the Gospel according to Matthew', which they call 'according to the Hebrews' and which they 'use to the exclusion of others' (*Pan.* 30.13.3). This does not appear to be entirely accurate because he himself goes on to speak of 'the beginning of their Gospel' and then cites a passage that is in fact taken not from Matthew but from Luke 3.1, 2. Either Epiphanius is mistaken in his identification of the Gospel he quotes or it harmonizes Matthew with Luke.[5] Epiphanius himself claims their 'Gospel, called according to Matthew' was 'not complete, but falsified and mutilated' (*Pan.* 30.13.13) and that they in fact removed the infancy narratives (*Pan.* 30.14.2–3). It remains interesting that this Gospel, like the *Gospel of the Hebrews* and the *Gospel of the Nazoreans* used by other Jewish Christian groups, was primarily dependent on Matthew[6] and that among them the tradition that Jesus was born naturally to Joseph and Mary was apparently preserved until at least the time of Epiphanius towards the end of the fourth century.

Textual emendations by later copyists of the Gospels may also reflect the view that Jesus' conception involved Joseph. A second- or third-century Old Syriac text (syr[s]) of Matthew 1.16 has, instead of 'Joseph, the husband of Mary, of whom Jesus was born, who is called the Messiah', the variant reading 'Joseph, to whom was betrothed Mary the virgin, begot Jesus who is called the Messiah'. This could be interpreted as a somewhat clumsy attempt to make clear that Joseph was the legal father of Jesus.[7] But the same scribe again adds 'to [or for] you' in 1.21 and 'to [or for] him' in 1.25 to the clause about Mary bearing a son in order to stress that this child is Joseph's child. It appears more likely therefore that in the variant reading of 1.16 *parthenos* is included in its more general sense, as would have been understood from the LXX rendering that Matthew takes up in 1.23, and that, despite what is said in Matthew 1.19, Joseph is thought of as the natural father. If, as we argued previously, the third century p[45] probably does not reflect the earliest text of Mark 6.3, then it has changed

---

[5] On the harmonizing tendencies of the *Gospel according to the Ebionites*, see A. F. J. Klijn, *Jewish-Christian Gospel Tradition* (Leiden: Brill, 1992), 28–9.

[6] Cf. Klijn, *Gospel Tradition*, 42.

[7] See R. E. Brown, *The Birth of the Messiah* (2nd edn New York: Doubleday, 1993), 62–4.

'Is not this the carpenter, the son of Mary?' to a reference to Jesus' origin from both parents with its reading of 'the son of the carpenter, [the son] of Mary'.

The tradition that Jesus had two human parents is taken in a different direction in the Gnostic *Gospel of Philip*. While Joseph and Mary are seen as Jesus' earthly parents, his true father is his heavenly Father and his true virgin mother is the Holy Spirit.

> Some said, 'Mary conceived by the Holy Spirit'. They are in error. They do not know what they are saying. When did a woman ever conceive by a woman? ... And the Lord would not have said, 'My Father who is in heaven', unless he had had another father; but he would have said simply, 'My Father'. (55.23)

Later it is made clear that Joseph is the human father:

> Philip the apostle said, 'Joseph the carpenter planted a garden because he needed wood for his trade. It was he who made the cross from the trees which he planted. His own offspring hung on that which he planted. His offspring was Jesus, and the planting was the cross ...' (73.8)

While the earlier *Gospel of Thomas* as a whole is not most appropriately characterized as gnostic, it appears to reflect a similar notion in two of its sayings. Logion 101 has Jesus say,

> Whoever does not hate his father and mother as I do cannot become my disciple. And whoever does [not] love his father and mother as I do cannot become my disciple, for my mother [gave me falsehood] but [my] true [mother] gave me life.

while Logion 105 states, 'Jesus said, "Whoever knows the father and the mother shall be called the son of a harlot."' The latter saying most plausibly means that, because Jesus knows his true heavenly father and mother and is dismissive of his human parents, he lays himself open to the charge of illegitimacy from those who fail to understand this. More generally, Irenaeus depicts Cerinthus and the Carpocratians as believing that Jesus was the son of Joseph and Mary, upon whom the Christ descended at his baptism (*Haer.* 1.25.1; 1.26.1) and similarly some gnostics as holding a view like that of the Ebionites, namely, that 'Jesus was born from Joseph and Mary and that the Christ from above descended upon him, being without flesh and impassible' (*Haer.* 3.11.3). As late as the third century, Origen still knows of Gentile Christians who do not believe Jesus was born of a virgin (*Comm. Matt.* 16.12). As suggested above in relation to the teaching of the Ebionites, nearly all these views would have originally been developed independently of any knowledge of the virgin birth tradition. That we know of some of them only through the eyes of later apologists for the virgin birth can tend to make them appear to have been formulated in explicit opposition to the idea of a virginal conception. They should more probably be seen, instead, as witnesses to the continuation of what we have claimed was the dominant tradition about Jesus' birth in the first century.[8] This witness was maintained, primarily among Jewish Christians, into at least the fourth century, but with the continuing increase of Gentiles joining the Christian movement from the end of the first century major developments in thinking about Jesus' conception took a quite different direction.

As we have said, the two notable exceptions to the lack of any mention of the virgin birth in the extant writings from the early part of the second century are the letters of Ignatius and the *Ascension of Isaiah*. Already in the second decade of the second century conviction about the virginal conception had become for Ignatius a highly significant element in his stress on Christ's incarnation.[9] In the *Epistle to the Ephesians* there are two extended passages in which this becomes clear. In warning against false teachers Ignatius asserts that 'there is one Physician who is possessed both of flesh and spirit; both made and not made; God existing in flesh; true life in death; both of Mary and of God . . .' He goes on to explain that Christ, the only-begotten Son and Word,

> became also man, of Mary the virgin. For 'the Word was made flesh'. Being incorporeal, He was in the body; being impassible, He was in a passible body; being immortal, He was in a mortal body; being life, He became subject to corruption, that He might free our souls from death and corruption, and heal them . . .   (*Eph.* 7)

Here the virgin birth tradition is already linked with John 1.14 and the incarnation, and birth from Mary the virgin is seen as securing Christ's full humanity and therefore his ability to heal and save other humans. Later, in extolling salvation through the cross, Ignatius declares,

> For our God, Jesus Christ, was, according to the appointment of God, conceived in the womb by Mary, of the seed of David, but by the Holy Spirit. He was born and baptized, that by His passion He might purify the water.

---

[8] Or, as H. von Campenhausen, *The Virgin Birth in the Theology of the Ancient Church* (London: SCM, 1964), 22, puts it, 'they are . . . further evidence of how little the virgin birth was taken as a matter of course, even at the beginning and up to the middle of the second century'.
[9] On Ignatius, cf. also von Campenhausen, *Virgin Birth*, 29–30.

and then speaks of three mysteries hidden from the prince of this world: Mary's virginity, her childbearing and the death of the Lord.[10] These have brought about the destruction of magic, wickedness and death, 'God Himself being manifested in human form for the renewal of eternal life' (*Eph.* 18–19). The mention of the seed of David in connection with Mary suggests that Ignatius, as in later more explicit assertions by others, sees the Davidic line as secured through Mary, but, more significantly, what is again apparent is the linking of the beginning and end of Jesus' life to stress the solidarity with humanity that enabled him to achieve its renewal. Writing to the Magnesians, having mentioned docetic teachers who deny Jesus' death and others who advocate continuing Jewish customs, Ignatius says he warns them because he wants them 'to be unshakably convinced of the birth, the passion and the resurrection which were the true and indisputable experiences of Jesus Christ, our hope, in the days of Pontius Pilate's governorship' (*Magn.* 10, 11).

Already we see in the first patristic writer to mention the virgin birth the key elements that will be taken up into the later creeds and the reasons why they were considered to be so crucial. They are reflected again in the warnings to the Trallians:

> Stop your ears, therefore, when any one speaks to you at variance with Jesus Christ, who was descended from David, and was of Mary; who was truly born, and ate and drank. He was truly persecuted under Pontius Pilate; He was truly crucified, and died, in the sight of beings in heaven, and on earth, and under the earth. (*Trall.* 9)

For Ignatius genuine faith will not tolerate any hint that the Christ was incompatible with the realm of the flesh and that therefore his entire earthly life constituted no more than an appearance of reality. Accordingly, over against those who maintain that Christ only seemed to suffer but are themselves of no substance, the Smyrneans are praised for

> being fully persuaded with respect to our Lord, that He was truly of the seed of David according to the flesh, and the Son of God according to the will and power of God; that He was truly born of a virgin, was baptized by John, in order that all righteousness might be fulfilled by Him; and was truly, under Pontius Pilate and Herod the tetrarch, nailed for us in His flesh. (*Smyrn.* 1.2)

---

[10] The mention of Mary's childbearing as the second mystery separate from her virginity in 19.1 may well imply that Ignatius thinks of the birth as miraculous as well as the conception and therefore is likely to be the first extant witness to the notion of *virginitas in partu*.

In addition, this passage is noteworthy for its apparent awareness of apostolic writings – Paul's distinctive formulation about the resurrection (Rom. 1.3–4), now correlated with Christ's birth, Matthew's distinctive gloss on Jesus' baptism (Matt. 3.15) and Luke's distinctive framing of the ministry and passion (Luke 3.1; 23.6–12).[11] This knowledge of redactional elements of Matthew and Luke suggests that Ignatius' convictions about the virginal conception itself come from acquaintance, direct or indirect, with the birth narratives of these two Gospels, where any ambiguities in Matthew's account have no longer been found problematic in the light of Luke's.

The other main early account of a virginal conception is found in the *Ascension of Isaiah*, which may be dated to within the second to fourth decades of the second century.[12] Isaiah is given a vision of the circumstances of Jesus' birth and this is related in 11.1–14. As in Matthew's annunciation story, the setting is Bethlehem and Joseph considers divorcing Mary when it becomes clear she is pregnant. Here, however, both Joseph and Mary are said to be of the family of David. The resolution of Joseph's dilemma is similar: 'the angel of the Spirit appeared in this world, and after this Joseph did not divorce Mary' (11.4a). Instead he 'kept her as a holy virgin, although she was pregnant' and did not live with her for two months. Now matters take a decidedly more miraculous turn. Immediately after the two months, when Joseph and Mary come under the same roof, she looks and to her astonishment sees a baby. 'And after her astonishment had worn off, her womb was found as (it was) at first, before she had conceived' (11.9). When this becomes known, some see this as the virgin Mary having borne a child after two months, while others say she has not actually given birth because they saw no midwife and heard no cries of labour pains (11.13–14). This text, then, appears to be familiar with Matthew's account or possibly the developing pre-Matthean tradition but has taken it further in a legendary and docetic direction, since Jesus

---

[11] A. Gregory, *The Reception of Luke and Acts in the Period before Irenaeus: Looking for Luke in the Second Century* (Tübingen: Mohr Siebeck, 2003), 74, is prepared, in connection with Ignatius, only to talk of 'the use of Luke-like material' that 'need not provide evidence of the knowledge and use of Luke', but does not consider this passage. Pontius Pilate and Herod are both, of course, names from the tradition but only Luke links them in his provision of a setting for the mission of Jesus.

[12] Cf. J. Knight, *The Ascension of Isaiah* (Sheffield: Sheffield Academic, 1995), 21: 'The apocalypse may ... provisionally be assigned to the period 112–138 CE, and it may possibly come from the period before the Second Revolt.' For an argument that the traditions behind the ascension of Isaiah go back into the first century, see E. Norelli, 'Les plus anciennes traditions sur la naissance de Jésus et leur rapport avec les *testimonia*', in eds C. Clivaz et al., *Infancy Gospels* (Tübingen: Mohr Siebeck, 2011), 47–66.

does not experience a real gestation in Mary's womb or a usual birth but simply appears as a fully formed baby. And 11.17 will go on to say, 'And I saw (that) in Nazareth he sucked the breast like an infant, as was customary, that he might not be recognized'. In common with Ignatius, *Ascension of Isaiah* has Mary's Davidic descent and probably the birth itself as miraculous, though now it is made even clearer that after the birth Mary is still virginal. It may be no accident that both Ignatius and the *Ascension of Isaiah* come from Syrian Antioch and that that location is also considered to be the most likely setting for Matthew's Gospel, whose tradition they develop.

There are other mentions of the virginal conception in writings from around 140 such as the confessional statements in the Syriac version of Aristides, *Apology* 3, and in the *Epistula Apostolorum* 3.[13] But it is shortly after the middle of the second century before we find again any extensive attention being paid to the virgin birth and it is in the writings of Justin Martyr in Rome.[14] As we have seen, Justin does not think that the alternative view that Jesus had a natural father puts those who hold it outside the pale of saving faith but he is himself strongly convinced of the truth of his own view and defends it robustly against both Jewish and pagan objections. He undoubtedly held this view on the basis of the accounts in what he calls 'the memoirs of the apostles' that were read in the assembly every Lord's day: 'having afterwards become man through the virgin, as we have learned from the memoirs' (*Dial.* 105). In one place he can say,

> The angel of God who was sent to this virgin at the time brought her this good news, saying, 'Behold, you shall conceive in the womb by the Holy Spirit and will bear a son, and he will be called Son of the Highest and you shall call his name Jesus, for he will save his people from their sins', as those who recorded everything about our Saviour Jesus Christ have taught us.
>
> (*1 Apol.* 33)

This shows awareness of texts distinctive to Luke (1.32) and Matthew (1.21) reproduced in a harmonizing version, where Luke's account with the annunciation to Mary is dominant and where the instruction to Joseph from Matthew's account can now simply be employed to fill out the message to Mary.[15]

---

[13] For a recent argument for this dating of *Epistula Apostolorum*, see D. R. Hannah, 'The Four Gospel "Canon" in the Epistula Apostolorum', *JTS* 59 (2008), 598–633, esp. 628–32.

[14] On Justin, cf. also von Campenhausen, *Virgin Birth*, 30–3.

[15] For a listing of the correspondences between Justin's writings as a whole and Matthew's and Luke's birth narratives, see Gregory, *Reception*, 265.

Justin's main arguments in defence of the virginal conception, however, strike us now as strained and unconvincing. As we saw in an earlier chapter, the fulfilment formula in Matthew is best interpreted in many instances as the evangelist finding, on the basis of his present beliefs about Jesus, motifs, terminology and events in the Jewish Scriptures whose original writers had no conception of their predicting the life of the Messiah but whose deeper meaning can now be seen as anticipating that life. Justin, like others of his contemporaries, is convinced that such Old Testament texts are actual predictions and thereby constitute proof from prophecy. So Jacob's blessing on Judah who is to wash his garments in the blood of grapes (Gen. 49.11) is a prediction of the virgin birth:

> that the Scripture mentions the blood of the grape has been evidently designed, because Christ derives blood not from the seed of man, but from the power of God. For as God, and not man, has produced the blood of the vine, so also [the Scripture] has predicted that the blood of Christ would be not of the seed of man, but the power of God. But this prophecy, sirs, which I repeated, proves that Christ is not man of men, begotten in the ordinary course of humanity. (*Dial.* 54, repeated in 63)

But his key text in all this is Isaiah 7.14:

> Now it is evident to all, that in the race of Abraham according to the flesh no one has been born of a virgin, or is said to have been born [of a virgin], save this our Christ. But since you and your teachers venture to affirm that in the prophecy of Isaiah it is not said, 'Behold, the virgin shall conceive', but, 'Behold, the young woman shall conceive, and bear a son'; and [since] you explain the prophecy as if [it referred] to Hezekiah, who was your king, I shall endeavour to discuss shortly this point in opposition to you, and to show that reference is made to Him who is acknowledged by us as Christ. (*Dial.* 43)

What Justin thinks is going on in this text is explained elsewhere:

> For things which were incredible and seemed impossible with men, these God predicted by the Spirit of prophecy as about to come to pass, in order that, when they came to pass, there might be no unbelief, but faith, because of their prediction. (*1 Apol.* 33)

Here in the debate with Trypho he repeats and expands on this particular proof from prophecy at some length (*Dial.* 66–68). Trypho also repeats that the passage says 'young woman' and not 'virgin' and refers to Hezekiah's time, and then adds the objection,

Moreover, in the fables of those who are called Greeks, it is written that Perseus was begotten of Danae, who was a virgin; he who was called among them Zeus having descended on her in the form of a golden shower. And you ought to feel ashamed when you make assertions similar to theirs, and rather [should] say that this Jesus was born man of men.

(Dial. 67)

Justin's reply to this is first to go back to arguing from the Scriptures that he and Trypho have in common. Trypho, unconvinced, then raises the reasonable and obvious question, which assumes the straightforward meaning of 'seed of David' that, we argued earlier, would have been the dominant early Christian understanding: 'How then does the Word say to David, that out of his loins God shall take to Himself a Son, and shall establish His kingdom, and shall set Him on the throne of His glory?' (*Dial.* 68). In his answer to this Justin concedes that this would indeed be a difficult problem were it not for the fact that Isaiah 7.14 is addressed to the house of David but nevertheless speaks of a virgin birth. The presupposition here that the virgin is herself of Davidic descent is spelled out when, elsewhere in interaction with Trypho, Justin, like Ignatius, reconciles virgin birth and Davidic lineage by having Mary be of Davidic descent. In offering one explanation of Jesus' self-designation as Son of Man, he talks of 'his birth by the Virgin, who was, as I said, of the family of David, and Jacob, and Isaac, and Abraham' (*Dial.* 100). But at this earlier stage in the debate, after giving his version of Isaiah 7.14 in context, he does now return to Trypho's point about Greek fables and, citing Bacchus' birth from the union of Jupiter and Semele and Hercules' birth from the union of Zeus and Alcemene and his ascension to heaven after death, dismisses such stories, which we discussed earlier in connection with Luke's account as influential parallels, as simply deliberate imitations of the Christian claim devised ahead of time by the devil in order to deceive (*Dial.* 69). This section concludes, '"And when I hear, Trypho," said I, "that Perseus was begotten of a virgin, I understand that the deceiving serpent counterfeited also this"' (*Dial.* 70), but the same argument is also found in more developed form in Justin's first Apology (*1 Apol.* 21–23, 54). Here the debate eventually returns again to Isaiah 7.14 (*Dial.* 77), where Justin quotes extensively from the Matthean account in which it is taken up and weaves into this Luke's narrative of Joseph taking Mary to Bethlehem for the census (*Dial.* 78). He goes on to argue that only the virgin birth is suited to the language of 'sign' in the Isaiah passage:

that which is truly a sign, and which was to be made trustworthy to mankind, – namely, that the first-begotten of all creation should become incarnate by the Virgin's womb, and be a child, – this he anticipated by the Spirit of prophecy, and predicted it, as I have repeated to you, in various ways.

(*Dial.* 84)

For Justin, then, the virgin birth is crucially important because it was narrated in Matthew and Luke,[16] it was predicted in Scripture and it ensures that, while Christ is certainly human, he is not simply a man like other men. While for Paul and for John in the previous century, belief in the incarnation was completely compatible with Jesus being born naturally to human parents, for Justin, when the pre-existent Son and Word, who had been manifested previously in the theophanies described in Scripture (cf. e.g. *Dial.* 127), became flesh, this was not to be thought of as a generation through ordinary means but through the direct intervention of God's power. In one brief mention only Justin anticipates what would become a major feature in later discussions of the virginal conception, namely, its association with Jesus' sinlessness: 'after that, according to the will of God, Jesus Christ the Son of God has been born without sin, of a virgin sprung from the stock of Abraham' (*Dial.* 23). And similarly in one other reference he foreshadows what would become a major motif in connection with the virgin birth, namely, the link between the virgin Mary and the virgin Eve and speaks of the former's obedience that undoes the latter's disobedience (*Dial.* 100).

A generation later than Justin's writings, those of Irenaeus (*c.*180) contain even more references to the virgin birth and develop elements that have already appeared in Ignatius and Justin: an appeal to the apostolic writings, which are now given similar authoritative status to the Jewish Scriptures, a polemic against opposing views, and a focus particularly on Isaiah 7.14 and the term 'virgin'.[17] In countering the views of Valentinian Gnostics, Irenaeus mentions some who hold that the Demiurge

produced Christ as his own proper son, but of an animal nature, and that mention was made of him by the prophets. This Christ passed through Mary just as water flows through a tube; and there descended upon him in the form of a dove at the time of his baptism, that Saviour who belonged to the Pleroma.

(*Haer.* 1.7.2)

---

[16] For the case that Justin also knows John's prologue in his treatment of the virgin birth, see C. E. Hill, *The Johannine Corpus in the Early Church* (Oxford: OUP, 2004), 316–24.

[17] On Irenaeus, cf. also von Campenhausen, *Virgin Birth*, 34–44.

So Christ was born of Mary but his temporary fleshly form had no real generation from her; instead her body was simply a receptacle through which his passed. Over against such docetic thinking, Irenaeus appeals to John's statement about the incarnation:

'And the Word was made flesh, and dwelt among us.' But, according to their hypothesis, the Word did not become flesh at all, inasmuch as He never went outside of the Pleroma, but that Saviour [became flesh] who was formed by a special dispensation [out of all the Æons], and was of later date than the Word.

Jesus has not come from the Pleroma via Sophia and the Demiurge but is the embodiment of the Word, and his flesh is the same as that of Adam, which God formed (*Haer.* 1.9.2–3).

Here at the outset of his work, we see much of what will be the burden of Irenaeus' treatment of the virgin birth: a concern to teach the true doctrine of the incarnation, and for him a virginal conception was integral to this, in the face of all opposing views.

Irenaeus is known for his advocacy of 'the rule of faith' and immediately after this discussion he outlines the universal Church's one faith received from the apostles and their disciples in a formulation that provides the basis for the later creeds. It consists of belief

in one God, the Father Almighty, Maker of heaven, and earth, and the sea, and all things that are in them; and in one Christ Jesus, the Son of God, who became incarnate for our salvation; and in the Holy Spirit, who proclaimed through the prophets the dispensations of God, and the advents, and the birth from a virgin, and the passion, and the resurrection from the dead, and the ascension into heaven in the flesh of the beloved Christ Jesus, our Lord, and His manifestation from heaven in the glory of the Father 'to gather all things in one,' and to raise up anew all flesh of the whole human race, in order that to Christ Jesus, our Lord, and God, and Saviour, and King, according to the will of the invisible Father, 'every knee should bow, of things in heaven, and things in earth, and things under the earth, and that every tongue should confess' to Him, and that He should execute just judgment towards all ...   (*Haer.* 1.10.1)

Noteworthy about this statement of faith is its trinitarian shaping, with creation by the Father providing the framework within which the incarnation of the Son takes place and then the work of the Spirit taking place through the prophets pointing to the key events in Christ's life as the fulfilment of the history of salvation, culminating in the recapitulation of all things in Christ (cf. Eph. 1.10). In relation to our topic, the incarnation of the Son is the major theological category and the prophetically pre-dicted virgin birth the historical means by which this incarnation takes place. For Irenaeus, it is this faith that is to be preserved by churches throughout the world and from which no deviation should be permitted (*Haer.* 1.10.2–3).[18]

Irenaeus is so concerned to have Christ in solidarity with humanity in order to save it that he insists Christ had to pass through every age – infant, child, boy, youth and old man – and since the decline towards old age begins when a man is 40 or 50, he holds, quite extraordinarily, that Jesus was 50 when he died, apparently having a 20-year ministry after his baptism, and claims to have received this information from those who had been conversant with John, the disciple of the Lord, who had conveyed it to them (*Haer.* 2.22.4–5). For those who might find this claim to apos-tolic tradition hard to believe, it does not particularly help the case he will go on to make that the 'heretics' have no tradition behind them, whereas even for the unlettered, the one faith is accessible in the Church through the preservation of apostolic tradition (*Haer.* 3.4.2–3). Again this ancient tradition involves belief

> in one God, the Creator of heaven and earth, and all things therein, by means of Christ Jesus, the Son of God; who, because of His surpassing love towards His creation, condescended to be born of the virgin, He Himself uniting man through Himself to God . . .   (*Haer.* 3.4.2)

In the context of refuting those who hold there is some God, such as the Pleroma or the Demiurge, other than the one God of Scripture, Irenaeus uses Matthew's citation of Isaiah 7.14 to make the point that

> therefore there is one and the same God, who was proclaimed by the pro-phets and announced by the Gospel; and His Son, who was of the fruit of David's body, that is, of the virgin of [the house of] David, and Emmanuel.
>   (*Haer.* 3.9.2)

After using all four Gospels to make this point about the unity of the God of Scripture with the God of Jesus Christ, Irenaeus makes his famous statement about the fourfold Gospel: 'It is not possible that the Gospels can be either more or fewer in number than they are' (*Haer.* 3.11.8). Those who destroy the fourfold form of the Gospel by representing its aspects as more, like Valentinus, or as fewer, like Marcion, are said to be vain and unlearned (*Haer.* 3.11.9).

---

[18] In *Haer.* 1.22.1 a similar formulation of belief is called 'the rule of truth'.

Matthew's use of Isaiah 7.14 is employed not only to show the unity between God and Christ but also between Jesus and Christ. Quoting the Matthean passage, beginning with 'And the birth of Christ was on this wise . . .', he goes on to state that this clearly signifies that

> both the promise made to the fathers had been accomplished, that the Son of God was born of a virgin, and that He Himself was Christ the Saviour whom the prophets had foretold; not, as these men assert, that Jesus was He who was born of Mary, but that Christ was He who descended from above. (*Haer.* 3.16.2)

As with Justin, so for Irenaeus, Matthew's use of Isaiah 7.14 is a key instance of the fulfilment of inspired prophecy and so those that viewed Joseph as the father of Jesus simply 'knew not the Scriptures nor the promise of God, nor the dispensation of Christ' (*Haer.* 4.23.1).

For Irenaeus all of this is ultimately important because a true incarnation was necessary for human salvation: 'For unless man had overcome the enemy of man, the enemy would not have been legitimately vanquished. And again: unless it had been God who had freely given salvation, we could never have possessed it securely' (*Haer.* 3.18.7). The virgin birth relates to both aspects of the incarnation. It shows that Christ's human nature was generated from Mary. But at the same time it is a sign that that which was born was not merely a man but 'God with us' and so

> those who assert that He was simply a mere man, begotten by Joseph, remaining in the bondage of the old disobedience, are in a state of death having been not as yet joined to the Word of God the Father.
> (*Haer.* 3.19.1, 3; 3.21.6)

> Or how shall man pass into God, unless God has [first] passed into man? And how shall he (man) escape from the generation subject to death, if not by means of a new generation, given in a wonderful and unexpected manner (but as a sign of salvation) by God – [I mean] that regeneration which flows from the virgin through faith? (*Haer.* 4.33.4)

Like Justin, Irenaeus goes into battle over whether the text of Isaiah is about a virgin or a young woman. He appeals to the miraculous account of the origin of the LXX where the 70 elders each independently came up with the same translation:

> For all of them read out the common translation [which they had prepared] in the very same words and the very same names, from beginning to end, so that even the Gentiles present perceived that the Scriptures had been interpreted by the inspiration of God.

This is to be accepted as divinely inspired and as giving 'a just interpreta-tion of that which had been truly prophesied' over against the 'impudent and presumptuous' Theodotion and Aquila who produced different Greek translations of Scripture where the term in Isaiah 7.14 is rendered as *neanis*, 'young woman', rather than *parthenos*, 'virgin' (*Haer.* 3.21.2–4). As part of his argument for the virgin birth as the fulfilment of the pro-phecy, he refers to it being addressed to 'the house of David' in Isaiah 7.13 and then brings in the promise to David in Psalm 132.11 to explain this:

> He whom God promised David that He would raise up from the fruit of his belly an eternal King, is the same who was born of the Virgin, herself of the lineage of David. For on this account also, He promised that the King should be 'of the fruit of his belly,' which was the appropriate [term to use with respect] to a virgin conceiving, and not 'of the fruit of his loins,' nor 'of the fruit of his reins,' which expression is appropriate to a generating man, and a woman conceiving by a man. In this promise, therefore, the Scripture excluded all virile influence. (*Haer.* 3.21.5)

This overturns the force of the original in an interesting fashion. 'The fruit of David's belly', that is, the descendants he has generated, now has refer-ence to Mary's womb and the exclusion of male generation, but it is still applicable to Jesus' descent from David because Mary herself is deemed to be of Davidic lineage. This interpretation is so convincing to Irenaeus that he challenges those who hold that Jesus was Joseph's son to alter this text too in the way he alleges they have altered the virgin passage! His other arguments against Jesus being the son of Joseph are likely to be equally unpersuasive to present-day readers. The first is: 'For if He were the son of Joseph, how could He be greater than Solomon, or greater than Jonah, or greater than David, when He was generated from the same seed, and was a descendant of these men?' (*Haer.* 3.21.8; cf. also 4.33.4). The second is to the effect that if Jesus were indeed the son of Joseph, then, according to Matthew's genealogy, he would be the descendant of Jechoniah, but that would disqualify him from being David's heir because Jeremiah 22.24–30 and 36.30–31 assert that the descendants of Joachim, his father, and of Jechoniah himself are to be disinherited (*Haer.* 3.21.9). Unfortunately, whatever the merits of this point,[19] it tells against Matthew's own account and appears to have passed the evangelist by, since he thought that by including Jechoniah in the genealogy he was in fact establishing Joseph's and therefore Jesus' authentic Davidic descent.

---

[19] For discussion of the confusion around this name, Jechoniah, in Matthew's genealogy, see Brown, *Birth*, 61, 83.

At the end of this section Irenaeus' more substantial argument, which will be taken up and elaborated by later writers and is still influential, has to do with the pattern of the history of salvation with its correspondence between the first man and Christ as the second Adam. While Paul applied this typology to what Christ achieved in his death (Rom. 5) and to his resurrection life (1 Cor. 15), Irenaeus now applies it to his virgin birth. Adam came from the untilled virgin soil and Christ from the virgin Mary.

> If, then, the first Adam had a man for his father, and was born of human seed, it were reasonable to say that the second Adam was begotten of Joseph. But if the former was taken from the dust, and God was his Maker, it was incumbent that the latter also, making a recapitulation in Himself, should be formed as man by God, to have an analogy with the former as respects His origin. (*Haer.* 3.21.10; cf. also 5.2.3)

The analogy with Adam allows Irenaeus also to reject again the view that Christ took nothing from Mary, the view depicted earlier as passing through her like water through a tube. Just as God gave Adam form and substance from the earth, so God gave Christ form and substance from Mary.

> For if He did not receive the substance of flesh from a human being, He neither was made man nor the Son of man; and if He was not made what we were, He did no great thing in what He suffered and endured.
> (*Haer.* 3.22.1; cf. also 5.1.2)

It also allows him to go on to make the typological contrast, seen already in Justin, between Eve, the disobedient virgin, and Mary, the obedient one: 'the knot of Eve's disobedience was loosed by the obedience of Mary. For what the virgin Eve had bound fast through unbelief, this did the virgin Mary set free through faith' (*Haer.* 3.22.4; cf. also 5.19.1).

Irenaeus' catholic vision, in which 'the path of those belonging to the Church circumscribes the whole world, as possessing the sure tradition from the apostles, and gives unto us to see that the faith of all is one and the same' (*Haer.* 5.20.1), soon began to prevail, not only in the Latin West but also in the East, where different concerns, which will be mentioned briefly below, had begun to attach themselves to the accounts of Jesus' birth. Accompanying the need to preserve the apostolic tradition was the rejection as false teaching of any other views of what were seen as its key elements, including, of course, different views about the incarnation, particularly those that did not teach the virgin birth and that now had the taint of association with docetists, Ebionites, Marcion and Valentinus.

The view that Jesus was born naturally did not, however, simply die out at the end of the second century, as can be seen in the continued efforts of later apologists to combat it, but the virgin birth tradition was now clearly dominant and it is worth reviewing the factors that had brought about this change from the diversity within the New Testament and apparent at the end of the first century. One basic factor was that the infancy narratives in the Gospels were now becoming widely known. When Irenaeus made his statement about there being four Gospels, no more and no fewer (*Haer.* 3.11.8), he was not advocating a new view but providing theological support for a phenomenon that had already been occurring. The four Gospels of our New Testament had already been singled out by many as those that were authoritative. Justin had talked of 'the memoirs of the apostles', a designation that recalls the title of Xenophon's life of Socrates, *Memorabilia*, and indicates that the Gospels were similarly seen as ancient biographies. Describing what takes place in weekly Christian worship, whether in the cities or in the country, he says that these 'memoirs of the apostles or the writings of the prophets are read, as long as time permits' (*1 Apol.* 67.1). The Gospels, then, had already begun to be put on the same level of authority as the Jewish Scriptures and were becoming widely known through their public reading. Furthermore, the *Epistula Apostolorum* provides evidence of this knowledge of the four Gospels and acceptance of their authority from around the same time.[20] Tatian's *Diatessaron*, constructed out of the four Gospels at around the time of Irenaeus' writing, also confirms the status of these four. Aiding this whole process of the wide circulation of the four Gospels in the latter part of the second century was the unusual Christian use of the codex, probably adopted because, unlike the rolls favoured by others, it was able to contain the texts of all four Gospels.[21]

Once the four Gospels were seen as the authoritative sources for the life of Jesus, it became natural, when thinking about Jesus' birth, to assume that these were the only relevant sources within the apostolic writings. Materials that can now be seen to offer different perspectives were ignored, not only because they were primarily linked with groups and teachers who in any case had clearly deficient positions on God as Creator or on the person of Christ or on the role of the Jewish law in the Christian dispensation, but also because only the actual accounts of the birth in the Gospels' lives of Jesus were thought to be significant. Diverging perspectives in Paul or elsewhere in the writings of Luke himself were read and interpreted in the light of what was taken to be the agreement between

---

[20] Cf. Hannah, 'Four Gospel "Canon"', 598–633.
[21] On this, see G. N. Stanton, 'The Fourfold Gospel', *NTS* 43 (1997), 317–46.

the birth narratives of Matthew and Luke about a virginal conception, and the latter was read into John's account, despite elements of his narrative that should have given pause. Other factors were at work in pressing the readers of the Gospels to find agreement at this point. The four Gospels were in a deeper sense to be viewed as one – one Gospel in fourfold form. The titles that were added underline this point. They were designated not as 'the Gospel *of* Matthew' or of Mark, Luke and John but as 'the Gospel *according to* Matthew' or according to the other evangelists. One Gospel was unfolded according to four different perspectives. As Irenaeus puts it, God 'has given us the Gospel under four aspects but bound together by one Spirit' (*Haer.* 3.11.8). So for the majority of churches the four different Gospels held the day against the one Gospel of Marcion (a truncated version of Luke) and of certain other groups and over against the one Gospel reconstructed from the four by Tatian with his *Diatessaron*, which, however, remained popular in Syriac-speaking churches for another 200 years. But, despite the preservation of four different Gospels rather than one, the drive was to stress the unity rather than to appreciate the diversity within the unity. One reason for this was that Christians were uneasy about their critics pointing out discrepancies and contradictions in their authoritative documents. This had been a factor in Tatian's attempt to produce one comprehensive and coherent narrative that would iron out some of these problems. Another reason lay in the sense that, since God had given a fourfold Gospel, its unity would be not only at a deep level but also on its surface. Irenaeus gives expression to this sense in his discussion of the four Gospels that produce a fourfold Gospel: 'since God made all things in due proportion and adaptation, it was fit also that the outward aspect of the Gospel should be well arranged and harmonized' (*Haer.* 3.11.8).

It should not be surprising, then, that the dominant way of interpreting a harmonized Gospel was to read the four Gospels in a harmonizing fashion. Earlier in the second century Matthew's Gospel had achieved the widest circulation and appears to have been most popular, probably because it was attributed to an eyewitness and because of its comprehensive and ordered treatment of Jesus' life and teaching. It was also to the fore in harmonizing versions of the Gospels. Tatian's *Diatessaron* as a whole is dependent primarily on John's Gospel with its three-year ministry for its chronological frame and on Matthew's for its content. But the main exception to this was in the treatment of the birth narratives. We have already encountered in Justin a harmonized quotation where the Matthean material is subsumed under the Lukan. On the topic of Jesus' birth Luke provided the larger framework, beginning with the birth of John the Baptist and concluding with the incident of Jesus in the Temple at the age of 12, and into this framework the key elements of Matthew's story could be fitted. This could also make some chronological sense, since it provided the opportunity to have the story of the annunciation to Mary before that of the dream appearance to Joseph when Mary was already pregnant. But we do not need to speculate about this, because it was in just such a fashion that Tatian's *Diatessaron*, which appears to have omitted the genealogies, treated the accounts. Granted the difficulties of establishing the original text of the *Diatessaron* and therefore its content in precise detail, it is nevertheless reasonably clear that, having begun with the first five verses of John's prologue, it then moved to the material in Luke 1.5–80, and after this inserted the account from Matthew 1.18–25. Tatian then returns to Luke 2.1–39 for the stories of the census visit to Bethlehem, the shepherds, Jesus' circumcision, and Simeon and Anna, ending with the return to Nazareth. Without sensing any incongruity, he follows this with Matthew's story of the magi in 2.1–23, where Jesus' parents are still in Bethlehem and a series of dreams warns them to flee into Egypt, then to return to Israel and only after that to go to Galilee, where they end up in Nazareth. Finally, Tatian rounds off this part of his harmony by returning to Luke 2.40–52. Any obscurities in Matthew's account of Jesus' birth disappear on this reading, because the harmony has already established that Mary is the sort of virgin who has not had intercourse with a man and who will therefore give birth miraculously before it moves to the account of Joseph's dilemma. The *Diatessaron* dates from around 175 CE, but in all probability it gives expression to what was already the popular option in interpreting the birth narratives – a continuing attempt to bring them together in a single coherent synthesis. Justin was Tatian's teacher and his harmonized quotations, to which we have drawn attention, are likely to reflect a broader prior harmonization of the Synoptic Gospels.[22] Luke's dominance in harmonizing interpretations of the birth stories may also owe something to the Christian movement having become a

---

[22] Indeed H. Koester, *Introduction to the New Testament: History and Literature of Early Christianity* Vol. 2 (Berlin: de Gruyter, 2000), 344, can go so far as to say, 'On the basis of the gospel quotations of the *First Apology* and the *Dialogue with Trypho*, one can conclude with great certainty that Justin also had composed a harmony of the Gospels of Matthew, Mark, and Luke (he did not know the Gospel of John), which is lost but was used by his student Tatian for the composition of his famous and influential four-gospel harmony known as the *Diatessaron*.' On this and on the likelihood of Gospel harmonies before Justin, cf. also A. Bellinzoni, *The Sayings of Jesus in the Writings of Justin Martyr* (Leiden: Brill, 1967), 139–42.

predominantly Gentile one. We have argued that Luke's own adaptation of the tradition in the direction of a virginal conception is related to his addressing a Gentile audience familiar with this beginning to the lives of great figures. In any case his presentation of the annunciation soon became the determinative one for Gentile Christians. Instead of this perspective sitting side by side with the more Jewish one of descent in the patrilineal line of David without the need for explanation, as in Luke's own writings, it became the single lens through which other perspectives were interpreted.

Matthew's account was very soon relieved of any ambiguities and the difficulties it raised, because it proved eminently amenable to being read in harmony with Luke's birth narrative on this basic point of Jesus' conception. In particular, *parthenos* from Isaiah 7.14 in Matthew's scriptural quotation could now be understood not in its LXX sense but as a virgin in Luke's more technical sense, a young woman who had not known a man. References to Jesus as 'the seed of David' continued to be taken in their natural sense by Jewish Christian groups and others, but in the prevailing harmonizing tradition Davidic descent could now be interpreted either in the way Matthew had responded to the charge of suspect paternity, namely that Jesus was Joseph's son through some form of adoption, or, as we have seen with Ignatius, the *Ascension of Isaiah*, Justin and Irenaeus, by still assuming that 'David's seed' required a physical reference but holding that this was provided through Jesus' mother's side of his genealogy, a notion of which there had been no hint in the earliest writings.

But what about the theological work that, by the end of the second century, the virgin birth tradition was being required to do and that would ensure its central place in future discussion of Jesus' beginnings? The New Testament writings, as we have seen, clearly reflect a process in which views about these beginnings were the end product of reflection that began with belief that because of Jesus' death and God's vindication of this in the resurrection, he must have been Messiah and Lord and that, if this were the case, he must have had this identity from the start of his life and, furthermore, his unique relationship with God must entail that he was the incarnate revelation of the pre-existent Word or Son of God. The consequence was that the individual human being Jesus of Nazareth was therefore to be seen as somehow at one and the same time one with God in his identity. John's Gospel provides the fullest attempt to express this conviction in its presentation of Jesus' life and does so, as we have seen, on the assumption of Jesus' natural birth. Luke's depiction in his annunciation story of the Son of God being born from a virgin, adapted from the conventions of ancient biography, is his way of presenting a similar conviction about the status and identity of the crucified and exalted Jesus. The New Testament Gospels hold this cluster of convictions together in their narratives. Once, however, these presentations had been made and were received as authoritative documents, it was perhaps inevitable that different depictions of the significance of elements in the life of Jesus, such as his beginnings, would tend to take on a life of their own, independent of both the overall narratives in which they were embedded and the process that had led to their articulation in this fashion in the first place. How far is this true of the rise of the virgin birth tradition in second-century developments?

For Ignatius there was one way of viewing Jesus' beginnings – that depicted in the virgin birth story – and so this is now seen as *the* means of incarnation. But this story is still firmly part of the cluster of significant events – 'the birth, the passion and the resurrection' – that resulted in life for humanity. He can mention Mary's virginity as one of three mysteries but he shows no other interest in it in its own right. Instead he is primarily concerned with the birth from Mary as a means of establishing, in combat with docetic teachings, that the one who redeems humanity himself truly suffered and truly died as a human being and was truly human from the beginning of his earthly existence. So birth from Mary stands for incarnation and originating from a human mother guarantees the genuineness of this incarnation. But in Justin the virgin birth tradition has certainly begun to take on a theological life of its own. Instead of the tradition being one of the ways of depicting the prior conviction, arrived at on the basis of the resurrection, that Jesus was uniquely one with God, now it is presented as the sign that establishes that Jesus is not merely a man, and the virginal conception is associated with the conviction that Jesus led a sinless life. One particular aspect of the virgin birth tradition, however, takes on extraordinary significance in its own right – the citation of Isaiah 7.14 in Matthew 1.23, interpreted in the light of the Lukan annunciation story. Since Justin shared a view of Scripture as predictive prophecy that was not content to point to its more clearly messianic passages and since this met with understandable resistance from the non-Christian Jews with whom he wished to dialogue, Isaiah 7.14 in the first part of Matthew's quotation, and not, arguably, the more significant second part with the name 'Emmanuel', became a primary focus of attention. 'A virgin shall conceive' is now made to bear the theological weight of proof from prophecy, resulting both in what are, for most contemporary exegetes, quite unpersuasive arguments about the original meaning of the LXX and, perhaps more importantly, the need felt by subsequent Christian writers to defend against unbelieving opposition the virgin birth tradition as seen in Matthew by all means possible. Justin also plays his part then in the process that has made it second nature for most Christian readers simply to assume that Matthew's account must be referring to a virginal conception.

An assessment of the theological role of the virgin birth tradition in Irenaeus in comparison with the New Testament writings has to be more mixed. On the one hand, there is a further singling out of the virginal conception, so that it now becomes the only permissible perspective on Jesus' birth, and a strengthening of its equivalence with the originally broader notion of incarnation. There is also its elevation to confessional or credal status through its inclusion in Irenaeus' statements of the catholic faith. In one of these, as we have seen, there is no mention of the incarnation but this has been replaced as the content of faith by a statement about 'the Son of God who condescended to be born of the virgin'. In addition, Irenaeus pursues enthusiastically Justin's concern with Isaiah 7.14, its LXX meaning and its fulfilment in Mary's virginal conception, producing further unpersuasive, to present-day readers, supporting arguments about this and about why Joseph was not Jesus' father. He also develops the virgin Eve–virgin Mary typology that we noted Justin had employed briefly. On the other hand, in one major credal statement belief in 'the Son of God who became incarnate for our salvation' does remain the major Christological affirmation and 'the birth from a virgin' takes a secondary role as the initial key event in the Son's incarnate life. Elsewhere, given the virtual equivalence of incarnation and the virgin birth as its means in Irenaeus' thought, the latter remains integrated both with the whole of Christ's life, particularly, as in Ignatius, in arguing against docetic views, and then with the whole history of God's dealings with humanity, beginning with Adam. On occasion the discussion of Isaiah 7.14 is also integrated into larger theological arguments – about the unity between the God of Scripture and the God of the gospel and the unity between the Christ and the human Jesus. More centrally, the virginal conception now plays an even bigger role than it had in Justin in establishing both elements of Christology – Jesus is fully human through his birth from the virgin Mary but he is also much more than human through his generation from God and not from Joseph. Yet, at the same time, it has to be noted again that this is a narrowing of perspectives in comparison with the New Testament. While certainly Luke, and then Matthew, probably in its own right but certainly when read in the light of Luke, can be seen as making a similar point about Jesus being both human and divine through their annunciation stories, elsewhere, in Paul and John, this Christological conviction is secured through statements about incarnation or its equivalent. And when Irenaeus draws the virgin birth into his important schema of the correspondence between the end and the beginning of the history of salvation with the Adam–Christ typology, as his discussion moves away from Paul's focus on the death and resurrection to the birth, he is not content to draw a general analogy about God being directly involved in both instances but his insistence on the virginity of Jesus' mother drives him to find a speculative connection with the virgin earth from which he claims Adam came.

In the narrowing of incarnation to the one means, that of the virgin birth, in the harmonizing readings of the New Testament documents that allowed them to do so, in the insistence that Isaiah 7.14 was originally predicting this one means, in seeing the virginal conception as crucial for combating docetic views that Jesus was less than fully human and other views that he was merely human, and in integrating the virgin birth into the larger Adam/Eve–Christ/Mary schema, the development from Ignatius to Irenaeus not only enabled the dominance of this tradition by the end of the second century but also provided the major elements that would ensure its central place in future belief about Jesus' birth, including its incorporation into the creeds.

It is worth observing at this point, however, that in more recent developments in the Christian tradition as a whole a number of these crucial major elements have been called into question. Historical and literary studies have emphasized the diversity within the unity of the New Testament writings and undermined a harmonizing approach that does not give due consideration to the distinctive presentations of each of these documents in its own right. They have shown that the Gospels are likely to contain a mix of historical tradition and theological elaboration and cast doubt on whether in particular the infancy narratives can be taken as straightforward history in the way that these early interpreters assumed. Such studies have also complicated the issue of how to understand the New Testament writers' claims to see fulfilment from prophecy in the life of Jesus and stress that the scriptural texts must be allowed as far as possible their original context and meaning in any attempt to see how far they may have a fuller meaning in the light of Christian beliefs. Appreciation of diversity within unity also opens up the likelihood of differing ways of presenting the incarnation, and theological scholarship now underlines the distinction that needs to be made between incarnation as a primary category and virgin birth as a particular mode of expressing its means. What has become especially problematic, however, is precisely what was so important in the early stages of the virgin birth tradition's rise to prominence, namely, that the birth from a virgin secured Jesus' full humanity over against docetic views of his origins. As will be discussed more fully later, this depended on ancient views of procreation that contemporary biology no longer shares.

From Irenaeus to Augustine and Chalcedon

Since we have seen the major lines along which the virgin birth tradition will be maintained now set, a briefer overview of further developments in the early centuries can be provided. In the discussions so far the clear focus has been on the relation of Jesus' conception to his origins and identity. Mary and her virginity have, to be sure, played their part in the arguments but almost exclusively only insofar as they provided the necessary accompaniment to Jesus' unique conception. Towards the end of the second century (possibly as late as c.190), however, there is a dramatic contrast to this state of affairs provided by the *Protevangelium of James*. In this popular and legendary account of Jesus' birth we find for the first time a story, in which Mary is the centre of attention and in which the concerns about her virginity that will be the object of later more theological discussion already surface. The story takes the reader from the birth of Mary to the attempt by Herod to kill both her baby and John, the son of Elizabeth and Zechariah, an incident that results in Zechariah's death. It elaborates greatly on a harmonized version of the accounts in Matthew and Luke, where again Luke provides the framework, the announcement to Joseph in Matthew can be incorporated into the announcement to Mary in Luke (11.3), as in Justin, and Mary herself is 'of the tribe of David' (10.1). It also supplies for the first time background details that would be included in many later versions of the virgin birth tradition, such as the names of Mary's parents – Joachim and Anna (1.1; 2.1) – and the characterization of Joseph as an aged widower who already has children (9.2; 17.1; 18.1). The latter detail prepared the way for the interpretation that Mary remained a virgin and that children ascribed to her in the Gospel accounts were not in fact hers but Joseph's.

More importantly, in the *Protevangelium* itself the concern with Mary's virginity in conception becomes expanded to an insistence on her total purity. She herself is born miraculously to childless parents (1.1—5.1) and dedicated to the service of God (4.2). When she is born the bedchamber is turned into a sanctuary through which nothing unclean is allowed to pass (5.2) and then, quite implausibly but continuing the preservation of her purity in a sanctuary, she is transferred to the Jerusalem Temple where she remains from the age of 3 to 12 and 'received food from the hand of an angel' (7.2—8.1). At this point, she is given as wife to the widower Joseph, who will be the guardian of her sacred purity. When Joseph discovers that, at the age of 16 and therefore after four more years of virginity, she has become pregnant and she protests her continued purity, he is assured by an angel that her child is 'of the holy Spirit' (13.1—14.2). But he is nevertheless accused by the high priest of having defiled her and both are subjected to the test of bitter waters, which they pass (16.1–2).[23] On the way to Bethlehem for the census Mary is ready to give birth and a Hebrew midwife is summoned (17.3—19.1). The midwife announces to another woman, Salome, that the birth itself is virginal: 'a virgin has brought forth, a thing which her nature does not allow' (19.3). Salome then tests with her finger to see whether Mary is still a virgin but her hand is consumed by fire until she touches the child and is healed (20.1–3). Here we have then far more explicit evidence than even in the *Ascension of Isaiah* for the belief that Mary's virginity was not only *ante partum* (before giving birth) but also *in partu* (in giving birth).[24] The physical evidence of her virginity miraculously remains intact. With this level of concentration on Mary and her purity, 'a reader who knew only the *Protevangelium* might reasonably conclude that Mary is the holy figure and that Jesus' holiness derives from her'.[25] There is no explicit attempt to depict Mary as a model for others to follow and the most likely motive for this presentation is an apologetic one. In response to the continuing illegitimacy tradition used by opponents, particularly the allegation that Mary had illicit relations with a Roman soldier, this depiction would not only exclude such a possibility before her virginal marriage to Joseph through her containment in sacred space and then afterwards through his guardianship of her and her passing the bitter waters test but also show that, as an integral part of the overall purity she embodied, her virginity remained even throughout the birth of Jesus.

---

[23] Cf. Num. 5.11–28, where, however, the test is applied only to a woman suspected of infidelity.

[24] For an earlier assertion about the miraculous in the birth itself elsewhere, cf. *Odes Sol.* 19.4–9.

[25] B. R. Gaventa, *Mary: Glimpses of the Mother of Jesus* (Columbia, SC: University of South Carolina Press, 1995), 119. Gaventa, *Mary*, 101–45 provides a close analysis of the role of Mary in the *Protevangelium* and also the text of the *Protevangelium* as found in W. Schneemelcher, ed., *New Testament Apocrypha* Vol. 1 (Louisville: Westminster John Knox, 1991), 426–39. For a complementary analysis that compares Mary's portrait with other cultural constructions of virginity, cf. M. F. Foskett, *A Virgin Conceived* (Bloomington, IN: University of Indiana Press, 2002), 141–64.

By contrast with the *Protevangelium*, Tertullian at the beginning of the third century,[26] while maintaining the virginal conception in similar fashion to his predecessors and seeing it as involving a new beginning in God's dealings with humanity, will have nothing to do with the actual birth being virginal (*Carn. Chr.* 23) and will make clear that Jesus' brothers were real brothers (and thus the product of Mary's later union with Joseph) (*Carn. Chr.* 7; *Mon.* 8). In his various writings he insists on the rule of faith, repeats the interpretation of Isaiah 7.14 as a miraculous sign involving a virgin, and develops the Adam/Eve–Christ/Mary analogies. He differs from earlier writers only in the intensity of his rhetoric against docetic, Marcionite and gnostic opponents when insisting on a real incarnation and has well-known passages where he goes into great detail about the messy physical aspects of the normal birth that Jesus would also have had.

> But how can that Christ of yours be liable to a shame, which it is impossible for him to experience? Since he was never condensed into human flesh in the womb of a woman, although a virgin; never grew from human seed, although only after the law of corporeal substance, from the fluids of a woman; was never deemed flesh before shaped in the womb; never called foetus after such shaping; was never delivered from a ten months' writhing in the womb; was never shed forth upon the ground, amidst the sudden pains of parturition, with the unclean issue which flows at such a time through the sewerage of the body, forthwith to inaugurate the light of life with tears, and with that primal wound which severs the child from her who bears him; never received the copious ablution, nor the medication of salt and honey; nor did he initiate a shroud with swaddling clothes; nor afterwards did he ever wallow in his own uncleanness, in his mother's lap; nibbling at her breast; long an infant; gradually a boy; by slow degrees a man. (*Marc.* 4.21; cf. also 3.9)

What is also of interest here is that, because Tertullian, who was an avid reader of the medical texts of his day, gets physical, he allows us to see his biological assumptions and his version of the ancient view of procreation. Jesus can be considered to have come from human seed in a qualified sense that nevertheless allows him to have full corporeal substance supplied by his mother. As will be discussed further in a later chapter, no clear distinction was drawn between male and female fluids, semen, milk and blood were seen as interchangeable discharges, and all bodily fluids were basically forms of blood. It was only the heat supplied to the blood by

---

[26] On Tertullian, cf. also von Campenhausen, *Virgin Birth*, 46–9.

male bodies that produced semen as a distinctive emission. But there was no idea that both male semen and a female ovum were needed to constitute the bodily form of a new human being. Mary's fluids were seen as enough to ensure this outcome. Such graphic depictions on Tertullian's part serve a robust view of the incarnation. Against Marcion's expunging of Luke's birth narrative and his view that the Christ appeared later fully formed, Tertullian is adamant that the incarnation was real and involved a fully human body from birth. In a similar passage to that cited above, he imagines Marcion's horror at 'the uncleanness of the generative elements within the womb, the filthy concretion of fluid and blood, of the growth of the flesh for nine months long out of that very mire' and then goes on to assert of Christ that 'loving man He loved his nativity also, and his flesh as well' and so took on their humiliation, which he links with the humiliation of the passion and crucifixion, in order to redeem them (*Carn. Chr.* 4).

Tertullian and the ancients knew of course that what made a virginal conception miraculous was the absence of male input. But what the male semen supplied to the 'corporeal substance' that came from the female fluids was the formative or generative principle, that which shaped the flesh. It is on this basis that Tertullian appeals to the Genesis story:

> A word of caution, however, must be addressed to all who refuse to believe that our flesh was in Christ on the ground that it came not of the seed of a human father, let them remember that Adam himself received this flesh of ours without the seed of a human father. As earth was converted into this flesh of ours without the seed of a human father, so also was it quite possible for the Son of God to take to Himself the substance of the selfsame flesh, without a human father's agency.   (*Carn. Chr.* 16)

So, in order to be fully God in the flesh, Christ needed the divine seed or generative principle rather than a human one:

> it was not fit that the Son of God should be born of a human father's seed, lest, if He were wholly the Son of a man, He should fail to be also the Son of God, and have nothing more than 'a Solomon' or 'a Jonas', as Ebion thought we ought to believe concerning Him. In order, therefore, that He who was already the Son of God – of God the Father's seed, that is to say, the Spirit – might also be the Son of man, He only wanted to assume flesh, of the flesh of man without the seed of a man; for the seed of a man was unnecessary for One who had the seed of God. As, then, before His birth of the virgin, He was able to have God for His Father without a human mother, so likewise, after He was born of the virgin, He was able to have a

woman for His mother without a human father. He is thus man with God, in short, since He is man's flesh with God's Spirit – flesh (I say) without seed from man, Spirit with seed from God. For as much, then, as the dispensation of God's purpose concerning His Son required that He should be born of a virgin, why should He not have received of the virgin the body which He bore from the virgin? Because, (forsooth) it is something else which He took from God, for 'the Word' say they, 'was made flesh'.

(Carn. Chr. 18)

Christ's flesh or body comes from his mother but God supplies the life principle through the Spirit or Word. Tertullian also provides evidence for the reading of John 1.13 in the singular as applying to Christ's virginal birth rather than believers' spiritual birth and claims that some have changed this to the plural to avoid such a reference. But this interpretation would raise a problem on ancient views of biology, because it denies Christ was 'born of blood'. Tertullian, therefore, finds himself forced to explain this:

For it did not disavow the substance of the flesh when it denied His being 'born of blood' but only the matter of the seed, which, as all know, is the warm blood as convected by ebullition into the coagulum of the woman's blood. In the cheese, it is from the coagulation that the milky substance acquires that consistency, which is condensed by infusing the rennet. We thus understand that what is denied is the Lord's birth after sexual intercourse (as is suggested by the phrase, 'the will of man and of the flesh'), not His nativity from a woman's womb. *(Carn. Chr.* 19)

These views about Jesus' human substance coming from Mary also aid Tertullian in bringing together Jesus' descent from David with his birth from a virgin. Commenting on Elizabeth's acclamation, 'Blessed is the fruit of your womb' (Luke 1.42), he can say,

What is this fruit of the womb, which received not its germ from the womb, which had not its root in the womb, which belongs not to her whose is the womb, and which is no doubt the real fruit of the womb – even Christ? Now, since He is the blossom of the stem which sprouts from the root of Jesse; since, moreover, the root of Jesse is the family of David, and the stem of the root is Mary descended from David, and the blossom of the stem is Mary's son, who is called Jesus Christ, will not He also be the fruit? For the blossom is the fruit, because through the blossom and from the blossom every product advances from its rudimental condition to perfect fruit . . . for every step indeed in a genealogy is traced from the latest up to the first, so that it is now a well-known fact that the flesh of Christ is inseparable, not merely from Mary, but also from David through Mary, and from Jesse through David. *(Carn. Chr.* 20)

And on 'seed of David' terminology in Romans 1.3 he can say, 'Christ's flesh, then, is of David's seed. Since He is of the seed of David in consequence of Mary's flesh, He is therefore of Mary's flesh because of the seed of David' (*Carn. Chr.* 22).

Given his view that the virgin birth indicates that Jesus is both God and man, it is not surprising to find that for Tertullian, as for Irenaeus, it is established as an important part of the Church's creed.

> The rule of faith, indeed, is altogether one, alone immoveable and irreformable; the rule, to wit, of believing in one only God omnipotent, the Creator of the universe, and His Son Jesus Christ, born of the Virgin Mary, crucified under Pontius Pilate, raised again the third day from the dead, received in the heavens, sitting now at the right (hand) of the Father, destined to come to judge quick and dead through the resurrection of the flesh as well (as of the spirit).　　　　　　　　　　　　　　　　　　　(*Virg.* 1)

For the next additions of any substance to the virgin birth tradition, we turn to the writings of Origen.[27] We have already encountered his *Contra Celsum* in connection with the addition to the illegitimacy tradition of the name of Pantera as the father. Origen's response to this allegation about Jesus' origins on the part of Jewish objectors is to see it as an acknowledgement on their part that Jesus had had an unusual conception but also a refusal to acknowledge its true divine source. He then questions Greeks, who would also reject the virgin birth, about the plausibility of one who accomplished such excellence as Jesus having had a disgraceful beginning rather than having been given a superior body invested with such excellence, a body that enabled his soul to remain untainted by sin (*Cels.* 32–33). Like others he has recourse to Isaiah 7.14 and its prediction but, in response to the usual Jewish objections about the meaning of the term *parthenos*, has a rather better argument by showing occasions (e.g. Deut. 22.23–24) on which even the original Hebrew word *almah* could be used of a virgin and claiming that as a sign it would be more fitting for a virgin rather than a young married woman to give birth to Emmanuel (*Cels.* 34–35). However, he then introduces into the discussion in support of a virgin birth an analogy from parthenogenesis in the animal realm and also suggests that it ill becomes Celsus to pour scorn on a virgin birth when the Greeks are prepared to believe fables about Plato having been born from the union of Apollos with a woman (*Cels.* 36). If the reply is that these myths of divine origin for heroic figures were a means of showing that they had accomplished deeds beyond those of other mortals, then

---

[27] On Origen, cf. also von Campenhausen, *Virgin Birth*, 57–63.

Origen claims that Jesus' deeds, grounded in reliable accounts, are superior to those of such heroes, based primarily on fables (*Cels.* 67).

Elsewhere Origen's well-known asceticism has apparently influenced his interpretation of the tradition on occasions. So he is an advocate of Mary's perpetual virginity, whereby Mary and Joseph never consummated their marriage and those who are called Jesus' brothers were in fact his stepbrothers, and in this Mary becomes a model for ascetic women:

> And I think it in harmony with reason that Jesus was the first-fruit among men of the purity which consists in chastity, and Mary among women; for it were not pious to ascribe to any other than to her the first-fruit of virginity.
>
> (*Comm. Matt.* 10.17)

Origen remains primarily concerned with the larger issue of incarnation and, as emerged from the debate with Celsus, in his reflections on this topic employs the anthropology that sees humans as constituted by both a body and a rational soul (cf. *Cels.* 33). The divine Word or Son therefore enters both a human body and rational soul and in so doing unites body and soul perfectly (*Princ.* 2.6.3). The soul that Christ assumed was like that of other humans in every respect but one – 'we must believe that there existed in Christ a human and rational soul, without supposing that it had any feeling or possibility of sin' (*Princ.* 2.6.5) – and, as we have seen, for Origen Jesus' acquiring of his body from a virgin enabled this to be the case for the soul with which his body was one. Here sinlessness, a matter touched on in passing in Justin's discussion, begins to play a larger role in the theology of the virginal conception.

It is not until over a century later that this is developed further in the writings of Ambrose.[28] In the meantime figures such as Basil, Athanasius and Ephraem the Syrian had made it customary to talk of Mary as the Mother of God in connection with the virgin birth and to find it offensive to the faith of the devout to think that after the conception of Jesus she would have had sexual relations with Joseph. Athanasius tended to think of Christ's body as the instrument through which the Logos chose to manifest himself (e.g. *Inc.* 43) and in this regard saw the virgin birth as proof of the divinity of the Logos:

> even to begin with, when He was descending to us, He fashioned His body for Himself from a Virgin, thus to afford to all no small proof of His Godhead . . . For who, seeing a body proceeding forth from a Virgin alone without man, can fail to infer that He Who appears in it is Maker and Lord of other bodies also? (*Inc.* 18.5)

---

[28] On Ambrose, cf. von Campenhausen, *Virgin Birth*, 76–80.

Lactantius had also formulated the distinction between the two births or two nativities of the Son – the first was spiritual when he was begotten by the Father alone in eternity and the second was in the flesh when he was born from a virgin (*Inst.* 4.8, 13). Against Arians who deny the divine generation of the Son from the Father, Ambrose employs this distinction and can in fact argue backwards from the virgin birth, claiming that if there was no visible cause in this second birth, then it should not be expected there would be any such cause in the first (*Fid.* 1.12). Elsewhere he argues from the virgin birth to believers' rebirth through baptism. In both grace is at work, not nature:

> for we confess that Christ the Lord was conceived of a Virgin, and reject the order of nature . . . If, then, the Holy Spirit coming down upon the Virgin wrought the conception, and effected the work of generation, surely we must not doubt but that, coming down upon the Font, or upon those who receive Baptism, He effects the reality of the new birth. (*Myst.* 9)

In relation to the matter of Christ's sinlessness, Ambrose begins to link the virginal conception not just with the absence of any taint of sin but also more explicitly with the absence of original sin. So, in contrast to the rest of us who 'are all born under sin, and our very origin is in evil, as we read in the words of David: "For lo, I was conceived in wickedness, and in sin did my mother bring me forth"', Christ

> was not begotten, as is every man, by intercourse between male and female, but born of the Holy Spirit and of the Virgin; He received a stainless body, which not only no sins polluted, but which neither the generation nor the conception had been stained by any admixture of defilement.
> (*Paen.* 1.3.13)

In such discussions Ambrose makes clear his biological assumptions. On the one hand, Jesus does not experience the contagion of earthly corruption, because 'male intercourse did not open the secret places of the virginal vulva, but the Holy Spirit infused the immaculate seed into the inviolable womb' (*Exp. Luc.* 2.56). On the other hand, Mary contributes something to Jesus' conception – his human flesh.

> For the virgin had something of her own that she transmitted . . . she conferred on him her own from her own flesh, indeed in an unusual way, but by a normal function. For the virgin had flesh, which she conferred on the fruit. (*Incarn.* 104)

In this way, Ambrose sees the seed as being of divine origin and the substantial human flesh as deriving from Mary.

In a number of his writings Ambrose shows himself to be a great champion of virginity and the celibate life. The author of virginity is Christ, since the immaculate Son of God was a virgin before the Virgin. Then, after birth from the Virgin, he became the spouse of the Virgin Church (*Virg.* 1.5). But it is, above all, Mary from whom virgins are to take their pattern of life, since the life of the Mother of God is the greatest of all teachers. Ambrose states that he has no need to go into detail about her purity but then displays apparent knowledge of virtually everything about her life and its blamelessness. Her eating, sleeping and reading habits, her harmonious relations with her neighbours, and her response to the needy, all show 'how worthy she was that the Son of God should be born of her' (*Virg.* 2.2). Her virginity is perpetual and that means for Ambrose that she was virginal in the birth itself (*in partu*). Citing Ezekiel 44.1–2, he writes,

> Then he brought me back to the outer gate of the sanctuary, facing the east; but it was closed. He said to me: 'This gate is to remain closed; it is not to be opened for anyone to enter by it; since the Lord, the God of Israel, has entered by it, it shall remain closed' ... Who is this gate, if not Mary? Is it not closed because she is a virgin? Mary is the gate through which Christ entered this world, when he was brought forth in the virginal birth and the manner of His birth did not break the seals of virginity ... There is a gate of the womb, although it is not always closed; indeed only one was able to remain closed, that through which the One born of the Virgin came forth without the loss of genital intactness. (*Instit.* 8.52)

Despite his attachment to Mary, Ambrose is clear about the difference between her and her Son. In a passage about the work of the Spirit in the incarnation, he can state that the incarnate Son is to be adored: 'for Christ is not divided but is one; nor, when He is adored as the Son of God, is He denied to have been born of the Virgin'. Likewise the Spirit who effected the incarnation is to be adored. But the same response is not to be extended to the Virgin Mary: 'Mary was the temple of God, not the God of the temple. And therefore He alone is to be worshipped who was working in His temple' (*Spir.* 3.11).[29]

It is Ambrose's concern for virginity in general and Mary's virginity in particular that also helps us to chart the course of the virgin birth's relation to the Church's creeds, since in all probability the first clear reference

---

[29] This may indicate that Ambrose is already aware of some who are in danger of taking devotion to Mary too far. The first extant reference to praying to Mary is apparently in Ambrose's contemporary, Gregory of Nazianzus, *Or. Bas.* 24.11, cf. von Campenhausen, *Virgin Birth*, 78n4.

to what came to be known as 'The Apostles' Creed' is to be associated with
him. Around 390 CE a letter was written in reply to Pope Siricius from
a council in Milan agreeing with his condemnation of, among others,
Jovinian, who denied Mary's virginity during birth (*in partu*). Milan was
of course Ambrose's area of ecclesiastical jurisdiction and he is thought
to have drafted the letter that certainly reflects the views he expressed
elsewhere. It acknowledges that marriage is good but sees virginity as
better, for 'by a woman care entered the world; by a virgin salvation was
brought to pass' (*Ep.* 42.3). Against those who dispute Mary's virginity in
giving birth, it offers a number of arguments. The precise wording of the
scriptural text is pointed out: '"Behold a Virgin shall conceive and bear a
Son"; declaring not only that she should conceive as a virgin, but also that
she bring forth as a virgin'; the interpretation of the closed gate of the
sanctuary in Ezekiel 44 in terms of Mary's womb is repeated; and appeal
is made to other incidents in Scripture that 'are contrary to the usage of
nature' (*Ep.* 42.5–7). But towards the beginning of these arguments the
letter asserts that if those who deny Mary's full virginity will not believe
the teachings of the clergy, 'let them give credit to the Creed of the Apostles
[Symbolicum Apostolorum], which the Roman Church has always kept
and preserved undefiled' (*Ep.* 42.5). This clearly assumes that the Apostles'
Creed contains the terminology of being born from a virgin. While the
form of the Apostles' Creed which is widely employed today may only
date back to the seventh century, it had its precursor in what is known as
the Old Roman Creed, which contained the bulk of the later version and
is what Ambrose's letter is likely to have in view. The credal statements
we have noted in Irenaeus and Tertullian are likely to approximate closely
to the earlier form of the Apostles' Creed which was an expansion of
catechumens' and baptismal candidates' confession of belief in Father,
Son and Holy Spirit. All contain assertions about Christ being born of the
virgin.[30] It is perhaps significant that Ambrose's letter refers to this creed,
when elsewhere in his writings he can appeal to the Council of Nicea (e.g.
Fid. 1.18). The credal statement issued by the Council (325) concentrated
on the questions raised by Arianism and therefore on Christ's relation
to the Father – 'begotten, not made, of one substance with the Father' –
taking up the term *ousia* to refer to Christ's ontological status as *homoousios*,
one in being, with the Father. It then simply went on to affirm of him:
'who for us men, and for our salvation, came down and was incarnate

---

[30] When Augustine preaches on this creed to catechumens, it contains the clause 'born of the Holy
Spirit and of the Virgin Mary' (*Symb.* 6) but not 'he descended into hell'.

and was made man'. It would have assumed that the incarnation was by means of the virgin birth, but it was left to the revision of the creed in 381 – the Niceno-Constantinopolitan Creed – to make this explicit when it also filled out the statement about belief in the Holy Spirit. It is this later form of the Council's creed that has 'who for us men, and for our salvation, came down from heaven, and was incarnate by the Holy Ghost of the Virgin Mary, and was made man'.

The final figure we shall consider here is Augustine, who owed a great debt to his mentor, Ambrose, and built on his teaching.[31] Augustine's writings are numerous and lengthy, but one place from which to gain orientation for his treatment of the virgin birth is his *Enchiridion*, written in 422, the handbook on faith, hope and love, in which he summarizes much of his thinking.[32] In it he refers early on to the Apostles' Creed and will then go on, in discussing the incarnation, to cite this creed's wording about the virgin birth (*Enchir.* 7, 34). Leading up to the treatment of the incarnation, Augustine sets the scene of the human plight with its origin in the defection of the will, its condemnation under the just verdict of God and the necessity of grace alone if there is to be deliverance from the bondage of sin. Integral to the plight are the consequences of the sin of the first man, whereby

> all those descended from him and his wife (who had prompted him to sin and who was condemned along with him at the same time) – all those born through carnal lust, on whom the same penalty is visited as for disobed-ience – all these entered into the inheritance of original sin.   (*Enchir.* 26)

For those in this state of original sin under divine wrath, a Mediator was required, of whom Augustine says:

> For who can unfold in cogent enough fashion this statement, that 'the Word became flesh and dwelt among us,' so that we should then believe in 'the only Son of God the Father Almighty, born of the Holy Spirit and Mary the Virgin.' Yet it is indeed true that the Word was made flesh, the flesh being assumed by the Divinity, not the Divinity being changed into flesh . . . Yet certainly we must say that in that assumption nothing was lacking that belongs to human nature. But it was a nature entirely free from the bonds of all sin. It was not a nature born of both sexes with fleshly desires, with the burden of sin, the guilt of which is washed away in regeneration. Instead, it was the kind of nature that would be fittingly born of a virgin, conceived

---

[31] On Augustine, cf. also von Campenhausen, *Virgin Birth*, 80–6.

[32] This resulted from a request from a certain Laurentius in 421 for a brief exposition of Christian teaching.

by His mother's faith and not her fleshly desires. Now if in his being born, her virginity had been destroyed, he would not then have been born of a virgin. It would then be false (which is unthinkable) for the whole Church to confess him 'born of the Virgin Mary.' This is the Church which, imitating his mother, daily gives birth to his members yet remains virgin.

(*Enchir.* 34)

In making a transition from the discussion of the incarnation to that of the significance of baptism, he makes a similar point:

> Since he was begotten and conceived in no pleasure of carnal appetite – and therefore bore no trace of original sin – he was, by the grace of God (operating in a marvelous and an ineffable manner), joined and united in a personal unity with the only-begotten Word of the Father, a Son not by grace but by nature. And although he himself committed no sin, yet because of 'the likeness of sinful flesh' in which he came, he was himself called sin and was made a sacrifice for the washing away of sins. (*Enchir.* 41)

Here, then, we see succinctly stated Augustine's continuation of Ambrose's insistence on the perpetual virginity of Mary,[33] including *in partu*, and his far greater development of the link between the virgin birth and original sin, transmitted between the generations through the carnal lust entailed in the act of procreation.[34] In this context he deals with a further matter that had become a topic of debate. He has to point out that the assertion that Christ 'was born of the Holy Spirit and the Virgin Mary' does not mean that the Spirit was the father of the human Christ. This, he claims, would be to confuse two senses of the term 'born'. Jesus Christ is the Son of the Father not of the Spirit. In his human nature he was born of Mary with no father, and 'born of the Holy Spirit' instead stands for

> the grace of God by which a certain human person, no merit whatever preceding, at the very outset of his existence, was joined to the Word of God in such a unity of person that the selfsame one who is Son of Man should be Son of God, and the one who is Son of God should be Son of Man. Thus, in his assumption of human nature, grace came to be natural to that nature, allowing no power to sin. (*Enchir.* 38–40)

As elsewhere in his writings, here the confession of the virgin birth is related lucidly to the central issue of the incarnation, to Jesus being fully divine

---

[33] Indeed Augustine interprets Luke 1.34 – 'How can this be, seeing that I do not know a man?' – as indicating Mary's vow of virginity even before the conception and therefore enabling her to be a model for Christian virgins (*Virginit.* 4).

[34] Augustine cites Ambrose on original sin, including some writings no longer extant, in *C. du. ep. Pelag.* 4.29.

and fully human. But why had original sin and the virgin birth's establishing of Jesus' freedom from its power come to play such a central role?

The major factors in Augustine's development of this approach are undoubtedly his attempt to understand his own experience of sexual desire in its conflict with his will and his controversy with Pelagius and his followers. Pelagius, the monk who wanted to lay down rules for those aspiring to a holy life, held that it was necessary that humans were capable of carrying out such rules. For him the freedom of the human will and moral accountability implied that humans were able to obey God's law and he resisted Augustine's conviction that God's grace was necessary in order to perform what God commands and therefore also rejected Augustine's teaching about original sin. For Augustine the sovereign grace of God was at stake in this debate and he insisted on original sin as the backdrop for such grace.

> Now, whoever maintains that human nature at any period required not the second Adam for its physician, because it was not corrupted in the first Adam, is convicted as an enemy to the grace of God; not in a question where doubt or error might be compatible with soundness of belief, but in that very rule of faith which makes us Christians ... From the moment, then, when 'by one man sin entered into the world, and death by sin, and so death passed upon all men, in whom all sinned', the entire mass of our nature was ruined beyond doubt, and fell into the possession of its destroyer. And from him no one – no, not one – has been delivered, or is being delivered, or ever will be delivered, except by the grace of the Redeemer.
>
> (*Pecc. orig.* 34(29))

Although he sees that original sin has its focus in the will and affects the whole of human life, his continuing reflection on the power of sexual desire and the call to celibacy that he experienced along with his conversion led him, building on the views of Ambrose, to view the transmission of original sin as taking place in the body and tied particularly to the sexual act of procreation.[35] It should be added that Augustine did not hold that original sin made marriage *per se* evil and indeed wrote a treatise *On the Good of Marriage* (*Bon. conj.*). Nevertheless, he claimed that the good of married life was 'that conjugal chastity, by which carnal lust is reduced to the good purposes of the appointed procreation of children' (*Pecc. orig.* 38(33)) and that, if within marriage there was carnal pleasure in acts open to procreation, then this was only a venial and not a mortal sin (*Nupt.*

---

[35] For an account of the key stages in the development of Augustine's views on concupiscence, see P. Brown, *The Body and Society* (London: Faber and Faber, 1990), 387–427.

17(15); 27(24)). As Brown observes, 'Augustine never found a way, any more than did any of his Christian contemporaries, of articulating the possibility that sexual pleasure might, in itself, enrich the relations between husband and wife.'[36]

From a later perspective, his belief about transmission through the carnal lust of procreation is, of course, one of the major problems with Augustine's version of original sin, but once this notion was in place the virgin birth tradition could, of course, be seen to fit Christology beautifully. The absence of procreation in Christ's conception guarantees his freedom from original sin and therefore his ability to deliver those who are caught up in its bondage. At the same time Mary's submission to conceiving without concupiscence could be seen as an act that restored the pre-fall harmony of the relation between the will and the body. Augustine did not tire of making such points:

> His virgin mother, therefore, whose conception was not according to the law of sinful flesh (in other words, not by the excitement of carnal concupiscence), but who merited by her faith that the holy seed should be framed within her, He formed in order to choose her, and chose in order to be formed from her.   (*Pecc. merit.* 2.38)

Or:

> All born carnally in the flesh of the flesh are born subject to this bond, to be freed from the debt of it by the blood of Him who was born in the flesh and of the flesh indeed – yet not carnally but spiritually, for He was born of the Holy Spirit and the Virgin Mary.
> (*C. Jul.* 5.19.62; cf. also e.g. *C. Jul.* 5.15.52; *Enchir.* 34, 41; *Nupt.* 27(24)))

The controversy with Pelagius also provoked at one point a response from Augustine that was itself to become a topic of controversy. Pelagius had given a list of those he considered to have been without sin and this included Joseph and the Virgin Mary. Augustine's reply was

> We must except the holy Virgin Mary, concerning whom I wish to raise no question when it touches the subject of sins, out of honour to the Lord; for from Him we know what abundance of grace for overcoming sin in every particular was conferred upon her who had the merit to conceive and bear Him who undoubtedly had no sin. Well, then, if, with this exception of the Virgin, we could only assemble together all the forementioned holy men and women, and ask them whether they lived without sin whilst they were in this life, what can we suppose would be their answer? . . . I put it to you,

---

[36] Brown, *Body*, 402.

whether, on having such a question submitted to them, however excellent
might have been their sanctity in this body, they would not have exclaimed
with one voice: 'If we say we have no sin, we deceive ourselves, and the truth
is not in us? (*sic*)'   (*Nat. grat.* 42(36))

Elsewhere, as we have already seen, Augustine repeatedly makes the point
that, with the exception of Christ, all humans are in bondage to original sin
and therefore all are in need of redemption through Christ and regeneration by the Spirit. Mary is presumably among those to be redeemed by
her Son. But what, then, of this particular response to Pelagius? Is Mary
without original sin or simply without later sins in addition to original
sin, since he talks of 'the subject of sins' (plural)? If only the latter, then
has not Augustine failed to respond adequately to Pelagius' point, since
his list was meant to refute the doctrine of original sin? And if Mary is
only without later sins, does not birth from her still mean that original
sin affects Christ's conception? Or is it only the carnal concupiscence of
procreation that passes on original sin? But then what of Mary herself
whose birth would have transmitted original sin to her?

Augustine was forced to come back to these matters in his later years
with his escalating exchange with the Pelagian Julian of Eclanum, who
accused him of having returned to his early Manicheanism, which deni-
grated God's good creation, and pressed such questions and other issues
about procreation upon him. Although he had already begun to respond
to Julian in earlier works, he replied more fully in 422 in *Contra Julianum*
(*C. Jul.*) and then in 429–30 in his final unfinished major writing, *Contra
secundam Juliani responsionem opus imperfectum* (*C. Jul. op. imp.*).[37] It
emerges from this debate, where we know Julian's views through Augustine's
citation of them, that both men held to the view we discussed earlier that
three parties were involved in procreation: God, the man, who provides
the seed, and the woman, who receives it and whose menstrual fluids are
formed by it into a foetus. For Julian, this means that since God uses the
seed, it must be good and not contaminated by sin, and concupiscence is
a natural phenomenon in this process and only its excess in fornication
is to be condemned (*C. Jul.* 3.26). But Augustine holds that the seed is in

---

[37] On the relation between Augustine and Julian, see also P. Brown, *Augustine of Hippo: A Biography*
(London: Faber and Faber, 1967), 381–97. For a detailed analysis of this exchange, see E. A. Clark,
'Vitiated Seeds and Holy Vessels: Augustine's Manichean Past', in ed. K. L. King, *Images of the
Feminine in Gnosticism* (Philadelphia: Fortress, 1988), 367–401 and 'Generation, Degeneration,
Regeneration: Original Sin and the Conception of Jesus in the Polemic between Augustine and
Julian of Eclanum', in eds V. Finucci and K. Brownlee, *Generation and Degeneration* (Durham, NC:
Duke University Press, 2001), 17–40.

essence good but has already become condemned and vitiated (*C. Jul.* 3.33). It is in essence good because it is created by God directly and does not receive its initial formation from 'lust' and so the resulting child can be said to be a merciful divine work and not simply a human one (*C. Jul.* 4.12; 5.34; 6.59). As Clark comments, 'If God were to withdraw his good action in producing seeds, caring for them, and quickening the fetus, there would be no begetting, and what was already begotten would lapse into nothingness.'[38] Julian later accused Augustine of ignorance of medical science in his interpretation of sin coming into the world 'through one man' in Romans 5.12 as entailing through generation, as it was common knowledge that procreation also involves the woman (cf. *C. Jul. op. imp.* 2.56). As part of his rejoinder, Augustine replies in kind,

> For everyone knows that the parent who sows the seed is the one who most of all or first of all generates a child and that the woman either does not generate, but bears a child – or, if bearing a child is correctly called generation, she first conceived from the man who generates the child and afterwards generates the child she has conceived. (*C. Jul. op. imp.* 3.85.4)

So Augustine finds nothing in the medical knowledge of the day to shift him from his view that original sin is passed on from Adam through the man who generates and that the woman receives from the man a seed that is good in essence but already vitiated, conceives and then gives birth.[39]

Julian was an upholder of the virgin birth, but he thought that Augustine's view of procreation adversely affected his view of Christ. If Christ was not born through a human male and thus lacked concupiscence, as Augustine held, this surely meant that Christ was unlike all other humans and that Augustine held a Manichean, and therefore docetic, view of Christ. Augustine here repeats his notion that Christ had all the senses that humans have and could have fathered children but would have done so without concupiscence, because he was exempt from the struggle between flesh and spirit that other humans experience (cf. *C. Jul. op. imp.* 4.47–50). Whether this was a satisfactory response is another matter. But Julian presses a further question. Even though, as Augustine appears to hold, it is the male seed that passes on original sin, then Mary must have contracted original sin from her father and if sin is a condition of the flesh, as he certainly holds, then Christ should have contracted sin through his mother's flesh (cf. *C. Jul. op. imp.* 4.51). Here Augustine goes further than his earlier somewhat ambiguous statement, when he concedes in response

---

[38] Clark, 'Vitiated Seeds', 376.
[39] Cf. Clark, 'Vitiated Seeds', 387.

that Mary would have acquired original sin and thereby been 'submitted to the devil', if the grace of regeneration had not loosed that condition (*C. Jul. op. imp.* 4.122). As Clark observes,

> This is as close as Augustine comes to espousing the later doctrine of the immaculate conception of Mary, a doctrine necessary if Augustine and others want to avoid the conclusion that Mary could have transmitted to Christ the sin present in her from her own birth.[40]

'The debate between Julian and Augustine can thus be seen as an early stage of the discussion that eventually led to the 1850 dogmatic proclamation.'[41]

If Augustine in his concern not to dishonour Mary left her own relation to original sin without clear resolution,[42] his teaching on Christ's birth and original sin certainly established the tradition of the virginal conception even more firmly in Latin Christendom. And, as we have seen in his debate with Julian, Augustine believed he had shown that such teaching was in line with the accepted biological views about procreation of his day. His remorse about his own past with its constant need for sexual pleasure, his views on the concupiscence of the sexual act and the high value he placed on celibacy all contributed to this emphasis in his teaching about Christ's incarnation and sexuality. Despite attempts by both Julian and John Cassian to refute his views on concupiscence by arguing that it was implanted by God rather than the product of a fallen and distorted will,[43] Augustine's combining of a virgin birth without carnal desire with a theory of the transmission of original sin 'was bound to appeal to all the monks and celibate clergy who made up his following and were to provide all the ecclesiastical leaders of the future'.[44] On a more popular level, Augustine's view had appeal as providing an explanation both for the sense of the misery of the human condition and for the Church's practice of baptizing infants.[45]

---

[40] Clark, 'Vitiated Seeds', 388.

[41] Clark, 'Generation', 39.

[42] The dispute about Mary's immaculate conception did not reach any sort of resolution in the Latin West until as late as the Council of Basel in 1439, which declared it to be 'a pious doctrine, in conformity with the worship of the church, the Catholic faith, right reason, and Scripture', required it to be 'professed by all Catholics', and did not permit any teaching contrary to it, cf. J. Pelikan, *Mary through the Centuries* (New Haven: Yale University Press, 1996), 198. It subsequently became papal dogma through the bull of Pius IX, *Ineffabilis Dei*, in 1850.

[43] It was only with Anselm's work *On the Virgin Conception and Original Sin* (*c.*1100) with its distinction between desire and sin that a break began to be made in later theologies of original sin from Augustine's view that it was imparted through the sexual act.

[44] Von Campenhausen, *Virgin Birth*, 85.

[45] Cf. Brown, *Augustine*, 385, 388.

Only two additional matters need to be mentioned in this overview of the virgin birth in the early tradition. They relate to the virginal conception only indirectly but have significance for the overall notion of incarnation of which the virgin birth was now an integral part and will play their role in more recent discussions of whether there can be an adequately orthodox view of incarnation without belief in a literal virgin birth. Both involve decisions of the early councils. At Ephesus in 431 the title that had already become attached to Mary – 'Mother of God' (*Theotokos*, literally 'God-bearer') – now became required. The issue was not a Mariological but a Christological one. As opposed to Nestorius, who thought that what was appropriate was talk of Mary as the mother of Christ's human nature and therefore as 'the mother of Christ', Cyril of Alexandria interpreted this as creating too great a separation between Christ's divine and human natures and, since Christ held the two together as one hypostasis ('subsistence' or 'person'), Mary should be considered as the 'Mother of God' in order to do justice to one divine Son who had become incarnate as a human. Mary was the bearer of the incarnate Son, not just of his human nature. The attempt to hold a council at Ephesus was a shambles. A first meeting was convened without the representatives from the East, who were late, and this was the meeting that condemned Nestorius. When the Eastern delegates arrived they convened their own meeting and excommunicated Cyril. But papal legates later ratified the decision of the first meeting, upholding Cyril's position, and so the Council's first anathema could pronounce, 'If anyone does not confess that Emmanuel is God in truth, and therefore that the holy Virgin is the Mother of God (for she bore in a fleshly way the Word of God become flesh), let him be anathema.'

The same issue of the relation of Christ's two natures and their union in one person, as is well known, underwent further deliberation at the Council of Chalcedon in 451. The Council reaffirmed the creeds of 325 and 381 but added a 'definition' meant to explain the right interpretation of the Christological section. *The Definition of Faith of the Council of Chalcedon* set the boundaries for acceptable articulation of the belief that Jesus Christ is God incarnate in response to the major competing viewpoints at the time. At the heart of *The Definition* is a statement that mentions the virgin birth as part of a much broader issue:

> as regards his Godhead, begotten of the Father before the ages, but yet as regards his manhood begotten, for us men and for our salvation, of Mary the Virgin, the God-bearer; one and the same Christ, Son, Lord,

Only-begotten, recognized in two natures, without confusion, without change, without division, without separation; the distinction of natures being in no way annulled by the union, but rather the characteristics of each nature being preserved and coming together to form one person and subsistence, not as parted or separated into two persons, but one and the same Son and Only-begotten God the Word, Lord Jesus Christ . . .

Its authors wished to preserve what they regarded as true but partial emphases in the various viewpoints while excluding their more dangerous and extreme elements. So oneness was applied to the hypostasis of the Son and duality to his natures. What was more contentious was the relation among these categories. In regard to the natures, the first two qualifiers – 'without confusion, without change' – were aimed at certain Alexandrian, and especially Monophysite, teachings that so stressed the oneness of Christ with the eternal Son that his humanity was absorbed into his divinity. The last two qualifiers – 'without division, without separation' – were aimed at Antiochene approaches, represented by someone like Nestorius, that so emphasized the distinctness of the divine and the human in Christ that the unity of the life of the incarnate Son was severely threatened. The incarnation, whereby Jesus Christ is both fully human and fully divine, remains, of course, a profound mystery. The result of Chalcedon was an attempt to preserve both elements in the paradox – to ensure that the divinity was not seen as diminishing the full humanity and that the humanity was not seen as set off against the oneness of the eternal Son but assumed into his divinity in such a way that believers, in their humanity, could also become partakers in the divine nature.

In *The Definition* the virgin birth is simply assumed as part of the talk about Christ's 'manhood' and we have seen why this assumption could be made. But it has been worth dwelling briefly on the Chalcedonian formulation, because, when that assumption is brought into question, as it will be in later developments, questions can also be raised about whether its defence or its reinterpretation remain within the boundaries set by Chalcedon about the broader issue of the incarnation. Do interpretations that wish to have incarnation without a literal virgin birth fall into a new Nestorianism that draws too sharp a divide between the human and the divine? Do some contemporary defences of the virgin birth actually involve a confusion between the two natures that diminishes Christ's full humanity? But there are also more radical questions that arise when the attempt is made to bring Chalcedon to bear on more recent Christological discussion. One such is whether the repetition of its terminology too readily leads to confusion. When, for instance, someone now asks, 'How can the human person of Jesus of Nazareth also have been divine?', it has to be recognized that what is meant by 'person' in that question is very different from what was meant by *hypostasis* ('person' or 'subsistence') in *The Definition*. At that time the latter term was applied to divine beings rather than human persons and so present-day insistence on the fully human person of Christ is by no means the same as Chalcedon's insistence on the person of the Son and is not easily adjusted to its formulation in terms of one person and two natures. This question is, in turn, part of a broader and perennial issue about the translation of Scripture and creed into different languages and cultures. Can there be a distinction between elements of a creed that belong to the cultural matrix in which it was originally formulated and other elements that are essential to its main concerns? Or does the whole package, as simultaneously a product of its time and place and transcending its originating factors, have to be negotiated in a more holistic way?

These observations lead into this section's final reflection. In this chapter we have travelled from the stories, embryonic confessions and diverse perspectives of the New Testament writings and of early traditions to Augustine's writings on sex and original sin and the formulation of Chalcedon with its adaptation of Greek philosophical categories to aid understanding of what was entailed in the incarnation. Such a journey inevitably raises the issue of continuity and change within the tradition. And, just as inevitably, a developing tradition will include both features, accompanied by disputes about whose interpretation is faithful to the tradition, how much flexibility is to be permitted, and whether any particular change is in line with preceding tradition and necessary precisely in order to preserve basic continuity with that tradition in new settings with their different challenges. In the case of the virgin birth there has been an added complication if, as we have argued, there was not, as later stages retrospectively asserted, simply one version of the tradition about Jesus' birth at the beginning of this process. Here the movement of continuity and change has to include at its start a change from a plurality of traditions to one of these becoming the normative tradition. Change that is in line with continuity can on occasion include real breaks within the tradition, justified as being necessary in order to remain faithful in changed circumstances. More frequently, the change is by way of reinterpretation of earlier elements. Here we have seen reinterpretation of the significance of Jesus' birth, and, once the virgin birth tradition became dominant, of a virginal conception and of Mary's virginity, all in response to changing circumstances and disputes. This leaves us with one of the key questions

212

in our exploration. In the name of continuity with an incarnational Christology, can faithful change appeal back to earlier elements in the tradition before the virgin birth became central and therefore involve further and more radical reinterpretation of that one element that for a variety of reasons had become established as the norm?

8

Reconceiving the tradition:
the case of Schleiermacher

In nearly all accounts of the beginnings of modern theology Friedrich Schleiermacher (1768–1834) figures prominently and, before entering into the theological discussion about the virgin birth in our own context, it will repay attending to Schleiermacher in order to appreciate why that discussion took a significantly new turn after the Enlightenment. In doing so, we take what, even in a very selective exploration, is a huge leap from Augustine and Chalcedon to the late eighteenth and early nineteenth century. It is not that figures such as Anselm, Aquinas, Luther and Calvin and their successors had nothing interesting to say on the topic but rather that these were simply elaborations on a tradition whose basic contours had remained unchanged.[1] Nothing in the new settings in which such figures expounded the faith had required them to rethink the tradition's assumptions about a virginal conception. But by the time Schleiermacher was reflecting on both the life of Jesus of Nazareth and Christology, the situation had changed considerably. The reason that Schleiermacher provides such an apt case for study is not only because he remains 'perhaps the most famous critic of the virgin birth tradition'[2] but also because, as Barth was to put it:

> Theologically the 'genius' of the major part of the church is that of Schleiermacher. All the so-to-speak official impulses and movements of the centuries since the Reformation find a center of unity in him: orthodoxy, pietism, the Enlightenment. All the official tendencies of the Christian present emanate from him like rays: church life, experiential piety, historicism, psychologism, and ethicism ... with a good conscience we can call him a type of what was determinative for a whole century, and are indeed forced to see in him the most brilliant representative not only of a theological past but also of the theological present.[3]

---

[1] For summaries of the views of Aquinas, Luther and Calvin, see D. Resch, *Barth's Interpretation of the Virgin Birth: A Sign of Mystery* (London: Ashgate, 2012), 15–26.

[2] Resch, *Barth's Interpretation*, 26.

[3] K. Barth, *The Theology of Schleiermacher: Lectures at Göttingen, Winter Semester of 1923/24* (ed. D. Ritschl; tr. G. W. Bromiley; Grand Rapids: Eerdmans, 1982), xv.

Within the scope of this book, then, the present chapter serves to under-line that, although there have been some recent distinctive twists in the discussion, the concerns we are exploring are by no means new but arise genuinely from any serious attempt to bring together critical study of Scripture and systematic theology.

Christmas Eve

Schleiermacher himself enables us to catch a glimpse of the changed situa-tion at the very beginning of the nineteenth century in Europe, when he depicts how an educated, religious and cultured group of people might have thought about the birth of Christ. Well before his more systematic treatment of Christology in 1821–2 in *The Christian Faith*, he wrote an engaging little book about the celebration of Christmas whose title in the latest English translation is *Christmas Eve: A Dialogue on the Incarnation*.[4] This was written just before Christmas in 1805 and published in 1806 and is a fictional account of a German gathering of families and friends, who, in the midst of decorations, presents, festive food and music, engage in banter and talk about what the season means to them. After the first part of the book has set the Christmas Eve scene, in the second part the main characters respond in various ways to the excited delight and the religious, artistic and musical expressions of devotion of the precocious young 10- or 11-year-old daughter of one of the couples, who is named Sophie. At one point in the good-humoured conversation a somewhat sceptical young lawyer, Leonhardt, expresses concern about her active imagination being exposed to the Bible's mythological stories that were never meant to be placed in the hands of children. Her father, Eduard, responds by recounting what had happened when she had heard that Joseph was only the foster-father of Christ.

> She had asked who his real father was, then. Her mother answered that he had no other Father than God. To this she replied that she believed God was her Father too, but that she would not like on that account to be with-out me, and that maybe it already belonged to the sufferings of Christ that he had no real father, for it was a wonderful thing to have one.

He then adds ironically, 'You can see from this what a penchant she has for dogmatics, and how extraordinarily predisposed she is toward becoming

---

[4] F. Schleiermacher, *Christmas Eve: A Dialogue on the Incarnation* (tr. T. N. Tice; Richmond, VA: John Knox, 1967). This is a translation of Schleiermacher's second revised edition of *Die Weihnachtsfeier: Ein Gespräch* from 1826.

a martyr for the belief in conception by the Virgin Mary!' To defend the family further against the charge that exposing her to biblical stories is leading to an incipient fanaticism, Eduard goes on,

> What is more, she really does take the sacred story in somewhat the aspect of a tale. For there are moments when the young girl wins the upper hand over the child, when she has her doubts about certain factual details in the story and asks whether they are to be understood literally. As you can see, this is 'bad' enough, and she has come very close to the allegorical interpretation of some of the church fathers.[5]

In the third and fourth parts of the book, in what strikes us now as sexual stereotyping,[6] the women first illustrate the meaning of Christmas for them by telling stories of the birth and baptism of children and by playing and singing Christmas hymns, while the men then discourse on the topic from various points of view. It is Leonhardt who opines that the festival is admirable but that its celebration of the Redeemer's birth is better preserved in and propagated by the festival itself than through any alleged connection with the biblical stories. The life of Jesus was entirely subordinate to the early Christian proclamation, in which in any case 'Christ's supernatural birth, however, seems to have been broadcast through narratives still less, otherwise there could not have been so many Christians at the time who took him to be a man begotten naturally.'[7] What is more, 'the divergence of accounts is so great that however we may designate it every claim or report undoes the others'.[8] For Leonhardt there is a gulf between what might be known about the life of Jesus and the apostolic testimony about him, and any actual history in relation to Jesus' birth is so precarious that it is better to see the tradition of the festival as having generated the story. But for that reason there can be no point in changing any of its details, all of which can be seen as full of meaning. And so he proposes 'a toast to an unending continuation of the Christmas festival!' Another of the men, Ernst, contributes by suggesting that the excellence of the festival lies in the disposition of joy and giving that it effects and that this occurs only because there is already a prior great cause for rejoicing and this cause is the birth of the Redeemer.

---

[5] Schleiermacher, *Christmas Eve*, 43.
[6] Though one of Schleiermacher's contributions to the literary journal *Athenaeum* was what might be seen as a proto-feminist piece entitled 'Idea for a Catechism of Reason for Noble Ladies'.
[7] Schleiermacher, *Christmas Eve*, 73.
[8] Schleiermacher, *Christmas Eve*, 74.

However unsatisfactory the historical traces of his life may be when one examines it critically . . . nevertheless the festival does not depend on this. It rests on the necessity of a Redeemer, and hence upon the experience of a heightened existence, which can be derived from no other beginning than him.[9]

Ernst is inclined, however, to see more small traces in the historical tradition than Leonhardt and so to be convinced that the powerful contemporary attraction of Christmas and participation in its joys must have a ground beyond themselves and owe their formation to the life of Christ and the beginning of that life. The final discourse is assigned to Sophie's father, Eduard, who moves the discussion beyond the perspectives of both Leonhardt and Ernst. He notes that in his historical comments Leonhardt had 'the more external biographers of Christ in mind' but that he himself would turn to the Fourth Gospel.

The Gospel according to John hasn't any Christmas even, recounted as an external event. . . . This is how I prefer to regard the object of this festival: not a child of such and such an appearance, born of this or that parent, here or there, but the Word become flesh, which was God and was with God.[10]

Eduard takes Ernst's views further by relating the experience of new life in the Christian community that is grounded in the individual life of Christ to 'the perspective of the divine'. God is seen as the transcendent source and foundation of Christ's life, and, with John's prologue, this entails the union of eternal being and the ever-changing process of becoming. Fallen humanity finds redemption in that same union that comes to expression in the living community of the Church. That community has its starting point in the one who is 'the man-in-himself, the God-man, from birth . . . all human life is related to his life, and only through this relation does it partake of goodness and divinity'. It retains its relationship with Christ through the Spirit.

In Christ, then, we see the Spirit, according to the nature and means of our world, originating contact with us and forming his presence within the genuine self-consciousness of individual persons . . . Devotion and love are his essence. Thus it is that every mother who, profoundly feeling what she has done in bearing a human being, knows as it were by an annunciation from heaven that the Spirit of the church, the Holy Spirit, dwells within her . . . And in like manner each one of us beholds in the birth of Christ his

---

[9] Schleiermacher, *Christmas Eve*, 79–80.
[10] Schleiermacher, *Christmas Eve*, 82.

own higher birth whereby nothing lives in him but devotion and love; and in him too the eternal Son of God appears . . . This is the very glory of the festival, which you wished also to hear me praise.[11]

If Eduard's contribution ends with an emotional, and indeed sermonic, rhetorical flourish, this is not where the evening ends. During his speech another friend, Josef, arrives. He has been roaming about 'the whole evening, everywhere taking part most heartily in every little happening and amusement' and soon breaks up the serious atmosphere, chiding the men for their tedious speech-making by teasingly blaming it on the presence of the over-intellectual Leonhardt and reminding them all of the speechless and childish joy of Christmas that is able to soothe away pain and grieving. His are the words that close the account of the evening: 'Come, then, and above all bring the child if she is not yet asleep, and let me see your glories, and let us be glad and sing something religious and joyful!'[12]

In this very selective exposition some of the theologically significant dimensions of the dialogue have been highlighted for obvious reasons. But it should be emphasized that this work was not, of course, primarily intended as a piece of theology so much as an open-ended celebration of the joy of ordinary living in the company of family and male and female friends, which, for Schleiermacher, was an expression of Christian community. Of all the times when the loves and joys of human living are apparent he particularly valued Christmas and so these partial reflections on the birth of Jesus and his later more extended historical and theological treatments were by no means carried out in abstraction from the actual celebrations of that event in everyday life in Church and society. More generally, they already indicate how far his thought always attempted to be rooted in experience. Insofar as Schleiermacher's own views are reflected here, there are elements in all the characters that echo his own personality, disposition and opinions, while the words of Eduard approximate most closely to his later systematic account of the incarnation.[13] More importantly, *Christmas Eve* reflects how Schleiermacher's thinking is shaped by the dialogical interplay between different approaches, here the approaches of the three major discourses with their emphases on the historical critical (Leonhardt), on the experience of new life in the Christian

---

[11] Schleiermacher, *Christmas Eve*, 84–5.
[12] Schleiermacher, *Christmas Eve*, 85–6.
[13] For an analysis of the characters in relation to their author, Schleiermacher, see T. N. Tice, 'Schleiermacher's Interpretation of Christmas: "Christmas Eve", "The Christian Faith", and the Christmas Sermons', *Journal of Religion* 47 (1967), 100–26 (102–10).

community and in continuity with the originating experience of Christ (Ernst), and on humanity, with Christ as its archetype, having as its essence an ontological relationship with the divine, a God-consciousness (Eduard).

Clearly, however, this fictional dialogue about the meaning of Christmas is taking place in the wake of the Enlightenment with its massive shift in ways of viewing the world and the place of humans within it. What is striking, and what makes Schleiermacher a key representative figure for our exploration, is that its range of topics is not at all dissimilar to what one might expect to be covered in a dinner-table conversation or media discussion about Christmas in our day. What is the meaning of this festival? How far do its celebration, its rituals, its music, the emotions it evokes have their own value? Is its meaning or value dependent on the original stories about Jesus' birth and does it matter whether those stories have any historical foundation that can be determined with any certainty? What relation does Christmas have to core Christian beliefs? What should adults responsibly tell children about these matters?

Schleiermacher's characters inhabit an intellectual and cultural world in which the impact of applying reason to religion in a particular way is taken for granted. Through the influence of English Deism and the writings of such figures as Reimarus, Lessing and Kant in Germany, it was now acknowledged that traditional authority and dogma could and should be questioned and criticized in the light of developing human under-standing. The Bible also, whatever else might be claimed about it, was to be treated as a human document, to which could be applied the historical and literary analysis employed on other texts. Erasmus and the reformers had, of course, used such tools but they were now applied in a more thoroughgoing fashion. Instead of a predominantly harmonizing approach to differences in the biblical texts, there was an emphasis on diversity, variety of literary genres, including legend and myth, contradictions, and discrepancy between what texts claimed and what actually happened. For Reimarus it was evident that natural or rational religion should not con-tain contradiction and so his version of the new approach was at the same time an attack on Christianity as revelation. For Lessing contradictions simply showed the historically conditioned character of the texts. But he is also well known for his view that there is an 'ugly ditch' between the accidental truths of history and the necessary truths of reason. He held that the probable truths of history might be the occasion for but could never legitimize religious truth and that the truth of Christianity could be established independently by reason's comprehending it. In *Christmas Eve* the discussion provoked by this more critical historical approach to the Bible is clearly reflected in Leonhardt's comments and the responses of the other characters about the value of the stories of Jesus' birth in the Gospels, the differences among the Gospels, whether a historical basis is needed for belief in the incarnation and, if so, how much historical evidence is required. Again, Schleiermacher was a key figure in the development of this discussion. He was the first person actually to give public academic lectures on the life of Jesus, and the topic of historical study of the life of Jesus first became part of the theological curriculum with his lecture series in 1819. These lectures were also to be influential in the subsequent quest for the historical Jesus, since they attracted David Friedrich Strauss, whose later *The Life of Jesus Critically Examined* (1835) was in part a response to the Schleiermacher lectures of 1831 which he had attended.[14] Interestingly, Schleiermacher shows himself to be aware of the more radically critical views exemplified by Strauss, since the character of Leonhardt in *Christmas Eve* foreshadows some of these.

The insistence on the historical conditionedness of all thought was part and parcel of post-Enlightenment views of human knowledge. While some had applied reason to revelation in such a way that all that was left was the natural or rational religion that reason was in any case able to posit independently, Kant had stressed both the limits of reason and the existence of radical evil. He distinguished between the realm of phenomena, the world of the senses, in which things appear to us, and the realm of the noumena, things in themselves, the basic realities behind sensory experience. The latter cannot be known because they cannot be perceived, but they are nevertheless thinkable because scientific investigation and moral decision-making cannot proceed without presupposing them. In this way Kant undercut traditional metaphysics by arguing that the concept of God functions only as a regulative or limiting principle in causal accounts of the order within the world. Yet at the same time this view of God did have a positive role in the moral sphere where Kant held that, by the practical use of reason, humans need to choose the highest good by actions based on the categorical imperative. Schleiermacher had wrestled with Kant's thought and learned from his epistemology but was dissatisfied with the resultant marginal place for religion within the limits of reason in which God was the necessary postulate for a morality of duty. Others too had reacted against the dominance of this mix of rationalism and morality. Schleiermacher had been closely associated with leading figures in the

---

[14] Strauss's later work, *The Christ of Faith and the Jesus of History* (1865; tr. L. E. Keck. Philadelphia: Fortress, 1977), is an explicit critique of Schleiermacher's lectures.

Romantic movement, especially Schlegel, and was also influenced by the Idealism of Fichte and Schelling. Such thinkers had championed the more intuitive and aesthetic senses of emotion, imagination and self-awareness as part of the attempt to find harmony between humans and the world of nature. Again *Christmas Eve* reflects this aspect of the intellectual culture with its emphasis on the child, on the emotions, especially joy, and on aesthetic sensibilities, including the appreciation of the beauty of the Christmas decorations, of art and of music.

Schleiermacher was a polymath who had not only absorbed but also contributed to these recent cultural developments, yet by no means uncritically. He remained distinctive in wanting to give a central place to religion. Here his own Christian Protestant experience came into play. His father was a Prussian army chaplain who belonged to the Reformed Church but had had his son educated in a Moravian college, part of the pietistic Herrnhuter renewal movement founded by Count von Zinzendorf. In *Christmas Eve* this group is mentioned as part of Leonhardt's warning against fanaticism, when he fears Sophie's piety will lead her later to join a convent or become one of the dully dressed women of the Herrnhuter community, but the group is then defended by other participants in the dialogue. Despite his intellectual struggles and the abandonment of important elements of the Moravians' theology during his student days, their emphasis on the religion of the heart with its profound sense of the grace of God mediated through Jesus remained part of Schleiermacher's own Christian experience when, after his studies, he became a pastor in the Reformed Church. Together with the influences of Romanticism and Idealism, it enabled him to forge a view of religion that he made famous in his *On Religion: Speeches to Its Cultured Despisers* (1799), the apologetic work in which he argued for the feeling or consciousness of absolute dependence as the common human experience of religion with its sense and taste for the infinite. In this way he attempted to restore religion, threatened by marginalization and oblivion, to an essential role within the thinking and life of his day.

At the time of the writing of *Christmas Eve* Schleiermacher was not only a Reformed pastor and preacher but also taught at the University of Halle. Shortly after, in 1808, he was appointed as the first professor of theology in the newly founded University of Berlin. But this statement about his academic appointments gives no indication of his remarkable scholarly range that included classical and New Testament studies, contemporary literature, culture and politics, and philosophy and ethics. So, for example, by the time of taking up his position in Berlin, he had not only produced

On Religion: Speeches to Its Cultured Despisers, but also, among other writings, a book on love and marriage, two volumes of translations of Plato, whose dialogues influenced the form of *Christmas Eve,* a study of Heraclitus, a treatise on philosophical ethics, a critical and exegetical work on 1 Timothy, a volume of sermons, and works on the position of the Jews and on the relations between Church and state in Prussia. In addition, he had already begun his lectures in hermeneutics, which continued until 1833 and which were to make him such a hugely significant figure in that discipline. Equally remarkable is that, in the midst of this prodigious intellectual activity, Schleiermacher remained a warm and engaging human being who had a wide circle of friends, as reflected in the correspondence that has been preserved, and who placed the highest value on celebrating the joys and empathizing with the sorrows of ordinary human life in families, physical intimacies and close friendships.

All of this meant that Schleiermacher, as both a public intellectual and a Christian theologian, was uniquely equipped to rethink the Christian faith from within the tradition but in a way that did justice to the present state of knowledge. Just as the patristic writers had interpreted the apostolic tradition by employing the thought forms of their day, so Schleiermacher sought to expound the faith in terms intelligible within a world of thought that had undergone a sea change. His lectures on the life of Jesus and, more especially, *The Christian Faith,*[15] first published in 1821–2, represent his attempt to do precisely this. It is in the former that we see some of his more detailed treatment of the historical issues and in the latter that his mature thinking on the virgin birth in relation to incarnation is to be found.

The Life of Jesus

Although his lectures on Jesus' life were not published until 1864,[16] some 30 years after his death, he had given the lecture series twice – in 1819 and 1821 – before the publication of *The Christian Faith* and his treatment of the birth narratives in them certainly fed into the latter's more systematic exposition of the incarnation. Treatment comes as might be expected

---

[15] F. Schleiermacher, *The Christian Faith,* (eds H. R. Mackintosh and J. S. Stewart; London: T. & T. Clark, 1999), which is a translation of the second edition of the original from 1830.

[16] F. Schleiermacher, *Das Leben Jesu: Vorlesungen an der Universität zu Berlin im Jahr 1932,* ed. K. A. Rütenik (Berlin: Georg Reimer, 1964); ET *The Life of Jesus* (ed. J. C. Verheyden; tr. S. M. Gilmour; Philadelphia: Fortress, 1975). As the German title indicates, the published volume of the lectures is based primarily on Schleiermacher's outline notes and student notebook material from the last time the series was given in 1832.

in the section entitled 'The Life of Christ before His Public Appearance'. What might not be expected, in the light of many present-day lives of Jesus, is the extent to which Schleiermacher's faith perspective dominates the discussion. He uses the methods of his day to investigate the Gospels historically but does not do so simply in order to come up with some supposedly neutral or objective account but subordinates such investigation to an overriding Christological concern that comes from faith. He assumes that what is at stake in studying the life of Jesus is what he calls 'the peculiar dignity of Christ'.[17] While being clear that Jesus must be studied as a historically conditioned individual who shared the common life of his time, he holds that his peculiar dignity, grounded in his absolute knowledge of God, can be maintained by showing that this inward ground was able to influence directly the common life and its conditions. On the one hand, he says of the task of historical research, 'We must undertake it as we should any other similar one with respect to a man who is no longer in any way an object for faith for us'.[18] On the other hand, while by no means assuming later orthodox formulae about the person of Christ and always remaining alert to the dangers of docetism, Schleiermacher nevertheless holds that 'it must also be possible with respect to our task to present the divinity of Christ in such a way that the human element in the whole phenomenon of Christ in his whole life remains unimperiled'.[19] So he summarizes his basic approach:

> everything that appears in Christ's individuality as a life-moment appears as a deed and an action, and it must be able to be apprehended in its historical connection in a purely human way; but nevertheless, we conceive it as the expression or effect of God which was internal.[20]

This is clearly an attempt to integrate faith and historical criticism, to use the methods and assumptions of his time as critically as possible but to do so as someone situated within the life and tradition of the Church. Throughout the lectures there is a creative tension between honest historical investigation and adherence to the significance of the life of Jesus for Christians, which makes it worthy of investigation in the first place. Whatever may be said about the strengths and weaknesses of his particular execution of this project,[21] such an approach is in line with our

---

[17] Schleiermacher, *Life of Jesus*, 13.
[18] Schleiermacher, *Life of Jesus*, 21.
[19] Schleiermacher, *Life of Jesus*, 34.
[20] Schleiermacher, *Life of Jesus*, 34.
[21] See Verheyden, 'Introduction' to Schleiermacher, *Life of Jesus*, lii–lvii on some of these.

own exploration and to be preferred to those that assume that questions of historical investigation and those of faith commitment and theological concern operate in two entirely separate spheres.

Having begun his lectures by setting out his basic assumptions, Schleiermacher then makes clear his views on the nature of the materials on which the task has to be carried out. The Synoptic Gospels 'are more aggregates of individual narratives than continuous presentations' and so it becomes important to ascertain the principles on which each evangelist has placed them in a particular temporal sequence. Here we have the rudiments of what would later be called source, tradition and redaction criticism. The Gospel of John is another matter. Schleiermacher takes it as coming from an eyewitness and offering a more coherent and comprehensive account, but its major differences from the Synoptics complicate matters further and so he is clear that the New Testament Gospels by themselves do not allow us to 'achieve a connected presentation of the life of Jesus'.[22] All we can do is to divide the life into its major periods: before the public ministry, the public ministry, the passion, and the resurrection to the ascension, and then by historical investigation assess the traditions relating to each of these periods. A word about Schleiermacher's view of John is necessary here. He rejects the ideas that Matthew's Gospel came from a disciple or that Mark's was written under the influence of Peter, but nevertheless holds that John's goes back to the disciple of that name, who wrote all of it apart from the last chapter. This strikes us as quite uncritical, but, in terms of Schleiermacher's own time, that would be an unfair judgement. Undoubtedly, John's perspective on Jesus would have been congenial to Schleiermacher's own view of Jesus' absolute knowledge of his God-consciousness, though that view is not simply dependent on the Fourth Gospel. But, during his lifetime, the notion that this perspective came from an eyewitness, John as the Beloved Disciple, would have been shared by most scholars. Ironically, it was shortly after Schleiermacher's death that this consensus view came under fire and it has remained a decidedly minority opinion ever since. Schleiermacher may have been wrong on this and it may have skewed his judgement in places but it does not mean that, when judged by the standards of his day, he was uncritical or unhistorical.[23]

Indeed in his treatment of the infancy narratives in *The Life of Jesus* he raises many of the issues discussed in our earlier chapters. He takes seriously the Fourth Gospel's statement that the Beloved Disciple (for him,

---

[22] Schleiermacher, *Life of Jesus*, 41–3.
[23] See Verheyden, 'Introduction', lii–liv.

John) took Mary to his own home after Jesus' death, yet he finds it highly improbable that any of the accounts of Jesus' birth stemmed originally from her. John's Gospel does not have any and, if the sources for Matthew and Luke are alleged to go back to conversations of the disciples with her, it is extremely strange that she provided them with no other information about Jesus' further development before his public appearance.[24] In any case, Schleiermacher is clear that Matthew and Luke could not have drawn from the same source because their accounts are contradictory at major points. He discusses at some length the incongruity between Matthew's account, which assumes that Joseph and Mary lived in Bethlehem and then gets them to Nazareth via Egypt, and Luke's, which has them living in Nazareth and then has to get them to Bethlehem for the birth before they return to Nazareth.[25] Further, because of this major difference, Luke's story of a presentation in the Temple in Jerusalem conflicts with Matthew's narrative about the visit of the magi, Herod's attempt to exterminate all newly born male children and the flight to Egypt. If the presentation is earlier than the visit of the magi, then the former cannot be accommodated to Luke's narrative because the return to Nazareth follows immediately upon the presentation. If the visit of the magi preceded the presentation, then it makes no sense that after that the child would have been taken to Jerusalem and 'practically delivered into the hands of Herod'.[26]

Schleiermacher is also prepared to discuss the historicity of that which Matthew and Luke have in common, namely, the assertion that Christ was born in Bethlehem. At one point in the lectures, he pauses to underline that, because Matthew and Luke are in the New Testament, this does not exempt them from scrutiny about their historical content.

> You see how skeptically I go to work. If we cannot recognize any original authentic source and it is improbable that the narrative as it stands has come from immediate eyewitnesses, then we are obliged, because we are engaged in a piece of historical research, to place no weight on the difference between canonical and apocryphal writings. On the contrary, we must presuppose as possible that these narratives have an apocryphal character because they are based on such a definite tendency.[27]

In connection with the birth in Bethlehem he raises issues that, as we have seen, continue to be discussed in historical-critical scholarship: the question

---

[24] Cf. Schleiermacher, *Life of Jesus*, 46–7, 62–3.
[25] Cf. Schleiermacher, *Life of Jesus*, 49–50.
[26] Schleiermacher, *Life of Jesus*, 69–70.
[27] Schleiermacher, *Life of Jesus*, 66.

whether 'they believed he must have been born in Bethlehem because Bethlehem was the ancestral seat of the Davidic family' and the further question whether the 'son of David' designation for Jesus was 'due to the supposition that the Messiah ought to come from the house of David'. But, as always, he relates these issues of historical study with their uncertainties to matters of faith and concludes,

> For our faith it is in itself of no consequence whether Christ was born in Bethlehem or in Nazareth ... whether his parents lived in one place or the other, whether one of the two accounts is literally correct or neither of them.[28]

In one place, however, Schleiermacher's theological interests appear to skew his historical judgement. He is willing to make an exception to his doubts about Mary being the source of material in the narratives when it comes to Luke's account of Jesus in the Temple at the age of 12. The account, he says, strikes him as authentic because of its naturalness, and Mary's reproach of Jesus is part of this naturalness because it does not harmonize with the earlier account of the supernatural birth of the child as Son of God. What is of major interest to him, however, is the saying of Jesus: 'Did you not know that I must be in my Father's house?' (Luke 2.49). Though he entertains the possibility that the utterance does not consist of the actual words of Jesus but is a reading back of the later way in which he expressed himself, he nevertheless concludes that Mary must have remembered these remarkable words.[29] One cannot help thinking that his conclusion is dictated by his wanting to find some foothold for his speculation about the gradual development of the God-consciousness in Jesus, because there then follows an extended discussion of the origin in time of that consciousness and the manner of its development over against credal formulations of a twofold nature in Christ.[30]

In dealing with the actual conception of Jesus, Schleiermacher begins by pointing out the diversity within the New Testament.

> There are passages where the Evangelists themselves are not the narrators but where other speakers are introduced who declare that Joseph was Jesus' father and where the Evangelists do not contradict the statement and appear [as it were] indifferent to it. Two Gospels make no conception of Christ's conception and birth, and this silence concerning the assertion of his supernatural origin is accompanied with a silent overlooking of the contrary assertion.[31]

---

[28] Schleiermacher, *Life of Jesus*, 52–5.
[29] Cf. Schleiermacher, *Life of Jesus*, 74–8.
[30] Cf. Schleiermacher, *Life of Jesus*, 78–88.
[31] Schleiermacher, *Life of Jesus*, 56.

Interestingly, and in contrast to our earlier discussion, he holds Matthew to be unequivocal about the supernatural conception of Jesus because of the mistrust of Joseph that demonstrates his awareness that he was not the cause of the origin of this life, while he finds Luke to be more ambiguous because 'Mary's statement that she had no husband' that follows the angel's promise 'cannot be taken so literally that one could relate the promise only to it, since she was betrothed to Joseph and knew of a man from whom she could bring a child into the world'. So Schleiermacher is inclined to see the promise as related more to the fact that the child would be the Messiah 'than to any assertion that he would begin life without Mary having been impregnated by a man'.[32] But, in any case, the two narratives do not agree with one another.

> If Mary had received such a promise it would have been contrary to the nature of the relationship for her not to have told Joseph of it, and then Joseph's mistrust could not be reconciled with it, since in the other narrative he is represented as receptive to such phenomena and to the truth they bring to light.[33]

Even in Matthew's more explicit account Schleiermacher sees the extraordinary birth presented not so much in relation to Christ's peculiar dignity as in relation to the fulfilment of the promise of a scriptural text. Accordingly,

> there is no presupposition that the Son of God would have to enter into life only in a supernatural way. This, to be sure, has frequently become part of Christian doctrine, and we must always take such a state of affairs into consideration, although it cannot be for us the determining factor.[34]

Here Schleiermacher reminds his students that the reason this presupposition was thought necessary was because it was connected to the theory of hereditary sin. He too holds that, to accomplish redemption, the Redeemer must be free from sin but finds a virginal conception simply cannot guarantee this.

> Because Christ was begotten without the cooperation of a man, therefore he was free of hereditary sin! No such concept can be imagined for, if one understands by it a transference of subjection to sin by the physical influence of one creature in the begetting of another, that is only half a step, for there is still the influence of Mary to be considered.[35]

---

[32] Schleiermacher, *Life of Jesus*, 57.
[33] Schleiermacher, *Life of Jesus*, 57.
[34] Schleiermacher, *Life of Jesus*, 58.
[35] Schleiermacher, *Life of Jesus*, 58.

If one attempts to rescue such a view by asserting that Mary had no physical influence in Christ's birth and her body was simply a channel through which Christ passed, this is nothing other than docetism. The other attempted way out is to claim that Mary herself had a supernatural conception, but this is equally unsatisfactory because then sinlessness would have to be carried all the way back and reckoned to Eve. He concludes, therefore,

> no concept of hereditary sin can be in agreement with the idea of redemption through Christ which makes the indispensable demand that, in order to be free from sin, also the first beginning of life must have been free of every physical influence.

So even though 'it cannot be maintained that the narrative of the supernatural conception of Christ is a wholly historically founded statement', the matter can be discussed 'without having to fear a disadvantage for the Christian faith'.[36]

As in our own day, there were various alternative theories about Jesus' birth in Schleiermacher's time and he describes two of these that involve conspiracies to establish the Messiah and deals with their speculations swiftly. He gives more serious consideration to the proposal that if Jesus was not conceived through Joseph, as Matthew records, this was through another man and that this other, as Celsus asserts, on the basis of Jewish accounts, was the Roman soldier Panthera. He rejects this, however, on the curious grounds that in the writings of John of Damascus there is a genealogy of Mary that has the name Panthera for Mary's great-grandfather and so the name provided by Celsus' informant must have derived from this source.[37] John of Damascus, however, was writing at the beginning of the eighth century and while his genealogy may have been influenced by that of Epiphanius in the fourth century, who has Panthera as the name of Joseph's father, it remains far more likely that these were responses to the charge reported by Celsus, extant from the second century, and meant to explain how Jesus could be called ben Panthera.

Despite his significant historical and theological observations about the accounts in Matthew and Luke, it has to be said that Schleiermacher's actual interpretation of the accounts of Jesus' conception as they now stand is not very convincing. It appears that he is unable to make a clear enough distinction between what the narratives assert and their likely historicity

---

[36] Schleiermacher, *Life of Jesus*, 58–9.
[37] Cf. Schleiermacher, *Life of Jesus*, 59–60.

or present theological appropriation. Instead he claims that Luke permits the interpretation that 'Christ was conceived with the cooperation of Joseph' and that the language of being overshadowed by the power of the Most High has reference to 'his becoming Son of God'. On Matthew he asserts that, since this evangelist reports a dream, it remains to be demonstrated that the dream was divinely communicated, and since such a demonstration is not part of the narrative, 'the matter remains uncertain'.[38] This latter point does not take seriously enough that dreams were considered to be a divine means of communication in the Jewish Scriptures and Second Temple Jewish writings and that the one who makes the announcement in the dream is designated as 'an angel of *the Lord*' (Matt. 1.20, emphasis added).

The Christian Faith

A number of these issues will be taken up again in a different form in *The Christian Faith*, to which we now turn. Although it cannot be part of this chapter's exploration to treat or evaluate Schleiermacher's theology and Christology as a whole, any adequate attempt to indicate how and why he came to his view of the virgin birth will need, however briefly, to place it in its broader context in this work, which Schleiermacher makes clear is a work of Christian dogmatics, a theological discipline that belongs within the Church. If all humans have a consciousness of God reflected in a feeling of absolute dependence, this takes on its distinctive and superior form in the Christian faith in which everything is related to the redemption accomplished by Jesus of Nazareth. He also makes clear that this dogmatics is situated within the Protestant Church. His discussion is therefore carried out in relation not only to the ancient creeds and conciliar definitions but also to more recent Protestant dogmatic statements found in such major documents of both the Lutheran and Reformed Churches as the Augsburg, Belgic and Helvetic Confessions. This reflected his conviction that any dogmatic system must establish its connection with language that has been approved by the Church and yet that 'the ecclesiastical formulae concerning the Person of Christ need to be subjected to constant criticism'.[39] So a dialectic of accountability to and yet criticism of the tradition characterizes his theology. He is aware of the historical conditioning of ecclesiastical formulae and their emergence from earlier

---

[38] Schleiermacher, *Life of Jesus*, 59.
[39] Schleiermacher, *Christian Faith*, 389.

controversy and thinks that, when such formulae were elaborated later, also partly to guard against misunderstandings, there was a tendency, seen especially in scholasticism, to an oversubtlety liable to produce complicated distinctions simply for the sake of definition. Instead

> the task of the critical process is to hold the ecclesiastical formulae to strict agreement with the foregoing analysis of our Christian self-consciousness, in order, partly, to judge how far they agree with it at least in essentials, partly (in regard to individual points), to inquire how much of the current form of expression is to be retained, and how much, on the other hand, had better be given up, either because it is an imperfect solution of the problem or because it is an addition not in itself essential, and harmful because the occasion of persistent misunderstandings.[40]

One might query whether Schleiermacher is sometimes too impatient with earlier definitions, not always making sufficient effort to understand them in their contexts, but some such process of discernment is indeed necessary for critical loyalty to the tradition. As we might now expect, the virginal conception is one part of the formulae that he will find an imperfect solution, an inessential addition, and possibly harmful because of the misunderstandings it perpetuates.

Schleiermacher intends his dogmatics to avoid what he considers the four major types of heresy: the docetic, the Nazarean (or Ebionite), the Manichean and the Pelagian. The latter two refer to depictions of the human situation in relation to redemption. The former two refer to views about the person of Christ. Here he is concerned to remain within the constraints of orthodoxy by avoiding formulations that make the difference between Christ and those in need of redemption so great that an essential likeness is jeopardized and 'His participation in human nature vanishes into a mere appearance' (docetism) or that make his likeness to those to be redeemed 'so unlimited that no room is left for a distinctive superiority as a constituent of His being' (Nazarean or Ebionite).[41] It is important at this point not to make the mistake of thinking that, when Schleiermacher talks of the God-consciousness of humans and, as he will now do, of Christ, he reduces theology to mere subjective experience. One of the influences of Plato's thought was to enable Schleiermacher to view God not just as the presupposition for human awareness of absolute dependence but as disclosed and present in such an experience. Certainly in a Christian context the disposition of absolute dependence that he posits as the religious

---

[40] Schleiermacher, *Christian Faith*, 390.
[41] Schleiermacher, *Christian Faith*, 99.

consciousness is not simply a description of an immanent human experience. It is where the reality of the infinite being of God meets with our own being.[42] So he can say of Christ, 'The Redeemer, then, is like all men in virtue of the identity of human nature, but distinguished from them all by the constant potency of His God-consciousness, which was a veritable existence of God in him.'[43]

He holds, then, that for an appropriate Christology that sees Christ as fully human but does justice to the unique distinctiveness of Christ from other humans, the cardinal issues are the nature of his God-consciousness and his sinlessness and that the two are intimately connected.

> That the Redeemer should be entirely free from all sinfulness is no objection at all to the complete identity of human nature in Him and others, for we have already laid down that sin is so little an essential part of the being of man that we can never regard it as anything other than a disturbance of nature.[44]

In the case of Christ, 'the ground of His sinlessness was not external to Himself, but . . . essentially grounded in Himself, if He was to take away, through what He was in Himself, the sinfulness of the corporate life'.[45] And what enables Christ to have the grounds within himself for overcoming sin is the nature of his God-consciousness that continually determines his life.

> To ascribe to Christ an absolutely powerful God-consciousness, and to attribute to Him an existence of God in Him, are exactly the same thing . . . It is only through Him that the human God-consciousness becomes an existence of God in human nature.[46]

So from the beginning of his life, the Redeemer has to be seen as free from the influences of earlier generations that disseminated sin, thereby disturbing the God-consciousness. 'The beginning of His life was a new implanting of the God-consciousness which creates receptivity in human nature.' In this regard Christ is to be seen as the Second Adam.

> The appearance of the first man constituted at the same time the physical life of the human race; the appearance of the Second Adam constituted for this nature a new spiritual life, which communicates and develops itself by spiritual fecundation.[47]

---

42 Cf. e.g. Schleiermacher, *Christian Faith*, 131–41.
43 Schleiermacher, *Christian Faith*, 385.
44 Schleiermacher, *Christian Faith*, 385.
45 Schleiermacher, *Christian Faith*, 386.
46 Schleiermacher, *Christian Faith*, 387–8.
47 Schleiermacher, *Christian Faith*, 389.

What Paul attributes to the resurrection, Schleiermacher, like John, attributes to the incarnation.

Schleiermacher finds this expression of Christology more satisfactory than others based on the formulations of Chalcedon, which he critiques on three counts. First, he points out problems with statements that assert that in Jesus Christ divine nature and human nature were combined into one person. In particular, they lead to a confusion about the terms 'nature' and 'person'. For Schleiermacher the problem with the former is that

> the expression 'nature' is used indifferently for the divine and the human ... For how can divine and human be thus brought together under any single conception, as if they could both be more exact determinations, coordinated to each other, of one and the same universal?[48]

He should not be misunderstood here.[49] Schleiermacher is not saying that it is impossible for the divine and human, the transcendent and immanent, to be brought together. After all, that is precisely what his own construal attempts to do. He is objecting to the frequent talk in Christology of two natures as if they were precisely the same in each case, to the term being used univocally instead of analogically. He is pointing to the faulty assumptions that the divine and the human are on the same plane of being and that we know what a nature is and that without further ado this can be applied to the divine and to the human in the same way in Christ. Second, and here, for him, matters become worse '... in utter contradiction to the use elsewhere, according to which the same nature belongs to many individuals or persons, here one person is to share in two quite different natures'.[50] He concludes, then, that

> the results of the endeavour to achieve a living presentation of the unity of the divine and the human in Christ, ever since it was tied down to this expression, have always vacillated between the opposite errors of mixing the two natures to form a third which would be neither of them, neither divine nor human, or of keeping the two natures separate, but either neglecting the unity of the person in order to separate the two natures more distinctly, or, in order to keep firm hold of the unity of the person, disturbing the necessary balance, and making one nature less important than the other and limited by it.[51]

His third criticism of the way the tradition has developed is that there is further confusion when this formula about Christ is related to the

---

[48] Schleiermacher, *Christian Faith*, 392.
[49] As is arguably the case in the discussion in C. E. Gunton, *Yesterday and Today: A Study of Continuities in Christology* (London: Darton, Longman & Todd, 1983), 89–90.
[50] Schleiermacher, *Christian Faith*, 393.
[51] Schleiermacher, *Christian Faith*, 394.

formula about the Trinity. In regard to the Trinity the talk was not of a unity of nature but of a unity of essence, but that raises the question

> what the relation is between what in Christ we call His divine nature and that unity of essence which is common to all three Persons of the Trinity, and whether each of the three Persons, outside their participation in the Divine Essence, has also a nature of its own as well, or whether that is a peculiarity of the Second Person.

In addition, the formula about the Trinity introduced another usage of the term 'person' so that we have three Persons in one essence alongside the Christological formula about one Person with two natures. If 'Person' means the same in each case – the Son of God taking up human nature into his Person – 'then the three Persons must have had an independent anterior existence in themselves; and if each Person is also a nature, we come almost inevitably to three divine natures for the three divine Persons in the one Divine Essence'. If, on the other hand, it is held that the same word 'person' means something different in each case, then, says Schleiermacher, 'the confusion is just as great'.[52]

For these reasons Schleiermacher avoids talk of the two natures in one Person. In doing so, he can claim that

> if this form of expression is very different from that of the language of the Schools as used hitherto, yet it rests equally upon the Pauline phrase 'God was in Christ' and the Johannine 'the Word became flesh' . . . In so far as all human activity of the Redeemer depends, as a connected whole, upon this existence of God in Him and represents it, the expression (that in the Redeemer God became man) is justified as true exclusively of Him; and similarly every moment of His existence, so far as it can be isolated, presents just such a new incarnation and incarnatedness of God, because always and everywhere all that is human in Him springs out of that divine.[53]

What is more, he asserts, there is nothing either docetic or Ebionite about such a way of putting the matter.

The preceding discussion has been necessary in order to show how Schleiermacher rethinks Christology in his new intellectual setting while attempting to maintain an appropriate balance between humanity and divinity and in order to see how his views on the virgin birth relate to belief in Christ as the incarnation of God. He will argue that the virgin

---

[52] Schleiermacher, *Christian Faith*, 395.
[53] Schleiermacher, *Christian Faith*, 397.

birth is not essential to a robust Christology that affirms that Jesus is fully divine and fully human. As might be expected from the dialogue in *Christmas Eve*, and in comparison with some more recent discussions, his handling of the topic is eirenic and conciliatory in its tone but makes his own position clear. He tackles the doctrine from two angles: the New Testament evidence and its dogmatic value. In regard to the former, he points out that the accounts in Matthew and in Luke 'are never again referred to in the further course of the history of the Christ; nor does any apostolic passage appeal to them'. When he adds, 'They conflict with the two genealogies, which go back to Joseph in a simple and straightforward way without taking any account of these stories',[54] this would need to be qualified. As we have seen, the ending of Matthew's genealogy and, arguably, the introduction to Luke's do seem to make adjustments in the light of their annunciation accounts. It is the genealogical traditions that they have employed with which the conception stories would be in conflict. His next observation, already made in *The Life of Jesus*, requires no qualification:

> So far as John is concerned, they conflict not only with his silence concerning the fact itself, but also with the way in which he relates, without any corrective remark, that Jesus was called the son of Joseph by His countrymen and acquaintances.

Having treated the New Testament data more extensively in his lectures on Jesus, Schleiermacher is content to leave matters here before attempting to be even-handed towards the two responses to these observations. He suggests that those who want to take the virgin birth stories as literally exact should probably not be seen as introducing into the faith something that is at variance with its true nature, while adding that 'certainly those who delight in parallels between these birth-narratives and the various Jewish and heathen legends of the supernatural conception of distinguished men go as far as they can in that direction', that is, of seeing it as introducing an alien element.[55] Of those who are doubtful about basing a doctrine solely on such stories and about making it an indispensable part of the creed and who conclude from the available evidence that the earliest followers of Christ set no great weight on this version of Christ's birth and that there was for a considerable time 'no fixed and generally recognized tradition on the subject', he says, 'we are bound to grant them that it is quite possible to believe

---

[54] Schleiermacher, *Christian Faith*, 403.
[55] Schleiermacher, *Christian Faith*, 403.

in Christ as Redeemer without believing in His supernatural conception in this sense'.[56]

Schleiermacher is more forthright about the dogmatic value of belief in the virginal conception; there is none. It would only have value if it affected Christ's relation to original sin or the presence of the divine in Christ's human nature. But, for him, it does not, since he sees the working of God in Christ as supernatural in a way quite different from a biological miracle. If Christ is to be sinless and if the divine is to be introduced into the human species in an individual for the first time, then it is necessary for divine creative activity to be combined with any human reproductive activity. Natural procreation will suffice neither to ensure the Redeemer's sinlessness, because 'the sinfulness of every individual has its roots in the previous generation', nor to produce the union of the divine with the human in a new creation. But the partial neutralization of this process through the absence of any paternal share in the new life will also not suffice to explain the being of God in Christ's life or the absence of sinfulness 'so long as the maternal share remains altogether what it is by nature'.[57] As Schleiermacher rightly observes, echoing the same point in the lectures, the idea very soon had to be supplemented by Mary too having been free from inherited sinfulness and yet to have any coherence would need to be extended further, back though the generations. Instead 'everything rests upon the higher influence which, as a creative divine activity, could alter both the paternal and maternal influence in such a way that all ground for sinfulness was removed, and this although procreation was perfectly natural'. If 'supernatural' refers to God's ability to work in the creation to achieve the divine purposes, then

> the general idea of a supernatural conception remains . . . essential and necessary, if the specific pre-eminence of the Redeemer is to remain undiminished. But the more precise definition of this supernatural conception as one in which there was no male activity has no connexion of any kind with the essential elements in the peculiar dignity of the Redeemer.

For Schleiermacher, therefore, 'the assumption of a Virgin Birth is superfluous'.[58] He had earlier explained this creative divine activity in the union of the divine and the human in Christ, which he describes as supernatural in the more general sense, as an eternal activity.

---

[56] Schleiermacher, *Christian Faith*, 403–4.
[57] Schleiermacher, *Christian Faith*, 404–5.
[58] Schleiermacher, *Christian Faith*, 405.

This eternal activity means for us simply a divine decree, identical as such with the decree to create man and included therein; but the aspect of this decree which is turned towards us as activity, or its manifestation in the actual beginning of the life of the Redeemer, through which that eternal decree realized itself . . . is temporal. So that the temporality has reference purely to the person-forming activity of the human nature, during which it was taken up into the union.[59]

There need then be no further special divine activity that in this case alters the person-forming activity of humans by excluding the male involvement in such activity. So, asserts Schleiermacher, belief in the virgin birth is not a matter of Christology but 'belongs solely to the doctrine of Scripture; and everyone has to reach a decision about it by the proper application of those principles of criticism and interpretation which approve themselves to Him (*sic*)'.[60] While Schleiermacher himself clearly accepts critical methods that do not require a literal interpretation of the accounts, he again acknowledges that there will be those who are not yet able to do so. Nevertheless he concludes this part of his discussion strongly.

But if it is superfluous to set up a doctrine of the Virgin Birth proper, it is also inadvisable to do so, for this involves one all too easily in investigations of a purely scientific character which lie quite outside our sphere.[61]

This is presumably a reference to entanglement in the biological implications of the miracle, a matter he never addresses specifically.

Since Schleiermacher recognizes that belief in a virginal conception is still to this point the dominant view of Jesus' birth in Christendom, he finishes his treatment by making a number of points that those who wish to continue to hold it should bear in mind. (i) 'This physiologically supernatural element does not, in itself, imply what we demand of the divine influence in the conception of the Redeemer.' (ii) It does not eradicate 'the racial character of Jesus' personality', robbing him of his historicity. (iii) It should not be spun out any further than the narratives in which it is found; 'hence the assertion that Mary remained a virgin is to be rejected as completely baseless'. This is, of course, a rejection of much of the patristic development that we have set out in the previous chapter. (iv) The notion must not be based on or give rise to 'a condemnation of the sexual impulse, as if its satisfaction were something sinful and

---

[59] Schleiermacher, *Christian Faith*, 401–2.
[60] The English translation has mistakenly employed a capital letter here, changing the original reference to the reader of Scripture to a reference to a divine person.
[61] Schleiermacher, *Christian Faith*, 406.

productive of sin'. Here Augustine's influential view is rejected. (v) Even if stories of the virginal conception are taken as historical, it should not be assumed that 'their terminology is pedantically exact'. So, for instance, the angel should not be thought of as speaking to Mary 'of the Holy Spirit in the more precise New Testament sense', let alone implying that Jesus was the son of the Holy Spirit.[62]

Having revised the traditional notion of how the union of the divine and the human in Christ was established, Schleiermacher then notes that the distinction between the original divine assumptive activity and the divine activity during the union that was part of the traditional discussion is also no longer necessary.

> It is not a special nature which comes into being in this way, one which could and must be distinguished from other human existence; what comes into existence through the being of God in Christ is all perfectly human, and in its totality constitutes a unity, the unity of a natural life-story, in which everything that emerges is purely human, and one thing can be deduced from another, since every moment presupposes those which have gone before, yet in which everything can be completely understood only upon the presupposition of that union through which alone this Person could come into being, so that every moment also reveals the divine in Christ as that which conditions it.[63]

Schleiermacher as agenda setter

A proper assessment of how adequately Schleiermacher's overall Christology achieves his aims of rethinking the Christian faith while maintaining its essential notion of Christ as both fully God and fully human cannot be our concern here. It has been criticized, on the one hand, for not being explicit enough about the ontology of the category of 'God-consciousness', and, on the other, for not paying sufficient attention, in depicting the person of Christ, to his identification with the poor and oppressed and the significance of his death. But by any standards it remains a magnificent attempt and one can see why it earned him the designation of 'the father of modern theology'.[64]

---

[62] Schleiermacher, *Christian Faith*, 406–7.

[63] Schleiermacher, *Christian Faith*, 409.

[64] The judgement of J. Macquarrie, *Jesus Christ in Modern Thought* (London: SCM, 1990), 386, is worth repeating: 'although Schleiermacher rejects the traditional formulations of the "two-natures" Christology, I do not think that he rejects its "governing intention" and would say that his own Christology says in his language no less than the ancient formulation said in its language'.

Our interest, however, has been in exploring why and how the virgin birth became problematic for Christian theologians after the Enlightenment and here Schleiermacher has proved to be a helpful case study. The factors affecting his treatment of this topic included the questions being raised about the role of reason in relation to religion and revelation, the new stress on the humanity and historical conditionedness of Scripture, and the need for reformulating theology and Christology in the light of problems with the language of earlier doctrinal statements, such as nature, substance and person, and with the traditional metaphysical assumptions behind them. In this context Schleiermacher's specific critique of the virgin birth tradition is a telling one and he makes a very strong case for seeing it as both superfluous and possibly harmful to adhering to the confession that Christ is God incarnate. Whether his alternative construal of the beginnings of Christ's life in relation to the matter of his sinlessness is entirely satisfactory may be questioned. It certainly contains some ambiguities. As we saw, before addressing the doctrine of the virgin birth explicitly, he can say of Christ at one point that 'the beginning of His life was a new implanting of the God-consciousness'.[65] Even allowing for the use of metaphor here, it sounds as though this involves a special divine intervention, whereby, in distinction from other humans, Christ was given a new God-consciousness that guaranteed him freedom from sin.[66] If not a contradiction of his primary intention, this appears at least to be an unfortunate formulation, because earlier he has insisted,

> That the Redeemer should be entirely free from all sinfulness is no objection at all to the complete identity of human nature in Him and others, for we have already laid down that sin is so little an essential part of the being of man that we can never regard it as anything other than a disturbance of nature.[67]

As we have seen, when he does talk of the virgin birth, he is also careful to distinguish his own notion of the supernatural divine activity involved in Christ's birth from any notion of a supernatural intervention in history. It would surely have been better, within his own terms, to have avoided the idea of a new implanting and instead have talked about Christ as unique in being enabled from the beginning to experience the God-consciousness that he shared with other humans as in entire and uninhibited alignment with God. It may well be that the matter of Christ's sinlessness is, in any

---

[65] Schleiermacher, *Christian Faith*, 389.
[66] On this see also Macquarrie, *Modern Thought*, 208–9.
[67] Schleiermacher, *Christian Faith*, 385.

case, better handled, as we shall indicate later, by placing greater emphasis on the work of God's Spirit and by a more thorough rethinking of sinlessness in dynamic terms than Schleiermacher managed to achieve.

Rather than debating the details of Schleiermacher's alternative to the virgin birth, it is perhaps more important at this point to stress that, just as the creeds and Chalcedon had set the agenda for reflection on our topic up until the Enlightenment, now Schleiermacher's thinking is added to that agenda and the issues he raises will figure prominently in more recent discussion. In particular, the questions that Schleiermacher raises and that will not go away include the following. (i) If Scripture is the primary source for theology, what difference does it make to the doctrine of the virgin birth once its human and historical conditionedness is properly recognized and literary and historical criticism is applied to the birth narratives? How is the diversity of views on the incarnation in the New Testament among the witnesses of Paul, the Synoptics and John to be handled and what impact does this have on the virgin birth tradition? (ii) What difference, if any, does a questioning of the historicity of a virginal conception make to an orthodox Christological confession of the full humanity, full divinity and sinlessness of Christ? (iii) How is a rethinking of the virgin birth in relation to incarnation to be treated in relation to the Church's tradition as expressed in the creeds and formulations of the early councils? (iv) What role in the rethinking of the tradition is played by the relation of the doctrine of the virgin birth to contemporary knowledge and thought forms? Such questions will be among the key issues to be revisited in our next chapter.

9

Reconceiving Jesus: Scripture
and hermeneutics

The burden of the book so far has been to indicate why and how the
traditional doctrine of the virginal conception of Christ needs to be
rethought in the light of serious biblical scholarship with its fuller understanding of both the genres employed by the biblical writers and the
diversity of the perspectives of the biblical witnesses. This exploration has
also indicated from time to time no longer shared assumptions that under-
lie the traditional doctrine, including those about what is involved in the
production of a human foetus, recognition of which undermines a major
function that the virgin birth was traditionally meant to serve, namely,
to safeguard the humanity of Christ against docetic views of his nature.
This chapter will begin by elaborating on these two issues. How do the
implications of critical scholarship on the conception of Jesus relate to
the authority of Scripture in the Christian tradition? What more precisely is the pressure exerted on the tradition by the difference between
our own assumptions about biology and those operative for the ancients?
In the light of the latter question, we shall then turn in the final chapter
to exploring more positively some of the implications of a revised understanding of the conception of Jesus for contemporary Christology and
conclude with reflections on how the discussion as a whole might be seen
in its place within the ongoing Christian tradition and in particular how
it is related to the matter of reciting the creed as part of Christian worship.

Scriptural truth and critical/post-critical reading

Whatever the tensions that may arise between holding that the Bible is an
authoritative source of truth and being persuaded that it needs to be read
critically, the two convictions are by no means incompatible. But, again,
we need to be clear here what is meant by critical reading. 'Critical' does
not mean assuming some position of superiority over against the text,
adopting a negative stance towards it, being dismissive of anything that
cannot be shown to be factual, or automatically being suspicious of its
claims. It means using all the tools available, whether they be historical,

linguistic, literary, theological, in order to gain as full an understanding of the text as possible, and it means being as aware as possible of one's own commitments and perspectives in doing so. A considerable period of time has elapsed since the beginnings of biblical criticism in the modern period after the Enlightenment and since Schleiermacher's particular use of the critical tools available to him. Those two centuries have seen the elaboration and refinement of historical and literary methods in particular but have also allowed perspective to be obtained on how such critical methods have been employed and on the various ideological assumptions that have accompanied and influenced their use. Part of this perspective has been a growing humility among scholars about what can be achieved by critical methods. While considerable achievements and some solid conclusions have resulted from their use, scholars are less inclined to talk of the 'assured results' of critical enquiry or to claim objectivity for their work. This has been due to an increased awareness that all histories are narrations of the past constrained by the sources employed and by the perspectives and social and cultural locations of the historians who employ them and to the accompanying recognition that, in regard to the results of historical methods, one has to be talking in terms of probabilities rather than certainties. The areas that remain under debate and the variety of interpretations of textual sources after 200 years of employing critical methods should underline that, while *a* critical reading remains necessary, there can be no presumption that one's own reading is *the* critical reading.

Some scholars have indeed used critical tools from a rationalistic perspective in a conscious attempt to undermine the Bible's authority or to establish an unbridgeable chasm between 'the historical Jesus' and both the early and the later Church's understanding of him. But the critical tools themselves by no means entail such consequences. For a stance of 'faith seeking understanding' they have a significant role to play. Having a confident faith that Jesus Christ, as witnessed to in Scripture, is the locus of God's revelation does not mean that one knows in advance of actual investigation the nature of Scripture and the means of its witness. These matters and others remain to be discovered and critical methods have an essential part to play in that discovery. This follows also from holding that Scripture is God's word that comes to us through human words, human words that are articulated in particular languages, presented in particular literary forms, shaped by their writers' particular perspectives and conditioned by those writers' historical and cultural settings. A critical reading is necessary because the Bible is a fully human document. Scripture's truth claims are mediated through all that is entailed in divine revelation taking this form, and investigation of this limited human form is essential for a responsible interpretation of such claims. But this also means that the understanding that faith seeks will inevitably have to be provisional and open to correction. A robust faith in Christ is to be distinguished from certainty in the areas of historical and literary interpretation and is able to live with probabilities and unresolved questions.

It is from this stance that our earlier exploration of the biblical material about Jesus' birth has been undertaken. It underscored that the various questions about the virgin birth in the biblical data, with which Schleiermacher and his contemporaries were engaging, are indeed valid ones that arise from the biblical witnesses themselves. Are there differing views about Jesus' conception within the New Testament and early Christianity? What are the nature and status of the stories about a virgin birth? How are they to be related to a responsible and coherent account of history and how far does this matter for the truth of these stories? Our study of the New Testament material has attempted both to summarize and to take forward many of the results of the last 200 years of critical enquiry on these matters and to be as honest as possible about the ambiguities in the materials, disputed interpretations and the levels of probability involved in conclusions about historical tradition, including those places where historical investigation has not been able to arrive at clear-cut decisions.

In brief, it has become apparent that, despite some voices to the contrary, further exploration does indeed support and enhance Schleiermacher's view that within the New Testament the virginal conception is not the only perspective on Jesus' birth. As we have observed previously, it might appear natural to give the virginal conception pride of place because it is in actual narratives about Jesus' birth and then to read the rest of the New Testament either as if it were silent about Jesus' conception or in a way that consciously or unconsciously harmonizes its data with the notion of a virginal conception. But this does not do justice to first hearing the message of each of the New Testament documents on its own terms. When we do this, then writers like Paul or John are no longer silent about a virginal conception, either because they do not know of it or have no cause to allude to it, but in fact become positive witnesses to a different view through their references to the seed of David or their straightforward acknowledgement of Joseph as Jesus' father. Parts of Luke–Acts also join this group of witnesses. In addition, the view that assumes that Matthew's and Luke's infancy narratives are the norm to which other New Testament material should be subordinated is frequently accompanied by the further assumption that, since these are in Gospels, they are the accounts that are meant to be historical and should therefore be given primacy. But, in addition to some ambiguity about whether Matthew does in fact assert a virginal conception and to the appearance in Luke of a virginal conception alongside material that assumes a normal birth, there is another major reason why assigning priority to Matthew and Luke on such grounds is not appropriate. Their infancy narratives are the least historical sections of their ancient biographies with their content far more substantially informed than the rest of their narratives both by their post-resurrection convictions about the significance of Jesus and by models from Jewish Scripture and its interpretation. In other words, such an approach tends to ignore the genre of these stories where, in line with the convention of other ancient biographies and their accounts of their heroes' beginnings, readers would have expected to find not what we would see as straight-forward history but history-like material with substantial legendary embellishment. A critical reading, then, raises theological and hermeneutical issues about diversity within the New Testament, to which we shall return, but it also raises historical questions in relation to Jesus' birth. Because of the genre of the stories in Matthew and Luke, these questions would arise for the attempt to construct a historical account even if the New Testament were uniform in its witness to the virginal conception. The presence of different views in the New Testament writings themselves simply means there are more sources for the historian to compare and assess in his or her task. In Chapter 6 we set out our positive reasons for considering that the material that witnesses to Jesus' birth from both Joseph and Mary most probably reflects the earliest tradition, that this earliest tradition can provide a plausible explanation of the development of the other traditions and that it is most likely to represent what was historically the case. In the process we also supplied reasons for considering that the virginal conception view of Jesus' birth was most probably a later tradition and unlikely to be historical, indicating how and why the tradition developed in this form.

For some, to cast doubt on the historicity of any biblical account is already to reject the authority and truth of the Bible. In regard to the virgin birth, their argument runs: the New Testament is authoritative as divinely inspired, therefore the Gospels should be accepted as historically reliable, therefore we should accept the claim of a virginal conception. It is a theological argument in which historical claims are embedded. But it is a fallacious one. Its initial premise, though one that would be accepted by a Christian approaching our topic, is incomplete and the consequences it draws from the premise simply do not follow. It omits from its premise the corresponding Christian belief about Scripture that it is the word of God through the words of humans, humans who lived in particular historical contexts and who used the modes of communication available to them in their particular cultures. As a consequence, it holds to a historical virginal conception by simply ignoring the issues of interpretation and genre, and with them the results of the serious study of the documents by New Testament scholars. Such study enables us to discern how specific parts of the Gospels are constructing the past, whether as reliable memories of events or in a way that is consonant with the conventions for writing the life of a subject in the first century CE or in some combination of these alternatives, and therefore also to discern the nature of the divine claim that is being made through such narratives. Again, this does not detract from their authority or truth but is simply to recognize the form in which divine revelation has been given us. When a theologian, such as Crisp, inveighs against the findings of historical critics about the infancy narratives by asserting, 'And the fact is, the birth narratives are canonical Scripture. This means that there is a very good theological reason for trusting them: they are divine revelation',[1] he is confusing what is at stake. That they are part of canonical Scripture tells us nothing about their literary genre and therefore what sort of history they may or may not contain. Trusting them as divine revelation entails trusting their witness to the significance of Jesus and does not necessarily mean taking them literally as straightforward, historically accurate accounts.

Insistence on the latter within evangelical circles is frequently still influenced by the legacy of the fundamentalist–modernist controversy from the beginning of the twentieth century. In reaction to what were seen as the corroding effects of rationalistic theology and the use of 'higher criticism' on orthodox Christianity, the fundamentals were frequently reduced to five: the inerrancy of Scripture, the deity of Jesus Christ, the virgin birth, the bodily resurrection of Christ and the personal return of Christ. In the process of taking what was considered a necessary defensive and apologetic stance over against liberal tendencies, the virgin birth and the inerrancy of Scripture, which historically had been more minor doctrines, were raised to the level of touchstones for authentic Christian orthodoxy. The virgin birth had, of course, always been there in the creeds and traditionally been seen as the means of the incarnation but now it became the key test of whether a person believed in the supernatural activity of God

---

[1] O. D. Crisp, *God Incarnate: Explorations in Christology* (London: T. & T. Clark, 2009), 91.

244

in the world. If modernists tended to deny miracles in the sense of God violating the laws of nature, then fundamentalist defenders of the orthodox faith held that if a person were able to assert the reality of the virgin birth, he or she would be sound on any lesser miracles recorded in Scripture. One of the problems with the controversy was that both sides were operating on a set of assumptions which are themselves culturally conditioned and questionable, such as a positivistic view of history, a primarily propositional view of revelation and a dualism between the 'natural' and the 'supernatural'. But given this relatively recent history, it is not too hard to understand why raising questions about the virgin birth on whatever grounds has remained a particularly sensitive area.

Throughout the earlier part of our exploration we have interacted at key points with the work of Machen on the virgin birth. This is not only because, although dated, it remains an erudite classic defence of this doctrine but also because, as such a classic, it continues to exercise significant influence among evangelical Christians. Machen was himself a major figure in the playing out of the fundamentalist–modernist controversy in the American Presbyterian Church and its institutions with its resulting denominational splits,[2] and, for all its scholarship, his book *The Virgin Birth of Christ* bears the unmistakable marks of that controversy. In the midst of detailed interaction with both the German- and English-language scholarship of his day, Machen's approach is determined by his view that 'the Bible is a record of facts'[3] and therefore the virgin birth is either an historical fact or an error,[4] either true or false.[5] One either accepts Luke's account of the annunciation as historical or views it as mistaken because one rejects the supernatural.[6] No ground can be given to those who maintain that, whether the account is reliable history or not, it still would be expressing a truth about Christ. That would be to split the authority of the Bible unacceptably into two different spheres: one to do with a spiritual religion and one to do with matters of science and history. But since the authority of the Bible extends to external fact, such a view, whatever it may claim, is a rejection of the Bible's authority.[7] What is more, for Machen, belief in the virgin birth, rather than belief in Christ's divinity

---

[2] Cf. also his *Christianity and Liberalism* (Grand Rapids: Eerdmans, 1923), in which he argues that orthodox Protestantism and modern liberal Christianity are two antithetical religions.

[3] J. G. Machen, *The Virgin Birth of Christ* (2nd edn New York: Harper and Row, 1932), 385.

[4] Machen, *Virgin Birth*, 1, 272.

[5] Machen, *Virgin Birth*, 382.

[6] Machen, *Virgin Birth*, 45.

[7] Cf. esp. Machen, *Virgin Birth*, 383–4.

or his resurrection, which are open to diverse interpretations, is to be seen as the only unambiguous test of whether a person has a true super-naturalistic view of Jesus Christ. Cast doubt on the historicity of the virgin birth and in principle – practice will inevitably follow – you have abandoned Christ and Christianity.[8]

Whatever sympathy one might have for Machen's stance in its context,[9] one cannot help but sense that something has gone profoundly wrong when the question of the historicity of the virgin birth is elevated to a status and role it had never had in the history of the Church and made to bear this amount of weight. Among the factors that make this wrong are matters we have already mentioned: a failure to distinguish between the crucial belief in the incarnation and the secondary matter of the precise means of incarnation and a failure to see that not all biblical narrative can simply be assumed to be recounting historical 'fact'. The influence among evangelicals of Machen's approach in making the virgin birth a test for genuine Christian belief has, however, been hard to shake off, although some are now prepared to admit that the virgin birth is not absolutely necessary for maintaining the reality of the incarnation and is a secondary doctrine that is not necessary for salvation.[10] Granted that Machen wrote before the positive results of redaction criticism about the evangelists' perspectives and before the rise of narrative criticism, one of the ironies of his work is that, for all its emphasis on biblical authority and its scholarly debate about textual detail, its reader is never actually confronted with the distinctive messages of the annunciation passages. Their message is apparently assumed to be that these things happened as told and so what in fact becomes decisive for believing them is not so much their overall message about the significance of Jesus but Machen's own harmo-nized reconstruction that supposedly shows their historical reliability. In the attempt to establish that reliability, Machen shared the modernist assumptions of his opponents about history but employed them within a supernaturalistic perspective.

---

[8] Cf. Machen, *Virgin Birth*, 287–97.

[9] See e.g. the chapter on 'Understanding J. Gresham Machen', in G. M. Marsden, *Understanding Fundamentalism and Evangelicalism* (Grand Rapids: Eerdmans, 1991), 182–201, which also sets Machen's views on 'facts' within the context of the historiography of the time.

[10] Cf. e.g. M. Erickson, *Christian Theology* (2nd edn Grand Rapids: Baker, 1998), 757–60, 772; S. Grenz, *Theology for the Community of God* (Carlisle: Paternoster, 1994), 324–5, concludes, 'we do well to accept the majority opinion of the church throughout its history. We affirm that the virgin birth was indeed a historical event.' However, the weak connection with other doctrines means that 'the virgin birth is not christologically indispensable ... it is not the historical founda-tion of our christological confession'.

In contrast to modernism's confidence that historical investigation enabled one to declare evidence true or false and to establish the facts, reflection on historical method in late modernity has rightly complicated matters by pointing out, among other issues, if not the impossibility of ever knowing whether our construct of past reality corresponds with that external reality, then at least the limits of historiography as a way of knowing, the distinction that must always be made between the historian's construction of the past and what is likely to have actually happened, the relation between evidence about the past and the literary form in which it is expressed, the inevitability of subjective perspectives at work in both the historian's construction and his or her narrative sources, and thus the involvement of interpretation in any talk of facts or historical data and the presence of fictive as well as more factual elements in both history writing and its narrative source material. All of these factors are particularly in play when it comes to ancient historiography, where, as we have seen, the notion of genre is crucial for alerting us to the difference between what is expected of modern histories in terms of establishing what in all probability happened and what was expected of ancient histories, and particularly biographies, in terms of plausibility. In the case of ancient biographies, in the mix of more factual and more legendary materials they contained, the accounts of the beginnings of a subject's life are always the most legendary. This should not be surprising. The only public interest in the birth of children in the ancient world would be if they already had the likelihood of being important because they were being born into a royal family and were heirs to a position that would affect the future of a dynasty or nation. Birth narratives about others do not so much supply reliable information as serve as a commentary on their significance once it has become clear that they have made an important impact as adults. They are retrospective interpretations of that impact, frequently not emerging until well after their subjects' deaths and involving from the start legendary elements that tended to increase in the passing on of traditions gathered around figures whose births themselves are now seen as having a major impact foreshadowing their future greatness. Matthew's and Luke's annunciation stories are of just this sort and readers are referred back to the extended discussion of the genre of the infancy narratives in Chapter 3.

The point to be made here is that it will, therefore, not do to point to the preface of Luke's Gospel and consider that that settles the question of historicity. Luke, it is said, must have been writing factual history because he claims to be dealing with that which was passed on by eyewitnesses and to have investigated his sources carefully and so his annunciation story must be factual history.[11] Ancient biography, as we have noted, overlaps at one end of its range with ancient historiography, and the sort of claims found in Luke's preface, including references to eyewitnesses, were standard fare in ancient historiography where they were part of the rhetorical arsenal of those who wanted to be able to legitimate the accounts they produced in order to persuade their audiences.[12] Some writers may have actually done what they claim as best they could. But, whether or not the claims were carried out and to whatever extent this was done, they were still employed to introduce works of widely different quality, judged by modern standards of historicity, ranging from those that conform more approximately to such standards to those that contain far more popular, anecdotal and legendary material. Ancient biographical writing tended to be closer to the latter end of this range than to the former. On a critical historical reading, once it is observed that Luke's preface places his work somewhere within this range, it remains to be determined, so far as this is possible, on a case-by-case basis which parts of it are more factual and which parts more legendary.[13] It is simply a category mistake to assume that the writers of the Gospels give straightforward factual history on the basis of which their accounts can be judged either true or false. Cox makes this point clearly:

> In antiquity biography . . . had its own unique characteristics and sustained historical veracity was not one of them. To impugn the integrity of a Greco-Roman biography on the basis of factual discrepancy is to misconceive the literary tradition of the genre to which it belongs.[14]

As we have seen, a legendary account of the announcement of its subject's birth would fall well within the conventions of ancient biography.[15] In the case of Matthew and Luke such an account is in the service of a truth larger than that of historical accuracy – the truth about the significance of the beginning of the life of Jesus, the Messiah and Son of God.

---

[11] Cf. e.g. Machen, *Virgin Birth*, 385–6; J. Redford, *Born of a Virgin: Proving the Miracle from the Gospels* (London: St Paul, 2007), 127–9.

[12] Cf. S. Byrskog, *Story as History – History as Story* (Tübingen: Mohr Siebeck, 2000), 199–223.

[13] For a careful discussion of the limited help the claims of Luke's preface can provide in determining the extent of fact or fiction in his work, see L. C. A. Alexander, 'Fact, Fiction and the Genre of Acts', *NTS* 44 (1998), 380–99.

[14] P. Cox, *Biography in Late Antiquity: A Quest for the Holy Man* (Berkeley: University of California Press, 1983), 5.

[15] R. E. Brown, *The Birth of the Messiah* (2nd edn New York: Doubleday, 1993), 562, also states clearly that 'one may not classify the infancy narratives as belonging to the literary genre of factual history', though rightly adding that this does not preclude the possibility of them containing some items of historical worth.

On a critical reading the question of genre, then, turns out to be crucial not only for the discussion of historicity but also for reflection on scriptural truth. In their infancy narratives the Gospels tell the truth about what God is accomplishing in Jesus through one particular means of conveying such truth that was available to their writers. The content of scriptural truth depends on the type of literature through which it is mediated. There is, for example, the truth of poetry, the truth of parable, and the truth of ancient biography, which includes the truth of legend. To this extent, and whether we employ the term legend or myth, we can agree with Spong's assertion, 'To assign the birth narratives to mythology is not to dismiss them as untrue. It is rather to force us to see truth in dimensions larger than literal truth . . .'[16] Accompanying the modernist positivist notion of history, which was shared by Machen, was also a positivist view of language that reduced its varied functions and relations to the world primarily to one: assertions about states of affairs. Attention to genre reminds us that the language of Scripture has a variety of functions. The history-like narratives of the Gospels are not so much giving us facts to accept or reject as providing reconfigured worlds in which we participate and which shape our minds, imaginations and lives. Their function, and that of the infancy narratives within them, is ultimately more formative than informative. Information about people and events that they do provide is reconfigured in a plot that invites us to look at the world differently and to be transformed in the process. A critical reading concerned about scriptural truth will certainly not, then, be content with asking questions about the probable historicity of the annunciation accounts. These questions are only part of our discernment of their genre. But the recognition of a genre also requires that we go on to ask questions about how such a genre functions and therefore what is the appropriate response to such a genre on the part of the reader.

The diversity among the witnesses to Jesus' conception within the New Testament also raises questions about scriptural truth. Such questions are, of course, not new and are raised, for instance, by the existence of the four very different Gospel narratives about the life of Jesus as a whole. Each can be seen as drawing out different aspects of the significance of God's action through that life and thereby allowing the gospel message to speak again to a variety of different situations. Rather than assuming that scriptural truth has to be monolithic or uniform, readers can appreciate its plural and dialogical nature as, for example, they allow the different perspectives

---

[16] J. S. Spong, *Born of a Woman: A Bishop Rethinks the Birth of Jesus* (San Francisco: HarperSanFrancisco, 1992), 45.

among Matthew, John, Paul, Hebrews and James on the nature of the salvation accomplished in Christ and on its relation to the Jewish law to be what they are and to challenge and interact with one another. Such an approach, while eschewing simple harmonization or synthesis, need not lead to contentment with incoherence. The New Testament canon has a differentiated unity in its witness to the salvific revelation of God accomplished uniquely in the life, death and resurrection of Christ. In regard to Jesus' conception, the diverse witnesses point in different ways to both the divine and the human elements at play from the outset of his life. The witnesses to his being the seed of David and having Joseph as his father emphasize the latter element and do so in the context of other claims about Jesus' unique relationship to God, as would also the further witness, if there is thought to be such, to his illegitimacy. The witnesses to his virginal conception in the annunciation stories of Matthew and Luke emphasize through the genre of ancient biography the divine element and its sovereign initiative and do so in the context of the assumption that Mary's involvement alone safeguards his humanity and of narratives that assume that fully mortal humanity in accounts of Jesus' death and burial. What are contradictory historical perspectives, if genre is not taken into account, can be seen to be strikingly different, in form and content, witnesses within the testimony of the New Testament as a whole to God becoming incarnate in the human life of Jesus of Nazareth. The re-examination of the New Testament provides the opportunity to appreciate, take seriously and return to its majority, dominant witness, represented particularly by Paul, Hebrews and John, where the subject of the incarnation was born naturally. It also enables us to see that the minority witness, found in the annunciation stories, gives graphic expression to the conviction that the life of Jesus, seen in the light of the resurrection, demands to be seen as, from its outset, the result of God's sovereign initiative for the redemption of the world. The overall impression from the New Testament – its unified witness, one might say – is of dual fatherhood – human and divine. This makes it particularly significant that, as we have argued, the two modes of presentation are combined in one of the witnesses, Luke–Acts. By holding together both the notion of a virginal conception and the assumption that Joseph was Jesus' biological father, Luke reinforces the dialogical and polyphonic nature of scriptural truth about the significance of what God has done and is doing in Christ. The later rise to dominance of the annunciation stories, read as unambiguously requiring a literal virginal conception, eventually suppressed the majority witness, closed down the possibility of dialogue and led to the set of problems we have been exploring.

As far as Scripture is concerned, the goal of our exploration with its combination of confessional stance and critical reading is to be able to move beyond simply trying to make sense of the text and instead to allow Scripture's narrative and its subject matter to make sense of us. Yet it should also be clear that this latter engagement with Scripture will need to be a post-critical one, that is, in the case of the annunciation stories, one that involves awareness of and confrontation with the sort of issues engaged here so that it has some clarity about whether a particular biological miracle has to be taken as part of the subject matter of the text.[17] Some recent attempts at such theological interpretation of Scripture have also been dubbed 'post-critical' but can turn out to exhibit neither a post-critical stance nor good theology. The treatment of the annunciation story in one recent theological commentary on Matthew is a case in point.[18] For all its insights on a variety of other matters, it chooses to ignore the real exegetical and historical problems we have outlined in Chapter 4 and instead dubious theological rhetoric triumphs. The commentary asserts, 'There is no way to prove Mary's virginity other than to observe that without Mary's virginity the story cannot be told. Mary's virginity is simply required by the way the story runs.' Yet this ignores what is the major exegetical issue for interpretation of the passage. No ambiguities about Matthew's story are noted and instead the only problem is taken to be attempts 'to render the virgin birth explicable in naturalistic terms', to which the response is offered that we 'should not try to explain how Jesus can at once be fully human and fully God'. But confessing Christians in wrestling with this passage are not simply attempting to find a naturalistic explanation, let alone to solve the mystery of the incarnation. Worse, however, is the way the depiction of the problem and what is thought to be the appropriate response to it simply conflate incarnation and virgin birth. This theological mistake of treating the virgin birth as the necessary mechanism for incarnation is repeated, when it is then asserted, 'Mary had to be a virgin because Jesus is the Son of God' and the one who will be named Emmanuel 'can have no other father than the Father who is the first person of the Trinity'. This is to encourage taking 'Son of God' in the most literal sense and would have been news to other canonical writers like Paul or John who believed Jesus was the Son of God but did not think that that entailed that his mother was a virgin or that he did not have a

---

[17] This is the approach P. Ricoeur, *The Symbolism of Evil* (Boston: Beacon, 1969), 351, famously described as proceeding to a 'second naïveté', which is reached through hermeneutical moments of suspicion and retrieval.

[18] S. Hauerwas, *Matthew* (Grand Rapids: Brazos, 2006).

father who gave him his descent from David. Reinforcing the need to take the story as historical, the writer tells us without further explanation, 'that a virgin should give birth to the Son is crucial for our understanding of the character of the Father'.[19] There is no nuancing of such a statement in terms of the categories of the first century and no reflection on whether what a virgin birth might say about the character of the Father in our context is really something that we would want to attribute to the God of Jesus Christ. If this is a theological discussion that is 'post-critical', it is so only in the sense that it ignores all critical issues.

For teaching and preaching, the positive side of a genuine post-critical reading lies in the recognition that, whatever the events of the past behind the scriptural narratives, those narratives themselves are the vehicles that instruct and transform. Indeed, this is not dissimilar to Paul's perspective in Romans 15.4: 'whatever was written in former days was written for our instruction, so that by steadfastness and by the encouragement of the scriptures we might have hope'. So the infancy narratives need to be, and of course will be, told and retold in the context of the Church's worship and liturgy, as they continue to shape the lives of those who hear them. But for that very reason, it is important to know what sort of narratives they are and to tell them alongside the complete story of Luke–Acts about Jesus and his origins or the story of John where Joseph's paternity and the incarnation of the Logos are both featured. When it comes to the actual annunciation stories in Matthew and Luke, teacher and preacher will need to have done sufficient critical reflection on literary and historical issues to discern that their subject matter is not the straightforward relating of historical events but the differing narrative constructions – inspired by the Spirit and shaped by the faith of the community – of the significance of the one who will be the agent of God's salvation for Israel and the world. The necessary critical distinctions having been made, and honestly explained in a teaching session, the interpreter is freed from thinking that in proclamation the historical reliability or lack of it have to feature as the subject matter and instead can wrestle with the relevant central question: 'How do these imaginative narrative construals of the beginning of Jesus' life shape the convictions and life of the believing community in the midst of a world with different values?' If, as is unfortunately often the case, the occasion of preaching is also the only major context of teaching, then the sermon itself will need to indicate to some extent how and why the truth of the annunciation stories does not depend on their being reliable historical reporting.

---

[19] Hauerwas, *Matthew*, 35–6.

Conceiving then and now

Theology, and in this case Christology in particular, is an ongoing discipline, one that to remain vital has to respond to the challenges posed by its contemporary setting. In regard to the human origins of Christ, we have already sufficiently explored the challenge presented by developments in historical and literary methods. But just as much of a challenge is presented by advances in biological knowledge, which we shall explore below. Such challenges will often mean that reinterpretation of the tradition is required. They inevitably set an agenda for Christology and it is impossible for reflective Christians to proceed as if they were still living in a pre-Enlightenment culture or in isolation from the intellectual assumptions of their own day. Whatever we now make of the details of Schleiermacher's approach, it is to his credit that he recognized this clearly and wrestled with its implications for Christian faith. The issue in acknowledging one's place in the tradition but also being willing to re-evaluate that tradition is whether and in what way present-day modes of thought also determine such re-evaluation. Is it simply a matter of the tradition conforming to changed conditions? How far does the tradition also have a say in shaping the questions posed by contemporary understandings or in challenging aspects or assumptions of the questions put to it? So there are always dangerous as well as beneficial possibilities in ongoing theological reflection and reinterpretation. Judgement of the outcome is usually contested and is often only possible from a later perspective and from a growing consensus among the faithful. But awareness of the fraught nature of the enterprise should at least be taken as an indicator of the intent not to sell the tradition short in a particular effort at reinterpretation.

Before proceeding to the main biological issue, it is worth noting the difference between then and now in regard to thinking about miraculous conceptions in general. Our contemporary discussion about the possibility of an event such as the virginal conception is very different from that of the ancients. Over against positivist historians who argue that a miracle such as this is impossible and no critical account should include it in its reconstruction of history, contemporary defenders of the historicity of the virgin birth tradition begin by tackling such a bias against the miraculous. Christians especially, they claim, hold that with God all things are possible. If one does not balk at God bringing the world into existence or raising Jesus from the dead, then there should be no problem with a virginal conception. While Protestants use this argument with reference to the virginal conception, Roman Catholics go on to use it of other aspects of Jesus' birth, particularly Mary's perpetual virginity, including her virginity *in partu*. So von Balthasar can say,

> And how typical of our age of minimalistic faith is the conceding of a virginal conception while dispensing the believer from having to accept a virginal birth. As if the second would not be as easy for God to bring about as the first.[20]

But this appeal to the general possibility of miracle quickly becomes very limited. For defenders of the tradition, a virginal conception or a virginal birth does not normally happen but, exceptionally, it has taken place in the one case of God's activity in the birth of Jesus. They turn out to be just as biased against the miraculous when it comes to other miracles in the ancient world and no more willing than anyone else to accept at face value accounts of other miraculous conceptions in Graeco-Roman literature. This position is, in fact, dependent on a particular view of the authority of Scripture, one that again fails to recognize the nature of Scripture as the words of God in the words of humans of their own time and place.

But the point of these observations is that such an apologetic and its cultural assumptions are markedly different from those of ancient apologetic for the virgin birth. In the world of the first centuries CE there would have been a spectrum of responses to accounts of miraculous events that ranged from taking them literally to understanding them more metaphorically but, generally speaking, they were part of the plausibility structures for most people. The argument of Christians was not so much that such events had occurred uniquely in the case of Jesus but that they had parallels with what was claimed for other divinities yet were superior in the case of Jesus because of the quality of his life and its effects. As we have seen, this is how Justin proceeds when maintaining that Christian claims about the virgin birth are similar to what is said about Perseus, who was born of the relationship between Zeus and the virgin Danae (*1 Apol.* 21–22). On the other side, the argument of Celsus, as reported by Origen (*Cels.* 1.39, 67), also compares Jesus' divine birth to that of Greek heroes but disputes the former because of Mary's inferior social status and Jesus' inferior words and deeds. One of the other weapons in the Christian arsenal, of course, and it is one that Justin (*1 Apol.* 54; *Dial.* 69–70) also employs, was to claim that the demons had anticipated what was to occur in the life of Jesus and so had replicated its extraordinary features, including the virgin birth, in the lives of other heroes in order to lead astray those confronted by claims for Jesus.

---

[20] H. von Balthasar, *Credo* (Edinburgh: T. & T. Clark, 1990), 48.

The point again, however, is simply that, even if we hold that the created world remains supple and open to its Creator, the accounts of a virginal conception were produced in a cultural setting quite distinct from our own, in which it was viable to conceive of the interchange between the heavenly world and the earthly as *frequently* producing extraordinary events surrounding the births of great figures. We have seen how widespread the notions of a miraculous conception and also, for that matter, of a heavenly ascent were for such figures and how they became part of the conventions for the *bios*, the very genre of which the Gospels form a subdivision. Taking the difference in our situation as readers seriously at the very least raises the question whether it is sufficient to accept the claim of a supernatural birth in the case of Jesus and reject it in the case of Augustus, for example, simply on the grounds that the former is in Scripture.[21] Again Scripture itself, as the word of God in the words of humans, is conditioned by the culture and thought forms of its day.

One of the major factors that Schleiermacher did not have to confront but one that, as we have said, has become urgent for a contemporary Christology is our current knowledge about human biology and pro-creation. As has been noted in passing in earlier chapters, such knowledge substantially undermines one of the major ancient reasons for considering the virgin birth important. The larger issue here is the relation of beliefs about Christ to scientific understanding of the origin and development of the human species. If being authentically human entails being part of a continuing adaptive differentiation of our species, what does that mean for the humanity of Jesus?[22] If Jesus' humanity resulted from a miraculous divine intervention, this places him outside the evolutionary process that we now consider to be part of the way God as Creator relates to humans as living bodies. Important as this broader issue of evolution is, it cannot be engaged directly here. The focus will be on the narrower matter of scientific understandings of conception and procreation, while being aware of the implications for the wider discussion.

A major difference between the assumptions of the ancient world and those of our own about conception can be seen at work in the biblical depictions of barrenness. In relation to the texts considered earlier,

---

[21] U. Luz, *Matthew 1—7* (London: T. & T. Clark, 1990), 118, sees this, when he argues that there are better sources for the supernatural begetting of Plato by Apollos than for Jesus' conception, which, he concludes, 'Probably . . . is part of the attempt of Jewish-Christian communities to witness to the faith in Jesus, who was appointed as son of God according to his Spirit (Rom. 1.4) in analogy to other ancient narratives in the form of an infancy narrative. The virgin birth then belongs to the means for witnessing to the faith and has no direct historical background.'

[22] See F. LeRon Schults, *Christology and Science* (Aldershot: Ashgate, 2008), 21–62.

the situation of the parents of John the Baptist as depicted in Luke can serve as an example (1.5–7). Despite their high social status as a priestly family, there is a blemish. Elizabeth was barren and, as she says in 1.25, this was viewed as a disgrace. There appeared to be nothing that could be done any longer about this, since both were getting on in years. Underlying this depiction and other Jewish scriptural stories is the ancient biological view of infertility, in which infertility was always considered the woman's problem.[23] There was no notion that a man's sperm might be infertile. If the man's seed failed to produce children, the problem and fault had to be with the receptacle, the woman's womb, which was judged therefore to be unfruitful. The woman's womb was dead and unable to function to enable her to fulfil her primary purpose: to be a bearer of children. A barren woman would therefore be seen as somehow under God's disfavour or curse and as socially shamed. Any extraordinary reversal of this situation was viewed not as God doing something about the male's sperm count but as God opening rather than closing the womb (e.g. Gen. 29.31; 30.22; 1 Sam. 1.6).

Such assumptions were part of the dominant ancient understanding of conception, influenced by a patriarchal culture. That understanding was some variation of the Aristotelian theory whereby the male semen provided the formative principle, while the female menstrual blood supplied the matter for the foetus and the womb the medium for its nurture (cf. e.g. Aristotle, *Gen. An.* 2.4.738b 20–23). The man's seed transmits his *logos* and *pneuma*, for which the woman's body is the receptacle. In this way the male functions as the active, efficient cause of reproduction and the female functions passively as the provider of the matter to which the male seed gives life and definition. This was part of a larger understanding of sexuality that remained dominant until the eighteenth century, what Laqueur calls a 'one sex/flesh model'. On this model masculinity was at one end and femininity at the other within a hierarchical spectrum where women's sexual organs were viewed as essentially the same as men's but, because of women's lack of vital heat, they had been retained inside the body, and so women were essentially men who lacked anatomical perfection. On this understanding also there was no clear distinction or sharp boundary between male and female in regard to the fluids the body produced. Blood, semen, milk were seen as interchangeable discharges and all bodily fluids were basically forms of blood, their variety being determined by the heat

---

[23] On various aspects of embryology, including infertility, in the ancient Mediterranean world, see M. Stol, 'Embryology in Babylonia and the Bible', in eds V. R. Sasson and J. M. Law, *Imagining the Fetus* (Oxford: OUP, 2009), 137–55.

of that blood.[24] So Aristotle thought that the menses might be viewed as a type of impure sperm and the Hippocratic Corpus and Galen held that women produced sperm but it was less refined than that of men.[25] Within this continuum male heat, dryness and hardness is superior to female coldness, moistness and softness. Even though in general women were seen as lacking the necessary heat of men, the one place in the woman's body that was seen as hot was the woman's womb. Both Aristotle and the Hippocratic Corpus look upon the womb as an oven in which the male seed is cooked in order to enable its formation of the substance provided by the female. For Galen if the offspring was female, this was because it had been undercooked in the womb and had therefore not reached its full potential.[26]

While, as we have noted previously, the Jewish Scriptures include God as an active third partner in conception, they also assume the dominant biological understanding. Wisdom 7.1–2 and 4 Maccabees 13.19–20 make explicit the notion that the male seed is implanted in the womb and gives life to the blood, the substance contributed by the mother. Philo also states, 'the material of the female is supplied to the son from what remains over of the eruption of blood, while the immediate maker and cause of the son is the male' (*QG* 3.47). Later rabbinic traditions about embryology and procreation were also deeply embedded within this Graeco-Roman tradition, even while, like the Jewish Scriptures, adapting it to suit their own theological purposes.[27] The same holds for patristic views on these matters, as we have seen in an earlier chapter,[28] and the ancient understanding

---

[24] On this, see T. Laqueur, *Making Sex: Body and Gender from the Greeks to Freud* (Cambridge, MA: Harvard University Press, 1990), 4–8, for a summary of his thesis and 35–43 for his account of the interconvertibility of bodily fluids.

[25] Cf. A. Rousselle, *Porneia: On Desire and the Body in Antiquity* (Oxford: Blackwell, 1988), 30–1. P. W. van der Horst, 'Sarah's Seminal Emission: Hebrews 11:11 in the Light of Ancient Embryology', in eds E. Ferguson, A. J. Malherbe, D. L. Balch, W. A. Meeks, *Greeks, Romans and Christians: Essays in Honor of Abraham J. Malherbe* (Minneapolis: Fortress, 1990), 287–302, surveys the evidence for the ancient view that females produced their own seed.

[26] For a fuller discussion and nuancing of the views summarized here, see L. Dean-Jones, *Women's Bodies in Classical Greek Science* (Oxford: OUP, 1994) and for ancient constructions of the body in the Graeco-Roman world in the first century CE, see D. Martin, *The Corinthian Body* (New Haven: Yale University Press, 1995), 3–37, 198–228.

[27] See G. Kessler, *Conceiving Israel: The Fetus in Rabbinic Narratives* (Philadelphia: University of Pennsylvania Press, 2009), 65–126.

[28] For an account of how such views functioned in the second century CE, see P. Brown, *The Body and Society* (London: Faber and Faber, 1990), 5–32. For an anthropological account of how such views of procreation are related to beliefs about cosmology and affect cultural constructions of paternity and of gender, see C. Delaney, 'The Meaning of Paternity and the Virgin Birth Debate', *Man* 21 (1986), 494–513; and for an earlier view of the relation between anthropological and theological accounts, see J. A. Saliba, 'The Virgin-Birth Debate in Anthropological Literature: A Critical Assessment', *TS* 36 (1975), 428–54.

continued to be held by Aquinas: 'the female supplies the matter, while the male is the active principle of generation' (*Summa Theologiae* 3.31.5). These assumptions would have had two main effects in considering the virginal conception of Jesus. On the one hand, all the emphasis in thinking about his true nature could be placed on his relationship to God with Mary being made virtually superfluous in this regard, since the divine Spirit was the active principle of generation. An extreme version of this consequence is articulated in Aeschylus' presentation of Apollo's defence of Orestes:

> The mother of what is called her child is not its parent but only the nurse of the swelling new-sown seed . . . And I will offer you a sure proof of what I say: fatherhood there may be, when mother there is none. Here at hand is a witness, the child of Olympian Zeus . . .   (*Eum.* 658–65)

On the other hand, it meant that Mary could be thought to supply all that was necessary of Jesus' fleshly matter, including his male embodiment, and thus serve as a guarantee of his solidarity with the rest of the material world.

But from the late eighteenth century a huge shift in thinking about sexuality has taken place. The model that took over dominance was a 'two sex/flesh' one in which the biological difference between men and women became essential and an anatomy of incommensurability replaced a metaphysics of hierarchy. The biology of sex gradually became foundational for thinking about procreation, eventually producing its narrative of the more complementary roles of sperm and egg, and we are, of course, heirs of its later stages in molecular biology. We take it for granted that it needs a female ovum to combine with a male sperm in order to produce a child and that the sex of the resulting child results from the female supplying an X chromosome and the male either an X or a Y chromosome. Whereas the ancient view allowed a certain Christological coherence in which Jesus could be seen as fully divine and yet fully human, the shift in biological understanding has produced a major problem of coherence. According to our present knowledge, to be a fully human male Jesus would have needed an X chromosome from Mary and a Y chromosome from a human father. If we still wished to hold to a literal virginal conception, God would have had to supply *de novo* either the genes that had come from a male or both sets of genes. In the latter case Mary would have been simply the surrogate mother of this embryo, which would have no real continuity with the human race to this point, although it could have been a copy of a human being with its genetic endowments. In the former case, if God provided the Y chromosome, what does this say about the normal encoded genetic information a male as part of the evolving human species would have received from a father? Does one then have to say that God copied the sort of genetic information that Joseph or some other first-century Jewish male might have supplied? It appears to be extremely difficult to hold that a divinely supplied copy of this genetic endowment still allows for Jesus to share fully our evolved human embodiment.[29]

Two types of response have been made to this argument by defenders of the traditional doctrine of the virgin birth. The first is to attempt to dispute the clarity of the evidence from molecular biology by pointing to cases of parthenogenesis or virgin births in the natural world[30] and thereby to indicate that Jesus' virginal conception need not be thought to be intrinsically incredible and could have involved processes that are genetically possible. This is the thrust of a somewhat strange article by an evangelical professor of genetics, R. J. Berry.[31] He concedes that parthenogenesis by itself cannot account for Jesus' birth because human males need a Y chromosome, but indicates that there is a mutation that produces people who are genetically male with XY chromosomes but, because of an inability to respond to testosterone, appear as completely normal females, although sterile and without a uterus. Mary, he proposes, could have been such a person who went on to develop an ovum and uterus. 'If this happened, and *if* the ovum developed parthenogenetically, and *if* a back-mutation to testosterone sensitivity took place, we would have the situation of an apparently normal woman giving birth without intercourse to a son.'[32] Berry holds, of course, that acceptance of the virgin birth is a matter of faith, based on the testimony of the Bible, but wants to show that it goes beyond the evidence to claim it could never happen in the light of what we know about embryology. Whether he succeeds in demonstrating this must be extremely doubtful, when he himself acknowledges, 'the mechanisms I have outlined are unlikely, unproven, and involve the implication that either Jesus or Mary (or both) were developmentally abnormal.'[33] Richard Dawkins, in an article on the female komodo dragon that produces male offspring without mating, outlines the two main explanations

---

[29] For a fuller statement of this biological argument and its consequences, see A. Peacocke, *Theology for a Scientific Age* (2nd edn London: SCM, 1993), 275–9 and its later version in 'DNA of our DNA', in ed. G. J. Brooke *The Birth of Jesus* (Edinburgh: T. & T. Clark, 2000), 62–5.

[30] For a recent account of animals reproducing without sex, human mothers conceiving monstrous growths and a future where women fertilize their own eggs by using artificial sperm, see A. Prasad, *Like a Virgin: How Science Is Redesigning the Rules of Sex* (London: Oneworld, 2012).

[31] R. J. Berry, 'The Virgin Birth of Christ', *Science & Christian Belief* 8 (1996), 101–10.

[32] Berry, 'Virgin Birth', 107–8.

[33] Berry, 'Virgin Birth', 108.

for parthenogenesis in the natural world – cloning and selfing – and points out that, if a female mammal reproduces by selfing, the baby would have to be female, but in the case of creatures such as birds, butterflies and probably the komodo dragon the female would produce a male. In the course of a passing reference to Berry's argument he suggests Christian apologists would be very unwise to build anything on the komodo dragon phenomenon: 'The Virgin Mary being a mammal, whether she reproduced by cloning or by selfing, the result could only be a daughter. Jesus either had an earthly father, or Jesus was a woman.'[34]

The more usual recent defence of the traditional view in the light of knowledge of genetics is to accept its findings but to claim that they do not constitute a problem. The miracle of Jesus' virginal conception simply involved the divine provision of the missing male Y chromosome.[35] Kerr appeals to a statement of Aquinas: 'the divine power, which is boundless, completed what was necessary for the foetus' (*Summa Theologiae* 3.28.1).[36] But, as we have seen, for Aquinas the mother supplied all that was necessary for the humanity of the foetus and the divine power completed not its human substance but what was necessary for the gestation and birth of the foetus, the active principle usually supplied by the human male. In any case this response fails to meet the problem. If the Y chromosome supplied was a human one but miraculously transferred without sexual contact, what was the point of the miracle and what is the message it conveys about sexuality? Why not use that of Joseph or some other male through the normal means? If the response is that this was a Y chromosome untainted by previous genetic traits so that Jesus could be the beginning of a new creation, then two further objections remain. Does Jesus then really and fully share the human condition he was to redeem[37] and why could a normal X chromosome be employed, which would have been tainted by previous genetic traits? A traditional answer to the latter question would be to appeal to the immaculate conception of Mary

---

[34] R. Dawkins, 'The Komodo Dragon's Tale' <http://evolutiondiary.com/2006/12/24/dawkins-on-komodo-dragons-virgin-birth/>. Accessed 16/08/2012.

[35] Cf. e.g. F. Kerr, 'Questioning the Virgin Birth', *New Blackfriars* 75 (1994), 132–40; Crisp, *God Incarnate*, 79–85.

[36] Kerr, 'Questioning', 136.

[37] Crisp, *God Incarnate*, 84–5, believes he can avoid this issue by proposing what amounts to a genetic version of the ancient view, namely, that there is only a threshold amount of DNA that is necessary for being fully human and that was supplied by Mary's ovum. Apart from the problems of any consensus on determining what such a genetic threshold might be, on this view we would now be talking not, as the doctrine of the incarnation does, of the humanity of a specific person, Jesus of Nazareth, who needed a Y chromosome to be a human male, but of an abstract and speculative category of 'humanity', into which he is made to fit.

herself, but that logically involves one in an infinite regress of immaculate conceptions.

This point does not need to be laboured further. Given what we now understand about reproduction, a literal virginal conception means that Jesus would not have 'become like his brothers and sisters in every respect' (Heb. 2.17). This produces a major irony. As we have seen, the earliest interpreters of the virgin birth and those who formulated the later creeds were able to see in it a defence against docetism. Ignatius (*Eph.* 18–19; *Magn.* 11) uses the virgin birth to stress Christ's human experience, and, over against Marcion, whose denial of the virgin birth was part of a refusal to see Jesus as having any connection with the Adam created by the God of the Jewish Scriptures, Irenaeus insisted that Jesus was a human being like all others in his descent from Adam and that it was his birth from Mary that guaranteed this (*Haer.* 3.22.1). Because of assumptions about the female role in procreation, the absence of a human father was simply not an issue for whether Jesus was fully human and the virgin birth could become part of the rule of faith. For these early interpreters of the virgin birth Jesus was fully human because he shared in common human matter through the flesh of Mary and because the agents of his birth and death – Mary and Pontius Pilate – could be known and named. Interestingly, the Athanasian Creed, which does not explicitly mention the virgin birth, spells out this assumption in its Christological section:

> Now the right faith is that we should believe and confess that our Lord Jesus Christ, the Son of God, is equally both God and man. He is God from the Father's substance, begotten before time; and He is man from His mother's substance, born in time. Perfect God, perfect man composed of a human soul and human flesh, equal to the Father in respect of His divinity, less than the Father in respect of His humanity. Who, although He is God and man, is nevertheless not two, but one Christ. He is one, however, not by the transformation of His divinity into flesh, but by the taking up of His humanity into God; one certainly not by confusion of substance, but by oneness of person. For just as soul and flesh are one man, so God and man are one Christ.

Christ's humanity that is taken up into God is a full humanity and it is a full humanity because of his mother's substance. But we can simply no longer think that a mother's input alone is sufficient to constitute a fully human person. Understood in the light of present biological knowledge, instead of guaranteeing Jesus' real participation in humanity, the virgin birth has just the opposite effect and becomes positively damaging to the doctrine of incarnation. Without complete human DNA Jesus would be a semi-divine or wholly divine special creation that appeared to be human.[38] Frequently defenders of the virgin birth tradition fail to appreciate the force of the objection from current biological knowledge and do not realize that their defence actually changes the tradition and what it was thought to signify. At the risk of repetition let us be clear, therefore, about the difference between a present-day belief in the virgin birth and that of the major part of the tradition. The older tradition assumed that Jesus' full bodily humanity could come from Mary alone because the mother supplied what was necessary for this in the process of procreation. We do not share that assumption but hold that for the production of an individual human the genetic traits of both male and female are needed. Female chromosomes by themselves could at best only produce an anomaly not recognizable as male or female. So when the response to the biological argument is that God provided the Y chromosome in the case of Jesus, something quite different is being asserted than the formulations of writers such as Irenaeus and Tertullian or of the Athanasian Creed were expressing. Of course, uniquely supplying the necessary chromosome is possible for the Creator God but this is to miss the point. This is not an argument about the possibility of the miraculous but about the meaning of the alleged miracle. While the patristic writers held that what was necessary for humanity came from Mary, this response holds that God has to supply what is necessary for Jesus to be human. Jesus, therefore, is not properly human without a special act of God, according to this view, but this still makes his humanity significantly different from that of those with whom he is supposed to be in solidarity. While ancient Christian writers held that God's part in Jesus' conception was to provide the life principle to the human substance that came from Mary and that God did this in a non-physical way, the current interpretation requires that God acted in a biological fashion to provide the genetic material that a man normally provides and comes much closer to ancient pagan notions of the divine impregnating a woman than the patristic writers would ever countenance.

---

[38] D. Minns, 'Traditional Doctrine and the Antique World-View: Two Case Studies, the Virgin Birth and Original Sin', in eds V. Pfitzner and H. Regan, *The Task of Theology Today* (Edinburgh: T. & T. Clark, 1999), 153–4, asks, 'If we wanted to hold on to the idea that the humanity of Jesus is one with ours … would we not be obliged to accept that, like the rest of us, he derived approximately half his genetic make-up (including his maleness) from a male human being, and approximately half from a female human being?', while Peacocke, 'DNA of our DNA', 66, can conclude his essay with the blunter assertion, 'for Jesus to be fully human, he had, for both biological and theological reasons, to have a human father as well as a human mother … Any theology for a scientific age which is concerned with the significance of Jesus of Nazareth now has to start at this point.'

Some recent theologians have recognized the force of the arguments from our present state of biological knowledge. John Macquarrie, for example, states,

> Our understanding of human reproduction today is vastly different from what people in the ancient world believed to be the case . . . So even if today in the context of our modern scientific culture we were to think of anything so improbable to modern ears as a virginal conception we would be understanding it in quite a different way from what was in the minds of the evangelists.[39]

He concludes therefore that we have to get away from any biological understanding of the virgin birth and see that the scriptural birth stories are making the theological point that Jesus is not *simply* the product of evolutionary processes and human procreation but is 'God with us'. It is somewhat surprising, then, that Macquarrie holds that the modern theologian who 'has dealt most adequately with the doctrine of the virgin birth is Karl Barth'.[40] As we shall see in our next chapter, it is true that Barth can make the theological point that the virgin birth is a sign 'that denotes that God stands at the start where real revelation takes place – God and not the arbitrary cleverness, capability, or piety of man'. But this appeal to Barth fails to indicate that he also insists on the historicity of a virginal conception. It is possibly Barth's talk of this event as a 'sign' of the incarnation that produces some confusion about his views and he does assert that Scripture and creed do not treat the virgin birth as a 'biological explanation'. But he also makes very clear that he holds 'the fact' of the virgin birth to be 'of such a kind as to belong to the area of biological enquiry', an event 'that happens here in the field of biology', since in order to be a 'sign' it has to be an occurrence in space and time and this means 'taking place in the sphere of biological enquiry'.[41] Yet by that very insistence, Barth fails to appreciate the vital point, highlighted in Macquarrie's own exposition, that such biological enquiry now entails that the virgin birth no longer functions as that which he proposes, namely, the necessary sign of that which is signified, the true humanity and true divinity of Jesus Christ.

In the light of the change of assumptions about procreation, the question has to be raised, though briefly, about the implications for gender and the

---

[39] J. Macquarrie, *Christology Revisited* (London: SCM, 1998), 33–4.

[40] Macquarrie, *Christology*, 35.

[41] K. Barth, *Church Dogmatics* (*CD*) 1.2 (eds G. W. Bromiley and T. F. Torrance; tr. G. W. Bromiley; Edinburgh: T. & T. Clark, 1956), 182–4.

divine. There was an ambiguity about the virgin birth as understood within ancient assumptions. On the one hand, it reinforced patriarchy, since Mary's body is the passive receptacle of the active principle of life, now supplied by the divine Spirit rather than by a human male, while, on the other, in imagining that Mary contained within herself all that was necessary for Jesus' humanity, it had at least the potential for some subversion of patriarchy. But if belief in a literal virginal conception is retained and viewed within contemporary assumptions as entailing God supplying the missing male Y chromosome, then, at the very least, this is in danger of reinforcing the notion of a male God the Father who provides the complement to human motherhood in the origins of Jesus and of making this mother a quasi-woman, one who can conceive outside the realm of sexuality.

In the earlier stages of Christological discussion the incarnation was linked, as we have seen, with the two central concerns of monotheism and the redemption of the world. The first entailed the affirmation of this world as the trustworthy creation of the one beneficent Creator God, not originating from some subordinate demiurge, and the means of the second was the putting on of complete humanity by God in Christ, not some partial, temporary or ostensible incarnation. In this way the incarnation could also be seen as the reaffirmation of the goodness pronounced by God about the creation. The world and humanity thus were valorized and sanctified as the appropriate and worthy sphere of divine activity. A virgin birth was not incompatible with such concerns because Christ's humanity could be seen as safeguarded through his mother. Nevertheless, as we have seen, ideals of asceticism and virginity also played their part both in the coming to prominence of the virginal conception tradition and the maintenance of that prominence by celibate theologians. For many of those who viewed the human body and its sexual activities with at best suspicion, the virginal conception of the Son of God provided a means of thinking about his origins free of such contamination. In the popular imagination it has continued to play a role in a strand of the Christian tradition that remains uncomfortable with a full acceptance of human sexuality as part of the goodness of creation that the incarnation reaffirms. Certainly within a contemporary context a literal understanding of the virgin birth undermines the central earlier concerns about creation and redemption. It implies the normal processes of creation are not appropriate or worthy in the case of Jesus and it implies that he cannot be fully human as that is presently understood, since he had no normal male chromosome, and therefore is not fully at one with the humanity that is to be redeemed and 'that which he has not assumed he has not healed'.[42] So to hold the traditional belief in a context of quite different basic assumptions is not just marginally problematic or historically difficult; it is hugely unfitting for the central concerns of Christian faith that it undermines.

It is not altogether surprising, then, that some Christians, who in recent times have come to the conclusion that Jesus had two natural parents, have employed this historical deduction in the service of promoting the goodness of sex in marriage and of normal family life and indeed of 'family values'.[43] Parrinder concludes his book by asserting that it is essential to see the Christian ideal of marriage demonstrated in the family of Jesus.

> Joseph was the father of Jesus, Mary was Joseph's wife in the fullest sense, and the family at Nazareth completed the picture. Christmas and the Nativity are about the family, and they can be freed from fantasies that mislead in both theology and devotion.[44]

Using such a historical reconstruction in this way, however, results in a certain irony. The Jesus of the rest of the gospel tradition is anything but a simple upholder of family values. He asks for an allegiance to the kingdom of God, which he inaugurates, that transcends family ties and disrupts normal family life.[45] One can applaud the clearing away of fantasies through a critical reading of the Gospel accounts but, rather than attempting to build an ethics on the basis of a historical reconstruction behind the birth narratives, one would do far better to find its source in the canonical traditions themselves where the family is the issue under consideration and to provide a discerning reading of this material. Whatever Christmas has now come to mean, the birth narratives are about the uniqueness of Jesus and not about 'the family', and it is to the former that we now turn.

---

[42] The much quoted words of Gregory of Nazianzus, *Ep.* 101.32.

[43] Cf. T. Boslooper, *The Virgin Birth* (London: SCM, 1962), 227–37; G. Parrinder, *Son of Joseph: The Parentage of Jesus* (Edinburgh: T. & T. Clark, 1992), 11, 40, 123.

[44] Parrinder, *Son of Joseph*, 123.

[45] Cf. esp. S. C. Barton, *Discipleship and Family Ties in Mark and Matthew* (Cambridge: CUP, 1994) and *Life Together: Family, Sexuality and Community in the New Testament and Today* (Edinburgh: T. & T. Clark, 2001).

10

Reconceiving Jesus: Christology and creed

The virginal conception and contemporary Christology

Christology is a dauntingly vast and inevitably hugely contested area of theology. Even reminding ourselves that we are only concerned with the implications of interpretations of Jesus' conception for Christology does little to limit the scope of an adequate treatment, because, as the earlier discussions of patristic interpretation and of Schleiermacher have indicated, one's view of Jesus' conception is linked with questions about Christ's humanity and divinity and the relation between them. It is also associated with questions about Christ's work of salvation, not only because in general Christ's person and work should not be separated but also because the nature of his conception has been seen by some to be crucial for the sinlessness of Jesus, without which his atoning work would have been ineffective in dealing with the sin of humanity. These introductory remarks should make clear that a proper treatment of the topic of the conception of Jesus and contemporary Christology deserves a far more extensive treatment than can be offered here and that the discussion that follows will be necessarily highly selective and compressed and can do little more than suggest some lines of thought on the key areas that need much fuller elaboration and qualification.

What we have indicated so far is that there are different views of Christ's conception within the New Testament itself, including one that assumes a normal human birth with Joseph as Jesus' father and one that tells a story of a divine conception without the aid of the male parent. The latter, we have argued, was a way of indicating within the conventions of its time that God was involved in the life of Jesus from its very conception. The former means that seeing Jesus as a fully human first-century Jewish person is neither simply an anachronistic modern imposition on ancient scriptural texts nor part of an attempt to build a Christology on a reconstructed historical Jesus behind the texts. We have also indicated how one of the New Testament strands, the virginal conception, became the dominant one, primarily because, within the views of the time about procreation, it was able to serve not only to highlight the divine status of

Jesus but also to safeguard his humanity against a variety of docetic views. But we have also shown that, given the changes in our knowledge of pro-creation, to continue to have the virginal conception, understood literally, as the dominant or sole view has precisely the opposite result by suggesting that Jesus is not fully human and in real solidarity with those his mission was intended to save from their plight. For some, then, the key Christological questions for the perspective we have presented would be whether it is still compatible with saying Jesus was fully divine, whether an adequately coherent account can be given of the relationship between humanity and divinity as regards Jesus, and whether Jesus can still be said to be sinless if this is not guaranteed through his virginal conception.

One further preliminary observation may be helpful at this point in explaining what may appear to some to be a move to a different type of discussion in relation to the virginal conception, a discussion that is in danger of losing sight of the concrete historical reality of Jesus of Nazareth. In treating the topic of Christology it is important not to confuse two different questions. Earlier in this book we have devoted much attention to exploring how the notion of a virginal conception came about, how it contributed to later Christological discussion and how that discussion developed. But a treatment of incarnational Christology as part of system-atic theology is not the same thing as describing how that Christology came about. The latter might explore implicit and explicit claims on the part of the historical Jesus, in his mission of inaugurating the coming reign of Israel's God, to a unique relationship with this God, and how, on the basis of belief in Jesus' resurrection, such claims were seen by early Christians as vindicated by God and then more fully understood and developed so that they held that Jesus was to be viewed as included in the identity of the one God of Israel and worthy of the worship and obedience owed to this God. The crucial insight was that, if Jesus had divine status on the basis of the resurrection, then, seen retrospectively, he must always have had such status, not only throughout his earthly life but also even beyond that in somehow always belonging to the identity of God. The Christological and trinitarian controversies and formulations of the first few centuries of the Church's existence were, of course, further contribu-tions to the process of understanding and articulating this earlier insight. While this sort of account is significant in its own right, crucial for apologe-tic purposes, and illuminating in regard to the historical contingency of Christian belief, it is not the same thing as exploring the resultant belief itself. The product of this historical development was the ontological claim that the God of Israel was incarnate in Jesus and that Jesus Christ is therefore truly human and truly God. A systematic or constructive theology about Christ, while cognizant of and able to accommodate different versions of an historical account, takes this ontological claim, already partially expressed in a variety of ways in the New Testament canonical witnesses, as a given and explores its meaning, coherence, scope, implications and most appropriate articulation in relation to the thought of its own time and place. Here, then, we are asking whether and how the view that the virginal conception is a legendary aspect of the New Testament witness affects the construction of such a Christology that attempts to be faithful to the mystery of the incarnation whereby Christ is both divine and human. In asking these questions, it should be underlined, we are not simply attempting to explore incarnational Christology on the basis of a reconstruction of the historical Jesus and his origins that has come to the conclusion that his virginal conception was not historical. Rather we are acknowledging that the ontological status of Christ as God incarnate is already shown to be compatible with presentations of his conception both as miraculous and as normal within the New Testament canon and asking how taking seriously the latter, frequently ignored in the tradition, makes a difference to contemporary articulation of the ontological claim.

Since we have given considerable space to Schleiermacher's views, some might be surprised that we do not devote equivalent space to Barth's later defence of the virgin birth whose miracle he sees as a sign of the mystery of the incarnation. This might be thought to be a major omission in our exploration, especially since so much of Barth's work consists of a response to Schleiermacher and he is considered by some to have rehabilitated the virgin birth for the twentieth century. At least some brief, if inadequately justified, account of this lack of any extensive discussion is needed.[1] Barth's major treatment of the topic is found in the Christology section of his treatment of revelation in the *Church Dogmatics*.[2] Unfortunately, for this writer, it turns out to be one of the least satisfactory parts of Barth's magisterial theology. It begins promisingly enough with the affirmation that objections to the virgin birth cannot simply be attributed to a reluctance to accept the miraculous and that there are genuine difficulties in our sources. But the latter are quickly brushed aside with simplistic and

---

[1] A partial justification is that D. Resch, *Barth's Interpretation of the Virgin Birth: A Sign of Mystery* (London: Ashgate, 2012), provides a recent full-length treatment of Barth's views on the virgin birth that is a detailed, sympathetic, but not altogether uncritical exposition.

[2] K. Barth, *Church Dogmatics* (*CD*) 1.2 (eds G. W. Bromiley and T. F. Torrance; tr. G. W. Bromiley; Edinburgh: T. & T. Clark, 1956), 172–202, entitled 'The Miracle of Christmas'. Resch's work helpfully sets this material within the development of Barth's views and in relation to the treatment of its themes in other parts of the *Church Dogmatics*.

unconvincing responses, so that Barth can ignore any diversity in those sources and continue with the assumption that the traditional credal formulation is the only perspective found in the New Testament itself.[3] Unlike Schleiermacher, who was, among his many accomplishments, both a New Testament scholar, who recognized the diversity in the New Testament witness, and a theologian, Barth has no real interest in interpreting texts within their historical, cultural and narrative contexts. He claims to take seriously what he calls 'literary' investigation but this turns out to mean little more than concern with text-critical issues and matters of introduction, such as dating of documents.[4] But at the theological level, whereas Schleiermacher had concluded that the virgin birth not only served no distinctive dogmatic purpose but might also be detrimental, Barth claims that, as a miracle that actually occurred, it is not to be demoted to a nonbinding sub-statement within the New Testament message but is the necessary form of the mystery of incarnation, the indispensable sign of that which it signifies. It is not one way in which the incarnation is presented, not one sign but *the* sign. Barth is not completely clear about what he thinks follows from this stance. On the one hand, he suggests that those who do not hold it are in fact talking about a signified that is other than the mystery of the incarnation, but, on the other hand, he allows that it is possible for someone to recognize the mystery of the person of Christ without affirming the virgin birth, as long as, by keeping silent about this, he or she pays the Church dogma due respect.[5]

Barth makes the virgin birth in relation to the incarnation at the beginning of Jesus' life parallel to the empty tomb in relation to the resurrection at the end, so that denial of the former calls into question belief in the latter.[6] Some might argue that this comparison does not achieve its goal because the empty tomb is essential to a bodily resurrection in a way that a virgin birth is not in relation to the incarnation. But the comparison in any case ignores at this point that the resurrection, attested across the New Testament, is central to the Christian message, while the virgin birth is at best marginal, and it downplays the epistemological priority of the resurrection, which is the presupposition on which the birth announcements about Jesus' identity depend.

---

[3] Cf. Barth, *CD* 1.2, 174–6.
[4] Earlier in his work Barth had been prepared to talk of the infancy narratives in terms of myth and legend, cf. Resch, *Barth's Interpretation*, 126–8. It is not obvious that replacing these categories by the more theological notion of 'sign', as he does here, constitutes an advance.
[5] Cf. Barth, *CD* 1.2, 180–1.
[6] Cf. Barth, *CD* 1.2, 182–3.

Barth also simply assumes that the miracle of a virginal conception secures Jesus as fully human. He indulges in an extraordinary outburst against Brunner for suggesting that the virgin birth leads to a biological interpretation of the miracle, failing to see that asserting that the creeds never made the virginal conception a biological explanation is not a sufficient response to the charge that it does nevertheless have biological implications.[7] He does then concede that the miracle 'is, of course, of such a kind as to belong to the area of biological enquiry', but holds that any attempt to pursue that enquiry would detract from the mystery to which the miracle points, and so the questions that occupied us in the previous chapter are nowhere on his horizon.[8] Barth, of course, holds that what is human is to be seen in the light of Jesus Christ as presented in Scripture and creed and that our understanding of what it is to be human should not be allowed to judge this presentation of Christ's humanity. What he fails to see is that his credal axiom – the full humanity of the one born of a virgin – is already dependent for its coherence on human knowledge of what is human, in this case ancient knowledge of procreation, which held that the foetus was given its human substance by the mother. There is no realization that on a contemporary understanding of biology the virginal conception might no longer be a sign of that which it is meant to signify, namely, the identity of Jesus as truly God and truly human. Instead for Barth the virgin birth becomes the site for the exposition of some of the great themes of his theology. It is the decisive act of a sovereign God and, he claims, all other views of Jesus' human origins allow natural theology to intrude. This act is one of both grace and judgement. The miracle of new beginning is a sign of judgement because it excludes the sinful life of sex. This is excluded 'not because of the nature of sexual life nor because of its sinfulness, but because every natural generation is the work of willing, achieving, creative sovereign man'.[9] Mary's virginity, not of itself or by nature, is part of the sign, because it becomes by grace what the female represents, that is 'the form of non-willing, non-achieving, non-creative, non-sovereign man . . . who can merely receive, merely be ready, merely let something be done to and with himself'.[10] Even leaving aside its highly problematic gender essentialism, this appears

---

[7] It also ignores, of course, that, as we have seen in Chapter 7, ancient biological notions are explicit in and essential to much of the patristic discussion of the virgin birth that constitutes the background assumptions of the creeds.

[8] Cf. Barth, *CD* 1.2, 183–4.

[9] Barth, *CD* 1.2, 192.

[10] Barth, *CD* 1.2, 191.

theologically suspect on other grounds. On this exposition the sign of the virgin birth skews what should surely be the doctrine that both the male and the female are equally under judgement, in the active creativity and passive receptivity that can apply to both, and equally under grace with the potential of each to become what it was meant to be. Finally Barth returns to the positive aspect of the sign – 'conceived by the holy Spirit'. Here he stresses that this means that God was involved in an inconceivable act of creative power and asserts that this means that though the Spirit replaces the role of the male, the Spirit cannot be said to do what the male does, as in some of the parallels in the history of religions. In addition the involvement of the Spirit points to God's work of reconciliation, because the same work of the Spirit in preparing humanity for God 'can happen to us also, in the form of pure grace'.[11]

Barth, then, suppresses the problems and diversity within the New Testament canon, so that Scripture and creed are united. He takes the virginal conception to be a miracle taking place in space and time and believes he has rescued it from being theologically superfluous by his exposition of what he sees as the essential doctrines to which the sign, in pointing to the mystery of incarnation, also points. This is a hard-line version of the criterion of 'fittingness' because this doctrinal fit of the virgin birth is held not simply to be appropriate but essential, since the sign cannot be separated from the signified. Yet he wants to have it both ways. So he can also state that the sign can be separated from the signified,[12] enabling him to claim when it suits him that some objections do not hold because they have not understood that he is not talking about the ontological mystery of the incarnation but only about the noetic appropriateness of its sign for us. Two further observations, among others that could be made, will need to suffice. First, it is not at all clear, apart from Barth asserting it to be the case, why one could not take the virginal conception to be among the legendary features of the annunciation stories and still hold that they conveyed the mystery of the incarnation and the truth of whichever of Barth's theological points one deems to be valid, say, God's sovereign initiative and the grace necessary for redemption. To reject this as a faithful and responsible approach is to confuse a particular theological truth with the historical nature of the narrative in which this truth comes to expression. Nor is it clear why attempts, such as we shall make below, to propose the corollary to this approach, namely, that Christ

---

[11] Cf. Barth, *CD* 1.2, 199–201.
[12] Barth, *CD* 1.2, 189.

having been born through natural means does indeed preserve the mystery of the incarnation and its accompanying doctrines, should be ruled out rather than the relation between the two seen as fitting. After all, Paul, John and Hebrews appear to have been able to maintain the mystery of the incarnation without the benefit of a doctrine of the virgin birth. Second, if 'fittingness' is a reasonable way to categorize how Barth operates at this point,[13] then fittingness is in the end in the eye of the beholder, so that, of course, if one already has a particular theology in place various phenomena, in Barth's case, that of the virgin birth, can be seen through this lens and be thought or made to fit. On the basis of other theologies, Mary's immaculate conception and assumption or the ordination of only men to the teaching office and to the administration of the sacraments can be declared fitting. Whether what is claimed as fitting can be genuinely derived from the texts that originally interpreted these topics or are in coherent continuity with the centre of the Christian gospel is another matter altogether. In the end one cannot escape the impression that Barth's defence of the virgin birth turns out to be an employment of the virgin birth as an illustration of theological convictions that he already holds on other grounds.[14]

If Barth has not proved to be a helpful way into a discussion of contemporary Christology, then another tempting short cut would be to avail ourselves of help from what might appear a surprising source, the work of theologian Oliver Crisp, who has been cited so far in relation to his defence of a literal understanding of the virgin birth and his view that biblical accounts are to be taken as straightforwardly historical. In his discussion of 'The "Fittingness" of the Virgin Birth', Crisp, unlike Barth, asserts, 'defences of the Virgin Birth that claim that it is somehow a *requirement* for a doctrine of Incarnation, are, in my view, mistaken' and in the course of his treatment goes on to provide what he calls 'an outline of a robust doctrine of the Incarnation without the Virgin Birth',[15] based on the sort of views about the virginal conception expressed by Emil Brunner.[16]

---

[13] He talks of the virgin birth narratives in terms of 'a certain inward, essential rightness and importance in their connexion with the person of Jesus Christ' and of the miracle's 'essential appropriateness' (Barth, *CD* 1.2, 176, 184).

[14] Interestingly, these criticisms are among the questions raised independently by Resch, *Barth's Interpretation*, 200–3, in the brief critical section of his concluding chapter.

[15] O. D. Crisp, *God Incarnate: Explorations in Christology* (London: T. & T. Clark, 2009), 77–8.

[16] For Brunner's views, see E. Brunner, *The Mediator* (tr. O. Wyon; London: Lutterworth, 1934), 316–27; *The Christian Doctrine of Creation and Redemption* (tr. O. Wyon; London: Lutterworth, 1952), 350–7. One should note, of course, that Brunner is not particularly exceptional in his views and that there are other recent major theologians, such as Pannenberg, Moltmann and Macquarrie, who advocate an incarnational theology without a virginal conception.

The account that follows assumes 'a Christology entirely in keeping with the canons of Chalcedon, apart from the doctrine of the Virgin Birth', talks of Jesus being born to Mary and Joseph through a normal act of human procreation producing Jesus' human soul, which the Holy Spirit ensured was without original sin and which the Word of God assumed, and then defends this account against a number of possible objections.[17] Despite what he sees as the coherence of a No Virgin Birth version of the incarnation, Crisp's own view is that the traditional account is more fitting because 'a special birth signals the fact that it is a divine person taking on human nature, not the beginning of the life of a new individual, as a normal process of human generation from two human parents might suggest'.[18] Yet what Crisp has offered with one hand he takes back with the other. Having distinguished between the incarnation and its mode and proposed that the latter is not a requirement for the former, it turns out that 'requirement' has a weak sense. All that Crisp means is that in theory the incarnation could have taken place in some way other than a virginal conception. In fact, according to him, a virginal conception is *required* as the mode of incarnation on any adequate or orthodox Christian theological account, because, according to canonical Scripture and the ecumenical creeds, the virgin birth simply *is* how God brought about the incarnation.[19] Nevertheless, since we have already provided what appear to be good reasons for doubting both that canonical Scripture and the creeds can bear this sort of weight on the matter of a virginal conception and that the virgin birth can still be seen as a fitting mode for the incarnation, one can see that it might be tempting simply to point readers to Crisp if they doubt that taking a different stance towards the virgin birth is compatible with a robust perspective on the incarnation.

But while Crisp's account of the incarnation without a virgin birth in Chalcedonian terms might appeal to some, the exploration here will need to resist the temptation to take the olive branch Crisp apparently extends. His analytic theology approach with its starting point in a certain view of Scripture and the creeds[20] means that there is a huge gulf between the account he presents and that of someone who comes to the discussion from a theological perspective that pays greater attention to the historical

---

[17] Crisp, *God Incarnate*, 91–5.
[18] Crisp, *God Incarnate*, 100. This appears to be little different from Barth's view, which is not however mentioned by Crisp at this point.
[19] Cf. Crisp, *God Incarnate*, 78, 95, 101–2.
[20] Cf. Crisp, *God Incarnate*, 1–3, 32–3; cf. also his earlier *Divinity and Humanity* (Cambridge: CUP, 2007).

conditionedness of both the Bible and the credal traditions. It is one thing
to see the creeds and especially the Chalcedonian Definition as spelling
out what were seen as the implications of Scripture for their own time
and place in the cultural and philosophical categories available to them
and quite another for later interpreters to read Scripture in a way that has
to be made to fit with these precise categories.[21] To accept Crisp's account
of incarnation without a virgin birth involves, for example, taking as one's
starting point such questionable assumptions as that if Christ is a divine
person, he cannot be a human person, though he has a human nature,
and that human nature itself is composed of two substances, body and
soul, the former generated from its parents, the latter created out of nothing by God. These are the philosophical and anthropological assumptions
that informed the debates leading to and resulting from the Chalcedonian
Definition. In this 'substance metaphysics' divinity and humanity were
taken to be two substances, the former immutable and the latter mutable,
that were united in Jesus while remaining the same. The way that this
could happen was seen as analogous to a corresponding anthropology of
the two substances within humans, the immaterial substance of the soul
in relation to the material substance of the body, an anthropology that
is being increasingly challenged by developments in neurobiology. Given
contemporary understandings of personal identity and given that 'person'
as applied to members of the triune God is at best analogical, how much
sense does it make to insist on the basis of such problematic ancient
assumptions that the human Jesus was not a person, because that would
be incompatible with him also being the person of the Word or the Son,
and then to struggle to indicate how Jesus had sufficient genetic traits to
be somehow human without being a person? What is needed is an approach
that is not dismissive of serious contemporary biblical criticism and
respects the diversity within the biblical writings, allowing their distinctive
viewpoints to be heard together, that takes account of contemporary knowledge, and that at the same time, without necessarily being restricted to
its particular categories and formulations, follows Chalcedon's attempt to
safeguard the mystery of Christ being both fully human and fully divine.
Since the latter ontological truth claim is about a mystery, it should not

---

[21] In fact, in regard to Chalcedon, the categories become far more precise than the original formulators would have intended. As S. Coakley underscores, despite its being called in translation 'the
Definition', the Chalcedonian formulation itself is remarkably imprecise about the meaning of key
terms such as person (*hypostasis*), nature (*physis*) and substance (*ousia*) and about how they are
related (cf. 'What Does Chalcedon Solve and What Does it Not? Some Reflections on the Status
and Meaning of the Chalcedonian "Definition", in eds S. T. Davis, D. Kendall, G. O'Collins,
The Incarnation (Oxford: OUP, 2002), 143–63.

be surprising that Christology is an ongoing discipline with various contested approaches but it should also not be surprising that there can be a number of those approaches that can be considered relatively adequate in regard to their coherence and their faithfulness to the intent of the credal traditions.

In fact, as we have maintained throughout, the belief in the incarnation is not affected when a literal virginal conception is no longer in the picture.[22] Within the New Testament itself the conviction that God was incarnate in Christ is reflected in a variety of ways in the Pauline Corpus, in the Gospel of John and in Hebrews, where the virginal conception plays no part in its formation or expression. In its more developed form that conviction involves the second hypostasis of the triune God, the Word or the Son, assuming the human life of Jesus of Nazareth as its own. There is no reason to think that a non-historical perspective on the virgin birth leads to a non-incarnational Christology in which Jesus is simply a supremely Spirit-filled man or the highest example of the openness of the human consciousness to God. In order to stay in continuity with the distinctive claims of the Christian tradition, it is a basic requirement to maintain that in Jesus God as the eternal Word, that is, Godself and not simply some divinely inspired representative, is encountered by humans. This is especially critical for Christian notions of salvation, where this world's evils are dealt with in Christ, again not simply by a human representative of God but by God identifying with and taking on the world's suffering Godself. If a major purpose of the incarnation was to restore the damaged relationship between the Creator and creatures, then the salvation that that restoration entails is only effective if God was uniquely and decisively present and active in the life, death and resurrection of Jesus. The notion of a human prophet who was inspired by God's Spirit cannot do the same theological work as the doctrine of the incarnation.

It is neither more difficult nor any easier to believe this without an accompanying belief in the virgin birth. All the major issues in an incarnational Christology about the relation between the divinity and humanity of Jesus remain the same. How can the two be united in one life without damage to the integrity of each? How can there be two agents of one act? Is it

---

[22] We have already seen the way in which Schleiermacher held such a conviction and it is worth repeating at this point the view of Pope Benedict XVI in his earlier writings, cited in our introductory chapter: 'according to the faith of the Church the Sonship of Jesus does not rest on the fact that Jesus had no human father: The doctrine of Jesus' divinity would not be affected if Jesus had been the product of a normal marriage. For the Sonship of which faith speaks is not a biological but an ontological fact, an event not in time but in God's eternity' (J. Ratzinger, *Introduction to Christianity* (New York: Herder & Herder/London: Burns & Oates, 1969), 208.

adequate to talk of the divine and the human as two natures within one divine-human person? Is there a straightforward identity of the second member of the triune God, the Word or the Son, and the earthly Jesus? Does the notion of a *kenosis*, a self-emptying of the divine during the life of Jesus, help or hinder a coherent construal? Is there some transference of attributes between the divinity and the humanity of Jesus (*communicatio idiomatum*)? Does the Word assume not only a particular human, Jesus, but also, in doing so, sinful humanity? Does the particularity of the incarnation in a Jewish male preclude him from being the source of salvation for women? How does Jesus' pre-resurrection incarnate state relate to its post-resurrected glorified incarnate state? Removing the literal understanding of the virginal conception from the discussion of these and other Christological questions simply removes a few problems at the margins of some of these issues that have only made the main discussion more difficult than it needs to be. In pointing these out, we shall also inevitably touch on elements necessary for an adequate contemporary framing of the broader Christological discussion.

First, taking seriously the strand of the scriptural witness that indicates Jesus had two human parents removes any ambiguities in the traditional view of incarnation about whether Christ is truly human. As we have seen, contemporary defenders of the traditional view actually change its original assumptions by claiming that God supplied what we now view as part of what is necessary for being human. Whereas on ancient views what Mary's womb contributed was all that was necessary for the human substance of Jesus, to which only the divine animating principle needed to be applied, now God is said miraculously to contribute the male chromosome that is necessary for human DNA. On this revised account of the virgin birth what is miraculously supplied is still not, strictly speaking, human but a divine duplicate of the Y chromosome normally supplied by the human male. This makes Jesus' humanity exceptional and threatens to undermine any assertion that Jesus shared fully in the humanity that is the lot of the rest of humankind. This problem is not mitigated by speculating that, contrary to normal assumptions, there could be a threshold amount of genetic material that was supplied by Mary's ovum alone and that was sufficient for Christ to be counted as a member of the human race.[23]

Once there is no need to negotiate a literal virginal conception, there need be no doubts or ambiguities about the full humanity of Jesus as a first-century Jewish male and, in thinking about that humanity assumed

---

[23] As proposed by Crisp, *God Incarnate*, 81–4.

by the Word, no obstacles to applying our current theological under-standing of what it means to be human and no need to be confined to traditional discussions about whether it was a human body or soul or a combination of the two that the Word assumed and whether we can only talk of the assumption of a human nature rather than a fully human subject or person. While there need be no doubt that Jesus was a fully human person in the way in which in everyday language we take one another to be, there are two main reasons why unqualified use of this category for Jesus is still not problem-free. The first has to do with theo-logical categories and results from the confusion that has arisen from the Chalcedonian Definition's use of the term 'person' (*hypostasis*) to refer only to the one subject of the Word become flesh and not to his humanity and yet at the same time to refer to the Word or Son of God as one of the three persons (*hypostases*) of the Trinity. Schleiermacher, as we have seen, already correctly put his finger on this matter and we shall return to this part of the problem below. The second has to do with the variety of contemporary assumptions about personhood that are made once the notion of 'person' is given any content. So, for example, is what is essen-tial for personhood rationality, a subjective consciousness or individual autonomy? David Kelsey has provided one of the most helpful theological treatments both of this issue and of what it means to be human and that discussion can inform our thinking about Jesus' humanity and person-hood.[24] Kelsey negotiates the complexities of these concepts in interaction with various viewpoints and disciplines, but among his own insightful proposals is that in relating to human beings through creation, God relates to those who both are and have a living body. What distinguishes the bodies human creatures are from other living entities is the possession of human DNA and what is important about the distinction, but not separation, between human creatures and their bodies is that this makes them accountable to God for the exercise of the powers that their living bodies possess. This formulation makes it possible to avoid either reduc-tionist materialist accounts of humans where it is thought that the natural sciences can give a complete explanation of what humans are or meta-physically dualistic accounts where the real person is thought to be inde-pendent of his or her secondary bodily entity. On this view, then, 'person' is not to be contrasted with impersonal material bodies but humans are personal bodies and, theologically, what constitutes them as persons

---

[24] See D. H. Kelsey, *Eccentric Existence: A Theological Anthropology* (2 vols; Louisville: Westminster John Knox, 2009), esp. 204–8, 242–80, 286–308, 357–401.

is their addressability by God. In fact their personal identities consist in how they respond over time and in community to their ultimate context – God actively relating to them in creating, calling to eschatological con- summation and reconciling – in their proximate contexts – the everyday physical, social and cultural worlds in which they live – and this means that narrative is the most appropriate form for rendering such dynamic and unsubstitutable identities.

The upshot of this sort of theological analysis of humanity and person- hood is to underline that the humanity assumed in the incarnation is just such a personal body, that of Jesus of Nazareth. Indeed, as Kelsey himself asserts, 'what Jesus' humanity is must be the same as what any other human being's humanity is'. This is semantically required if 'humanity' is not to be used in a systematically ambiguous way and it is theologically required because, if Jesus is not an authentically human creature, the way he images God cannot be paradigmatic for other human creatures.[25] It is, of course, also theologically required if God is to reconcile humanity through Jesus' full solidarity in that humanity. The possession of human DNA, as Kelsey has made clear, is basic to this view of humanity and yet, if we retain a virginal conception, even one in which half of this DNA is supplied miracu- lously, there remains at very best both a semantic and a theological ambiguity about the humanity of the Word become flesh. On the other hand, taking seriously the strand of New Testament witness whereby Jesus is the seed of David through Joseph requires no semantic and theological gymnastics and no contested body–soul dualism in positing Jesus' full humanity.

As we have noted in reviewing the development of the tradition, a virginal conception has been related to the issue of Jesus' humanity at one further point, when Paul's contrastive comparison between Adam and Christ is elaborated and the virginal conception of the latter is seen as the beginning of a new humanity, a new creation. It is argued that the virgin birth was necessary for a new creation, because Jesus as its sinless inaugurator had to have had an entirely new beginning, indicated by God and not a human male being involved in his conception. But this appears not to recognize that 'new creation' is a metaphor. Creation out of nothing is a past act and so 'new creation' stands not for the type of further divine initiative in which God supplies created material, in this case, genetic endowment, *de novo*, but for the transformative initiative whereby God draws this created world to its eschatological consummation. Shifting the Christ and Adam comparison from Paul's application of it to Christ's death

---

[25] Kelsey, *Eccentric*, 1016.

and resurrection back to his conception gives the use of this language an entirely different, more literal, force. For Paul, the plight of a creation perverted through sin in the human race is not resolved by a miracle surrounding the birth of Jesus. Rather, it is supremely Christ's resurrection that both inaugurates the new creation and guarantees its consummation, and it is a fully human Christ and fully human creatures to whom God relates in this way.

In thinking about Jesus as truly divine, focus on the virgin birth as the mode of incarnation has had two main unfortunate consequences. One is the tendency to speak of the incarnation as though it refers to the inception of Jesus' life rather than its totality. Once Jesus' conception and birth are seen as a normal aspect of his being and having a personal body rather than entailing an extraordinary divine intrusion, the emphasis can fall where it should in talking of incarnation. Incarnation stands for the way in which the triune God relates to creaturely humanity in and through the entirety of the life of the particular human personal body of Jesus of Nazareth, which culminates in his death and resurrection and which is also part of the larger story of God's interaction with Israel. To speak of Jesus' divinity, then, is to claim that in and through this entire human life, not in special moments or events within it, God has chosen to identify Godself. The personal identity of Jesus in his humanity now decisively defines how God is most aptly characterized. Jesus is God precisely in the whole sequence of his historical human existence, where the humanity is not somehow appended to the divinity but is precisely where the divinity is ontologically located.

The second unfortunate consequence of the focus on the virgin birth as the mode of incarnation is the tendency of some to hold that one of the major indicators of that divinity is precisely that Jesus was miraculously conceived without a human male. But this is to introduce confusion. Jesus' divinity is not to be sought at particular moments or in particular aspects of Jesus' life, whether here his conception or elsewhere his miracles, but is to be seen in the pattern of his life as a whole as rendered in the various canonical narratives. It is the fully human personal body, Jesus of Nazareth, and not a hybrid or semi-divine figure, in whom the divine Word is incarnate. To claim that his divinity is seen in a miraculous conception is not only to propose a divine strain within the human subject that constitutes his humanity in a different fashion from that of other humans, akin to the infusion of superhuman powers into a hero, but also to suppose that the divine Logos or principle took the place of some aspect of the human life of Jesus. It is to predicate divinity of the human subject instead of predicating humanity of the Son of God, the Second Person of the Trinity.

It is worth noting that, according to the rules of Chalcedonian Christology, this is to confuse the two 'natures'. While this language is problematic and we need not be bound by the specifics of the terminology employed in the Chalcedonian Definition in articulating the doctrine of incarnation, to disregard its thinking about the appropriate and inappropriate ways to relate humanity and divinity in connection with Jesus may well be to fail to learn from earlier wisdom. Chalcedon insisted that Jesus is one with God and fully human and that he is both of these at the same time without separation or confusion. It did not realize that a literal virgin birth in fact introduces a confusion of the two. The birth of Jesus initiated by God without a human father but with a human mother confuses the categories of divine and human by identifying the divine aspect of Jesus with his conception in space and time and makes an exception to what was confessed about his full humanity. It replaces an aspect of normal human existence for Jesus with a divine property. Of course, those who formulated *The Definition* would themselves have seen no tension between their reflections on not confusing the two natures and a virginal conception, because their biological understanding was different from ours. As we have seen, their notions of procreation and reproduction were such that they could think of Jesus as a fully human subject simply on the basis of his mother's role in his conception and birth. What they wanted to safeguard was the claim that the whole of Jesus' human life has its origin and subsistence in his unique relationship to God.

The problem of confusing the humanity and the divinity of Jesus Christ in retaining a virginal conception is a modern one but a real one for those who wish to think coherently and plausibly in relation to the incarnation. Necessary for any such coherence is the recognition that what is divine about Jesus is simply that, unlike other humans, his entire being is assumed by and subsists in the Word, the Second Person of the Trinity. That does not mean that the one subject of the life of Jesus is the Word as such but that it is the incarnate Logos who is both divine and human. In other words, the human Jesus' relationship to the divine Word is one that leaves his human life essentially intact and therefore at one with the lives of other humans. There is distinction but no separation between the human and the divine – Jesus and the Word are one, but there is also no confusion – Jesus does not have a humanity that is made exceptional because divinity takes over at specific points in his life. Because the Word chooses to be identified with this particular human life, Jesus' entire human life is divine.

What Chalcedon talks of as a hypostatic union is not one that has a particular location in Jesus' psyche or in some temporal event in his life. The virgin birth inevitably ends up making his conception precisely such a point of confusion between the two natures. Arguably, therefore, declining to understand that conception literally enables one to do better justice to the intent of Chalcedon.

Confusing divinity and humanity in Jesus or for that matter thinking that the two have to remain discrete elements that can be isolated in describing his life are frequently part of a more basic mistake in construing the relation between God and all that is not God, namely, created reality. That construal puts the two in competition. Again, as we noted, this is a problem Schleiermacher rightly saw with the use of the two natures terminology.[26] It operates by subsuming divinity and humanity under the same category of 'nature', not realizing that the two are not on the same plane, and then attempts to referee the clash between them.[27] But God is not one being among other beings, one thing among other things. God is the radically transcendent source of all being and therefore not on the same plane of being and activity with creatures and not in competition with them. God's activity as the continuous giver of life does not come at the expense of human activity. In terms of Christology this means that taking seriously the full humanity of Christ need not entail downplaying his divinity, and asserting his divinity need not mean that his humanity is slighted or threatened. Because divinity is not a kind of being over against other kinds of being, 'God is not bound by apparent contrasts between divine and creaturely qualities; God is therefore free to enter into intimate communion with us, without loss to the divine nature, without sacrificing the difference between God and us.'[28] To assert divinity of Jesus does not therefore require also asserting a miraculous divine conception and is fully compatible with his being conceived in the usual way through two human parents.

The confusion between the humanity and divinity of Jesus has affected two further areas in which the virgin birth has played a role in the traditional

---

[26] See the earlier discussion of F. Schleiermacher, *The Christian Faith* (eds H. R. Mackintosh and J. S. Stewart; London: T. & T. Clark, 1999), 392.

[27] Cf. also W. Pannenberg, *Jesus – God and Man* (2nd edn Philadelphia: Westminster, 1977), 322: 'The problem results from speaking of "two" natures as if they were on the same plane. This poses the pseudotask of relating the two natures to one another in such a way that their synthesis results in a single individual in spite of the hindrances posed by the idea of a "nature".'

[28] K. Tanner, *Jesus, Humanity and the Trinity* (Edinburgh: T. & T. Clark, 2001), 11. Tanner's first chapter (1–31) expounds the implications of this view of the relation between God and creatures for Christology more fully. Kelsey, *Eccentric*, 125, 916, makes similar points about the relation between God and creation and between God's transcendence and immanence.

understanding of the incarnation. The first is the matter of the pre-existence of Christ as the Son. Pannenberg holds that the virgin birth stands in 'irreconcilable tension' with the doctrine of the pre-existence of Christ.[29] The annunciation accounts suggest the conception of Jesus as the absolute beginning of the life of the Son of God, while the pre-existence of the Son as part of the triune God obviously precludes such a notion. One can reply that the accounts in Matthew and Luke did not have pre-existence in view, that it is possible, as later Christians obviously did, to find ways in which the two perspectives are not irreconcilable, and that the issues he raises about the relationship between a pre-existent divine Son, who is more than simply a personification of God's purposes for redemption, and the beginnings of his life as a fully human individual are issues for any view of incarnation and thus not specific to the notion of a virginal conception. However, the real issue that lies behind Pannenberg's claim is that taking the virginal conception accounts as anything other than legendary elements within the conventions of ancient biography is hugely problematic for thinking about the relation between the triune God and the life of Jesus. It is one thing to talk of the Word or Son assuming the fully human Jesus from the beginning of his life; it is another to articulate coherently how the Son as one of the trinitarian relations was involved in the conception of Jesus along with the Father and the Spirit. What is important here, rather, is to be clear about the distinction within identity of the one person of Jesus Christ, which will shortly be discussed more fully, and to recognize that talk of the pre-existence of Christ, which becomes necessary when we hold that the human life of Jesus is to be identified as the incarnate expression of the life of the divine Logos, has reference to God the Son and not to the human existence of Jesus which had a beginning in historical time.

The second further aspect of Christology in which confusion between humanity and divinity has been in play is in regard to the sinlessness of Jesus. It is worth pointing out, though this is not decisive for systematic theological reflection, that those parts of the New Testament witness that have an account of a virginal conception do not link this in any way with the notion of Jesus' sinlessness, while those parts of the witness (Paul, Hebrews and the Johannine literature) that most strongly assert Jesus' sinlessness know nothing of a virginal conception. As we have seen, however, beginning especially with Augustine, who takes up earlier assertions in Ambrose, it has frequently been argued that the virgin birth is necessary

---

[29] Pannenberg, *Jesus*, 143–6.

in order to guarantee a break between human sinful nature and the sinless state of Jesus, which is a prerequisite if his offering of himself in death is to be effective in dealing with sin. Christ has to be in solidarity with humanity and yet free from its taint. Such a proposal, however, again introduces a discrete miraculous divine component into the life of Jesus of Nazareth. Even though he may have been tempted, he did not sin because his extraordinary conception meant that he was preserved from the full effects of human fallenness. In addition to its assumption of a dubious genetic explanation of original sin, tracing it back to the sin of the first humans, this is unsatisfactory on several other grounds. It adds, uniquely in the case of Christ, a special quality to his humanity, exemption from the inheritance of original sin, while at the same time it removes any real and full solidarity of Christ in the human condition he came to save. One part of the logic of the incarnation's soteriology is preserved – to be effective Christ's death must also be a divine act, to which no impurity can be ascribed. But this is at the expense of the other part, where for redemption to be effective the one through whom redemption comes must be fully at one with those he redeems.

In addition, when Christ's freedom from sin and its taint is tied to the virginal birth, it is evident that it too is shaped by the ancient view of procreation. Original sin was seen as transferred through the male's role in reproduction with the female only supplying the soil in which the sin that had been planted would grow. Taking up the comment of Augustine (*Gen. litt.* 10.20) that 'Christ took the visible substance of his flesh from the Virgin's flesh; but the principle of his conception did not spring from the seed of man', Aquinas can go on to say that Christ did not sin in Adam because he did not receive human nature from Adam actively but only from the Holy Ghost (cf. *Summa Theologiae* 3.15.1). Even on this ancient view, there appears to be an insuperable objection. The virgin's flesh itself has already been tainted through the seed of her father. So unless it is held that 'Christ passed through Mary as water flows through a tube', the heretical view opposed by Irenaeus (*Haer.* 1.7.2), his mother would have passed on to him the taint of sin. Once this problem was appreciated, a traditional response was, of course, to appeal to the immaculate conception of Mary herself. But, as we have noted, there can be no good reason to stop with Mary's conception. Once one embarks on this line of reasoning, its logic can only entail an infinite regress of immaculate conceptions. The problem is no different on a revised modern version of the virginal conception, where the Y chromosome is divinely rather than humanly supplied. How is it that the mother's normal X chromosome could be employed, when this would have been tainted by previous genetic traits?

A contemporary Christology would also insist on Christ's freedom from sin, but, once the virginal conception and ancient understandings of biology are no longer tied to the doctrine, there is freedom to explore this in a variety of other ways, while holding that Christ fully shares in the suffering and death that are part of the human condition, being vulnerable to the consequences of humans' estrangement from God and from one another. Barth, who did not think that it was a virginal conception that exempted Christ from sin, talked of the divine will and grace that enabled Christ to respond continuously and appropriately to that will and grace.[30] Gunton speaks of Christ's total faithfulness to his vocation.

> If that freedom is to be mediated to us, he must also share to the full the conditions of our taint. For that to be achieved, it is necessary that he be constituted of the same stuff of which we are made, part of a created order, subjected to vanity and in need of redemption. The taint does not indeed touch him, in the sense that he offers his humanity, through the eternal Spirit, perfect to the Father. But it must be through the Spirit: that is to say, through the process of a real life of struggle and temptation . . . to evade the implications of his human calling.[31]

Jesus' sinlessness, in other words, manifests itself through a historical struggle and is not guaranteed from the start by a virginal conception. Others point in a complementary fashion to the New Testament's insistent stress on Jesus' obedience to the Father for the sake of his kingdom mission, an obedience, of which sinlessness is simply the negative expression, that makes the whole pattern of his life transparent to God's will and purpose. If sin is a distorted resistant response to God, then Jesus' wholly dependent and faithful response to God entails sinlessness. If sin thereby also involves a distortion of our true human identity, Jesus lives out his identity authentically and thereby shows that to be human and to be without sin are not incompatible. He does this in interaction and solidarity with those who are estranged from what God has called them to be and thus estranged from Godself and he suffers the consequence of their estrangement, so that, in Paul's words, 'for our sake he made him to be sin who knew no

---

[30] Cf. Barth, *CD* 1.2, 92–3.

[31] C. E. Gunton, 'Dogma, the Church and the Task of Theology', in eds V. Pfitzner and H. Regan, *The Task of Theology Today* (Edinburgh: T. & T. Clark, 1999), 18–19. The citation is taken from Gunton's objections to another dogma, that of the immaculate conception. It is striking that the same objections apply to the virgin birth, once it is acknowledged that we no longer share the ancient assumptions about procreation.

sin, so that in him we might become the righteousness of God' (2 Cor. 5.21). It is not, then, that Jesus was incapable of sinning because of a special divine conception nor that we can somehow establish from the accounts of his life that his every act was morally pure but rather that, in the resurrection's vindication of the faithfulness of the whole course of his life lived under the conditions of sinful flesh, God established the sinlessness of that life and made its resulting death the means whereby God 'condemned sin in the flesh' (cf. Rom. 8.3).[32]

In the discussion of Jesus' humanity and divinity so far it has, of course, been assumed that the doctrine of incarnation predicates both of these of one and the same subject. How this can be so, its nature as a mystery, and yet necessary attempts to analyse and articulate it coherently have been at the heart of traditional and contemporary Christology.[33] It can be no part of our brief here to address such matters directly and for their own sake and, for the most part, their treatment remains the same whether or not a virgin birth is in the picture. Yet there is a way that the notion of a virginal conception intrudes, because it has often encouraged a faulty understanding of the relation between the triune God, who assumes the personal body of Jesus of Nazareth, and Jesus in his humanity, particularly when the term 'Son' is employed for both. This sometimes occurs in unqualified appeals to the tradition's endorsement of the title *Theotokos* (God-bearing) or its less precise equivalent, Mother of God, for Mary. It was controversy about this title that was a primary factor leading to Chalcedon. While the council held that the divine Son, begotten of the Father, and the Son born of Mary were 'one and the same', even on its own terms it complemented this 'without separation' by 'without confusion'. Unless the title is to be reduced to absurdity – the uncreated God having a created mother – it has to be understood to have in view the humanity assumed by the divine Son. Failing to make the distinction within the identity of the divine Son also leads to assertions that, as the Son, Jesus had to be born of a virgin; he could only have God as his Father, not some human male.[34] This is precisely the mistake against which Ratzinger warns in the earlier citation of his comment about the relation between incarnation and the virgin birth and to which Lash draws

---

[32] For a fuller account of Jesus' sinlessness in similar fashion, see Pannenberg, *Jesus*, 354–64.

[33] Tanner, *Jesus, Humanity*, 22–31, for example, provides one helpful recent attempt to articulate what she calls 'a mighty conundrum'.

[34] Such assertions can be found in unexpected places. A theologian, commenting on Matthew's narrative, can write, 'Mary had to be a virgin because Jesus is the Son of God' and Jesus 'can have no other father than the Father who is the first person of the Trinity'. See Hauerwas, *Matthew*, 36.

attention when he asserts, 'confessing Jesus to be Son of *God* most certainly does not entail denying that he was any other father's son'.[35] Since this reasoning is found so frequently, it is worth indicating in a little more detail why it is mistaken.

Part of the confusion lies in the language of the tradition, derived from the Chalcedonian Definition, in which the term 'person' (*hypostasis*) is applied both to the members of the triune God and to the one subject of the incarnation once humanity is assumed by the triune God. But, as is frequently observed, 'hypostasis' should be seen here as having two different senses that are not to be simply collapsed into one another. Clearly one cannot speak of the hypostases of the Trinity as having a personal identity in the same way that we have discussed Jesus of Nazareth as having such an identity as a living human personal body.[36] Trinitarian hypostases are 'persons' only in a very loose, extended analogical sense. They stand not for individual centres of consciousness but for relationships within the triune God, where each has its being or reality only in relation to the other two.[37]

Which sense of the term, then, is being employed when we speak of the life of the incarnate Word or Son? Here we need to remind ourselves of what the incarnation claim is asserting. It holds that in the depiction of the life of the personal human, Jesus, God is uniquely disclosed so that this particular life is God's own; this life is God's activity on behalf of the world. Without any detriment to Jesus' full humanity, therefore, both God and Jesus are the subjects of this life. This is a necessary identity because, as Tanner puts it, 'a human being's dying on a cross is not saving unless this is also God's dying; and God's dying does not save us (it is not even possible) unless God does so *as* a human being'.[38] But this is an identity within which there remain distinctions. In order to avoid simplistic, and ultimately docetic, notions of Jesus as God walking about on earth, this incarnational Christology has always required some sophistication. The old quip, 'Did Jesus know that he was God? No, but he was mistaken', contains some recognition, inadequate to be sure, of the traditional distinction between what can be said of the human subject Jesus and what can be said of the divine subject God the Son, who takes on the human

---

[35] N. Lash, *Believing Three Ways in One God* (London: SCM, 1992), 58.
[36] For this reason, Kelsey, *Eccentric*, 69–71, 358–9, 616, prefers to reserve 'personal' for the humanity of Jesus and to retain 'hypostasis' as a technical term for the distinctions within the triune God.
[37] Barth, *CD* 1.1, 353–68, therefore eschewed the use of 'persons' for the Trinity, preferring to speak of *Seinsweisen*, three distinct modes or ways of being within one indissoluble subject.
[38] Tanner, *Jesus, Humanity*, 21.

subject Jesus in the incarnation. While all that Jesus is and does can be attributed to God, not all that God is and does can be attributed to Jesus. In the New Testament witness Jesus is seen as the Son who is sent by the Father in the power of the Spirit, and so the Logos or Word as the second hypostasis is also seen as the Son. In this way the Son as the second hypostasis and Jesus of Nazareth who calls on God as Father can both be seen as the subject of the one human life assumed by the triune God. In the development of classical Christology the Second Person of the Trinity comes to be employed in talking of the way the triune God assumes Jesus because the second member's interaction within the Trinity corresponds most closely to Jesus' human relationship to God. But again this is a complex identity within which there remain distinctions.[39] While all that the human creature Jesus does in his dependence on God as Father can be attributed to the second hypostasis of the Son, not all that the Son is and does as the second hypostasis can be attributed to Jesus in his faithful human sonship. The Son as the second hypostasis remains on the Creator's side of the Creator–creature divide, while the humanity of Jesus of Nazareth as the Son is clearly a creaturely humanity. The two relationships of sonship come together but cannot be collapsed into each other without remainder. This is a further implication of the distinction between 'begotten' and 'created' or 'made' that Athanasius introduced into the early Christological debate. His point was that the relation between the Father and the Son as hypostases does not need to be construed as part of the more general Creator–creature distinction. The two terms 'begetting' and 'creating' should be seen as metaphors for two different sorts of relationship, the former a generative and derivative relationship characterized by distinction within identity and the latter a similar relationship but characterized by a difference that amounts to an ontological otherness. The Son as the second hypostasis is therefore 'eternally begotten'. But, by extension from this point, Jesus as the human Son is created but not begotten. The generative relationship between Father and Son in the Trinity cannot be directly transferred to talk of the relationship between God and the human Jesus and the relationship between God and the human Jesus as Son cannot be directly transferred to the relationship between the Father and the Son in the Trinity. The Son as the human Jesus was fully part of unadulterated

---

[39] Cf. Pannenberg, *Jesus*, 155: 'we . . . cannot escape distinguishing the *eternal Son* from the *man Jesus*. Certainly, in so doing we always remember that this involves nothing more than two different aspects of the one Jesus Christ'; Tanner, *Jesus, Humanity*, 47–8: 'Human and divine functions remain distinct in Christ's life, nothing like the unity of substance or nature found in the Trinity, though they have an identity of shape.'

creaturely reality, and, as we have argued, in contemporary understanding that means this Son had a human father.

It should now be clear where this all-too-compressed discussion has been leading. The relation between the human Jesus as the Son and the second hypostasis of the Trinity as Son is that of indirect identity, an identity that retains important distinctions. One of those is that it should not be said of the second hypostasis that God conceived this Son with the help of a human mother because the Son in this sense is always part of the essential life of the triune God. Only of the Son as the human Jesus can the language of conception and birth be employed. The whole life, including its conception and birth, of the human Jesus is taken up or assumed as its own by the second hypostasis but that is by no means the same as stating straightforwardly that the second hypostasis was humanly conceived. Jesus' humanity from its conception is the humanity of the Word or Son, distinct from the divinity but not separate from it. The unity of the one subject of the incarnation does not obliterate this distinction between his humanity and divinity. To declare, therefore, that since Jesus is the Son he could not have a human father and his mother had to be a virgin is to ignore the nature of the unity of the one subject of the incarnation and to fail to make the necessary distinction within the identity.

In case this whole discussion seems to have become too abstracted from its roots in the New Testament witness, it is, finally, worth briefly reminding ourselves that that witness, in its various forms, to Jesus' identity had already indicated that the story of Jesus was also the story of God and thereby raised just such questions about how to understand the one subject whose story is both stories. So, in relation to our topic, for example, Paul held that the one who shared equality with God was found in human form and, through the obedience of his death, exalted to share the status of Lord (Phil. 2.6–11), and that the one who is God's Son was also in terms of that human form 'the seed of David', David's physical descendant through Joseph. Hebrews also tells both stories about the same person. It opens with some of the strongest assertions about Jesus as the Son being God and Lord before stressing equally strongly that, in sharing flesh and blood, Jesus is like humans in every respect and taking for granted that that includes normal human descent, 'for it is evident that our Lord was descended from Judah' (7.14). Since all the Gospels are written from and shaped by post-resurrection perspectives, all four, though to differing degrees, have narratives that convey that the identity of their protagonist, whose full humanity is assumed, is uniquely aligned with that of God. As we have seen, one of the ways that Matthew conveys this is to insist that from his conception and birth Jesus is Emmanuel, God with us. In the thought forms of the day one of the means of expressing a similar conviction about a subject's relation to the gods was to retroject what was believed on the basis of the extraordinary nature of his life back to an account of his conception and birth that incorporated such a belief; Matthew does this for the one who is Israel's Saviour by supplying a virginal conception. Ancient notions of procreation, as we have seen, also played their part here. Since the male provided the generating principle, while the female was its receptor, an account in which God and not a human male was the decisive generator of Jesus' life provided an appropriate means of under-lining that this life was also the life of God. Luke's narrative binds the identities of Israel's God and of Jesus of Nazareth by presenting both as Lord.[40] In telling the story of the birth of this Lord (1.42; 2.11), Luke, as we have argued, does so in even greater conformity to similar stories of heroic figures in Graeco-Roman biography by combining a miraculous account of the conception and traditions about a normal human origin, in which Joseph is the father. John's Gospel has an even more explicit identification of its subject as both the human Jesus and Israel's God, so that the self-identification of the latter as 'I Am' is now to be found on the lips of the former. God's Logos who has become flesh needs no miraculous birth in this Gospel. The Son of God can also be depicted straight-forwardly as the son of Joseph. It is, therefore, these and other features of the apostolic witness about the one subject, whose story combines two identities, that provoke the discussion for later believers about how best to understand and articulate this mystery in their own time and place.

Inevitably this discussion has focused on the relation of the first two members of the Trinity to the incarnation. A fuller treatment would also need to do justice to the work of the divine Spirit. It is significant that, in emphasizing the divine initiative from the very beginning of Jesus' life, the stories of both Matthew and Luke identify the divine agent operative in his conception as the Holy Spirit. This remains important even if one no longer thinks it necessary to hold that the Spirit somehow replaces the role of a human male. The divine Spirit does not just come upon Jesus from his baptism onwards but is involved in his life from its inception. For the totality of the fully human life of Jesus the Spirit enables him uniquely to be, to say and to do precisely what God the Father intended. The Spirit does not overrule human agency but orders it to achieve God's

---

[40] Cf. esp. C. Kavin Rowe, *Early Narrative Christology: The Lord in the Gospel of Luke* (Berlin: De Gruyter/Grand Rapids: Baker Academic, 2006).

purposes. This applies as much to Jesus' conception, where the presence of the Spirit does not require the absence of a male agent, as to the rest of his life and mission, where his human agency retains its integrity. There is no need therefore to play off a Spirit Christology over against an incarnational Christology. The Spirit is supremely active in the man Jesus, but it is the Spirit who is also active in bringing about the unique identity between the divine Son and the human vehicle of the Son's self-disclosure. Trinitarian thinking, already implicit in John's Gospel, would go on to see the way in which Jesus, the incarnate Son, is filled by the Spirit as a reflection of the eternal indwelling of the Son by the Father through the Spirit. The unity of person of the incarnate Word is that of the human Jesus transfigured by constant immersion in the divine Spirit.

Tradition, critical loyalty and saying the creed

Some of those who have been patient enough to follow the discussion to this point might still harbour the suspicion that, with its emphasis on critical reading of Scripture and the problems presented by contemporary biological knowledge, and despite its alleged high view of Scripture, the exploration has turned out to be little different from modern or liberal views of the Christian faith that are prepared to water down its content by privileging the latest findings in historical, literary or scientific studies in order to make it accessible or attractive to a present-day audience. What, then, they might ask, of any attempt to take seriously one's situation as a reader of Scripture not only within contemporary critical and cultural perspectives but also, and primarily, within that community whose confessional tradition is articulated classically in the Apostles' and Nicene Creeds? The earlier chapter in which we attempted to understand why the virginal conception was thought important enough to become the dominant perspective on Jesus' birth and this chapter's preceding discussion of the virginal conception in the light of Chalcedonian and contemporary Christology ought to have allayed such suspicions and indicated that the tradition has been given serious attention, but it is worth responding more directly, if briefly, to the general issue.

The 'faith seeking understanding' stance that has driven this book's exploration is not simply an individual matter. It is both a faith shaped within the Church and, according to the Apostles' Creed, a belief in 'the holy catholic church: the communion of saints'. This places both faith and understanding within a tradition. Taking seriously our embodiment as finite and as situated within a particular space and time means that we are all inevitably placed somewhere within an unfolding historical and cultural tradition and that thinking we are able to attain a universal and timeless understanding through the exercise of critical reasoning is illusory. We are both shaped by tradition and shapers of tradition in that we construe our tradition in particular ways in order to guide our present and our future. Christians may inhabit a variety of traditions but clearly the determinative one is that shaped by God's revelation, given its decisive form in the life, death and resurrection of Christ, and by the Church's continuing attempt to respond to that revelation over time in its life and understanding. The tradition that results is not some dead weight from the past but a living tradition. As Barth reminds us, 'Augustine, Thomas Aquinas, Luther, Schleiermacher, and all the rest are not dead but living. They still speak and demand a hearing as living voices, as surely as we know that they and we belong together in the Church.'[41] The mention of Schleiermacher, of course, also serves as a reminder that, in regard to our topic, the ongoing living tradition is not a monolithic one and that from his time onwards the virgin birth has been one of the points of contestation.

In the context of the tradition Irenaeus and other pre-modern readers rightly assumed that interpretation of Scripture was a corporate project, taking place within the community of the Church and that to help it sort out the intricacies and complexities within Scripture the Church needed the guidance of the rule of faith. They also assumed that there was a body of apostolic doctrine passed on in the tradition of the Church's teaching that enabled discernment of a unified witness within Scripture. Along with the historical consciousness that helped to shape modern historical-critical methods, however, there has often gone an antagonism towards tradition and doctrinal formulations. It was considered necessary to strip away such distorting frameworks if the Bible was to be read accurately. Late modern or postmodern ways of thinking have now exposed clearly the flaws in such an approach and the illusion of holding that there can be some neutral, objective reading of texts that operates without an interpretative community and its framework. In this regard one of the benefits of working from within the doctrinal tradition of the Church is that this can act as a safeguard against succumbing uncritically to the variety of frameworks supplied by our contemporary setting and contribute to the recognition that all such frameworks and their discourses derive ultimately from commitments that are religious at root.

---

[41] K. Barth, *Protestant Theology in the Nineteenth Century: Its Background and History* (London: SCM, 1972), 17.

But it is not quite as clear-cut as this may sound. There is continuing discussion, for instance, of what does and does not belong to the content of Irenaeus' and others' rule of faith. Even if we specify the early creeds and decisions of ecumenical councils as that rule, then critical historical awareness still needs to be at play, because, as with the scriptural texts themselves, understanding of their formulations changes as later generations interpret them in settings removed from their original context. Inevitably discernment is required about what is central and what is time-conditioned in a way that is no longer helpful. Churches have recognized this issue by allowing a range of interpretations on some controversial issues. So, for example, while the doctrines of the Trinity or the incarnation are normally thought to be non-negotiable, whether the formulation that the Spirit proceeds from the Father and the Son is the most appropriate way of depicting the mutual interpenetration of the divine persons remains hotly disputed, as does what meaning is to be given to the statement that Christ descended into hell. Similarly, then, this study has been arguing, there should be room for different interpretations of the virginal conception, including that it is to be seen as one time-conditioned way of expressing belief in the incarnation, the conviction that God has been disclosed uniquely in the particular human life of Jesus of Nazareth, and one which for contemporary understanding may well undermine the authentic humanity of the one in whom God was disclosed.[42] We may be clear that at the heart of Christian doctrine is the Creator God, the God of Israel, who sends Christ as the Son to die for humans and their salvation and who by the power of the Spirit raises the crucified Christ and produces a people who by faith and baptism participate in the life of Christ in one body as the Church and fulfil the loving and just purposes of God in mission in the world. But this still allows much room for interpretation and leaves all sorts of other doctrinal issues unresolved. Those who rightly advocate theological interpretation of Scripture, therefore, do not for the most part think that there is a specific list of doctrinal statements that, when operative, decide in advance issues of exegesis and interpretation. They prefer to think of the doctrinal tradition as producing

---

[42] As one writer on the Nicene Creed puts it, 'The truth of the incarnation does not depend on Jesus not having had a human father. It may still be that the virginal conception was given to humankind as a sign of this unique self-presentation of God in human form. But not necessarily so. The Church cannot countenance denial of the reality of the incarnation, but it can be tolerant of a degree of agnosticism about its actual manner of occurrence. It makes perfect theological sense to suppose that God incarnate had both a human father and mother.' B. Hebblethwaite, *The Essence of Christianity: A Fresh Look at the Nicene Creed* (London: SPCK, 1996), 90–1.

rather a mindset or a disposition that reads Scripture in the light of its witness to the trinitarian God and in openness to the transforming impact of that witness in their own time and place. What role historical and critical thinking has in the outworking of such a disposition has to be negotiated on a case-by-case basis and in dialogue with the wider Christian community.

This is to take a different stance from that represented recently by Robert Jenson in his typically provocative reflections on the relation between study of the Scriptures and the creed.[43] While there is much to agree with on the failure of some biblical scholarship to pay attention to the theological subject matter of the texts under investigation and on the need for credal tradition to provide a hermeneutical lens, what he calls 'the creed as critical theory for Scripture',[44] in practice this does not mean for him that the outline of the creed provides guidance but that 'the plain sense' of particular credal statements is determinative for textual interpretation. This becomes clear because one of his worked examples is, in fact, Luke's annunciation story.[45] Here the statement of the Apostles' Creed – 'born of the virgin Mary' – simply trumps exegetical possibilities and suppresses canonical diversity without sufficient acknowledgement that the statement itself does not have a plain sense abstracted from its historical and cultural context and is dependent for its coherence within the creed on assumptions about procreation that we no longer share. The Spirit, we are told, 'can bestow human nature – whatever that actually is – as he wills' and having problems with this issue is due to thinking of modern science's warrants and results as an encompassing system of truth to which a virginal conception is to be accommodated. But it is by no means obvious that having a critical understanding of the creed that is in dialogue both with Scripture and with our understandings of cosmology and biology leaves us, as Jenson suggests, without 'one true metanarrative'.[46] Why is not the incarnation itself, rather than one interpretation of its means, sufficient as part of the overarching story within which the stories of modern cosmology and biology need to find their place?

Behind the stance adopted in our own reflections lies the recognition that while the reality of God and God's acts for human salvation in Christ remain constant, human apprehension of their truth and significance changes and develops. Our access to the truths is through historically,

---

[43] R. W. Jenson, *Canon and Creed* (Louisville: Westminster John Knox, 2010).
[44] Jenson, *Canon*, 79–87.
[45] Jenson, *Canon*, 99–107.
[46] Cf. Jenson, *Canon*, 104–5.

culturally and socially conditioned interpretations. Credal statements do not escape this and are therefore not immutable. That we live in different, and equally limited and partial, historical, cultural and social conditions entails, as we have seen with the virgin birth and its biological dimensions, that, even when we repeat the same words as the writers of Scripture or the formulators of the creeds, their meaning for us is not guaranteed to be the same as it was for them. The consequence is not that all doctrinal truth becomes relative but that the Church in succeeding generations through its theologians and teachers, through its worship and practice, is inevitably involved in the hard work of interpretation of the truths that shape its life. It should not be surprising that advances in knowledge throw up problems that require rethinking the tradition. After all, one of the tasks of theologians is to explore and restate central doctrines in the light of developments in human knowledge. The doctrine of creation is now rethought in the light of what is taken to be the case in respect to cosmology or evolution or genetics but nevertheless it is still a doctrine of creation when it affirms that the universe and its life as we know them depend for their existence on a divine Creator. Similarly there are various attempts to rethink and restate the doctrine of incarnation in the light of increased knowledge of the historical, cultural and social conditions of living in first-century Palestine and of what is entailed by personhood but they are still recognizably a doctrine of incarnation when they affirm that, without ceasing to be God, God identified Godself with humanity in the person of Jesus of Nazareth and became vulnerable to suffering and death. Determining what we are to make of the virgin birth in the light of our knowledge of New Testament diversity, literary genre and biology can be seen then as just one of those attempts to think again about an aspect of the tradition's depiction of the incarnation while reaffirming the essentials of the main doctrine of incarnation.

Being part of a tradition entails precisely such a process. A tradition is not static but displays continuities and discontinuities, as the tradition is contested and what is essential to it is debated. The Church has usually believed that through this process of discussion and debate, informed by reflection on Christian worship and practices and taking place among fallible and sinful humans, God's truth will prevail because in the midst of the process the Spirit is at work. This is not to suggest some guarantee of a simple continuing progress in apprehension of the truth but an expectation that over time and in the Church at large inappropriate and erroneous articulations of the faith will be exposed as inadequate. In practice, this works out in oscillating movements between the past and the present, going back to interpret the foundations in Scripture and creeds and coming forwards to re-express their significance in new ways for one's own time, then testing those new expressions in terms of both their adequacy for worship and practice in the present and their coherence with the foundational events of the faith in the past. It is in this way that Scripture primarily and the early creeds secondarily, in all their conditioned character as witnesses to truth, exercise a control over the development and modification of the tradition. On the one hand, these and other dogmatic formulations provide the boundaries within which one's theological interpretation operates. On the other, if the boundaries are not to become restrictive walls, theological, and in this case specifically Christological, interpretation has the freedom, in response to the work of the Spirit, to suggest the alteration or reinterpretation of the boundaries. Interpretations or reinterpretations of Scripture and creeds are therefore unavoidable but unless, in their modifications and applications, they commend themselves as essentially in continuity with their subject matter, the characteristic shape of Christian faith in terms of the incarnation, the Trinity and the redemption of humanity is in danger of being lost.

If freedom is not to become the licence to replace dogma with human speculation, then some agreed criteria are needed for evaluating whether a proposed change or reinterpretation is in continuity with the tradition. The following would be among the candidates. Does the credal or doctrinal formulation in question or its proposed modification express more adequately the witness of Scripture taken as a whole and have a place in a proper summary of the gospel? What essential implication of the Christian gospel was being safeguarded by the credal formulation and does retaining that historically conditioned formulation help or hinder the proclamation and defence of the same point today? Does the formulation of the traditional doctrine or its reinterpretation cohere better with other doctrines?[47] What has been proposed here is that the virgin birth part of the tradition is under severe pressure both from the recognition of Scripture's diversity on the matter of Jesus' conception and the place of the annunciation stories in the literary conventions of ancient biography and from our contemporary understanding of the biological make-up of the human male. No longer making it an essential doctrinal or credal element meets the criteria of discernment suggested above. It acknowledges more adequately the witness of the New Testament as a whole and how its writers summarize the gospel message. Insisting on the incarnation

---

[47] For a discussion along similar lines, cf. Gunton, 'Dogma', 1–22.

but not the historically conditioned presentation of a virginal conception both safeguards what is essential to the formulators of the creed, namely the divinity and humanity of Christ, and helps rather than hinders the proclamation of the incarnation for a contemporary audience, not least because it coheres better with other doctrines, particularly the full humanity of Jesus.

The mention of proclamation is a reminder that such hermeneutical development in the tradition can be seen more broadly as part of the Church's task in mission, translating a gospel to which witness has been borne in one historical and cultural context so as to be able to bear witness to the same message within the culture of another time and place. The expression of the gospel cannot be confined within the thought forms and assumptions of one particular culture. Merely to repeat the latter would become a form of cultural imperialism. Indeed, faithfulness to the tradition entails not simply using the same concepts as previous formulations but making similar judgements. Faithful proclamation of the faith in a new setting, then, requires evaluating which concepts and formulations in the tradition are based on assumptions that we no longer share and which are not essential to the gospel. Once it is seen that this applies to the virgin birth, the Church's proclamation can concentrate on a non-identical repetition of the basic message of the incarnation.

Given what has been said about the nature of tradition with its elements of stability and dynamism, there is no way that the Church can avoid the need to exercise discernment and to make critical judgements of this sort. The only alternatives are to allow the tradition to stultify and become irrelevant to changing times and their issues or to attempt to abandon the tradition. The recognition that one is part of a tradition that does not stand still inevitably involves a stance of critical loyalty to that tradition. This is very different from an impatience with its perceived imperfections that too readily turns its back on the tradition or an inflexible or nostalgic commitment to earlier formulations that amounts to blind loyalty.

But what does such critical loyalty mean for those whose worship involves actually repeating wording from the creed which, when taken at face value, is now considered inadequate, erroneous or damaging? While different churches may have slightly different English wordings of the creeds, the relevant parts of the Apostles' Creed and the Niceno-Constantinopolitan Creed are, for the former, 'I believe in Jesus Christ, God's only Son, our Lord, who was conceived by the Holy Spirit, born of the Virgin Mary' (the ecumenical version of the English Language Liturgical Consultation) and, for the latter, 'We believe in one Lord, Jesus Christ . . . For us and for our salvation he came down from heaven, was incarnate from the Holy Spirit and the Virgin Mary and was made man' (*Common Worship: Services and Prayers for the Church of England*). If, on the grounds we have explored above, one no longer holds to a literal virginal conception, can one say the creed with integrity? Or should one remain silent or work to have the creed changed? The question still has purchase if one is in an ecclesiastical tradition that does not give the creeds this prominence in public worship but that acknowledges that the creeds have a defining role in the Christian tradition. If, on historical, hermeneutical and theological grounds, one has problems with the virgin birth, can one still give assent to its formulation?

My response to such questions is similar to the argument I have made about Scripture. What was proposed was that the problems with taking Matthew 1 or Luke 1 literally in their talk of a virgin birth do not require a rejection of the authority or truth of Scripture at these points but rather lead to the recognition that Scripture's truth comes in culturally conditioned forms, in this instance through the literary form of ancient biography with its legendary features where claims about figures being born without a human father were means of asserting their extraordinary significance. In the case of Jesus, then, the stories of virginal conception express the convictions that only God's sovereign initiative could ultimately explain his life and that this God was wholly present in his fully human life from its inception. Similarly, the credal statements need to be seen as conditioned by the assumptions and categories of their day. The Niceno-Constantinopolitan Creed, for example, is clearly part of a process of debate and ecclesiastical politics, is made up of a patchwork of earlier scriptural formulations and credal fragments, employs categories from Graeco-Roman philosophy and responds polemically to alternative formulations.[48] The creeds, then, do not need to be changed but recognized for what they are. When we repeat them we are already interpreting them in our own terms, making adjustments, for example, for the ancient cosmology they presuppose. If the Apostles' Creed's statement that Jesus 'descended into hell' can be reinterpreted in the light of the shift away from an ancient cosmology as a way of depicting his full experience of death and its consequences or the Nicene Creed's statement that 'he came down from heaven' can be taken in a non-literal fashion as utilizing ancient cosmological mythology to articulate the notion of incarnation,

---

[48] For an excellent accessible account of the historical contingencies surrounding the Niceno-Constantinopolitan Creed, see A. Cameron, 'The Creed', in ed. S. Conway, *Living the Eucharist* (London: Darton, Longman & Todd, 2001), 56–71.

there should be no impediment to reinterpreting the virginal conception in the light of the shift away from an ancient biology.[49]

Whether the credal statement is 'conceived by the Holy Spirit, born of the Virgin Mary' or 'was incarnate by the Holy Spirit and the Virgin Mary', the important point of such an affirmation is that, through the divine Spirit, Jesus is the incarnation of God's Son. As we have seen in an earlier chapter, the two phrases in the Niceno-Constantinopolitan Creed were meant to declare that this incarnation was both fully divine – 'by the Holy Spirit' – and fully human – '[by] the Virgin Mary', but that was only possible given the assumptions of ancient culture about procreation. A present-day reciter of the creed would have little problem with saying 'and Mary', understanding that Mary simply stood for the two human parents of Jesus. It is obviously the presence of the term 'virgin' that is problematic and requires reinterpretation. But all that is necessary is to take the whole clause, whether 'who was . . . born of the Virgin Mary' or 'was incarnate . . . from the Virgin Mary and was made man', and realize that this was an ancient way of depicting the fully human conception and birth of the Son of God. There is no reason not to say the words, just as there is no reason not to read or proclaim the annunciation stories. We are conditioned into certain ways of thinking and so have no problem with saying with both creeds that Jesus Christ 'is seated at the right hand of the Father' and, if and when we pause to ask ourselves what we mean by that, we say something like: 'It points to Jesus as the supreme agent of divine authority.' If we are persuaded by the arguments about the status of formulations about the virgin birth, it requires no more adjustment to say those words and then, when asking ourselves what we mean by them, to say something like: 'It points to the mystery of the divine being experiencing a fully human life from its start.' And this, after all, is precisely what the framers of the creed, in the conceptuality of their own time, were intending to convey.

Sometimes the objection is raised that such an approach to saying the creed lacks transparency. So, for example, in responding to Pannenberg's similar claim that the virgin birth can be retained as part of the Church's liturgical confession because its formulation safeguards against adoptionism and docetism, Crisp declares that this 'seems more than a little disingenuous.

---

[49] Rowan Williams, *Open to Judgement* (London: Darton, Longman & Todd, 1994), 27, makes a similar point in relation to the formulation in the Niceno-Constantinopolitan Creed: 'If we can have some freedom in interpreting the vividly mythological language of "he came down from heaven", we can claim equal flexibility in our understanding of "incarnate by the Holy Ghost of the Virgin Mary".'

Better to come clean and give clear biblical and theological reasons for rejecting the doctrine than retain the pretence of confessing a doctrine that one no longer believes to be true.'[50] But the objection is confused and misunderstands the primary role of the creeds. As Pannenberg himself says in the context of the remarks to which Crisp takes exception,

> The repetition of a confession of the church is certainly something different from the statement of faith of an individual. Whoever joins in the confession of the church confesses the unity of Christianity by placing himself in the context of the intentions expressed in the formulations, even where the mode of expression must be perceived as inappropriate.[51]

Those who find this disingenuous appear to confuse creed and doctrine and to think that the Church affirming the creed is precisely the same as the individual believer giving his or her intellectual consent to each of a series of propositions. Certainly the creeds can be used to teach doctrine when the various beliefs are explained and elaborated, including exposition of 'born of the virgin Mary' and what it might mean today. But there are various doctrinal proposals that may comport with the creeds. The credal affirmations can be said to norm and shape such proposals but, strictly speaking, the creeds as statements of faith are not such doctrinal proposals in their own right.[52] Their primary function is within the Church's worship where believers, as part of the Church throughout the ages, affirm the nature of the God in whom the Church trusts and whose nature and acts have shaped and continue to shape their identity. In this context saying the creed is primarily taking a pledge of allegiance to the one God of which it speaks. As Nicholas Lash puts it, ' "I believe" does not express an opinion, however well founded or firmly held, concerning God's existence. It promises that life and love, mind, heart, and all my actions, are set henceforth steadfastly on God, and God alone.'[53] But in its place in the Church's worship recital of the creed also functions as 'a proclamation of belonging' to the community of the Church. Indeed, the English versions of the Nicene (or Niceno-Constantinopolitan) Creed have 'We believe' rather than 'I believe'. 'Saying things together is a badge of belonging.'[54] The Niceno-Constantinopolitan Creed is very much a product of the fourth century CE and as such preserves the collective memory of the Church. To approach it as a statement of contemporary faith is misguided,

---

[50] Crisp, *God Incarnate*, 95–6n44.
[51] Pannenberg, *Jesus*, 150.
[52] On this, see Kelsey, *Eccentric*, 61–2.
[53] Lash, *Believing*, 18.
[54] Cameron, 'The Creed', 58.

but 'for all its faults and curiosities, it is the outward symbol of unity, used by churches not unified in other respects'.[55]

Back in 1976 the Doctrine Commission of the Church of England endorsed the perspective proposed here by explicitly recognizing four different approaches to contemporary use of the creeds. These can be summarized as (i) acknowledging the creeds as a norm of Christian faith, embodying the permanent truth of the gospel; (ii) affirming them as a means of expressing one's identification with the general faith of the Church, while holding reservations about or questioning individual clauses, such as that relating to the virgin birth; (iii) acknowledging the past formation of the Church by the creeds but holding that one's primary loyalty is to the continuing Church of God as it testifies to the truth of God in new formulations today; (iv) holding that all credal affirmations are inadequate to express the essence of one's faith which is to be found in a life of discipleship in the sense of loyalty to Jesus and his values as depicted in the Gospels.[56] The Commission realizes that these differing approaches produce conflict that is sometimes painful but is convinced it would be disastrous to the health of the Church to rule out any of the competing attitudes. What it looks for is a creative tension, in which there is constant dialogue and cross-fertilization of insights and in which the creeds are seen as the classic formularies of Christendom but there is freedom to discuss and question them seriously.[57] Here, then, recognition is given to a spectrum of views, the last two of which sit quite loosely to any credal affirmation at all and three of which certainly envisage authentic Christian faith being able to take a form or expression that significantly reinterprets its historically and culturally conditioned origins in the Bible and creeds. Clearly what interests us most here is the second view that explicitly acknowledges differences of opinion over the virgin birth. It is to this sort of treatment of the creeds that the present study appeals, reminding readers of its mainstream status when all too often, even in some Anglican circles, raising questions about an affirmation such as the virgin birth is dismissed as heterodox.

The views of the 1976 Commission were not new. In a previous Doctrine Report in 1938 the Commission noted both the traditional view of the virgin birth and the view that 'a full belief in the historical Incarnation is more consistent with the supposition that our Lord's birth took place

---

[55] Cameron, 'The Creed', 68–9.
[56] The Doctrine Commission of the Church of England, *Christian Believing: The Nature of the Christian Faith and Its Expression in Holy Scriptures and Creeds* (London: SPCK, 1976), 35–8.
[57] Doctrine Commission, *Christian Believing*, 38–42.

under the normal conditions of human generation'. It went on to recognize that both views 'are held by members of the Church, as of the Commission, who fully accept the reality of our Lord's Incarnation, which is the central truth of the Christian faith'.[58]

As if these reports were not already clear enough, in the aftermath of the furore over the views of Bishop David Jenkins, in 1986 the House of Bishops issued a 'statement and exposition' on *The Nature of Christian Belief*. On our topic the bishops stated,

> It needs to be clearly acknowledged that those who feel compelled to regard the virginal conception as symbolic legend rather than history may do so in support of belief in the Incarnation, and regard the symbol of such conception as pointing to an unquestionably objective divine reality.

Different interpretations of the virginal conception were recognized as existing within the House of Bishops but these views were all accepted as

> expressing the faith of the Church of England and of its historic teaching, affirming the truth that in Christ God has taken the initiative for our salvation by uniting our human nature with himself, so bringing into being a new humanity.[59]

Though this is not as well known as it should be, the sort of critical loyalty to the Church's creeds and to the credal statement about the virginal conception in particular that we have been advocating in this book is in fact the clearly official stance of the Church of England. One may contrast this Church's carefully worked-out stance with some recent assertions by Dr R. Albert Mohler, Jr, President of the Southern Baptist Theological Seminary, the flagship school of America's largest Protestant denomination, the Southern Baptist Convention. He writes,

> Even if the Virgin Birth was taught by only one biblical passage, that would be sufficient to obligate all Christians to the belief . . . If Jesus was not born of a virgin, the Bible teaches a lie. Those who deny the Virgin Birth affirm other doctrines only by force of whim, for they have already surrendered the authority of Scripture. They have undermined Christ's nature and nullified the incarnation.[60]

---

[58] ed. G. W. H. Lampe, *Doctrine in the Church of England: The 1938 Report* (new edn London: SPCK, 1982), 82–3.

[59] The House of Bishops of the General Synod of the Church of England, *The Nature of Christian Belief: A Statement and Exposition* (London: Church House, 1986), 32–3.

[60] Mohler continues, 'This much we know: All those who find salvation will be saved by the atoning work of Jesus the Christ – the virgin-born Savior. Anything less than this is just not Christianity, whatever it may call itself. A true Christian will not deny the Virgin Birth.' See <http://www.albertmohler.com/2011/12/14/must-we-believe-in-the-virgin-birth/>. Accessed 15/12/2011.

These unqualified remarks reflect clearly that leaders in some ecclesial settings remain totally resistant to serious engagement with biblical and theological scholarship on our topic.

This brings us back full circle to the sort of divide over the issue sketched in our first chapter. Can it be bridged? In this book I have not laboured under the illusion of providing a comprehensive account of the topic or of supplying solutions that are bound to elicit agreement. I do hope to have indicated why it is high time that the old conservative–liberal divide on the virgin birth be left behind and why those with different views, not least those who disagree with the views expressed here, should be prepared to explore the issues further. I would be content to have persuaded some with a high view of Scripture and of the credal tradition that questions about the virginal conception are not able to be reduced to whether or not one believes God can do miracles with chromosomes, that Scripture's own diversity needs to be taken seriously, that the emphasis should be on the incarnation rather than its means, and that those engaged in such explorations as have been pursued here should at least not be dismissed as having retreated from orthodoxy and capitulated to rationalistic secular thought. I would, of course, be even happier to have convinced some that the stance that has been advocated can be critically embraced, refined and developed as part of the Church's ongoing attempt to be faithful in its interpretation and proclamation of Scripture and creeds for our own day. After all, it would be a great pity to get so caught up in debate over the means of incarnation that we lose sight of the still astonishing and potentially life-changing truth claim that in the fully human life of Jesus of Nazareth, son of Joseph and Mary, and for the sake of humanity and the world God became incarnate.

Bibliography

Primary sources

Aristotle. *Metaphysics*. Tr. H. Tredennick, G. C. Armstrong. 2 vols (Loeb Classical Library; Cambridge: Harvard University Press, 1933, 1935).

Aristotle ed. W. D. Ross. 2 vols (Chicago: Encyclopaedia Britannica, Inc., 1952).

Chadwick, H. ed. *Origen: Contra Celsum* (Cambridge: Cambridge University Press, 1953).

Charlesworth, J. H. ed. *The Old Testament Pseudepigrapha*. 2 vols (New York: Doubleday, 1983–5).

Diogenes Laertius. *Lives of Eminent Philosophers*. Tr. R. D. Hicks. 2 vols (Loeb Classical Library; Cambridge: Harvard University Press, 1925).

Early Christian Writings: The Apostolic Fathers. Tr. M. Staniforth (Harmondsworth: Penguin, 1968).

Eusebius. *Ecclesiastical History*. Tr. K. Lake, J. E. L. Oulton. 2 vols (Loeb Classical Library; Cambridge: Harvard University Press, 1926, 1932).

Iamblichus. *Life of Pythagoras*. Tr. T. Taylor (Rochester, VT: Inner Traditions, Bear & Company, 1986).

Joseph and Aseneth. Tr. D. Cook; in ed. H. F. D. Sparks, *The Apocryphal Old Testament* (Oxford: Oxford University Press, 1984), 473–503.

Philo. Tr. F. H. Colson, G. R. Whitaker, R. Marcus. 12 vols (Loeb Classical Library; Cambridge: Harvard University Press, 1929–62).

Philostratus. *Apollonius of Tyana*. Tr. C. P. Jones. 2 vols (Loeb Classical Library; Cambridge: Harvard University Press, 2005).

Plutarch. *Lives*. Tr. B. Perrin. 11 vols (Loeb Classical Library; Cambridge: Harvard University Press, 1914–26).

Plutarch. *The Lives of the Noble Grecians and Romans*. The Dryden Translation (Chicago: Encyclopaedia Britannica, Inc., 1952).

Roberts, A., J. Donaldson et al. eds *The Ante-Nicene Fathers*. 10 vols (Buffalo: The Christian Literature Publishing Company, 1887. Reprint Peabody, MA: Hendrickson, 1994).

Robinson, J. M. ed. *The Nag Hammadi Library in English* (Leiden: Brill; San Francisco: Harper & Row, 1977).

Schaff, P. et al. eds *The Nicene and Post-Nicene Fathers*. 1st series: 14 vols; 2nd series: 13 vols (Buffalo: The Christian Literature Publishing Company, 1886–98. Reprint Peabody, MA: Hendrickson, 1996).

Schneemelcher, W. ed. *New Testament Apocrypha*. Tr. R. McL. Wilson. 2 vols (Louisville: Westminster John Knox, 1991).

Suetonius. *Lives of the Caesars*. Tr. J. C. Rolfe. 2 vols (Loeb Classical Library; London: William Heinemann, 1913–14).

Bibliography

Vermes, G. *The Complete Dead Sea Scrolls in English* (7th edn London: Penguin, 2011).

Secondary sources

Alexander, L. C. A. 'Fact, Fiction and the Genre of Acts', *NTS* 44 (1998), 380–99.

Alexander, P. 'Jesus and his Mother in the Jewish Anti-Gospel (the *Toledot Yeshu*)', in eds C. Clivaz et al., *Infancy Gospels* (Tübingen: Mohr Siebeck, 2011), 588–616.

Allison, D. C. *The New Moses: A Matthean Typology* (Minneapolis: Augsburg Fortress, 1994).

Allison, D. C. *Studies in Matthew* (Grand Rapids: Baker Academic, 2005).

Allison, D. C. 'The Historians' Jesus and the Church', in eds B. R. Gaventa and R. B. Hays, *Seeking the Identity of Jesus* (Grand Rapids: Eerdmans, 2008), 79–95.

Allison, D. C. *Constructing Jesus: Memory, Imagination and History* (London: SPCK, 2010).

Anglican–Roman Catholic International Commission, *Mary: Grace and Hope in Christ* (London: Morehouse, 2005).

Aus, R. D. *Matthew 1—2 and the Virginal Conception* (Lanham, MD: University Press of America, 2004).

Balthasar, H. von *Credo* (Edinburgh: T. & T. Clark, 1990).

Barrett, C. K. *The Gospel according to St. John* (Philadelphia: Westminster, 1978).

Barrett, C. K. *A Critical and Exegetical Commentary on the Acts of the Apostles* Vol. 2 (Edinburgh: T. & T. Clark, 1998).

Barth, K. *Church Dogmatics* 1.2 (eds G. W. Bromiley and T. F. Torrance; tr. G. W. Bromiley; Edinburgh: T. & T. Clark, 1956).

Barth, K. *Protestant Theology in the Nineteenth Century: Its Background and History* (London: SCM, 1972).

Barth, K. *Church Dogmatics* 1.1 (2nd edn eds G. W. Bromiley and T. F. Torrance; tr. G. W. Bromiley; Edinburgh: T. & T. Clark, 1975).

Barth, K. *The Theology of Schleiermacher: Lectures at Göttingen, Winter Semester of 1923/24* (ed. D. Ritschl; tr. G. W. Bromiley; Grand Rapids: Eerdmans, 1982).

Barton, S. C. *Discipleship and Family Ties in Mark and Matthew* (Cambridge: Cambridge University Press, 1994).

Barton, S. C. *Life Together: Family, Sexuality and Community in the New Testament and Today* (Edinburgh: T. & T. Clark, 2001).

Bauckham, R. *Jude and the Relatives of Jesus in the Early Church* (Edinburgh: T. & T. Clark, 1990).

Bellinzoni, A. *The Sayings of Jesus in the Writings of Justin Martyr* (Leiden: Brill, 1967).

Berry, R. J. 'The Virgin Birth of Christ', *Science & Christian Belief* 8 (1996), 101–10.

Bockmuehl, M. 'The Son of David and his Mother', *JTS* 62 (2011), 476–93.

Borg, M. J. and J. D. Crossan. *The First Christmas: What the Gospels Really Teach about Jesus's Birth* (New York: HarperCollins, 2007).

Borg, M. J. and N. T. Wright. *The Meaning of Jesus: Two Visions* (San Francisco: HarperCollins, 1999).

Boslooper, T. *The Virgin Birth* (London: SCM, 1962).

Bovon, F. *Luke 1* (Minneapolis: Fortress, 2002).

Boyarin, D. *Border Lines: The Partition of Judaeo-Christianity* (Philadelphia: University of Pennsylvania Press, 2004).

Braaten, C. E. and R. W. Jenson eds *Mary, Mother of God* (Grand Rapids: Eerdmans, 2004).

Brooke, G. J. ed. *The Birth of Jesus* (Edinburgh: T. & T. Clark, 2000).

Brown, P. *Augustine of Hippo: A Biography* (London: Faber and Faber, 1967).

Brown, P. *The Body and Society* (London: Faber and Faber, 1990).

Brown, R. E. 'Luke's Description of the Virginal Conception', *TS* 35 (1974), 360–2.

Brown, R. E. *The Birth of the Messiah* (2nd edn New York: Doubleday, 1993).

Brown, R. E., K. P. Donfried, J. A. Fitzmyer, J. Reumann eds *Mary in the New Testament* (Philadelphia: Fortress, 1978).

Brunner, E. *The Mediator* (tr. O. Wyon; London: Lutterworth, 1934).

Brunner, E. *The Christian Doctrine of Creation and Redemption* (tr. O. Wyon; London: Lutterworth, 1952).

Bultmann, R. *History of the Synoptic Tradition* (tr. J. Marsh; San Francisco: Harper, 1976).

Burridge, R. A. *What Are the Gospels? A Comparison with Graeco-Roman Biography* (2nd edn Grand Rapids: Eerdmans, 2004).

Byrskog, S. *Story as History – History as Story* (Tübingen: Mohr Siebeck, 2000).

Caird, G. B. *The Gospel of Luke* (Oxford: Clarendon, 1963).

Cameron, A. 'The Creed', in ed. S. Conway, *Living the Eucharist* (London: Darton, Longman & Todd, 2001), 56–71.

Campenhausen, H. von *The Virgin Birth in the Theology of the Ancient Church* (London: SCM, 1964).

Catchpole, D. J. *Resurrection People: Studies in the Resurrection Narratives of the Gospels* (London: Darton, Longman & Todd, 2000).

Catchpole, D. J. *Jesus People: The Historical Jesus and the Beginnings of Community* (London: Darton, Longman & Todd, 2006).

Chilton, B. *Rabbi Jesus: An Intimate Biography* (New York: Doubleday, 2000).

Clark, E. A. 'Vitiated Seeds and Holy Vessels: Augustine's Manichean Past', in ed. K. L. King, *Images of the Feminine in Gnosticism* (Philadelphia: Fortress, 1988), 367–401.

Clark, E. A. 'Generation, Degeneration, Regeneration: Original Sin and the Conception of Jesus in the Polemic between Augustine and Julian of Eclanum', in eds V. Finucci and K. Brownlee, *Generation and Degeneration* (Durham, NC: Duke University Press, 2001), 17–40.

Clivaz, C., A. Dettwiler, L. Devillers, E. Norelli with the assistance of B. Bertho eds *Infancy Gospels* (Tübingen: Mohr Siebeck, 2011).

Bibliography

Coakley, S. 'What Does Chalcedon Solve and What Does it Not? Some Reflections on the Status and Meaning of the Chalcedonian "Definition"', in eds S. T. Davis, D. Kendall, G. O'Collins, *The Incarnation* (Oxford: Oxford University Press, 2002), 143–63.

Coleridge, M. *The Birth of the Lukan Narrative* (Sheffield: Sheffield Academic, 1993).

Cox, P. *Biography in Late Antiquity: A Quest for the Holy Man* (Berkeley: University of California Press, 1983).

Cranfield, C. E. B. 'Some Reflections on the Subject of the Virgin Birth', *SJT* 41 (1988), 177–89.

Crisp, O. D. 'On the "Fittingness" of the Virgin Birth', *Heythrop Journal* 49 (2008), 197–221.

Crisp, O. D. *God Incarnate: Explorations in Christology* (London: T. & T. Clark, 2009).

Crossan, J. D. *Jesus: A Revolutionary Biography* (San Francisco: HarperCollins, 1994).

Crossan, J. D. 'Virgin Mother or Bastard Child?', in ed. A.-J. Levine, *A Feminist Companion to Mariology* (London: T. & T. Clark, 2005), 37–55.

Crossan, J. D. 'Response to Robert M. Price', in eds J. K. Beilby and P. R. Eddy, *The Historical Jesus: Five Views* (London: SPCK, 2010), 84–8.

Davies, W. D. and D. C. Allison, *The Gospel according to Saint Matthew* Vol. 1 (Edinburgh: T. & T. Clark, 1988).

Dean-Jones, L. *Women's Bodies in Classical Greek Science* (Oxford: Oxford University Press, 1994).

Deissmann, A. 'Der Name Panthera', in ed. C. Bezold, *Orientalische Studien: Theodor Nöldeke zum siebzigsten Geburtstag gewidmet* (Giessen: Töpelmann, 1906), 871–5.

Delaney, C. 'The Meaning of Paternity and the Virgin Birth Debate', *Man* 21 (1986), 494–513.

Dennis, T. *The Christmas Stories* (London: SPCK, 2007).

Doctrine Commission of the Church of England, *Christian Believing: The Nature of the Christian Faith and its Expression in Holy Scriptures and Creeds* (London: SPCK, 1976).

Downing, F. G. 'Mary: Between Minimal History and Maximal Myth', *Theology* 110 (2007), 163–70.

Dunn, J. D. G. *Jesus Remembered* (Grand Rapids: Eerdmans, 2003).

Ehrhardt, A. 'The Disciples of Emmaus', *NTS* 10 (1963–4), 187–201.

Erickson, M. *Christian Theology* (2nd edn Grand Rapids: Baker, 1998).

Farrer, A. *The Brink of Mystery* (London: SPCK, 1976).

Fitzmyer, J. A. 'The Virginal Conception of Jesus in the New Testament', *TS* 34 (1973), 541–75.

Fitzmyer, J. A. *The Gospel according to Luke I—IX* (New York: Doubleday, 1981).

Fitzmyer, J. A. *The Acts of the Apostles* (New York: Doubleday, 1998).

Foskett, M. F. *A Virgin Conceived* (Bloomington: Indiana University Press, 2002).

Freed, E. D. *The Stories of Jesus' Birth* (Sheffield: Sheffield Academic, 2001).

Frey, J. 'How Could Mark and John Do without Infancy Stories? Jesus' Humanity and His Divine Origins in Mark and John', in eds C. Clivaz et al., *Infancy Gospels* (Tübingen: Mohr Siebeck, 2011), 189–215.

Gaventa, B. R. *Mary: Glimpses of the Mother of Jesus* (Columbia, SC: University of South Carolina Press, 1995).

George, T. 'The Blessed Virgin Mary in Evangelical Perspective', in eds C. E. Braaten and R. W. Jenson, *Mary, Mother of God* (Grand Rapids: Eerdmans, 2004), 100–22.

Goodacre, M. *The Synoptic Problem* (London: Sheffield Academic Press, 2001).

Goodacre, M. *The Case Against Q* (Harrisburg, PA: Trinity Press International, 2002).

Gordon, C. H. 'Paternity at Two Levels', *JBL* 96 (1977), 101.

Goulder, M. D. *Luke: A New Paradigm* Vol. 1 (Sheffield: JSOT Press, 1989).

Green, J. B. *The Gospel of Luke* (Grand Rapids: Eerdmans, 1997).

Gregory, A. *The Reception of Luke and Acts in the Period before Irenaeus: Looking for Luke in the Second Century* (Tübingen: Mohr Siebeck, 2003).

Grenz, S. *Theology for the Community of God* (Carlisle: Paternoster, 1994).

Guignard, C. 'Jesus' Family and their Genealogy according to the Testimony of Julius Africanus', in eds C. Clivaz et al., *Infancy Gospels* (Tübingen: Mohr Siebeck, 2011), 67–93.

Gunton, C. E. *Yesterday and Today: A Study of Continuities in Christology* (London: Darton, Longman & Todd, 1983).

Gunton, C. E. *The Triune Creator* (Edinburgh: Edinburgh University Press, 1998).

Gunton, C. E. 'Dogma, the Church and the Task of Theology', in eds V. Pfitzner and H. Regan, *The Task of Theology Today* (Edinburgh: T. & T. Clark, 1999), 1–22.

Hannah, D. R. 'The Four Gospel "Canon" in the Epistula Apostolorum', *JTS* 59 (2008), 598–633.

Hardy, T. *Time's Laughingstocks and Other Verses* (London: Macmillan, 1909).

Hauerwas, S. *Matthew* (Grand Rapids: Brazos, 2006).

Hebblethwaite, B. *The Essence of Christianity: A Fresh Look at the Nicene Creed* (London: SPCK, 1996).

Hill, C. E. *The Johannine Corpus in the Early Church* (Oxford: Oxford University Press, 2004).

Horst, P. W. van der 'Sarah's Seminal Emission: Hebrews 11:11 in the Light of Ancient Embryology', in eds E. Ferguson, A. J. Malherbe, D. L. Balch, W. A. Meeks, *Greeks, Romans and Christians: Essays in Honor of Abraham J. Malherbe* (Minneapolis: Fortress, 1990), 287–302.

House of Bishops of the General Synod of the Church of England. *The Nature of Christian Belief: A Statement and Exposition* (London: Church House, 1986).

Hurtado, L. W. *Lord Jesus Christ* (Grand Rapids: Eerdmans, 2003).

Bibliography

Ilan, T. '"Man Born of Woman . . ." (Job 14.1): The Phenomenon of Men Bearing Metronymes at the Time of Jesus', *NovT* 34 (1992), 23–45.

Jenson, R. W. *Systematic Theology* Vol. 2 (Oxford: Oxford University Press, 1999).

Jenson, R. W. *Canon and Creed* (Louisville: Westminster John Knox, 2010).

Johnson, E. A. *Truly Our Sister: A Theology of Mary in the Communion of Saints* (London: Continuum, 2003).

Kelsey, D. H. *Eccentric Existence: A Theological Anthropology.* 2 vols (Louisville: Westminster John Knox, 2009).

Kerr, F. 'Questioning the Virgin Birth', *New Blackfriars* 75 (1994), 132–40.

Kessler, G. *Conceiving Israel: The Fetus in Rabbinic Narratives* (Philadelphia: University of Pennsylvania Press, 2009).

Klijn, A. F. J. *Jewish-Christian Gospel Tradition* (Leiden: Brill, 1992).

Klutz, T. E. 'The Value of Being Virginal: Mary and Anna in the Lukan Infancy Prologue', in ed. G. J. Brooke, *The Birth of Jesus* (Edinburgh: T. & T. Clark, 2000), 71–87.

Klutz, T. E. *The Exorcism Stories in Luke–Acts* (Cambridge: Cambridge University Press, 2004).

Knight, J. *The Ascension of Isaiah* (Sheffield: Sheffield Academic, 1995).

Koester, H. *Introduction to the New Testament: History and Literature of Early Christianity* Vol. 2 (Berlin: de Gruyter, 2000).

Kupp, D. D. *Matthew's Emmanuel: Divine Presence and God's People in the First Gospel* (Cambridge: Cambridge University Press, 1996).

Lampe, G. W. H. ed. *Doctrine in the Church of England: The 1938 Report* (new edn London: SPCK, 1982).

Landry, D. T. 'Narrative Logic in the Annunciation to Mary (Luke 1:26–38)', *JBL* 114 (1995), 65–79.

Laqueur, T. *Making Sex: Body and Gender from the Greeks to Freud* (Cambridge, MA: Harvard University Press, 1990).

Lash, N. *Believing Three Ways in One God* (London: SCM, 1992).

Leaney, A. R. C. *The Gospel according to St. Luke* (London: A. & C. Black, 1958).

Le Donne, A. *The Historiographical Jesus: Memory, Typology and the Son of David* (Waco: Baylor University Press, 2009).

Le Donne, A. *Historical Jesus: What Can We Know and How Can We Know It?* (Grand Rapids: Eerdmans, 2011).

Levin, Y. 'Jesus, "Son of God" and "Son of David": The "Adoption" of Jesus into the Davidic Line', *JSNT* 28 (2006), 415–42.

Lewis, A. E. *Between Cross and Resurrection: A Theology of Holy Saturday* (Grand Rapids: Eerdmans, 2001).

Lincoln, A. 'Born of a Virgin: Credal Affirmation and Critical Reading', in eds A. Lincoln and A. Paddison, *Christology and Scripture: Interdisciplinary Perspectives* (London: T. & T. Clark International, 2007), 84–103.

Lincoln, A. 'Contested Paternity and Contested Readings: Jesus' Conception in Matthew 1.18–25', *JSNT* 34 (2012), 211–31.

Bibliography

Lincoln, A. 'Luke and Jesus' Conception: A Case of Double Paternity?' *JBL* 132 (2013), 639–58.

Louw, J. P. and E. A. Nida. *Greek–English Lexicon of the New Testament: Based on Semantic Domains* Vol. 1 (New York: United Bible Societies, 1998).

Lüdemann, G. *Virgin Birth? The Real Story of Mary and Her Son Jesus* (London: SCM, 1998).

Luz, U. *Matthew 1—7* (London: T. & T. Clark, 1990).

McGrath, J. 'Was Jesus Illegitimate? The Evidence of His Social Interactions', *JSHJ* 5 (2007), 81–100.

Machen, J. G. *Christianity and Liberalism* (Grand Rapids: Eerdmans, 1923).

Machen, J. G. *The Virgin Birth of Christ* (2nd edn New York: Harper and Row, 1932).

McNicol, A. J., D. L. Dungan, D. B. Peabody. *Beyond the Q Impasse: Luke's Use of Matthew* (Valley Forge, PA: Trinity Press International, 1996).

Macquarrie, J. *Jesus Christ in Modern Thought* (London: SCM, 1990).

Macquarrie, J. *Christology Revisited* (London: SCM, 1998).

Marcus, J. *Mark 1—8* (New York: Doubleday, 2000).

Marohl, M. J. *Joseph's Dilemma: 'Honor Killing' in the Birth Narrative of Matthew* (Eugene, OR: Cascade, 2008).

Marsden, G. M. *Understanding Fundamentalism and Evangelicalism* (Grand Rapids: Eerdmans, 1991).

Martin, D. *The Corinthian Body* (New Haven: Yale University Press, 1995).

Matlock, R. B. 'The Birth of Jesus and Why Paul Was in Favour of It', in ed. G. J. Brooke, *The Birth of Jesus* (Edinburgh: T. & T. Clark, 2000), 47–57.

Meier, J. P. *A Marginal Jew* Vol. 1 (New York: Doubleday, 1991).

Meier, J. P. *A Marginal Jew* Vol. 3 (New York: Doubleday, 2001).

Menken, M. J. J. *Matthew's Bible: The Old Testament Text of the Evangelist* (Leuven: Leuven University Press, 2004).

Metzger, B. M. *A Textual Commentary on the Greek New Testament* (London: United Bible Societies, 1971).

Miller, R. J. *Born Divine: The Births of Jesus and Other Sons of God* (Santa Rosa, CA: Polebridge, 2003).

Minns, D. 'Traditional Doctrine and the Antique World-View: Two Case Studies, the Virgin Birth and Original Sin', in eds V. Pfitzner and H. Regan, *The Task of Theology Today* (Edinburgh: T. & T. Clark, 1999), 139–62.

Moltmann, J. *The Way of Jesus Christ* (London: SCM, 1990).

Momigliano, A. *The Development of Greek Biography* (Cambridge, MA: Harvard University Press, 1971).

Moyise, S. *Was the Birth of Jesus According to Scripture?* (Eugene, OR: Cascade, 2013).

Nadella, R. *Dialogue not Dogma: Many Voices in the Gospel of Luke* (London: T. & T. Clark, 2011).

Norelli, E. 'Les plus anciennes traditions sur la naissance de Jésus et leur rapport avec les testimonia', in eds C. Clivaz et al., *Infancy Gospels* (Tübingen: Mohr Siebeck, 2011), 47–66.

Bibliography

O'Loughlin, T. 'Losing Mystery in History: The Challenge of Recalling the Nativity', in ed. J. Corley, *New Perspectives on the Nativity* (London: T. & T. Clark, 2009), 180–99.

Pannenberg, W. *Jesus – God and Man* (2nd edn Philadelphia: Westminster, 1977).

Parrinder, G. *Son of Joseph: The Parentage of Jesus* (Edinburgh: T. & T. Clark, 1992).

Peacocke, A. *Theology for a Scientific Age* (2nd edn London: SCM, 1993).

Peacocke, A. 'DNA of our DNA', in ed. G. J. Brooke, *The Birth of Jesus* (Edinburgh: T. & T. Clark, 2000), 59–67.

Pelikan, J. *Mary through the Centuries* (New Haven: Yale University Press, 1996).

Pelling, C. B. R. 'Truth and Fiction in Plutarch's *Lives*', in ed. D. A. Russell, *Antonine Literature* (Oxford: Clarendon, 1990), 19–52.

Pfitzner, V. and H. Regan eds *The Task of Theology Today* (Edinburgh: T. & T. Clark, 1999).

Porton, G. 'Defining Midrash', in ed. J. Neusner, *The Study of Ancient Judaism* (New York: Ktav, 1981), 55–92.

Prasad, A. *Like A Virgin: How Science Is Redesigning the Rules of Sex* (London: Oneworld, 2012).

Prescendi, F. 'Divine Fathers, Virgin Mothers and Founding Children: Italic Myths about Conception and Birth', in eds C. Clivaz et al., *Infancy Gospels* (Tübingen: Mohr Siebeck, 2011), 3–14.

Räisänen, H. 'Begotten by the Holy Spirit', in eds M. Nissinen and R. Uro, *Sacred Marriages: The Divine–Human Sexual Metaphor from Sumer to Early Christianity* (Winona Lake, IN: Eisenbrauns, 2008), 321–42.

Ranke-Heinemann, U. *Eunuchs for the Kingdom of Heaven* (Harmondsworth: Penguin, 1991).

Ratzinger, J. *Introduction to Christianity* (New York: Herder & Herder/London: Burns & Oates, 1969).

Redford, J. *Born of a Virgin: Proving the Miracle from the Gospels* (London: St Paul, 2007).

Resch, D. *Barth's Interpretation of the Virgin Birth: A Sign of Mystery* (London: Ashgate, 2012).

Ricoeur, P. *The Symbolism of Evil* (Boston: Beacon, 1969).

Robinson, B. P. 'Matthew's Nativity Stories: Historical and Theological Questions for Today's Readers', in ed. J. Corley, *New Perspectives on the Nativity* (London: T. & T. Clark, 2009), 110–31.

Robinson, J. A. T. *The Human Face of God* (London: SCM, 1973).

Rousselle, A. *Porneia: On Desire and the Body in Antiquity* (Oxford: Blackwell, 1988).

Rowe, C. K. *Early Narrative Christology: The Lord in the Gospel of Luke* (Berlin: De Gruyter/Grand Rapids: Baker Academic, 2006).

Runesson, A. 'Giving Birth to Jesus in the Late First Century: Matthew as Midwife in the Context of Colonisation', in eds C. Clivaz et al., *Infancy Gospels* (Tübingen: Mohr Siebeck, 2011), 301–27.

Runia, D. T. *Philo in Early Christian Literature: A Survey* (Assen: van Gorcum, 1993).

Russell, D. A. *Essays on Plutarch's Lives* (ed. B. Scardigli; Oxford: Clarendon, 1995).

Saliba, J. A. 'The Virgin-Birth Debate in Anthropological Literature: A Critical Assessment', *TS* 36 (1975), 428–54.

Schaberg, J. *The Illegitimacy of Jesus: A Feminist Theological Interpretation of the Infancy Narratives* (Sheffield: Sheffield Academic Press, 1995; original edn San Francisco: Harper & Row, 1987).

Schaberg, J. 'Feminist Interpretations of the Infancy Narrative of Matthew', in ed. A.-J. Levine, *A Feminist Companion to Mariology* (London: T. & T. Clark, 2005), 15–36.

Schleiermacher, F. *Christmas Eve: A Dialogue on the Incarnation* (tr. T. N. Tice; Richmond, VA: John Knox Press, 1967).

Schleiermacher, F. *The Life of Jesus* (ed. J. C. Verheyden; tr. S. M. Gilmour; Philadelphia: Fortress, 1975).

Schleiermacher, F. *The Christian Faith* (eds H. R. Mackintosh and J. S. Stewart; London: T. & T. Clark, 1999).

Schults, F. LeRon *Christology and Science* (Aldershot: Ashgate, 2008).

Skarsaune, O. and R. Hvalvik eds *Jewish Believers in Jesus* (Peabody, MA: Hendrickson, 2007).

Smit, P.-B. 'Something about Mary? Remarks about the Five Women in the Matthean Genealogy', *NTS* 56 (2010), 191–207.

Smith, M. *Jesus the Magician* (New York: Harper & Row, 1978).

Soares Prabhu, G. M. *The Formula Quotations in the Infancy Narrative of Matthew* (Rome: Biblical Institute Press, 1976).

Spong, J. S. *Born of a Woman: A Bishop Rethinks the Birth of Jesus* (San Francisco: HarperSanFrancisco, 1992).

Stanton, G. N. 'The Fourfold Gospel', *NTS* 43 (1997), 317–46.

Stol, M. 'Embryology in Babylonia and the Bible', in eds V. R. Sasson and J. M. Law, *Imagining the Fetus* (Oxford: Oxford University Press, 2009), 137–55.

Strauss, D. F. *The Christ of Faith and the Jesus of History* (tr. L. E. Keck; Philadelphia: Fortress, 1977).

Strauss, M. L. *The Davidic Messiah in Luke–Acts* (Sheffield: Sheffield Academic, 1995).

Tabor, J. D. *The Jesus Dynasty* (London: HarperElement, 2006).

Talbert, C. H. 'The Concept of Immortals in Mediterranean Antiquity', *JBL* 94 (1975), 419–36.

Talbert, C. H. *Reading Luke–Acts in Its Mediterranean Milieu* (Leiden: Brill, 2003).

Talbert, C. H. 'Miraculous Conceptions and Births in Mediterranean Antiquity', in eds A.-J. Levine, D. C. Allison, J. D. Crossan, *The Historical Jesus in Context* (Princeton: Princeton University Press, 2006), 79–86.

Tanner, K. *Jesus, Humanity and the Trinity* (Edinburgh: T. & T. Clark, 2001).

Taylor, V. *The Historical Evidence for the Virgin Birth* (Oxford: Clarendon, 1920).

Bibliography

Tice, T. N. 'Schleiermacher's Interpretation of Christmas: "Christmas Eve", "The Christian Faith", and the Christmas Sermons', *Journal of Religion* 47 (1967), 100–26.

Torrance, T. F. 'The Doctrine of the Virgin Birth', *Scottish Bulletin of Evangelical Theology* 12 (1994), 8–25.

Vermes, G. *Jesus the Jew* (London: Collins, 1973).

Vermes, G. *The Nativity: History and Legend* (London: Penguin, 2006).

Wainwright, E. *Towards a Feminist Critical Reading of the Gospel of Matthew* (New York: De Gruyter, 1991).

Wansborough, H. 'The Infancy Stories of the Gospels since Raymond E. Brown', in ed. J. Corley, *New Perspectives on the Nativity* (London: T. & T. Clark, 2009), 4–22.

Watson, F. '*Veritas Christi*: How to Get from the Jesus of History to the Christ of Faith without Losing One's Way', in eds B. R. Gaventa and R. B. Hays, *Seeking the Identity of Jesus* (Grand Rapids: Eerdmans, 2008), 96–114.

Welburn, A. J. *From a Virgin Womb: The Apocalypse of Adam and the Virgin Birth* (Leiden: Brill, 2008).

Whitehead, J. *The Panther* (Springfield, MO: Moon City Press, 2008).

Williams, R. *Open to Judgement* (London: Darton, Longman & Todd, 1994).

Index of ancient sources

Index of ancient sources

Index of ancient sources

Index of modern authors

Alexander, L. C. A. 248
Alexander, P. 155
Allison, D. C. 13, 46, 76, 86, 87, 94, 127, 149, 165
Aus, R. D. 94

Balthasar, H. von 254
Barclay, J. 97
Barrett, C. K. 29, 118
Barth, K. 10, 214, 263, 268, 269, 270, 271, 272, 273, 284, 286, 291
Barton, S. C. xi, 265
Bauckham, R. 161, 162
Bellinzoni, A. 188
Berry, R. J. 259, 260
Blake, W. 158
Bockmuehl, M. 32, 161, 163
Borg, M. J. 2, 8, 66, 94
Boslooper, T. 265
Bovon, F. 65, 118
Boyarin, D. 144
Brown, P. 113, 205, 206, 207, 209, 257
Brown, R. E. 8, 14, 15, 23, 26, 27, 36, 49, 74, 77, 78, 86, 87, 90, 99, 105, 106, 107, 117, 119, 129, 132, 134, 139, 140, 148, 160, 162, 172, 184, 248
Brunner, E. 270, 272
Bultmann, R. 119
Burridge, R. A. xi, 58, 60
Byrskog, S. 248

Caird, G. B. 104
Cameron, A. 297, 299, 300
Campenhausen, H. von 30, 174, 177, 180, 195, 198, 199, 201, 203, 209
Catchpole, D. J. xi, 68, 73, 76, 77, 99, 151
Chilton, B. 81, 152
Clark, E. A. 207, 208, 209
Clivaz, C. 14
Coakley, S. 274
Coleridge, M. 107
Cox, P. 248

Cranfield, C. E. B. 22, 23, 24, 25, 34
Crisp, O. D. 1, 2, 244, 260, 272, 273, 274, 276, 299
Crossan, J. D. 2, 66, 94, 131

Davies, W. D. 86, 87, 93, 149
Dawkins, R. 259, 260
Dean-Jones, L. 257
Deissmann, A. 156, 157
Delaney, C. 257
Dennis, T. 150
Downing, F. G. 27
Dungan, D. L. 130
Dunn, J. D. G. 159

Ehrhardt, A. 110
Erickson, M. 246

Farrer, A. 19, 129
Fitzmyer, J. A. 26, 49, 99, 103, 116, 117, 118, 119, 132, 134, 139
Foskett, M. F. 76, 112, 113, 194
Freed, E. D. 99
Frey, J. 30

Gaventa, B. R. 13, 194
George, T. 10
Goodacre, M. 130
Gordon, C. H. 122
Goulder, M. D. 129, 130
Green, J. B. 57, 131
Gregory, A. 176, 177
Grenz, S. 8, 246
Guignard, C. 161
Gunton, C. E. 232, 284, 295

Hannah, D. R. 177, 186
Hardy, T. 158
Hauerwas, S. 251, 252, 285
Hebblethwaite, B. 292
Hill, C. E. 180
Horst, P. W. van der 257

320

Index of modern authors

Index of modern authors

CPSIA information can be obtained
at www.ICGtesting.com
Printed in the USA
LVHW112343091122
732800LV00018B/95

9 780802 869258